THE VIKING BOOK OF

Poetry

OF THE ENGLISH-SPEAKING WORLD

VOLUME TWO

REVISED, MID-CENTURY EDITION

THE VIKING BOOK OF

Poetry

OF THE
ENGLISH-SPEAKING
WORLD

Edited by Richard Aldington

VOLUME TWO

New York · The Viking Press

The Viking Book of Poetry of the English-Speaking World
Revised, Mid-Century Edition

PUBLISHED IN 1958 BY THE VIKING PRESS, INC.
625 MADISON AVENUE, NEW YORK 22, N. Y.

ORIGINAL ONE-VOLUME EDITION PUBLISHED IN 1941

Note to the Revised, Mid-Century Edition

The additions and revisions in this edition were most kindly undertaken for me by the editorial staff of The Viking Press, assisted by Malcolm Cowley, since pressure of work made it impossible for me to give the time for an adequate revision. Since no two persons ever think alike or choose alike in anthology-making, I leave to them all the responsibility and praise for the alterations and additions from page 1122 on.

RICHARD ALDINGTON

PRINTED IN THE UNITED STATES OF AMERICA

CONTENTS OF VOLUME TWO

THE VIKING BOOK OF

Poetry

OF THE ENGLISH-SPEAKING WORLD

VOLUME TWO

WILLIAM WORDSWORTH

(1770–1850)

"My Heart Leaps Up..."

My heart leaps up when I behold
   A rainbow in the sky;
So was it when my life began;
So is it now I am a man;
So be it when I shall grow old.
   Or let me die!
The Child is father of the Man;
And I could wish my days to be
Bound each to each by natural piety.

"Strange Fits of Passion..."

Strange fits of passion have I known:
And I will dare to tell,
But in the Lover's ear alone,
What once to me befell.

When she I loved looked every day
Fresh as a rose in June,
I to her cottage bent my way,
Beneath an evening-moon.

Upon the moon I fixed my eye,
All over the wide lea;
With quickening pace my horse drew nigh
Those paths so dear to me.

And now we reached the orchard plot;
And, as we climbed the hill,
The sinking moon to Lucy's cot
Came near, and nearer still.

In one of those sweet dreams I slept,
Kind Nature's gentlest boon!
And all the while my eyes I kept
On the descending moon.

[655]

My horse moved on; hoof after hoof
He raised, and never stopped:
When down behind the cottage roof,
At once, the bright moon dropped.

What fond and wayward thoughts will slide
Into a Lover's head!
"O mercy!" to myself I cried,
"If Lucy should be dead!"

"She Dwelt among the Untrodden Ways"

She dwelt among the untrodden ways
    Beside the springs of Dove,
A Maid whom there were none to praise
    And very few to love:

A violet by a mossy stone
    Half hidden from the eye!
—Fair as a star, when only one
    Is shining in the sky.

She lived unknown, and few could know
    When Lucy ceased to be;
But she is in her grave, and, oh,
    The difference to me!

"She Was a Phantom..."

She was a Phantom of delight
When first she gleamed upon my sight;
A lovely Apparition, sent
To be a moment's ornament;
Her eyes as stars of Twilight fair;
Like Twilight's, too, her dusky hair;
But all things else about her drawn
From May-time and the cheerful Dawn;
A dancing Shape, an Image gay,
To haunt, to startle, and way-lay.

I saw her upon nearer view,
A Spirit, yet a Woman too!
Her household motions light and free,
And steps of virgin-liberty;
A countenance in which did meet
Sweet records, promises as sweet;
A Creature not too bright or good
For human nature's daily food;
For transient sorrows, simple wiles,
Praise, blame, love, kisses, tears, and smiles.

And now I see with eye serene
The very pulse of the machine;
A Being breathing thoughtful breath,
A Traveller between life and death;
The reason firm, the temperate will,
Endurance, foresight, strength, and skill;
A perfect Woman, nobly planned,
To warn, to comfort, and command;
And yet a Spirit still, and bright
With something of angelic light.

"A Slumber Did My Spirit Seal"

A slumber did my spirit seal;
    I had no human fears:
She seemed a thing that could not feel
    The touch of earthly years.

No motion has she now, no force;
    She neither hears nor sees;
Rolled round in earth's diurnal course,
    With rocks, and stones, and trees.

"I Wandered Lonely..."

I wandered lonely as a cloud
That floats on high o'er vales and hills,
When all at once I saw a crowd,

A host, of golden daffodils;
Beside the lake, beneath the trees,
Fluttering and dancing in the breeze.

Continuous as the stars that shine
And twinkle on the milky way,
They stretched in never-ending line
Along the margin of a bay:
Ten thousand saw I at a glance,
Tossing their heads in sprightly dance.

The waves beside them danced; but they
Out-did the sparkling waves in glee:
A poet could not but be gay,
In such a jocund company:
I gazed—and gazed—but little thought
What wealth the show to me had brought:

For oft, when on my couch I lie
In vacant or in pensive mood,
They flash upon that inward eye
Which is the bliss of solitude;
And then my heart with pleasure fills,
And dances with the daffodils.

Sonnets

1.

Nuns fret not at their convent's narrow room;
And hermits are contented with their cells;
And students with their pensive citadels;
Maids at the wheel, the weaver at his loom,
Sit blithe and happy; bees that soar for bloom,
High as the highest peak of Furness-fells,
Will murmur by the hour in foxglove bells:
In truth the prison, unto which we doom
Ourselves, no prison is: and hence for me,
In sundry moods, 'twas pastime to be bound
Within the Sonnet's scanty plot of ground;
Pleased if some Souls (for such there needs must be)
Who have felt the weight of too much liberty,
Should find brief solace there, as I have found.

2.   TO SLEEP

A flock of sheep that leisurely pass by,
One after one; the sound of rain, and bees
Murmuring; the fall of rivers, winds and seas,
Smooth fields, white sheets of water, and pure sky;
I have thought of all by turns, and yet do lie
Sleepless! and soon the small birds' melodies
Must hear, first uttered from my orchard trees;
And the first cuckoo's melancholy cry.
Even thus last night, and two nights more, I lay
And could not win thee, Sleep! by any stealth:
So do not let me wear to-night away:
Without Thee what is all the morning's wealth?
Come, blessed barrier between day and day,
Dear mother of fresh thoughts and joyous health!

3.

Surprised by joy—impatient as the Wind
I turned to share the transport—Oh! with whom
But Thee, deep buried in the silent tomb,
That spot which no vicissitude can find?
Love, faithful love, recalled thee to my mind—
But how could I forget thee? Through what power,
Even for the least division of an hour,
Have I been so beguiled as to be blind
To my most grievous loss!—That thought's return
Was the worst pang that sorrow ever bore,
Save one, one only, when I stood forlorn,
Knowing my heart's best treasure was no more;
That neither present time, nor years unborn
Could to my sight that heavenly face restore.

4.

It is a beauteous evening, calm and free,
The holy time is quiet as a Nun
Breathless with adoration; the broad sun
Is sinking down in its tranquillity;
The gentleness of heaven broods o'er the Sea:

Listen! the mighty Being is awake,
And doth with his eternal motion make
A sound like thunder—everlastingly.
Dear Child! dear Girl! that walkest with me here,
If thou appear untouched by solemn thought,
Thy nature is not therefore less divine:
Thou liest in Abraham's bosom all the year;
And worshipp'st at the Temple's inner shrine,
God being with thee when we know it not.

5.

The world is too much with us; late and soon,
Getting and spending, we lay waste our powers:
Little we see in Nature that is ours;
We have given our hearts away, a sordid boon!
This Sea that bares her bosom to the moon;
The winds that will be howling at all hours,
And are up-gathered now like sleeping flowers;
For this, for everything, we are out of tune;
It moves us not.—Great God! I'd rather be
A Pagan suckled in a creed outworn;
So might I, standing on this pleasant lea,
Have glimpses that would make me less forlorn;
Have sight of Proteus rising from the sea;
Or hear old Triton blow his wreathéd horn.

6.   WESTMINSTER BRIDGE, SEPTEMBER 3, 1802

Earth has not anything to show more fair:
Dull would he be of soul who could pass by
A sight so touching in its majesty:
This City now doth, like a garment, wear
The beauty of the morning; silent, bare,
Ships, towers, domes, theatres, and temples lie
Open unto the fields, and to the sky;
All bright and glittering in the smokeless air.
Never did sun more beautifully steep
In his first splendour, valley, rock, or hill;

Ne'er saw I, never felt, a calm so deep!
The river glideth at his own sweet will:
Dear God! the very houses seem asleep;
And all that mighty heart is lying still!

7. ON THE EXTINCTION OF THE VENETIAN REPUBLIC

Once did She hold the gorgeous east in fee;
And was the safeguard of the west: the worth
Of Venice did not fall below her birth,
Venice, the eldest Child of Liberty.
She was a maiden City, bright and free;
No guile seduced, no force could violate;
And, when she took unto herself a Mate,
She must espouse the everlasting Sea.
And what if she had seen those glories fade,
Those titles vanish, and that strength decay;
Yet shall some tribute of regret be paid
When her long life hath reached its final day:
Men are we, and must grieve when even the Shade
Of that which once was great is passed away.

8.

England! the time is come when thou shouldst wean
Thy heart from its emasculating food;
The truth should now be better understood;
Old things have been unsettled; we have seen
Fair seed-time, better harvest might have been
But for thy trespasses; and, at this day,
If for Greece, Egypt, India, Africa,
Aught good were destined, thou wouldst step between.
England! all nations in this charge agree:
But worse, more ignorant in love and hate,
Far—far more abject, is thine Enemy:
Therefore the wise pray for thee, though the freight
Of thy offences be a heavy weight:
Oh grief that Earth's best hopes rest all with Thee!

Ode

(INTIMATIONS OF IMMORTALITY
FROM RECOLLECTIONS OF EARLY CHILDHOOD)

The child is father of the Man;
And I could wish my days to be
Bound each to each by natural piety.

There was a time when meadow, grove, and stream,
The earth and every common sight,
  To me did seem
  Apparelled in celestial light,
The glory and the freshness of a dream.
It is not now as it hath been of yore;—
  Turn wheresoe'er I may,
  By night or day,
The things which I have seen I now can see no more.

  The Rainbow comes and goes,
  And lovely is the Rose,
  The Moon doth with delight
Look round her when the heavens are bare,
  Waters on a starry night
  Are beautiful and fair;
  The sunshine is a glorious birth;
  But yet I know, where'er I go,
That there hath passed away a glory from the earth.

Now, while the birds thus sing a joyous song,
  And while the young lambs bound
  As to the tabor's sound,
To me alone there came a thought of grief:
A timely utterance gave that thought relief,
  And I again am strong:
The cataracts blow their trumpets from the steep;
No more shall grief of mine the season wrong;
I hear the Echoes through the mountains throng,
The Winds come to me from the fields of sleep,
  And all the earth is gay;
  Land and sea
  Give themselves up to jollity,
  And with the heart of May

> Doth every beast keep holiday—
>   Thou child of Joy,
> Shout round me, let me hear thy shouts, thou
>   happy Shepherd-boy!

> Ye blessèd Creatures, I have heard the call
>   Ye to each other make; I see
> The heavens laugh with you in your jubilee;
>   My heart is at your festival,
>   My head hath its coronal,
> The fullness of your bliss, I feel—I feel it all.
>   Oh evil day! if I were sullen
>   While earth itself is adorning,
>   This sweet May-morning,
>   And the children are culling
>   On every side,
>   In a thousand valleys far and wide,
>   Fresh flowers; while the sun shines warm,
> And the babe leaps up in his mother's arm—
>   I hear, I hear, with joy I hear!
>   —But there's a tree, of many, one,
> A single field which I have looked upon,
> Both of them speak of something that is gone:
>   The pansy at my feet
>   Doth the same tale repeat:
> Whither is fled the visionary gleam?
> Where is it now, the glory and the dream?

> Our birth is but a sleep and a forgetting:
> The Soul that rises with us, our life's Star,
>   Hath had elsewhere its setting,
>   And cometh from afar:
>   Not in entire forgetfulness,
>   And not in utter nakedness,
> But trailing clouds of glory do we come
>   From God, who is our home:
> Heaven lies about us in our infancy!
> Shades of the prison-house begin to close
>   Upon the growing Boy,
> But He beholds the light, and whence it flows,
>   He sees it in his joy;

The Youth, who daily farther from the east
    Must travel, still is Nature's Priest,
    And by the vision splendid
    Is on his way attended;
At length the Man perceives it die away,
And fade into the light of common day.

Earth fills her lap with pleasures of her own;
Yearnings she hath in her own natural kind,
And, even with something of a Mother's mind,
    And no unworthy aim,
To make her Foster-child, her Inmate Man,
    Forget the glories he hath known,
And that imperial palace whence he came.
Behold the Child among his new-born blisses,
A six years' Darling of a pygmy size!
Fretted by sallies of his mother's kisses,
With light upon him from his father's eyes!
See, at his feet, some little plan or chart,
Some fragment from his dream of human life,
Shaped by himself with newly-learnéd art;
    A wedding or a festival,
    A mourning or a funeral;
      And this hath now his heart,
    And unto this he frames his song:
      Then will he fit his tongue
To dialogues of business, love, or strife;
    But it will not be long
    Ere this be thrown aside,
    And with new joy and pride
The little Actor cons another part;
Filling from time to time his "humorous stage"
With all the Persons, down to palsied Age,
That Life brings with her in her equipage;
    As if his whole vocation
    Were endless imitation.

Thou, whose exterior semblance doth belie
    Thy Soul's immensity;
Thou best Philosopher, who yet dost keep
Thy heritage, thou Eye among the blind,

That, deaf and silent, read'st the eternal deep,
Haunted for ever by the eternal mind—
        Mighty Prophet! Seer blest!
        On whom those truths do rest,
Which we are toiling all our lives to find,
In darkness lost, the darkness of the grave;
Thou, over whom thy Immortality
Broods like the Day, a Master o'er a Slave,
A Presence which is not to be put by;
        To whom the grave
Is but a lonely bed without the sense or sight
        Of day or the warm light,
A place of thought where we in waiting lie;
Thou little Child, yet glorious in the might
Of heaven-born freedom on thy being's height,
Why with such earnest pains dost thou provoke
The years to bring the inevitable yoke,
Thus blindly with thy blessedness at strife?
Full soon thy Soul shall have her earthly freight,
And custom lie upon thee with a weight,
Heavy as frost, and deep almost as life!

        O joy! that in our embers
        Is something that doth live,
        That nature yet remembers
        What was so fugitive!
The thought of our past years in me doth breed
Perpetual benediction: not indeed
For that which is most worthy to be blest;
Delight and liberty, the simple creed
Of Childhood, whether busy or at rest,
With new-fledged hope still fluttering in his breast—
        Not for these I raise
        The song of thanks and praise;
    But for those obstinate questionings
    Of sense and outward things,
    Fallings from us, vanishings;
    Blank misgivings of a Creature
Moving about in worlds not realised,
High instincts before which our mortal Nature
Did tremble like a guilty Thing surprised:

But for those first affections,
  Those shadowy recollections,
    Which, be they what they may,
Are yet the fountain-light of all our day,
Are yet a master-light of all our seeing;
  Uphold us, cherish, and have power to make
Our noisy years seem moments in the being
Of the eternal Silence: truths that wake,
    To perish never:
Which neither listlessness, nor mad endeavour,
    Nor Man nor Boy,
Nor all that is at enmity with joy,
Can utterly abolish or destroy!
  Hence in a season of calm weather
    Though inland far we be,
Our Souls have sight of that immortal sea
    Which brought us hither,
    Can in a moment travel thither,
And see the Children sport upon the shore,
And hear the mighty waters rolling evermore.

Then sing, ye Birds, sing, sing a joyous song!
    And let the young Lambs bound
    As to the tabor's sound!
We in thought will join your throng,
    Ye that pipe and ye that play,
    Ye that through your hearts to-day
    Feel the gladness of the May!
What though the radiance which was once so bright
Be now for ever taken from my sight,
  Though nothing can bring back the hour
Of splendour in the grass, of glory in the flower;
    We will grieve not, rather find
    Strength in what remains behind;
    In the primal sympathy
    Which having been must ever be;
    In the soothing thoughts that spring
    Out of human suffering;
    In the faith that looks through death,
In years that bring the philosophic mind.

And O, ye Fountains, Meadows, Hills, and Groves,
Forebode not any severing of our loves!
Yet in my heart of hearts I feel your might;
I only have relinquished one delight
To live beneath your more habitual sway.
I love the Brooks which down their channels fret,
Even more than when I tripped lightly as they;
The innocent brightness of a new-born Day
       Is lovely yet;
The Clouds that gather round the setting sun
Do take a sober colouring from an eye
That hath kept watch o'er man's mortality;
Another race hath been, and other palms are won.
Thanks to the human heart by which we live,
Thanks to its tenderness, its joys, and fears,
To me the meanest flower that blows can give
Thoughts that do often lie too deep for tears.

FROM *Tintern Abbey*

And now, with gleams of half-extinguished thought,
With many recognitions dim and faint,
And somewhat of a sad perplexity,
The picture of the mind revives again:
While here I stand, not only with the sense
Of present pleasure, but with pleasing thoughts
That in this moment there is life and food
For future years. And so I dare to hope,
Though changed, no doubt, from what I was when first
I came among these hills; when like a roe
I bounded o'er the mountains, by the sides
Of the deep rivers, and the lonely streams,
Wherever nature led: more like a man
Flying from something that he dreads than one
Who sought the thing he loved. For nature then
(The coarser pleasures of my boyish days,
And their glad animal movements all gone by)
To me was all in all.—I cannot paint
What then I was. The sounding cataract
Haunted me like a passion: the tall rock,

The mountain, and the deep and gloomy wood,
Their colours and their forms, were then to me
An appetite; a feeling and a love,
That had no need of a remoter charm,
By thought supplied, nor any interest
Unborrowed from the eye.—That time is past,
And all its aching joys are now no more,
And all its dizzy raptures. Not for this
Faint I, nor mourn nor murmur; other gifts
Have followed; for such loss, I would believe,
Abundant recompense. For I have learned
To look on nature, not as in the hour
Of thoughtless youth; but hearing oftentimes
The still, sad music of humanity,
Nor harsh, nor grating, though of ample power
To chasten and subdue. And I have felt
A presence that disturbs me with the joy
Of elevated thoughts; a sense sublime
Of something far more deeply interfused,
Whose dwelling is the light of setting suns,
And the round ocean and the living air,
And the blue sky, and in the mind of man:
A motion and a spirit, that impels
All thinking things, all objects of all thought,
And rolls through all things. Therefore am I still
A lover of the meadows and the woods,
And mountains; and of all that we behold
From this green earth; of all the mighty world
Of eye, and ear—both what they half create,
And what perceive; well pleased to recognise
In nature and the language of the sense
The anchor of my purest thoughts, the nurse,
The guide, the guardian of my heart, and soul
Of all my moral being.

FROM *The Prelude*

One summer evening (led by her) I found
A little boat tied to a willow tree
Within a rocky cave, its usual home.

Straight I unloosed her chain, and stepping in
Pushed from the shore. It was an act of stealth
And troubled pleasure, nor without the voice
Of mountain-echoes did my boat move on;
Leaving behind her still, on either side,
Small circles glittering idly in the moon,
Until they melted all into one track
Of sparkling light. But now, like one who rows,
Proud of his skill, to reach a chosen point
With an unswerving line, I fixed my view
Upon the summit of a craggy ridge,
The horizon's utmost boundary; far above
Was nothing but the stars and the grey sky.
She was an elfin pinnace; lustily
I dipped my oars into the silent lake,
And, as I rose upon the stroke, my boat
Went heaving through the water like a swan;
When, from behind that craggy steep till then
The horizon's bound, a huge peak, black and huge,
As if with voluntary power instinct
Upreared its head. I struck and struck again,
And growing still in stature the grim shape
Towered up between me and the stars, and still,
For so it seemed, with purpose of its own
And measured motion like a living thing,
Strode after me. With trembling oars I turned,
And through the silent water stole my way
Back to the covert of the willow tree;
There in her mooring-place I left my bark—
And through the meadows homeward went, in grave
And serious mood; but after I had seen
That spectacle, for many days, my brain
Worked with a dim and undetermined sense
Of unknown modes of being; o'er my thoughts
There hung a darkness, call it solitude
Or blank desertion. No familiar shapes
Remained, no pleasant images of trees,
Of sea or sky, no colours of green fields;
But huge and mighty forms, that do not live
Like living men, moved slowly through the mind
By day, and were a trouble to my dreams.

SIR WALTER SCOTT

(1771–1832)

FROM *The Lay of the Last Minstrel*

In peace, Love tunes the shepherd's reed;
In war, he mounts the warrior's steed;
In halls, in gay attire is seen;
In hamlets, dances on the green.
Love rules the court, the camp, the grove,
And men below, and saints above;
For love is heaven, and heaven is love.

FROM *Marmion*

SONG

Where shall the lover rest,
    Whom the fates sever
From his true maiden's breast,
    Parted for ever?
Where, through groves deep and high,
    Sounds the far billow,
Where early violets die,
    Under the willow.

Chorus:
Eleu loro, &c. Soft shall be his pillow.

There, through the summer day
    Cool streams are laving;
There, while the tempests sway
    Scarce are boughs waving.
There thy rest thou shalt take,
    Parted for ever,
Never again to wake,
    Never, O never!

Chorus:
Eleu loro, &c. Never, O never!

Where shall the traitor rest,
  He, the deceiver,
Who could win maiden's breast,
  Ruin, and leave her?
In the lost battle,
  Borne down by the flying,
Where mingles war's rattle
  With groans of the dying.

Chorus:
Eleu loro, &c. There shall he be lying.

Her wing shall the eagle flap
  O'er the false-hearted;
His warm blood the wolf shall lap,
  Ere life be parted.
Shame and dishonour sit
  By his grave ever;
Blessing shall hallow it—
  Never, O never.

Chorus:
Eleu loro, &c. Never, O never.

FROM *The Lady of the Lake*

1.

Harp of the North! that mouldering long hast hung
  On the witch-elm that shades Saint Fillan's spring,
And down the fitful breeze thy numbers flung,
  Till envious ivy did around thee cling,
Muffling with verdant ringlet every string—
  O minstrel harp, still must thine accents sleep?
Mid rustling leaves and fountains murmuring,
  Still must thy sweeter sounds their silence keep,
Nor bid a warrior smile, nor teach a maid to weep?

Not thus, in ancient days of Caledon,
    Was thy voice mute amid the festal crowd,
When lay of hopeless love, or glory won,
    Aroused the fearful, or subdued the proud.
At each according pause, was heard aloud
    Thine ardent symphony sublime and high.
Fair dames and crested chiefs attention bowed;
    For still the burden of thy minstrelsy
Was Knighthood's dauntless deed, and Beauty's matchless
        eye.

O wake once more! how rude soe'er the hand
    That ventures o'er thy magic maze to stray;
O wake once more! though scarce my skill command
    Some feeble echoing of thine earlier lay:
Though harsh and faint, and soon to die away,
    And all unworthy of thy nobler strain,
Yet if one heart throb higher at its sway,
    The wizard note has not been touched in vain,
Then silent be no more! Enchantress, wake again!

2.

Time rolls his ceaseless course. The race of yore,
    Who danced our infancy upon their knee,
And told our marvelling boyhood legends store
    Of their strange ventures happed by land or sea,
How are they blotted from the things that be!
    How few, all weak and withered of their force,
Wait on the verge of dark eternity,
    Like stranded wrecks, the tide returning hoarse,
To sweep them from our sight. Time rolls his ceaseless
        course.

3.   CORONACH

            He is gone on the mountain,
                He is lost to the forest,
            Like a summer-dried fountain,
                When our need was the sorest.

The font, reappearing,
    From the rain-drops shall borrow,
But to us comes no cheering,
    To Duncan no morrow.
The hand of the reaper
    Takes the ears that are hoary,
But the voice of the weeper
    Wails manhood in glory.
The autumn winds rushing
    Waft the leaves that are searest,
But our flower was in flushing
    When blighting was nearest.

Fleet foot on the correi,
    Sage counsel in cumber,
Red hand in the foray,
    How sound is thy slumber!
Like the dew on the mountain,
    Like the foam on the river,
Like the bubble on the fountain,
    Thou art gone, and for ever!

4.

The rose is fairest when 'tis budding new,
    And hope is brightest when it dawns from fears,
The rose is sweetest washed in morning dew,
    And love is loveliest when embalmed in tears.
O wilding rose, whom fancy thus endears,
    I bid your blossoms in my bonnet wave,
Emblem of hope and love through future years.

5.   SOLDIER'S SONG
Our vicar still preaches that Peter and Poule
Laid a swinging long curse on the bonny brown bowl,
That there's wrath and despair in the jolly black-jack,
And the seven deadly sins in a flagon of sack;
Yet whoop! Barnaby, off with thy liquor,
Drink upsees out, and a fig for the vicar!

Correi, *hollow of the hill, where game lies.*

Our vicar he calls it damnation to sip
The ripe ruddy dew of a woman's dear lip,
Says that Beelzebub lurks in her kerchief so sly,
And Apollyon shoots darts from her merry black eye;
Yet whoop! Jack, kiss Gillian the quicker,
Till she bloom like a rose, and a fig for the vicar!

Our vicar thus preaches—and why should he not?
For the dues of his cure are the placket and pot;
And 'tis right of his office poor laymen to lurch,
Who infringe the domains of our good Mother Church.
Yet whoop! bully-boys, off with your liquor
Sweet Marjorie's the word, and a fig for the vicar!

6.

Harp of the North, farewell! The hills grow dark,
   On purple peaks a deeper shade descending;
In twilight copse the glow-worm lights her spark,
   The deer, half-seen, are to the covert wending.
Resume thy wizard elm, the fountain lending
   And the wild breeze thy wilder minstrelsy;
Thy numbers sweet with nature's vespers blending,
   With distant echo from the fold and lea,
And herd-boy's evening pipe, and hum of housing bee.

Yet, once again, farewell, thou Minstrel harp.
   Yet, once again, forgive my feeble sway,
And little reck I of the censure sharp
   May idly cavil at an idle lay.
Much have I owed thy strains on life's long way,
   Through secret woes the world has never known,
When on the weary night dawned wearier day,
   And bitterer was the grief devoured alone.
That I o'erlive such woes, Enchantress, is thine own.

Hark! as my lingering footsteps slow retire,
   Some Spirit of the Air has waked thy string!
'Tis now a seraph bold, with touch of fire,
   'Tis now the brush of Fairy's frolic wing.

Receding now, the dying numbers ring
   Fainter and fainter down the rugged dell,
And now the mountain breezes scarcely bring
   A wandering witch-note of the distant spell—
And now 'tis silent all—Enchantress, fare thee well!

FROM *Rokeby*

SONG

A weary lot is thine, fair maid,
   A weary lot is thine.
To pull the thorn thy brow to braid,
   And press the rue for wine.
A lightsome eye, a soldier's mien,
   A feather of the blue,
A doublet of the Lincoln green—
   No more of me you knew,
         My love,
   No more of me you knew.

This morn in merry June, I trow,
   The rose is budding fain;
But she shall bloom in winter snow,
   Ere we two meet again.
He turned his charger as he spake,
   Upon the river shore,
He gave his bridle-reins a shake,
   Said: Adieu for evermore,
         My love!
   And adieu for evermore.

"False Love..."

False love, and hast thou played me this
   In summer among the flowers?
I will repay thee back again
   In winter among the showers.

Unless again, again, my love,
   Unless you turn again;
As you with other maidens rove,
   I'll smile on other men.

Waverley

"Hie Away..."

Hie away, hie away,
Over bank and over brae,
Where the copsewood is the greenest,
Where the fountains glisten sheenest,
Where the lady-fern grows strongest,
Where the morning dew lies longest,
Where the black-cock sweetest sips it,
Where the fairy latest trips it:
Hie to haunts right seldom seen,
Lovely, lonesome, cool, and green,
Over bank and over brae,
Hie away, hie away.

Waverley

"When Israel..."

When Israel, of the Lord beloved,
   Out from the land of bondage came,
Her fathers' God before her moved,
   An awful guide in smoke and flame.
By day, along the astonished lands
   The cloudy pillar glided slow;
By night, Arabia's crimsoned sands
   Returned the fiery column's glow.

There rose the choral hymn of praise,
   And trump and timbrel answered keen,
And Zion's daughters poured their lays,
   With priest's and warrior's voice between.
No portents now our foes amaze,
   Forsaken Israel wanders lone;
Our fathers would not know Thy ways,
   And Thou hast left them to their own.

But present still, though now unseen!
    When brightly shines the prosperous day,
Be thoughts of Thee a cloudy screen
    To temper the deceitful ray.
And oh, when stoops on Judah's path
    In shade and storm the frequent night,
Be Thou, long-suffering, slow to wrath,
    A burning and a shining light!

Our harps we left by Babel's streams,
    The tyrant's jest, the Gentile's scorn;
No censer round our altar beams,
    And mute are timbrel, harp, and horn.
But Thou hast said, The blood of goat,
    The flesh of rams I will not prize;
A contrite heart, a humble thought,
    Are Mine accepted sacrifice.

Ivanhoe

"Anna-Marie, Love, Up Is the Sun"

Knight: Anna-Marie, love, up is the sun,
    Anna-Marie, love, morn is begun,
    Mists are dispersing, love, birds singing free,
    Up in the morning, love, Anna-Marie.
    Anna-Marie, love, up in the morn,
    The hunter is winding blithe sounds on his horn,
    The echo rings merry from rock and from tree.
    'Tis time to arouse thee, love, Anna-Marie.

Wamba: O Tybalt, love, Tybalt, awake me not yet,
    Around my soft pillow while softer dreams flit;
    For what are the joys that in waking we prove,
    Compared with these visions, O Tybalt! my love?
    Let the birds to the rise of the mist carol shrill,
    Let the hunter blow out his loud horn on the hill,
    Softer sounds, softer pleasures, in slumber I prove,
    But think not I dream of thee, Tybalt, my love.

Ivanhoe

"March, March..."

March, march, Ettrick and Teviotdale,
  Why the deil dinna ye march forward in order!
March, march, Eskdale and Liddesdale,
  All the blue bonnets are bound for the Border.
    Many a banner spread
    Flutters above your head,
  Many a crest that is famous in story.
    Mount and make ready then,
    Sons of the mountain glen,
  Fight for the Queen and our old Scottish glory.

Come from the hills where your hirsels are grazing,
  Come from the glen of the buck and the roe;
Come to the crag where the beacon is blazing,
  Come with the buckler, the lance, and the bow.
    Trumpets are sounding,
    War-steeds are bounding,
Stand to your arms, and march in good order,
    England shall many a day
    Tell of the bloody fray,
When the Blue Bonnets came over the Border.

The Monastery

"Woman's Faith..."

Woman's faith, and woman's trust—
Write the characters in dust;
Stamp them on the running stream,
Print them on the moon's pale beam,
And each evanescent letter
Shall be clearer, firmer, better,
And more permanent, I ween,
Than the thing those letters mean.

I have strained the spider's thread
'Gainst the promise of a maid;
I have weighed a grain of sand
'Gainst her plight of heart and hand;

I told my true love of the token,
How her faith proved light, and her word was broken:
Again her word and truth she plight,
And I believed them again ere night.

The Betrothed

SAMUEL TAYLOR COLERIDGE
(1772–1834)

The Rime of the Ancient Mariner

PART I

An ancient mariner meeteth three gallants bidden to a wedding-feast, and detaineth one.

It is an ancient Mariner,
And he stoppeth one of three.
"By thy long grey beard and glittering eye,
Now wherefore stopp'st thou me?

The Bridegroom's doors are opened wide,
And I am next of kin;
The guests are met, the feast is set:
May'st hear the merry din."

He holds him with his skinny hand,
"There was a ship," quoth he.
"Hold off! unhand me, grey-beard loon!"
Eftsoons his hand dropt he.

The Wedding-Guest is spellbound by the eye of the old seafaring man, and constrained to hear his tale.

He holds him with his glittering eye—
The Wedding-Guest stood still,
And listens like a three years' child:
The Mariner hath his will.

The Wedding-Guest sat on a stone:
He cannot choose but hear;
And thus spake on that ancient man,
The bright-eyed Mariner.

The Mariner tells how the ship sailed southward with a good

"The ship was cheered, the harbour cleared,
Merrily did we drop
Below the kirk, below the hill,
Below the lighthouse top.

*wind and fair
weather, till it
reached the
line.*

The Sun came up upon the left,
Out of the sea came he!
And he shone bright, and on the right
Went down into the sea.

Higher and higher every day,
Till over the mast at noon—"
The Wedding-Guest here beat his breast,
For he heard the loud bassoon.

*The Wedding-
Guest heareth
the bridal
music; but
the Mariner
continueth
his tale.*

The bride hath paced into the hall,
Red as a rose is she;
Nodding their heads before her goes
The merry minstrelsy.

The Wedding-Guest he beat his breast,
Yet he cannot choose but hear;
And thus spake on that ancient man,
The bright-eyed Mariner.

*The ship
driven by a
storm toward
the south pole.*

"And now the STORM-BLAST came, and he
Was tyrannous and strong:
He struck with his o'ertaking wings,
And chased us south along.

With sloping masts and dipping prow,
As who pursued with yell and blow
Still treads the shadow of his foe,
And forward bends his head,
The ship drove fast, loud roared the blast,
And southward aye we fled.

And now there came both mist and snow,
And it grew wondrous cold:
And ice, mast-high, came floating by,
As green as emerald.

*The land of
ice, and of
fearful sounds
where no
living thing
was to be seen.*

And through the drifts the snowy clifts
Did send a dismal sheen:
Nor shapes of men nor beasts we ken—
The ice was all between.

The ice was here, the ice was there,
The ice was all around:
It cracked and growled, and roared and howled,
Like noises in a swound!

At length did cross an Albatross,
Thorough the fog it came;
As if it had been a Christian soul,
We hailed it in God's name.

It ate the food it ne'er had eat,
And round and round it flew.
The ice did split with a thunder-fit;
The helmsman steered us through.

And a good south wind sprung up behind;
The Albatross did follow,
And every day, for food or play,
Came to the mariner's hollo!

In mist or cloud, or mast or shroud,
It perched for vespers nine;
Whiles all the nights, through fog-smoke white,
Glimmered the white Moon-shine."

"God save thee, ancient Mariner!
From the fiends, that plague thee thus!—
Why look'st thou so?"—With my cross-bow
I shot the ALBATROSS.

PART II

The Sun now rose upon the right:
Out of the sea came he,
Still hid in mist, and on the left
Went down into the sea.

And the good south wind still blew behind,
But no sweet bird did follow,
Nor any day for food or play
Came to the mariners' hollo!

*His shipmates
cry out against
the ancient
Mariner, for
killing the
bird of good
luck.*

And I had done a hellish thing,
And it would work 'em woe:
For all averred, I had killed the bird
That made the breeze to blow.
Ah wretch! said they, the bird to slay,
That made the breeze to blow!

*But when the
fog cleared
off, they
justify the
same, and
thus make
themselves
accomplices
in the crime.
The fair
breeze con-
tinues; the ship
enters the
Pacific Ocean,
and sails north-
ward, even
till it reaches
the Line.
The ship hath
been suddenly
becalmed.*

Nor dim nor red, like God's own head,
The glorious Sun uprist:
Then all averred, I had killed the bird
That brought the fog and mist.
'Twas right, said they, such birds to slay,
That bring the fog and mist.

The fair breeze blew, the white foam flew,
The furrow followed free;
We were the first that ever burst
Into that silent sea.

Down dropt the breeze, the sails dropt down,
'Twas sad as sad could be;
And we did speak only to break
The silence of the sea!

All in a hot and copper sky,
The bloody Sun, at noon,
Right up above the mast did stand
No bigger than the Moon.

Day after day, day after day,
We stuck, nor breath nor motion;
As idle as a painted ship
Upon a painted ocean.

*And the Alba-
tross begins to
be avenged.*

Water, water, every where,
And all the boards did shrink;
Water, water, every where,
Nor any drop to drink.

The very deep did rot: O Christ!
That ever this should be!

Yea, slimy things did crawl with legs
Upon the slimy sea.

About, about, in reel and rout,
The death-fires danced at night;
The water, like a witch's oils,
Burnt green, and blue and white.

A Spirit had
followed
them; one of
the invisible
inhabitants of
this planet,
neither de-

And some in dreams assuréd were
Of the Spirit that plagued us so;
Nine fathom deep he had followed us
From the land of mist and snow.

parted souls nor angels; concerning whom the learned Jew, Josephus, and
the Platonic Constantinopolitan, Michael Psellus, may be consulted. They
are very numerous, and there is no climate or element without one or more.

And every tongue, through utter drought,
Was withered at the root;
We could not speak, no more than if
We had been choked with soot.

The shipmates
in their sore
distress, would
fain throw the
whole guilt on

Ah! well-a-day! what evil looks
Had I from old and young!
Instead of the cross, the Albatross
About my neck was hung.

the ancient Mariner; in sign whereof they hang the dead sea-bird round
his neck.

PART III

There passed a weary time. Each throat
Was parched, and glazed each eye.
A weary time! A weary time!

The ancient
Mariner be-
holdeth a sign
in the element
afar off.

How glazed each weary eye,
When looking westward, I beheld
A something in the sky.

At first it seemed a little speck,
And then it seemed a mist;
It moved and moved, and took at last
A certain shape, I wist.

At its nearer approach, it seemeth him to be a ship; and at a dear ransom he freeth his speech from the bonds of thirst.

A speck, a mist, a shape, I wist!
And still it neared and neared:
As if it dodged a water-sprite,
It plunged and tacked and veered.

With throats unslaked, with black lips baked,
We could not laugh nor wail;
Through utter drought all dumb we stood!
I bit my arm, I sucked the blood,
And cried, A sail! a sail!

With throats unslaked, with black lips baked,
Agape they heard me call:

A flash of joy;

Gramercy! they for joy did grin,
And all at once their breath drew in,
As they were drinking all.

And horror follows. For can it be a ship that comes onward without wind or tide?

See! See! (I cried) she tacks no more!
Hither to work us weal;
Without a breeze, without a tide,
She steadies with upright keel!

The western wave was all a-flame.
The day was well nigh done!
Almost upon the western wave
Rested the broad bright Sun;
When that strange shape drove suddenly
Betwixt us and the Sun.

It seemeth him but the skeleton of a ship.

And straight the Sun was flecked with bars,
(Heaven's Mother send us grace!)
As if through a dungeon-grate he peered
With broad and burning face.

And its ribs are seen as bars on the face of the setting Sun.

Alas! (thought I, and my heart beat loud)
How fast she nears and nears!
Are those *her* sails that glance in the Sun,
Like restless gossameres?

The Spectre-Woman and her Death-

Are those *her* ribs through which the Sun
Did peer, as through a grate?

mate, and no other on board the skeleton ship.

And is that Woman all her crew?
Is that a DEATH? and are there two?
Is DEATH that woman's mate?

Like vessel, like crew! Death and Life-in-Death have diced for the ship's crew, and she (the latter) winneth the ancient Mariner.

Her lips were red, *her* looks were free,
Her locks were yellow as gold.
Her skin was white as leprosy,
The Night-mare LIFE-IN-DEATH was she,
Who thicks man's blood with cold.

The naked hulk alongside came,
And the twain were casting dice;
'The game is done! I've won! I've won!'
Quoth she, and whistles thrice.

No twilight within the courts of the Sun.

The Sun's rim dips; the stars rush out:
At one stride comes the dark;
With far-off whisper, o'er the sea,
Off shot the spectre-bark.

At the rising of the Moon,

We listened and looked sideways up!
Fear at my heart, as at a cup,
My life-blood seemed to sip!
The stars were dim, and thick the night,
The steersman's face by his lamp gleamed
          white;
From the sails the dew did drip—
Till clomb above the eastern bar
The hornéd Moon, with one bright star
Within the nether tip.

One after another,

One after one, by the star-dogged Moon,
Too quick for groan or sigh,
Each turned his face with a ghastly pang,
And cursed me with his eye.

His shipmates drop down dead.

Four times fifty living men,
(And I heard nor sigh nor groan)
With heavy thump, a lifeless lump,
They dropped down one by one.

But Life-in-Death begins her work on the ancient Mariner.

The souls did from their bodies fly,—
They fled to bliss or woe!
And every soul, it passed me by,
Like the whizz of my cross-bow!

PART IV

The Wedding-Guest feareth that a Spirit is talking to him;

"I fear thee, ancient Mariner!
I fear thy skinny hand!
And thou art long, and lank, and brown,
As is the ribbed sea-sand.

I fear thee and thy glittering eye,
And thy skinny hand, so brown."—

But the ancient Mariner assureth him of his bodily life, and proceedeth to relate his horrible penance.

Fear not, fear not, thou Wedding-Guest!
This body dropt not down.

Alone, alone, all, all alone,
Alone on a wide wide sea!
And never a saint took pity on
My soul in agony.

He despiseth the creatures of the calm,

The many men, so beautiful!
And they all dead did lie:
And a thousand thousand slimy things
Lived on; and so did I.

And envieth that they should live, and so many lie dead.

I looked upon the rotting sea,
And drew my eyes away;
I looked upon the rotting deck,
And there the dead men lay.

I looked to heaven, and tried to pray;
But or ever a prayer had gusht,
A wicked whisper came, and made
My heart as dry as dust.

I closed my lids, and kept them close,
And the balls like pulses beat;
For the sky and the sea, and the sea and the
    sky
Lay like a load on my weary eye,
And the dead were at my feet.

*But the curse
liveth for him
in the eye of
the dead men.*

The cold sweat melted from their limbs,
Nor rot nor reek did they:
The look with which they looked on me
Had never passed away.

An orphan's curse would drag to hell
A spirit from on high;
But oh! more horrible than that
Is the curse in a dead man's eye!
Seven days, seven nights, I saw that curse,
And yet I could not die.

The moving Moon went up the sky,
And no where did abide:
Softly she was going up,
And a star or two beside—

*In his lone-
liness and
fixedness he
yearneth to-
wards the
journeying
Moon, and
the stars that
still sojourn,
yet still move
onward; and
everywhere
the blue sky
belongs to*

Her beams bemocked the sultry main,
Like April hoar-frost spread;
But where the ship's huge shadow lay,
The charméd water burnt alway
A still and awful red.

*them, and is their appointed rest, and their native country and their own
natural homes, which they enter unannounced, as lords that are certainly
expected and yet there is a silent joy at their arrival.*

*By the light
of the Moon
he beholdeth
God's crea-
tures of the
great calm.*

Beyond the shadow of the ship,
I watched the water-snakes:
They moved in tracks of shining white,
And when they reared, the elfish light
Fell off in hoary flakes.

Within the shadow of the ship
I watched their rich attire:
Blue, glossy green, and velvet black,
They coiled and swam; and every track
Was a flash of golden fire.

*Their beauty
and their
happiness.
He blesseth*

O happy living things! no tongue
Their beauty might declare:
A spring of love gushed from my heart,

*them in his
heart.*

And I blessed them unaware:
Sure my kind saint took pity on me,
And I blessed them unaware.

*The spell
begins to
break.*

The self-same moment I could pray;
And from my neck so free
The Albatross fell off, and sank
Like lead into the sea.

PART V

Oh sleep! it is a gentle thing,
Beloved from pole to pole!
To Mary Queen the praise be given!
She sent the gentle sleep from Heaven,
That slid into my soul.

*By grace of
the holy
Mother, the
ancient
Mariner is
refreshed
with rain.*

The silly buckets on the deck,
That had so long remained,
I dreamt that they were filled with dew;
And when I awoke, it rained.

My lips were wet, my throat was cold,
My garments all were dank;
Sure I had drunken in my dreams,
And still my body drank.

I moved, and could not feel my limbs:
I was so light—almost
I thought that I had died in sleep,
And was a blesséd ghost.

*He heareth
sounds and
seeth strange
sights and
commotions in
the sky and
the element.*

And soon I heard a roaring wind:
It did not come anear;
But with its sound it shook the sails,
That were so thin and sere.

The upper air burst into life!
And a hundred fire-flags sheen,
To and fro they were hurried about!
And to and fro, and in and out,
The wan stars danced between.

And the coming wind did roar more loud,
And the sails did sigh like sedge;
And the rain poured down from one black
    cloud;
The Moon was at its edge.

The thick black cloud was cleft, and still
The Moon was at its side:
Like waters shot from some high crag,
The lightning fell with never a jag,
A river steep and wide.

The bodies of
the ship's crew
are inspired
and the ship
moves on;

The loud wind never reached the ship,
Yet now the ship moved on!
Beneath the lightning and the Moon
The dead men gave a groan.

They groaned, they stirred, they all uprose,
Nor spake, nor moved their eyes;
It had been strange, even in a dream,
To have seen those dead men rise.

The helmsman steered, the ship moved on;
Yet never a breeze up-blew;
The mariners all 'gan work the ropes,
Where they were wont to do;
They raised their limbs like lifeless tools—
We were a ghastly crew.

The body of my brother's son
Stood by me, knee to knee:
The body and I pulled at one rope,
But he said nought to me.

But not by the
souls of the
men, nor by
daemons of
earth or
middle air,
but by a
blessed troop
of angelic
spirits sent
down by the

"I fear thee, ancient Mariner!"
Be calm, thou Wedding-Guest!
'Twas not those souls that fled in pain,
Which to their corses came again,
But a troop of spirits blest:

For when it dawned—they dropped their arms,
And clustered round the mast;

*invocation of
the guardian
saint.*

Sweet sounds rose slowly through their mouths,
And from their bodies passed.

Around, around, flew each sweet sound,
Then darted to the Sun;
Slowly the sounds came back again,
Now mixed, now one by one.

Sometimes, a-dropping from the sky
I heard the sky-lark sing;
Sometimes all little birds that are,
How they seemed to fill the sea and air
With their sweet jargoning!

And now 'twas like all instruments,
Now like a lonely flute;
And now it is an angel's song,
That makes the heavens be mute.

It ceased; yet still the sails made on
A pleasant noise till noon,
A noise like of a hidden brook
In the leafy month of June,
That to the sleeping woods all night
Singeth a quiet tune.

Yet noon we quietly sailed on,
Yet never a breeze did breathe:
Slowly and smoothly went the ship,
Moved onward from beneath.

*The lonesome
Spirit from
the south pole
carries on the
ship as far as
the Line, in
obedience to
the angelic
troop, but still
requireth
vengeance.*

Under the keel nine fathom deep,
From the land of mist and snow,
The spirit slid: and it was he
That made the ship to go.
The sails at noon left off their tune,
And the ship stood still also.

The Sun, right up above the mast,
Had fixed her to the ocean:
But in a minute she 'gan stir,

With a short uneasy motion—
Backwards and forwards half her length
With a short uneasy motion.

Then like a pawing horse let go,
She made a sudden bound:
It flung the blood into my head,
And I fell down in a swound.

The Polar Spirit's fellow daemons, the invisible inhabitants of the element, take part in his wrong; and two of them relate, one to the other, that penance long and heavy for the ancient Mariner hath been accorded to the Polar Spirit, who returneth southward.

How long in that same fit I lay,
I have not to declare;
But ere my living life returned,
I heard and in my soul discerned
Two voices in the air.

"Is it he?" quoth one, "Is this the man?
By him who died on cross,
With his cruel bow he laid full low
The harmless Albatross.

The spirit who bideth by himself
In the land of mist and snow,
He loved the bird that loved the man
Who shot him with his bow."

The other was a softer voice,
As soft as honey-dew:
Quoth he: "The man hath penance done,
And penance more will do."

PART VI

First Voice:

"But tell me, tell me! speak again,
Thy soft response renewing—
What makes that ship drive on so fast?
What is the ocean doing?

Second Voice:

"Still as a slave before his lord,
The ocean hath no blast;

His great bright eye most silently
Up to the Moon is cast—

If he may know which way to go;
For she guides him smooth or grim.
See, brothers, see! how graciously
She looketh down on him."

First Voice:

"But why drives on that ship so fast,
Without or wave or wind?"

Second Voice:

"The air is cut away before,
And closes from behind.

Fly, brother, fly! more high, more high!
Or we shall be belated:
For slow and slow that ship will go,
When the Mariner's trance is abated."

I woke, and we were sailing on
As in a gentle weather:
'Twas night, calm night, the moon was high;
The dead men stood together.

All stood together on the deck,
For a charnel-dungeon fitter:
All fixed on me their stony eyes,
That in the Moon did glitter.

The pang, the curse, with which they died,
Had never passed away:
I could not draw my eyes from theirs,
Nor turn them up to pray.

And now this spell was snapt: once more
I viewed the ocean green,
And looked far forth, yet little saw
Of what had else been seen—

The Mariner hath been cast into a trance, for the angelic power causeth the vessel to drive northward faster than human life could endure.

The supernatural motion is retarded; the Mariner awakes and his penance begins anew.

The curse is finally expiated.

Like one, that on a lonesome road
Doth walk in fear and dread,
And having once turned round walks on,
And turns no more his head;
Because he knows, a frightful fiend
Doth close behind him tread.

But soon there breathed a wind on me,
Nor sound nor motion made:
Its path was not upon the sea,
In ripple or in shade.

It raised my hair, it fanned my cheek
Like a meadow-gale of spring—
It mingled strangely with my fears,
Yet it felt like a welcoming.

Swiftly, swiftly flew the ship,
Yet she sailed softly too:
Sweetly, sweetly blew the breeze—
On me alone it blew.

*And the
ancient
Mariner be-
holdeth his
native
country.*

Oh! dream of joy! is this indeed
The light-house top I see?
Is this the hill? is this the kirk?
Is this mine own countree?

We drifted o'er the harbour-bar,
And I with sobs did pray—
O let me be awake, my God!
Or let me sleep alway.

The harbour-bay was clear as glass,
So smoothly it was strewn!
And on the bay the moonlight lay,
And the shadow of the Moon.

The rock shone bright, the kirk no less,
That stands above the rock:
The moonlight steeped in silentness
The steady weathercock.

And the bay was white with silent light,
The angelic spirits leave the dead bodies,   Till rising from the same,
Full many shapes, that shadows were,
In crimson colours came.

A little distance from the prow
And appear in their own forms of light.   Those crimson shadows were:
I turned my eyes upon the deck—
Oh, Christ! what saw I there!

Each corse lay flat, lifeless and flat,
And, by the holy rood!
A man all light, a seraph-man,
On every corse there stood.

This seraph-band, each waved his hand:
It was a heavenly sight!
They stood as signals to the land,
Each one a lovely light;

This seraph-band, each waved his hand,
No voice did they impart—
No voice; but oh! the silence sank
Like music on my heart.

But soon I heard the dash of oars,
I heard the Pilot's cheer;
My head was turned perforce away
And I saw a boat appear.

The Pilot and the Pilot's boy,
I heard them coming fast:
Dear Lord in Heaven! it was a joy
The dead men could not blast.

I saw a third—I heard his voice:
It is the Hermit good!
He singeth loud his godly hymns
That he makes in the wood.
He'll shrieve my soul, he'll wash away
The Albatross's blood.

PART VII

*The Hermit
of the Wood,*

This Hermit good lives in that wood
Which slopes down to the sea.
How loudly his sweet voice he rears!
He loves to talk with marineres
That come from a far countree.

He kneels at morn, and noon, and eve—
He hath a cushion plump:
It is the moss that wholly hides
The rotted old oak-stump.

The skiff-boat neared: I heard them talk,
"Why, this is strange, I trow!
Where are those lights so many and fair,
That signal made but now?"

*Approacheth
the ship with
wonder.*

"Strange, by my faith!" the Hermit said—
"And they answered not our cheer!
The planks look warped! and see those sails!
How thin they are and sere!
I never saw aught like to them,
Unless perchance it were

Brown skeletons of leaves that lag
My forest-brook along;
When the ivy-tod is heavy with snow,
And the owlet whoops to the wolf below,
That eats the she-wolf's young."

"Dear Lord! it hath a fiendish look—
(The Pilot made reply)
I am a-feared"—"Push on, push on!"
Said the Hermit cheerily.

The boat came closer to the ship,
But I nor spake nor stirred;
The boat came close beneath the ship,
And straight a sound was heard.

*The ship
suddenly
sinketh.*

Under the water it rumbled on,
Still louder and more dread:
It reached the ship, it split the bay;
The ship went down like lead.

*The ancient
Mariner is
saved in the
Pilot's boat.*

Stunned by that loud and dreadful sound,
Which sky and ocean smote,
Like one that hath been seven days drowned
My body lay afloat;
But swift as dreams, myself I found
Within the Pilot's boat.

Upon the whirl, where sank the ship,
The boat spun round and round;
And all was still, save that the hill
Was telling of the sound.

I moved my lips—the Pilot shrieked
And fell down in a fit;
The holy Hermit raised his eyes,
And prayed where he did sit.

I took the oars: the Pilot's boy,
Who now doth crazy go,
Laughed loud and long, and all the while
His eyes went to and fro.
"Ha! ha!" quoth he, "full plain I see,
The Devil knows how to row."

And now, all in my own countree,
I stood on the firm land!
The Hermit stepped forth from the boat,
And scarcely he could stand.

*The ancient
Mariner
earnestly en-
treateth the
Hermit to
shrieve him;
and the
penance of
life falls on
him.*

"O shrieve me, shrieve me, holy man!"
The Hermit crossed his brow.
"Say quick," quoth he, "I bid thee say—
What manner of man art thou?

Forthwith this frame of mine was wrenched
With a woful agony,

Which forced me to begin my tale;
And then it left me free.

And ever and
anon through
out his future
life an agony
constraineth
him to travel
from land to
land;

Since then, at an uncertain hour,
That agony returns:
And till my ghastly tale is told,
This heart within me burns.

I pass, like night, from land to land;
I have strange power of speech;
That moment that his face I see,
I know the man that must hear me:
To him my tale I teach.

What loud uproar bursts from that door!
The wedding-guests are there;
But in the garden-bower the bride
And bride-maids singing are:
And hark the little vesper bell.
Which biddeth me to prayer!

O Wedding-Guest! this soul hath been
Alone on a wide wide sea:
So lonely 'twas, that God himself
Scarce seeméd there to be.

O sweeter than the marriage-feast,
'Tis sweeter far to me,
To walk together to the kirk
With a goodly company!—

To walk together to the kirk,
And all together pray,
While each to his great Father bends,
Old men, and babes, and loving friends
And youths and maidens gay!

And to teach,
by his own
example, love
and reverence
to all things
that God made
and loveth.

Farewell, farewell! but this I tell
To thee, thou Wedding-Guest!
He prayeth well, who loveth well
Both man and bird and beast.

He prayeth best, who loveth best
All things both great and small;
For the dear God who loveth us,
He made and loveth all.

The Mariner, whose eye is bright,
Whose beard with age is hoar,
Is gone: and now the Wedding-Guest
Turned from the bridegroom's door.

He went like one that hath been stunned,
And is of sense forlorn:
A sadder and a wiser man,
He rose the morrow morn.

FROM *Christabel*

A little child, a limber elf,
Singing, dancing to itself,
A fairy thing with red round cheeks,
That always finds, and never seeks,
Makes such a vision to the sight
As fills a father's eyes with light;
And pleasures flow in so thick and fast
Upon his heart, that he at last
Must needs express his love's excess
With words of unmeant bitterness.
Perhaps 'tis pretty to force together
Thoughts so all unlike each other;
To mutter and mock a broken charm,
To dally with wrong that does no harm.
Perhaps 'tis tender too and pretty
At each wild word to feel within
A sweet recoil of love and pity.
And what, if in a world of sin
(O sorrow and shame should this be true!)
Such giddiness of heart and brain
Comes seldom save from rage and pain,
So talks as it's most used to do.

Kubla Khan

In Xanadu did Kubla Khan
A stately pleasure-dome decree:
Where Alph, the sacred river, ran
Through caverns measureless to man
   Down to a sunless sea.
So twice five miles of fertile ground
With walls and towers were girdled round:
And there were gardens bright with sinuous rills,
Where blossomed many an incense-bearing tree;
And here were forests ancient as the hills,
Enfolding sunny spots of greenery.

But oh! that deep romantic chasm which slanted
Down the green hill athwart a cedarn cover!
A savage place! as holy and enchanted
As e'er beneath a waning moon was haunted
By woman wailing for her demon-lover!
And from this chasm, with ceaseless turmoil seething,
As if this earth in fast thick pants were breathing,
A mighty fountain momently was forced:
Amid whose swift half-intermitted burst
Huge fragments vaulted like rebounding hail,
Or chaffy grain beneath the thresher's flail:
And 'mid these dancing rocks at once and ever
It flung up momently the sacred river.
Five miles meandering with a mazy motion
Through wood and dale the sacred river ran,
Then reached the caverns measureless to man,
And sank in tumult to a lifeless ocean:
And 'mid this tumult Kubla heard from far
Ancestral voices prophesying war!
   The shadow of the dome of pleasure
   Floated midway on the waves;
   Where was heard the mingled measure
   From the fountain and the caves.
It was a miracle of rare device,
A sunny pleasure-dome with caves of ice!

A damsel with a dulcimer
In a vision once I saw:
It was an Abyssinian maid,
And on her dulcimer she played,
Singing of Mount Abora.
Could I revive within me
Her symphony and song,
To such a deep delight 'twould win me,
That with music loud and long,
I would build that dome in air,
That sunny dome! those caves of ice!
And all who heard should see them there,
And all should cry, Beware! Beware!
His flashing eyes, his floating hair!
Weave a circle round him thrice,
And close your eyes with holy dread,
For he on honey-dew hath fed,
And drunk the milk of Paradise.

"Hear, Sweet Spirit..."

Hear, sweet spirit, hear the spell,
Lest a blacker charm compel!
So shall the midnight breezes swell
With thy deep long-lingering knell.

And at evening evermore,
In a chapel on the shore,
Shall the chaunter, sad and saintly,
Yellow tapers burning faintly,
Doleful masses chaunt for thee,
    Miserere Domine!

Hark! the cadence dies away
    On the quiet moonlight sea:
The boatmen rest their oars and say,
    Miserere Domine!

Remorse

JOSEPH BLANCO WHITE
(1775–1841)

To Night

Mysterious Night! when our first parent knew
Thee from report divine, and heard thy name,
Did he not tremble for this lovely frame,
This glorious canopy of light and blue?
Yet 'neath a curtain of translucent dew,
Bathed in the rays of the great setting flame,
Hesperus with the host of heaven came,
And lo! Creation widened in man's view.
Who could have thought such darkness lay concealed
Within thy beams, O sun! or who could find,
Whilst fly and leaf and insect stood revealed,
That to such countless orbs thou mad'st us blind!
Why do we then shun death with anxious strife?
If Light can thus deceive, wherefore not Life?

CHARLES LAMB
(1775–1834)

The Old Familiar Faces

I have had playmates, I have had companions,
In my days of childhood, in my joyful school-days—
All, all are gone, the old familiar faces.

I have been laughing, I have been carousing,
Drinking late, sitting late, with my bosom cronies—
All, all are gone, the old familiar faces.

I loved a Love once, fairest among women:
Closed are the doors on me, I must not see her—
All, all are gone, the old familiar faces.

I have a friend, a kinder friend has no man:
Like an ingrate, I left my friend abruptly;
Left him, to muse on the old familiar faces.

Ghost-like I paced round the haunts of my childhood,
Earth seemed a desert I was bound to traverse,
Seeking to find the old familiar faces.

Friend of my bosom, thou more than a brother,
Why wert not thou born in my father's dwelling?
So might we talk of the old familiar faces—

How some they have died, and some they have left me,
And some are taken from me; all are departed—
All, all are gone, the old familiar faces.

WALTER SAVAGE LANDOR
(1775-1864)

Proem to Hellenics

Come back, ye wandering Muses, come back home,
Ye seem to have forgotten where it lies:
Come, let us walk upon the silent sands
Of Simois, where deep footmarks show long strides;
Thence we may mount perhaps to higher ground,
Where Aphrodite from Athene won
The golden apple, and Here too,
And happy Ares shouted far below.

Or would ye rather choose the grassy vale
Where flows Anapos through anemones,
Hyacinths, and narcissuses, that bend
To show their rival beauty in the stream?

Bring with you each her lyre, and each in turn
Temper a graver with a lighter song.

To Robert Browning

There is delight in singing, though none hear
Beside the singer; and there is delight
In praising, though the praiser sit alone
And see the praised far off him, far above.

Shakespeare is not *our* poet, but the world's,
Therefore on him no speech; and short for thee,
Browning! Since Chaucer was alive and hale,
No man hath walked along our roads with step
So active, so inquiring eye, or tongue
So varied in discourse. But warmer climes
Give brighter plumage, stronger wing; the breeze
Of Alpine heights thou playest with, borne on
Beyond Sorrento and Amalfi, where
The Siren waits thee, singing song for song.

On Catullus

Tell me not what too well I know
About the bard of Sirmio . . .
   Yes, in Thalia's son
Such stains there are . . . as when a Grace
Sprinkles another's laughing face
   With nectar, and runs on.

To Shelley

Shelley! whose song so sweet was sweetest here,
We knew each other little; now I walk
Along the same green path, along the shore
Of Lerici, along the sandy plain
Trending from Lucca to the Pisan pines,
Under whose shadow scattered camels lie,
The old and young, and rarer deer uplift
Their knotty branches o'er high-feathered fern.
Regions of happiness! I greet ye well;
Your solitudes, and not your cities, stayed
My steps among you; for with you alone
Conversed I, and with those ye bore of old.
He who beholds the skies of Italy
Sees ancient Rome reflected, sees beyond,
Into more glorious Hellas, nurse of Gods
And godlike men: dwarfs people other lands.
Frown not, maternal England! thy weak child
Kneels at thy feet, and owns in shame a lie.

Dying Speech of an Old Philosopher

I strove with none, for none was worth my strife:
    Nature I loved, and next to Nature, Art:
I warmed both hands before the fire of Life;
    It sinks; and I am ready to depart.

FROM "In Clementina's Artless Mien"

In Clementina's artless mien
    Lucilla asks me what I see,
And are the roses of sixteen
    Enough for me?

Lucilla asks, if that be all,
    Have I not culled as sweet before . . .
Ah yes, Lucilla! and their fall
    I still deplore.

"Fate! I Have Asked..."

Fate! I have asked few things of thee,
    And fewer have to ask.
Shortly, thou knowest, I shall be
    No more . . . then con thy task.

If one be left on earth so late
    Whose love is like the past,
Tell her in whispers, gentle Fate,
    Not even love must last.

Tell her, I leave the noisy feast
    Of life, a little tired;
Amidst its pleasures few possest
    And many undesired.

Tell her, with steady pace to come
    And, where my laurels lie,
To throw the freshest on the tomb
    When it has caught her sigh.

Tell her, to stand some steps apart
  From others, on that day,
And check the tear (if tear should start)
  Too precious for dull clay.

"Sweet Was the Song..."

Sweet was the song that Youth sang once,
And passing sweet was the response;
But there are accents sweeter far
When Love leaps down our evening star,
Holds back the blighting wings of Time,
Melts with his breath the crusty rime,
And looks into our eyes, and says,
"Come, let us talk of former days."

"Years, Many Parti-Coloured Years"

Years, many parti-coloured years,
  Some have crept on, and some have flown,
Since first before me fell those tears
  I never could see fall alone.

Years, not so many, are to come,
  Years not so varied, when from you
One more will fall: when, carried home,
  I see it not, nor hear *adieu!*

"Ah, What Avails..."

Ah, what avails the sceptred race,
  Ah, what the form divine!
What every virtue, every grace!
  Rose Aylmer, all were thine.
Rose Aylmer, whom these wakeful eyes
  May weep, but never see,
A night of memories and sighs
  I consecrate to thee.

"Past Ruined Ilion..."

Past ruined Ilion Helen lives,
    Alcestis rises from the shades;
Verse calls them forth; 'tis verse that gives
    Immortal youth to mortal maids.

Soon shall Oblivion's deepening veil
    Hide all the peopled hills you see,
The gay, the proud, while lovers hail
    In distant ages you and me.

The tear for fading beauty check,
    For passing glory cease to sigh;
One form shall rise above the wreck,
    One name, Ianthe, shall not die.

Ianthe's Troubles

From you, Ianthe, little troubles pass
    Like little ripples down a sunny river;
Your pleasures spring like daisies in the grass,
    Cut down, and up again as blithe as ever.

"Twenty Years Hence..."

Twenty years hence my eyes may grow
If not quite dim, yet rather so,
Still yours from others they shall know
                Twenty years hence.
Twenty years hence though it may hap
That I be called to take a nap
In a cool cell where thunder-clap
                Was never heard;
There breathe but o'er my arch of grass
A not too sadly sighed *Alas,*
And I shall catch, ere you can pass,
                That wingéd word.

"Proud Word You Never Spoke..."

Proud word you never spoke, but you will speak
   Four not exempt from pride some future day.
Resting on one white hand a warm wet cheek
   Over my open volume you will say,
     "This man loved *me!*" then rise and trip away.

"Do You Remember Me?..."

"Do you remember me? or are you proud?"
Lightly advancing through her star-trimmed crowd,
   Ianthe said, and looked into my eyes.
"A *yes*, a *yes*, to both: for Memory
Where you but once have been must ever be,
   And at your voice Pride from his throne must rise."

"Well I Remember..."

Well I remember how you smiled
   To see me write your name upon
The soft sea-sand . . . "*O! what a child!*
   You think you're writing upon stone!"
I have since written what no tide
   Shall ever wash away, what men
Unborn shall read o'er ocean wide
   And find Ianthe's name again.

Dirce

Stand close around, ye Stygian set,
   With Dirce in one boat conveyed!
Or Charon, seeing, may forget,
   That he is old and she a shade.

A Foreign Ruler

He says, *My reign is peace,* so slays
    A thousand in the dead of night.
Are you all happy now? he says,
    And those he leaves behind cry *quite.*
He swears he will have no contention,
    And sets all nations by the ears;
He shouts aloud, *No intervention!*
    Invades, and drowns them all in tears.

FROM *Regeneration*

We are what suns and winds and waters make us;
The mountains are our sponsors, and the rills
Fashion and win their nursling with their smiles.
But where the land is dim from tyranny,
There tiny pleasures occupy the place
Of glories and of duties; as the feet
Of fabled faeries when the sun goes down
Trip o'er the grass where wrestlers strove by day.
Then Justice, called the eternal one above,
Is more inconstant than the buoyant form
That bursts into existence from the froth
Of ever-varying ocean: what is best
Then becomes worst; what loveliest, most deformed.
The heart is hardest in the softest climes,
The passions flourish, the affections die.

FROM *Corinna to Tanagra*

Tanagra! think not I forget
    Thy beautifully-storied streets:
Be sure my memory bathes yet
    In clear Thermodon, and yet greets
The blithe and liberal shepherd-boy,
Whose sunny bosom swells with joy
When we accept his matted rushes
Upheaved with sylvan fruit; away he bounds, and blushes.

I promise to bring back with me
    What thou with transport wilt receive,
The only proper gift for thee,
    Of which no mortal shall bereave
In later times thy mouldering walls,
Until the last old turret falls;
A crown, a crown from Athens won,
A crown no God can wear, beside Latona's son.

FROM *Pericles and Aspasia*

1.

Beauty! thou art a wanderer on the earth,
    And hast no temple in the fairest isle
Or city over-sea, where wealth and mirth
    And all the Graces, all the Muses, smile.

Thou art a wanderer, Beauty! like the rays
    That now upon the platan, now upon
The sleepy lake, glance quick or idly gaze,
    And now are manifold and now are none.

In more than one bright form hast thou appeared,
    In more than one sweet dialect hast thou spoken:
Beauty! thy spells the heart within me heard,
    Grieved that they bound it, grieves that they are broken.

2.

"Artemidora! Gods invisible,
While thou art lying faint along the couch,
Have tied the sandal to thy veinéd feet,
And stand beside thee, ready to convey
Thy weary steps where other rivers flow.
Refreshing shades will waft thy weariness
Away, and voices like thine own come nigh
Soliciting, nor vainly, thy embrace."

Artemidora sighed, and would have pressed
The hand now pressing hers, but was too weak.
Fate's shears were over her dark hair unseen
While thus Elpenor spake: he looked into
Eyes that had given light and life erewhile
To those above them, those now dim with tears
And watchfulness. Again he spake of joy
Eternal. At that word, that sad word, *joy,*
Faithful and fond her bosom heaved once more,
Her head fell back: one sob, one loud deep sob
Swelled through the darkened chamber; 'twas not hers:
With her that old boat incorruptible,
Unwearied, undiverted in its course,
Had plashed the water up the farther strand.

To Poets

My children! speak not ill of one another;
   I do not ask you not to hate;
Cadets must envy every elder brother,
   The little poet must the great.

"Leaf after Leaf..."

Leaf after leaf drops off, flower after flower,
Some in the chill, some in the warmer hour:
Alike they flourish and alike they fall,
And earth who nourished them receives them all.
Should we, her wiser sons, be less content
To sink into her lap when life is spent?

THOMAS MOORE

(1779–1852)

"The Harp That Once..."

The harp that once through Tara's halls
   The soul of music shed,
Now hangs as mute on Tara's walls
   As if the soul were fled.

So sleeps the pride of former days,
    So glory's thrill is o'er,
And hearts, that once beat high for praise,
    Now feel that pulse no more.

No more to chiefs and ladies bright
    The harp of Tara swells:
The chord alone, that breaks at night,
    Its tale of ruin tells.
Thus Freedom now so seldom wakes,
    The only throb she gives,
Is when some heart indignant breaks,
    To show that still she lives.

"At the Mid Hour of Night..."

At the mid hour of night, when stars are weeping, I fly
To the lone vale we loved, when life shone warm in thine eye;
    And I think oft, if spirits can steal from the regions of air
    To revisit past scenes of delight, thou wilt come to me there,
And tell me our love is remembered even in the sky.

Then I sing the wild song it once was rapture to hear,
When our voices commingling breathed like one on the ear;
    And as Echo far off through the vale my sad orison rolls,
    I think, O my love! 'tis thy voice from the Kingdom of Souls
Faintly answering still the notes that once were so dear.

Child's Song

I have a garden of my own,
    Shining with flowers of every hue;
I loved it dearly while alone,
    But I shall love it more with you:
And there the golden bees shall come,
    In summer time at break of morn,
And wake us with their busy hum
    Around the Siha's fragrant thorn.

I have a fawn from Aden's land,
  On leafy buds and berries nursed;
And you shall feed him from your hand,
  Though he may start with fear at first,
And I will lead you where he lies
  For shelter in the noon-tide heat;
And you may touch his sleeping eyes,
  And feel his little silvery feet.

JAMES HENRY LEIGH HUNT

(1784–1859)

The Nile

It flows through old hushed Egypt and its sands,
  Like some grave mighty thought threading a dream,
  And times and things, as in that vision, seem
Keeping along it their eternal stands,—
Caves, pillars, pyramids, the shepherd bands
  That roamed through the young world, the glory extreme
  Of high Sesostris, and that southern beam,
The laughing queen that caught the world's great hands.

Then comes a mightier silence, stern and strong,
As of a world left empty of its throng,
  And the void weighs on us; and then we wake,
And hear the fruitful stream lapsing along
  Twixt villages, and think how we shall take
  Our own calm journey on for human sake.

The Fish, the Man, and the Spirit

TO A FISH

You strange, astonished-looking, angle-faced,
  Dreary-mouthed, gaping wretches of the sea,
  Gulping salt water everlastingly,
Cold-blooded, though with red your blood be graced,
And mute, though dwellers in the roaring waste;
  And you, all shapes beside, that fishy be,—
  Some round, some flat, some long, all devilry,
Legless, unloving, infamously chaste:—

O scaly, slippery, wet, swift, staring wights,
　　What is't ye do? What life lead? eh, dull goggles?
How do ye vary your vile days and nights?
　　How pass your Sundays? Are ye still but joggles
In ceaseless wash? Still nought but gapes, and bites,
　　And drinks, and stares, diversified with boggles?

A FISH ANSWERS

Amazing monster! that, for aught I know,
　　With the first sight of thee didst make our race
　　For ever stare! O flat and shocking face,
Grimly divided from the breast below!
Thou that on dry land horribly dost go
　　With a split body and most ridiculous pace,
　　Prong after prong, disgracer of all grace,
Long-useless-finned, haired, upright, unwet, slow!

O breather of unbreathable, sword-sharp air,
　　How canst exist? How bear thyself, thou dry
And dreary sloth? What particle canst share
　　Of the only blessed life, the watery?
I sometimes see of ye an actual *pair*
　　Go by! linked fin by fin! most odiously.

THE FISH TURNS INTO A MAN, AND THEN INTO A SPIRIT, AND AGAIN SPEAKS

Indulge thy smiling scorn, if smiling still,
　　O man! and loathe, but with a sort of love;
　　For difference must its use by difference prove,
And, in sweet clang, the spheres with music fill.
One of the spirits am I, that at his will
　　Live in whate'er has life—fish, eagle, dove—
　　No hate, no pride, beneath nought, nor above,
A visitor of the rounds of God's sweet skill.

Man's life is warm, glad, sad, 'twixt loves and graves,
　　Boundless in hope, honoured with pangs austere,
Heaven-gazing; and his angel-wings he craves:—
　　The fish is swift, small-needling, vague yet clear,
A cold, sweet, silver life, wrapped in round waves,
　　Quickened with touches of transporting fear.

Rondeau

Jenny kissed me when we met,
    Jumping from the chair she sat in;
Time, you thief, who love to get
    Sweets into your list, put that in:
Say I'm weary, say I'm sad,
    Say that health and wealth have missed me,
Say I'm growing old, but add
    Jenny kissed me.

THOMAS LOVE PEACOCK

(1785–1866)

Song

In his last bin Sir Peter lies,
    Who knew not what it was to frown:
Death took him mellow, by surprise,
    And in his cellar stopped him down.
Through all our land we could not boast
    A knight more gay, more prompt than he,
To rise and fill a bumper toast,
    And pass it round with three times three.

None better knew the feast to sway,
    Or keep Mirth's boat in better trim;
For Nature had but little clay
    Like that of which she moulded him.
The meanest guest that graced his board
    Was there the freest of the free,
His bumper toast when Peter poured,
    And passed it round with three times three.

He kept at true good humour's mark
    The social flow of pleasure's tide:
He never made a brow look dark,
    Nor caused a tear, but when he died.
No sorrow round his tomb should dwell:
    More pleased his gay old ghost would be,
For funeral song, and passing bell,
    To hear no sound but three times three.

Headlong Hall

A Catch

Seamen three! What men be ye?
Gotham's three wise men we be.
Whither in your bowl so free?
To rake the moon from out the sea.
The bowl goes trim. The moon doth shine.
And our ballast is old wine;
And your ballast is old wine.

Who art thou, so fast adrift?
I am he they call Old Care.
Here on board we will thee lift.
No: I may not enter there.
Wherefore so? 'Tis Jove's decree,
In a bowl Care may not be;
In a bowl Care may not be.

Fear ye not the waves that roll?
No: in charméd bowl we swim.
What the charm that floats the bowl?
Water may not pass the brim.
The bowl goes trim. The moon doth shine.
And our ballast is old wine;
And your ballast is old wine.

Nightmare Abbey

Song

It was a friar of orders free,
A friar of Rubygill:
At the greenwood-tree a vow made he,
But he kept it very ill:
A vow made he of chastity,
But he kept it very ill.
He kept it, perchance, in the conscious shade
Of the bounds of the forest wherein it was made:
But he roamed where he listed, as free as the wind,
And he left his good vow in the forest behind:
For its woods out of sight were his vow out of mind,
With the friar of Rubygill.

In lonely hut himself he shut,
The friar of Rubygill;
Where the ghostly elf absolved himself,
To follow his own good will:
And he had no lack of canary sack,
To keep his conscience still.
And a damsel well knew, when at lonely midnight
It gleamed on the waters, his signal-lamp-light:
"Over! Over!" she warbled with nightingale throat,
And the friar sprung forth at the magical note,
And she crossed the dark stream in his trim ferry-boat,
With the friar of Rubygill.

Maid Marian

"Not Drunk Is He..."

Not drunk is he, who from the floor
Can rise alone, and still drink more;
But drunk is he, who prostrate lies,
Without the power to drink or rise.

The Misfortunes of Elphin

FROM *The War-Song of Dinas Vawr*

The mountain sheep are sweeter,
But the valley sheep are fatter;
We therefore deemed it meeter
To carry off the latter.

The Misfortunes of Elphin

Chorus

If I drink water while this doth last,
May I never again drink wine:
For how can a man, in his life of a span,
Do anything better than dine?
We'll dine and drink, and say if we think
That anything better can be;
And when we have dined, wish all mankind
May dine as well as we.

And though a good wish will fill no dish,
And brim no cup with sack,
Yet thoughts will spring, as the glasses ring,
To illume our studious track.
On the brilliant dreams of our hopeful schemes
The light of the flask shall shine;
And we'll sit till day, but we'll find the way
To drench the world with wine.

Crotchet Castle

Love and Age

I played with you 'mid cowslips blowing,
When I was six and you were four;
When garlands weaving, flower-balls throwing,
Were pleasures soon to please no more.
Through groves and meads, o'er grass and heather,
With little playmates, to and fro,
We wandered hand in hand together;
But that was sixty years ago.

You grew a lovely roseate maiden,
And still our early love was strong;
Still with no care our days were laden,
They glided joyously along;
Then I did love you, very dearly,
How dearly words want power to show;
I thought your heart was touched as nearly;
But that was fifty years ago.

Then other lovers came around you,
Your beauty grew from year to year,
And many a splendid circle found you
The centre of its glittering sphere.
I saw you then, first vows forsaking,
On rank and wealth your hand bestow;
Oh, then I thought my heart was breaking,—
But that was forty years ago.

And I loved on, to wed another:
No cause she gave me to repine;
And when I heard you were a mother,
I did not wish the children mine.
My own young flock, in fair progression,
Made up a pleasant Christmas row:
My joy in them was past expression;—
But that was thirty years ago.

You grew a matron plump and comely,
You dwelt in fashion's brightest blaze;
My earthly lot was far more homely;
But I too had my festal days.
No merrier eyes have ever glistened
Around the hearth-stone's wintry glow,
Than when my youngest child was christened:—
But that was twenty years ago.

Time passed. My eldest girl was married,
And I am now a grandsire grey;
One pet of four years old I've carried
Among the wild-flowered meads to play.
In our old fields of childish pleasure,
Where now, as then, the cowslips blow,
She fills her basket's ample measure,—
And that is not ten years ago.

But though first love's impassioned blindness
Has passed away in colder light,
I still have thought of you with kindness,
And shall do, till our last good-night.
The ever-rolling silent hours
Will bring a time we shall not know,
When our young days of gathering flowers
Will be an hundred years ago.

Gryll Grange

Glee—The Ghosts

In life three ghostly friars were we,
And now three friarly ghosts we be.
Around our shadowy table placed,
The spectral bowl before us floats;
With wine that none but ghosts can taste,
We wash our unsubstantial throats.
Three merry ghosts—three merry ghosts—three merry ghosts
        are we:
Let the ocean be Port, and we'll think it good sport
To be laid in that Red Sea.

With songs that jovial spectres chaunt,
Our old refectory still we haunt.
The traveller hears our midnight mirth:
"O list!" he cries, "the haunted choir!
The merriest ghost that walks the earth,
Is sure the ghost of a ghostly friar."
Three merry ghosts—three merry ghosts—three merry ghosts
        are we:
Let the ocean be Port, and we'll think it good sport
To be laid in that Red Sea.

Melincourt

GEORGE NOEL GORDON, LORD BYRON
(1788–1824)

FROM *To Woman*

Woman! experience might have told me,
That all must love thee who behold thee:
Surely experience might have taught
Thy finest promises are nought:
But, placed in all thy charms before me,
All I forget but to adore thee.
Oh memory! thou choicest blessing
When joined with hope, when still possessing;
But how much cursed by every lover
When hope is fled and passion's over.

"Farewell! If Ever Fondest Prayer"

Farewell! if ever fondest prayer
    For other's weal availed on high,
Mine will not all be lost in air,
    But waft thy name beyond the sky.
'Twere vain to speak, to weep, to sigh:
    Oh! more than tears of blood can tell,
When wrung from guilt's expiring eye,
    Are in that word—Farewell!—Farewell!

These lips are mute, these eyes are dry;
    But in my breast and in my brain,
Awake the pangs that pass not by,
    The thoughts that ne'er shall sleep again.
My soul nor deigns nor dares complain,
    Though grief and passion there rebel:
I only know we loved in vain—
    I only feel—Farewell!—Farewell!

"When We Two Parted"

When we two parted
    In silence and tears,
Half broken-hearted
    To sever for years,
Pale grew thy cheek and cold,
    Colder thy kiss;
Truly that hour foretold
    Sorrow to this.

The dew of the morning
    Sunk chill on my brow—
It felt like the warning
    Of what I feel now.
Thy vows are all broken,
    And light is thy fame;
I hear thy name spoken,
    And share in its shame.

They name thee before me,
 A knell to mine ear;
A shudder comes o'er me—
 Why wert thou so dear?
They know not I knew thee,
 Who knew thee too well—
Long, long shall I rue thee,
 Too deeply to tell.

In secret we met—
 In silence I grieve
That thy heart could forget,
 Thy spirit deceive.
If I should meet thee
 After long years,
How should I greet thee?
 With silence and tears.

"Remember Thee! Remember Thee!"

Remember thee! remember thee!
 Till Lethe quench life's burning stream
Remorse and shame shall cling to thee,
 And haunt thee like a feverish dream!

Remember thee! Aye, doubt it not.
 Thy husband too shall think of thee:
By neither shalt thou be forgot,
 Thou false to him, thou fiend to me!

FROM *Stanzas*

Could Love for ever
Run like a river,
And Time's endeavour
 Be tried in vain—
No other pleasure
With this could measure

And like a treasure
　　We'd hug the chain.
But since our sighing
Ends not in dying,
And, formed for flying,
　　Love plumes his wing;
Then for this reason
Let's love a season:
But let that season be only Spring.

When lovers parted
Feel broken-hearted,
And, all hopes thwarted,
　　Expect to die;
A few years older,
Ah! how much colder
They might behold her
　　For whom they sigh!
When linked together
In every weather
They pluck Love's feather
　　From out his wing—
He'll stay for ever
But sadly shiver
Without his plumage when past the Spring.

Wait not, fond lover!
Till years are over,
And then recover,
　　As from a dream.
While each bewailing
The other's failing,
With wrath and railing,
　　All hideous seem—
While first decreasing,
Yet not quite ceasing,
Wait not till teasing
　　All passion blight:
If once diminished
Love's reign is finished—
Then part in friendship—and bid good-night.

"So We'll Go No More a Roving"

So we'll go no more a roving
  So late into the night,
Though the heart be still as loving,
  And the moon be still as bright.

For the sword outwears the sheath,
  And the soul wears out the breast,
And the heart must pause to breathe,
  And Love itself have rest.

Though the night was made for loving,
  And the day returns too soon,
Yet we'll go no more a roving
  By the light of the moon.

FROM *Childe Harold's Pilgrimage*

1.

There was a sound of revelry by night,
And Belgium's capital had gathered then
Her beauty and her chivalry, and bright
The lamps shone o'er fair women and brave men;
A thousand hearts beat happily; and when
Music arose with its voluptuous swell,
Soft eyes looked love to eyes which spake again,
And all went merry as a marriage bell—
But hush! hark! a deep sound strikes like a rising knell!

Did ye not hear it? No, 'twas but the wind,
Or the car rattling o'er the stony street;
On with the dance! let joy be unconfined;
No sleep till morn, when youth and pleasure meet
To chase the glowing hours with flying feet—
But hark!—that heavy sound breaks in once more
As if the clouds its echo would repeat;
And nearer, clearer, deadlier than before!
Arm! Arm! it is—it is—the cannon's opening roar!

Ah! then and there was hurrying to and fro,
And gathering tears, and tremblings of distress,
And cheeks all pale, which but an hour ago
Blushed at the praise of their own loveliness;
And there were sudden partings, such as press
The life from out young hearts, and choking sighs
Which ne'er might be repeated; who could guess
If ever more should meet those mutual eyes,
Since upon night so sweet such awful morn could rise!

And there was mounting in hot haste: the steed,
The mustering squadron, and the clattering car,
Went pouring forward with impetuous speed,
And swiftly forming in the ranks of war;
And the deep thunder peel on peel afar;
And near, the beat of the alarming drum
Roused up the soldier ere the morning star;
While thronged the citizens with terror dumb,
Or whispering with white lips—"The foe! They come! they
    come!"

And Ardennes waves above them her green leaves,
Dewy with nature's tear-drops, as they pass,
Grieving, if aught inanimate e'er grieves,
Over the unreturning brave—alas!
Ere evening to be trodden like the grass
Which now beneath them, but above shall grow
In its next verdure, when this fiery mass
Of living valour, rolling on the foe
And burning with high hope, shall moulder cold and low.

Last noon beheld them full of lusty life,
Last eve in Beauty's circle proudly gay,
The midnight brought the signal-sound of strife,
The morn the marshalling in arms—the day
Battle's magnificently-stern array!
The thunder-clouds close o'er it, which when rent
The earth is covered thick with other clay,
Which her own clay shall cover, heaped and pent,
Rider and horse—friend, foe—in one red burial blent!

2.

The castled crag of Drachenfels
Frowns o'er the wide and winding Rhine,
Whose breast of waters broadly swells
Between the banks which bear the vine;
And hills all rich with blossomed trees,
And fields which promise corn and wine,
And scattered cities crowning these,
Whose far white walls along them shine,
Have strewed a scene, which I should see
With double joy wert thou with me.

And peasant girls, with deep blue eyes
And hands which offer early flowers,
Walk smiling o'er this paradise;
Above, the frequent feudal towers
Through green leaves lift their walls of gray;
And many a rock which steeply lowers,
And noble arch in proud decay,
Look o'er this vale of vintage-bowers;
But one thing want these banks of Rhine—
Thy gentle hand to clasp in mine.

I send the lilies given to me;
Though long before thy hand they touch,
I know that they must withered be,
But yet reject them not as such;
For I have cherished them as dear,
Because they yet may meet thine eye,
And guide thy soul to mine even here,
When thou behold'st them, drooping nigh,
And know'st them gathered by the Rhine,
And offered from my heart to thine!

The river nobly foams and flows,
The charm of this enchanted ground,
And all its thousand turns disclose
Some fresher beauty varying round:
The haughtiest breast its wish might bound

Through life to dwell delighted here;
Nor could on earth a spot be found
To nature and to me so dear,
Could thy dear eyes in following mine
Still sweeten more these banks of Rhine!

3.

I stood in Venice on the Bridge of Sighs,
A palace and a prison on each hand;
I saw from out the wave her structures rise
As from the stroke of the enchanter's wand:
A thousand years their cloudy wings expand
Around me, and a dying glory smiles
O'er the far times, when many a subject land
Looked to the wingéd Lion's marble piles,
Where Venice sat in state, throned on her hundred isles!

She looks a sea Cybele, fresh from ocean,
Rising with her tiara of proud towers
At airy distance, with majestic motion,
A ruler of the waters and their powers.
And such she was—her daughters had their dowers
From spoils of nations, and the exhaustless East
Poured in her lap all gems in sparkling showers:
In purple was she robed, and of her feast
Monarchs partook, and deemed their dignity increased.

In Venice Tasso's echoes are no more,
And silent rows the songless gondolier;
Her palaces are crumbling to the shore,
And music meets not always now the ear;
Those days are gone, but beauty still is here;
States fall, arts fade, but Nature doth not die,
Nor yet forget how Venice once was dear,
The pleasant place of all festivity,
The revel of the earth, the masque of Italy!

4.

Egeria, sweet creation of some heart
Which found no mortal resting-place so fair
As thine ideal breast! whate'er thou art
Or wert—a young Aurora of the air,

The nympholepsy of some fond despair,
Or, it might be, a beauty of the earth,
Who found a more than common votary there
Too much adoring; whatsoe'er thy birth,
Thou wert a beautiful thought, and softly bodied forth.

The mosses of thy fountain still are sprinkled
With thine Elysian water-drops; the face
Of thy cave-guarded spring, with years unwrinkled,
Reflects the meek-eyed genius of the place,
Whose green, wild margin now no more erase
Art's works; nor must the delicate waters sleep
Prisoned in marble; bubbling from the base
Of the cleft statue, with a gentle leap
The rill runs o'er, and round, fern, flowers, and ivy creep,

Fantastically tangled. The green hills
Are clothed with early blossoms, through the grass
The quick-eyed lizard rustles, and the bills
Of summer-birds sing welcome as ye pass;
Flowers fresh in hue, and many in their class,
Implore the pausing step, and with their dyes
Dance in the soft breeze in a fairy mass;
The sweetness of the violet's deep blue eyes,
Kissed by the breath of heaven, seems coloured by its skies.

5.

Oh Love! no habitant of earth thou art—
An unseen seraph, we believe in thee,
A faith whose martyrs are the broken heart,
But never yet hath seen, nor e'er shall see
The naked eye, thy form, as it should be;
The mind hath made thee, as it peopled heaven,
Even with its own desiring phantasy,
And to a thought such shape and image given,
As haunts the unquenched soul—parched—wearied—wrung—
          and riven.

Of its own beauty is the mind diseased,
And fevers into false creation—where,
Where are the forms the sculptor's soul hath seized?
In him alone. Can Nature show so fair?
Where are the charms and virtues which we dare
Conceive in boyhood and pursue as men,
The unreached paradise of our despair,
Which o'er-informs the pencil and the pen,
And overpowers the page where it would bloom again?

Who loves, raves—'tis youth's frenzy; but the cure
Is bitterer still. As charm by charm unwinds
Which robed our idols, and we see too sure
Nor worth nor beauty dwells from out the mind's
Ideal shape of such; yet still it binds
The fatal spell, and still it draws us on,
Reaping the whirlwind from the oft-sown winds;
The stubborn heart, its alchemy begun,
Seems ever near the prize—wealthiest when most undone.

We wither from our youth, we gasp away—
Sick—sick—unfound the boon—unslaked the thirst,
Though to the last, in verge of our decay,
Some phantom lures, such as we sought at first—
But all too late—so are we doubly cursed.
Love, fame, ambition, avarice—'tis the same,
Each idle, and all ill, and none the worst—
For all are meteors with a different name,
And Death the sable smoke where vanishes the flame.

6.

There is a pleasure in the pathless woods,
There is a rapture on the lonely shore,
There is society where none intrudes,
By the deep Sea, and music in its roar:
I love not Man the less, but Nature more,
From these our interviews, in which I steal
From all I may be or have been before,
To mingle with the universe, and feel
What I can ne'er express, yet can not all conceal.

Roll on, thou deep and dark blue ocean, roll!
Ten thousand fleets sweep over thee in vain;
Man marks the earth with ruin, his control
Stops with the shore; upon the watery plain
The wrecks are all thy deed, nor doth remain
A shadow of man's ravage, save his own,
When, for a moment, like a drop of rain,
He sinks into thy depths with bubbling groan,
Without a grave, unknelled, uncoffined, and unknown.

FROM Don Juan

1.

      . . . 'Tis sweet to hear
  At midnight on the blue and moonlit deep
The song and oar of Adria's gondolier,
  By distance mellowed, o'er the waters sweep;
'Tis sweet to see the evening star appear;
  'Tis sweet to listen as the night-winds creep
From leaf to leaf; 'tis sweet to view on high
The rainbow, based on ocean, span the sky.

'Tis sweet to hear the watch-dog's honest bark
  Bay deep-mouthed welcome as we draw near home;
'Tis sweet to know there is an eye will mark
  Our coming, and look brighter when we come;
'Tis sweet to be awakened by the lark,
  Or lulled by falling waters; sweet the hum
Of bees, the voice of girls, the song of birds,
The lisp of children, and their earliest words.

Sweet is the vintage, when the showering grapes
  In Bacchanal profusion reel to earth,
Purple and gushing; sweet are our escapes
  From civic revelry to rural mirth;
Sweet to the miser are his glittering heaps,
  Sweet to the father is his first-born's birth,
Sweet is revenge—especially to women,
Pillage to soldiers, prize-money to seamen.

But sweeter still than this, than these, than all,
   Is first and passionate love—it stands alone,
Like Adam's recollection of his fall;
   The tree of knowledge has been plucked—all's known—
And life yields nothing further to recall
   Worthy of this ambrosial sin, so shown,
No doubt in fable, as the unforgiven
Fire which Prometheus filched for us from heaven.

2.

    They tell me 'tis decided; you depart:
      'Tis wise—'tis well, but not the less a pain;
    I have no further claim on your young heart,
      Mine is the victim, and would be again;
    To love too much has been the only art
      I used—I write in haste, and if a stain
    Be on this sheet, 'tis not what it appears;
    My eyeballs burn and throb, but have no tears.

    I loved, I love you, for this love have lost
      State, station, heaven, mankind's, my own esteem,
    And yet can not regret what it hath cost,
      So dear is still the memory of that dream;
    Yet, if I name my guilt, 'tis not to boast,
      None can deem harshlier of me than I deem:
    I trace this scrawl because I cannot rest—
    I've nothing to reproach, or to request.

    Man's love is of man's life a thing apart,
      'Tis woman's whole existence; man may range
    The court, camp, church, the vessel, and the mart;
      Sword, gown, gain, glory, offer in exchange
    Pride, fame, ambition, to fill up his heart,
      And few there are whom these cannot estrange;
    Men have all these resources, we but one,
    To love again, and be again undone.

    You will proceed in pleasure, and in pride,
      Beloved and loving many; all is o'er
    For me on earth, except some years to hide
      My shame and sorrow deep in my heart's core;

These I could bear, but cannot cast aside
    The passion which still rages as before—
And so farewell—forgive me, love me—No,
That word is idle now—but let it go.

My breast has been all weakness, is so yet;
    But still I think I can collect my mind;
My blood still rushes where my spirit's set,
    As roll the waves before the settled wind;
My heart is feminine, nor can forget—
    To all, except one image, madly blind;
So shakes the needle, and so stands the pole,
As vibrates my fond heart to my fixed soul.

I have no more to say, but linger still,
    And dare not set my seal upon this sheet,
And yet I may as well the task fulfil,
    My misery can scarce be more complete:
I had not lived till now, could sorrow kill;
    Death shuns the wretch who fain the blow would meet,
And I must even survive this last adieu,
And bear with life, to love and pray for you!

3.

    'Tis pleasing to be schooled in a strange tongue
        By female lips and eyes—that is, I mean,
    When both the teacher and the taught are young,
        As was the case, at least, where I have been;
    They smile so when one's right, and when one's wrong
        They smile still more, and then there intervene
    Pressure of hands, perhaps even a chaste kiss—
    I learned the little that I know by this.

4.

    It was the cooling hour, just when the rounded
        Red sun sinks down behind the azure hill,
    Which then seems as if the whole earth it bounded,
        Circling all nature, hushed, and dim, and still,

With the far mountain-crescent half surrounded
   On one side, and the deep sea calm and chill
Upon the other, and the rosy sky,
With one star sparkling through it like an eye.

And thus they wandered forth, and hand in hand,
   Over the shining pebbles and the shells,
Glided along the smooth and hardened sand,
   And in the worn and wild receptacles
Worked by the storms, yet worked as it were planned
   In hollow halls, with sparry roofs and cells,
They turned to rest; and, each clasped by an arm,
Yielded to the deep twilight's purple charm.

They looked up to the sky, whose floating glow
   Spread like a rosy ocean, vast and bright;
They gazed upon the glittering sea below,
   Whence the broad moon rose circling into sight;
They heard the wave's splash, and the wind so low,
   And saw each other's dark eyes darting light
Into each other—and, beholding this,
Their lips drew near, and clung into a kiss;

A long, long kiss, a kiss of youth, and love,
   And beauty, all concentrating like rays
Into one focus, kindled from above;
   Such kisses as belong to early days,
Where heart, and soul, and sense, in concert move,
   And the blood's lava, and the pulse a blaze,
Each kiss a heart-quake—for a kiss's strength,
I think, it must be reckoned by its length.

By length I mean duration; theirs endured
   Heaven knows how long—no doubt they never reckoned;
And if they had, they could not have secured
   The sum of their sensations to a second:
They had not spoken; but they felt allured,
   As if their souls and lips each other beckoned,
Which, being joined, like swarming bees they clung—
Their hearts the flowers from whence the honey sprung.

They were alone, but not alone as they
   Who shut in chambers think it loneliness;
The silent ocean, and the starlight bay,
   The twilight glow which momently grew less,
The voiceless sands and dropping caves, that lay
   Around them, made them to each other press,
As if there were no life beneath the sky
Save theirs, and that their life could never die.

They feared no eyes nor ears on that lone beach,
   They felt no terrors from the night, they were
All in all to each other: though their speech
   Was broken words, they *thought* a language there—
And all the burning tongues the passions teach
   Found in one sigh the best interpreter
Of nature's oracle—first love—that all
Which Eve has left her daughters since her fall.

Haidée spoke not of scruples, asked no vows,
   Nor offered any; she had never heard
Of plight and promises to be a spouse,
   Or perils by a loving maid incurred;
She was all which pure ignorance allows,
   And flew to her young mate like a young bird;
And, never having dreamed of falsehood, she
Had not one word to say of constancy.

She loved and was belovéd—she adored
   And she was worshipped; after nature's fashion
Their intense souls, into each other poured,
   If souls could die, had perished in that passion—
But by degrees their senses were restored,
   Again to be o'ercome, again to dash on;
And, beating 'gainst his bosom, Haidée's heart
Felt as if never more to beat apart.

Alas! they were so young, so beautiful,
   So lonely, loving, helpless, and the hour
Was that in which the heart is always full,
   And, having o'er itself no further power,

Prompts deeds eternity can not annul,
  But pays off moments in an endless shower
Of hell-fire—all prepared for people giving
Pleasure or pain to one another living.

Alas! for Juan and Haidée! they were
  So loving and so lovely—till then never,
Excepting our first parents, such a pair
  Had run the risk of being damned for ever;
And Haidée, being devout as well as fair,
  Had, doubtless, heard about the Stygian river,
And hell and purgatory—but forgot
Just in the very crisis she should not.

They look upon each other, and their eyes
  Gleam in the moonlight; and her white arm clasps
Round Juan's head, and his around her lies
  Half buried in the tresses which it grasps;
She sits upon his knee, and drinks his sighs,
  He hers, until they end in broken gasps;
And thus they form a group that's quite antique,
Half naked, loving, natural, and Greek.

And when those deep and burning moments passed,
  And Juan sunk to sleep within her arms,
She slept not, but all tenderly, though fast,
  Sustained his head upon her bosom's charms;
And now and then her eye to heaven is cast,
  And then on the pale cheek her breast now warms,
Pillowed on her o'erflowing heart, which pants
With all it granted, and with all it grants.

An infant when it gazes on the light,
  A child the moment when it drains the breast,
A devotee when soars the Host in sight,
  An Arab with a stranger for a guest,
A sailor when the prize has struck in fight,
  A miser filling his most hoarded chest,
Feel rapture; but not such true joy are reaping
As they who watch o'er what they love while sleeping.

For there it lies so tranquil, so beloved,
　　All that it hath of life with us is living;
So gentle, stirless, helpless and unmoved,
　　And all unconscious of the joy 'tis giving;
All it hath felt, inflicted, passed and proved,
　　Hushed into depths beyond the watcher's diving;
There lies the thing we love with all its errors
And all its charms, like death without its terrors.

5.

　　The isles of Greece, the isles of Greece!
　　　　Where burning Sappho loved and sung,
　　Where grew the arts of war and peace,
　　　　Where Delos rose, and Phoebus sprung!
　　Eternal summer gilds them yet,
　　But all, except their sun, is set.

　　The Scian and the Teian muse,
　　　　The hero's harp, the lover's lute,
　　Have found the fame your shores refuse;
　　　　Their place of birth alone is mute
　　To sounds which echo further west
　　Than your sires' "Islands of the Blest."

　　The mountains look on Marathon,
　　　　And Marathon looks on the sea;
　　And musing there an hour alone,
　　　　I dreamed that Greece might still be free;
　　And standing on the Persians' grave,
　　I could not deem myself a slave.

　　A king sate on the rocky brow
　　　　Which looks o'er sea-born Salamis;
　　And ships, by thousands, lay below,
　　　　And men in nations—all were his!
　　He counted them at break of day—
　　And when the sun set where were they?

And where are they? and where art thou,
  My country? On thy voiceless shore
The heroic lay is tuneless now—
  The heroic bosom beats no more!
And must thy lyre, so long divine,
Degenerate into hands like mine?

'Tis something, in the dearth of fame,
  Though linked among a fettered race,
To feel at least a patriot's shame,
  Even as I sing, suffuse my face;
For what is left the poet here?
For Greeks a blush—for Greece a tear.

Must we but weep o'er days more blest?
  Must we but blush? Our fathers bled.
Earth! render back from out thy breast
  A remnant of our Spartan dead!
Of the three hundred grant but three
To make a new Thermopylae!

What, silent still? and silent all?
  Ah! no—the voices of the dead
Sound like a distant torrent's fall,
  And answer, "Let one living head,
But one arise—we come, we come!"
'Tis but the living who are dumb.

In vain—in vain: strike other chords;
  Fill high the cup with Samian wine!
Leave battles to the Turkish hordes,
  And shed the blood of Scio's vine!
Hark! rising to the ignoble call—
How answers each bold Bacchanal!

You have the Pyrrhic dance as yet,
  Where is the Pyrrhic phalanx gone?
Of two such lessons, why forget
  The nobler and the manlier one?
You have the letters Cadmus gave—
Think ye he meant them for a slave?

Fill high the bowl with Samian wine!
  We will not think of themes like these!
It made Anacreon's song divine:
  He served—but served Polycrates—
A tyrant; but our masters then
Were still, at least, our countrymen.

The tyrant of the Chersonese
  Was freedom's best and bravest friend;
That tyrant was Miltiades!
  Oh! that the present hour would lend
Another despot of the kind!
Such chains as his were sure to bind.

Fill high the bowl with Samian wine!
  On Suli's rock, and Parga's shore,
Exists the remnant of a line
  Such as the Doric mothers bore;
And there, perhaps, some seed is sown,
The Heracleidan blood might own.

Trust not for freedom to the Franks—
  They have a king who buys and sells:
In native swords, and native ranks,
  The only hope of courage dwells;
But Turkish force, and Latin fraud,
Would break your shield, however broad.

Fill high the bowl with Samian wine!
  Our virgins dance beneath the shade—
I see their glorious black eyes shine;
  But gazing on each glowing maid,
My own the burning tear-drop laves,
To think such breasts must suckle slaves.

Place me on Sunium's marbled steep,
  Where nothing, save the waves and I,
May hear our mutual murmurs sweep;
  There, swan-like, let me sing and die;
A land of slaves shall ne'er be mine—
Dash down yon cup of Samian wine!

On This Day I Complete My Thirty-Sixth Year

'Tis time this heart should be unmoved,
　　Since others it hath ceased to move;
Yet, though I cannot be beloved,
　　　　Still let me love!

My days are in the yellow leaf;
　　The flowers and fruits of love are gone;
The worm, the canker, and the grief
　　　　Are mine alone!

The fire that on my bosom preys
　　Is lone as some volcanic isle;
No torch is kindled at its blaze—
　　　　A funeral pile.

The hope, the fear, the jealous care,
　　The exalted portion of the pain
And power of love, I cannot share,
　　　　But wear the chain.

But 'tis not thus—and 'tis not here—
　　Such thoughts should shake my soul, nor now,
Where glory decks the hero's bier,
　　　　Or binds his brow.

The sword, the banner, and the field,
　　Glory and Greece, around me see!
The Spartan, borne upon his shield,
　　　　Was not more free.

Awake! (not Greece—she is awake!)
　　Awake, my spirit! Think through whom
Thy life-blood tracks its parent lake,
　　　　And then strike home!

Tread those reviving passions down,
　　Unworthy manhood! unto thee
Indifferent should the smile or frown
　　　　Of beauty be.

If thou regret'st thy youth, why live?
    The land of honourable death
Is here—up to the field, and give
    Away thy breath!

Seek out—less often sought than found—
    A soldier's grave, for thee the best;
Then look around, and choose thy ground,
    And take thy rest.

Missolonghi, January 22, 1824

CHARLES WOLFE

(1791–1823)

To Mary

If I had thought thou couldst have died,
    I might not weep for thee;
But I forgot, when by thy side,
    That thou couldst mortal be:
It never through my mind had past
    The time would e'er be o'er,
And I on thee should look my last,
    And thou shouldst smile no more!

And still upon that face I look,
    And think 'twill smile again;
And still the thought I will not brook,
    That I must look in vain.
But when I speak—thou dost not say
    What thou ne'er left'st unsaid;
And now I feel; as well I may,
    Sweet Mary, thou art dead!

If thou wouldst stay, e'en as thou art,
    All cold and all serene—
I still might press thy silent heart,
    And where thy smiles have been.

While e'en thy chill, bleak corse I have,
    Thou seemest still mine own;
But there—I lay thee in the grave,
    And now I am alone!

I do not think, where'er thou art,
    Thou hast forgotten me;
And I, perhaps, may soothe this heart
    In thinking too of thee:
Yet there was round thee such a dawn
    Of light ne'er seen before,
As fancy never could have drawn,
    And never can restore!

PERCY BYSSHE SHELLEY

(1792–1822)

from *Prometheus Unbound*

1.

Fourth Spirit:

On a poet's lips I slept
Dreaming like a love-adept
In the sound his breathing kept;
Nor seeks nor finds he mortal blisses,
But feeds on the aërial kisses
Of shapes that haunt thought's wildernesses.
He will watch from dawn to gloom
The lake-reflected sun illume
The yellow bees in the ivy-bloom,
Nor heed nor see, what things they be;
But from these create he can
Forms more real than living man,
Nurslings of immortality!

2.

Semichorus I of Spirits:

The path through which that lovely twain
    Have passed, by cedar, pine, and yew,
    And each dark tree that ever grew,
    Is curtained out from Heaven's wide blue;

Nor sun, nor moon, nor wind, nor rain
   Can pierce its interwoven bowers,
  Nor aught, save where some cloud of dew,
Drifted along the earth-creeping breeze,
Between the trunks of the hoar trees,
    Hangs each a pearl in the pale flowers
  Of the green laurel, blown anew;
And bends, and then fades silently,
One frail and fair anemone:
Or when some star of many a one
That climbs and wanders through steep night,
Has found the cleft through which alone
Beams fall from high those depths upon
Ere it is borne away, away,
By the swift Heavens that cannot stay,
It scatters drops of golden light,
Like lines of rain that ne'er unite:
And the gloom divine is all around,
And underneath is the mossy ground.

Semichorus II:

There the voluptuous nightingales,
  Are awake through all the broad noonday.
When one with bliss or sadness fails,
   And through the windless ivy-boughs,
  Sick with sweet love, droops dying away
On its mate's music-panting bosom;
Another from the swinging blossom,
   Watching to catch the languid close
  Of the last strain, then lifts on high
  The wings of the weak melody,
'Till some new strain of feeling bear
  The song, and all the woods are mute;
When there is heard through the dim air
The rush of wings, and rising there
  Like many a lake-surrounded flute,
Sounds overflow the listener's brain
So sweet, that joy is almost pain.

3.

    Voice in the Air, Singing:

Life of Life! thy lips enkindle
    With their love the breath between them;
And thy smiles before they dwindle
    Make the cold air fire; then screen them
In those looks, where whoso gazes
Faints, entangled in their mazes.

Child of Light! thy limbs are burning
    Through the vest which seems to hide them;
As the radiant lines of morning
    Through the clouds ere they divide them;
And this atmosphere divinest
Shrouds thee wheresoe'er thou shinest.

Fair are others; none beholds thee,
    But thy voice sounds low and tender
Like the fairest, for it folds thee
    From the sight, that liquid splendour,
And all feel, yet see thee never,
As I feel now, lost for ever!

Lamp of Earth! where'er thou movest
    Its dim shapes are clad with brightness,
And the souls of whom thou lovest
    Walk upon the winds with lightness,
Till they fail, as I am failing,
Dizzy, lost, yet unbewailing!

    Asia:

My soul is an enchanted boat,
    Which, like a sleeping swan, doth float
Upon the silver waves of thy sweet singing;
    And thine doth like an angel sit
    Beside a helm conducting it,
Whilst all the winds with melody are ringing.
    It seems to float ever, for ever,
    Upon that many-winding river,
    Between mountains, woods, abysses,
    A paradise of wildernesses!

Till, like one in slumber bound,
Borne to the ocean, I float down, around,
Into a sea profound, of ever ever-spreading sound:

Meanwhile thy spirit lifts its pinions
In music's most serene dominions;
Catching the winds that fan that happy heaven.
And we sail on, away, afar,
Without a course, without a star,
But, by the instinct of sweet music driven;
Till through Elysian garden islets
By thee, most beautiful of pilots,
Where never mortal pinnace glided,
The boat of my desire is guided:
Realms where the air we breathe is love,
Which in the winds and on the waves doth move,
Harmonizing this earth with what we feel above.

We have passed Age's icy caves,
And Manhood's dark and tossing waves,
And Youth's smooth ocean, smiling to betray:
Beyond the glassy gulfs we flee
Of shadow-peopled Infancy,
Through Death and Birth, to a diviner day;
A paradise of vaulted bowers,
Lit by downward-gazing flowers,
And watery paths that wind between
Wildernesses calm and green,
Peopled by shapes too bright to see,
And rest, having beheld; somewhat like thee;
Which walk upon the sea, and chant melodiously!

FROM *Lines Written among the Euganean Hills*

'Mid the mountains Euganean
I stood listening to the paean
With which the legioned rooks did hail
The sun's uprise majestical;
Gathering round with wings all hoar,

Through the dewy mist they soar
Like gray shades, till the eastern heaven
Bursts, and then, as clouds of even,
Flecked with fire and azure, lie
In the unfathomable sky,
So their plumes of purple grain,
Starred with drops of golden rain,
Gleam above the sunlight woods,
As in silent multitudes
On the morning's fitful gale
Through the broken mist they sail,
And the vapours cloven and gleaming
Follow, down the dark steep streaming,
Till all is bright, and clear, and still,
Round the solitary hill.

Beneath is spread like a green sea
The waveless plain of Lombardy,
Bounded by the vaporous air,
Islanded by cities fair;
Underneath Day's azure eyes
Ocean's nursling, Venice lies,
A peopled labyrinth of walls,
Amphitrite's destined halls,
Which her hoary sire now paves
With his blue and beaming waves.
Lo! the sun upsprings behind,
Broad, red, radiant, half-reclined
On the level quivering line
Of the waters crystalline;
And before that chasm of light,
As within a furnace bright,
Column, tower, and dome, and spire,
Shine like obelisks of fire,
Pointing with inconstant motion
From the altar of dark ocean
To the sapphire-tinted skies;
As the flames of sacrifice
From the marble shrines did rise,
As to pierce the dome of gold
Where Apollo spoke of old.

Stanzas Written in Dejection, near Naples

The sun is warm, the sky is clear,
    The waves are dancing fast and bright,
Blue isles and snowy mountains wear
    The purple noon's transparent might,
    The breath of the moist earth is light,
Around its unexpanded buds;
    Like many a voice of one delight,
The winds, the birds, the ocean floods,
The City's voice itself, is soft like Solitude's.

I see the Deep's untrampled floor
    With green and purple seaweeds strown;
I see the waves upon the shore,
    Like light dissolved in star-showers, thrown:
    I sit upon the sands alone,—
The lightning of the noontide ocean
    Is flashing round me, and a tone
Arises from its measured motion,
How sweet! did any heart now share in my emotion.

Alas! I have nor hope nor health,
    Nor peace within nor calm around,
Nor that content surpassing wealth
    The sage in meditation found,
    And walked with inward glory crowned—
Nor fame, nor power, nor love, nor leisure.
    Others I see whom these surround—
Smiling they live, and call life pleasure;—
To me that cup has been dealt in another measure.

Yet now despair itself is mild,
    Even as the winds and waters are;
I could lie down like a tired child,
    And weep away the life of care
    Which I have borne and yet must bear,
Till death like sleep might steal on me,
    And I might feel in the warm air
My cheek grow cold, and hear the sea
Break o'er my dying brain its last monotony.

Some might lament that I were cold,
  As I, when this sweet day is gone,
Which my lost heart, too soon grown old,
  Insults with this untimely moan;
  They might lament—for I am one
Whom men love not,—and yet regret
  Unlike this day, which, when the sun
Shall on its stainless glory set,
Will linger, though enjoyed, like joy in memory yet.

Song to the Men of England

Men of England, wherefore plough
For the lords who lay ye low?
Wherefore weave with toil and care
The rich robes your tyrants wear?

Wherefore feed, and clothe, and save,
From the cradle to the grave,
Those ungrateful drones who would
Drain your sweat—nay, drink your blood?

Wherefore, Bees of England, forge
Many a weapon, chain, and scourge,
That these stingless drones may spoil
The forced produce of your toil?

Have ye leisure, comfort, calm,
Shelter, food, love's gentle balm?
Or what is it ye buy so dear
With your pain and with your fear?

The seed ye sow, another reaps;
The wealth ye find, another keeps;
The robes ye weave, another wears;
The arms ye forge, another bears.

Sow seed,—but let no tyrant reap;
Find wealth,—let no impostor heap;
Weave robes,—let not the idle wear;
Forge arms,—in your defence to bear.

Shrink to your cellars, holes, and cells;
In halls ye deck another dwells.
Why shake the chains ye wrought? Ye see
The steel ye tempered glance on ye.

With plough and spade, and hoe and loom,
Trace your grave, and build your tomb,
And weave your winding-sheet, till fair
England be your sepulchre.

FROM *To the Lord Chancellor*

Oh, let a father's curse be on thy soul,
  And let a daughter's hope be on thy tomb;
Be both, on thy gray head, a leaden cowl
  To weigh thee down to thine approaching doom!

I curse thee by a parent's outraged love,
  By hopes long cherished and too lately lost,
By gentle feelings thou couldst never prove,
  By griefs which thy stern nature never crossed;

By those infantine smiles of happy light,
  Which were a fire within a stranger's hearth,
Quenched even when kindled, in untimely night
  Hiding the promise of a lovely birth:

By those unpractised accents of young speech,
  Which he who is a father thought to frame
To gentlest lore, such as the wisest teach—
  Thou strike the lyre of mind!—oh, grief and shame!

By all the happy see in children's growth—
  That undeveloped flower of budding years—
Sweetness and sadness interwoven both,
  Source of the sweetest hopes and saddest fears—

By all the days, under an hireling's care,
  Of dull constraint and bitter heaviness,—
O wretched ye if any ever were,—
  Sadder than orphans, yet not fatherless!

By the false cant which on their innocent lips
   Must hang like poison on an opening bloom,
By the dark creeds which cover with eclipse
   Their pathway from the cradle to the tomb—

By all the hate which checks a father's love—
   By all the scorn which kills a father's care—
By those most impious hands which dared remove
   Nature's high bounds—by thee—and by despair—

I curse thee—though I hate thee not.—O slave!
   If thou couldst quench the earth-consuming Hell
Of which thou art a daemon, on thy grave
   This curse should be a blessing. Fare thee well!

Ode to the West Wind

I

O wild West Wind, thou breath of Autumn's being,
Thou, from whose unseen presence the leaves dead
Are driven, like ghosts from an enchanter fleeing,

Yellow, and black, and pale, and hectic red,
Pestilence-stricken multitudes: O thou,
Who chariotest to their dark wintry bed

The wingéd seeds, where they lie cold and low,
Each like a corpse within its grave, until
Thine azure sister of the Spring shall blow

Her clarion o'er the dreaming earth, and fill
(Driving sweet buds like flocks to feed in air)
With living hues and odours plain and hill:

Wild Spirit, which art moving everywhere;
Destroyer and preserver; hear, oh, hear!

II

Thou on whose stream, mid the steep sky's commotion,
Loose clouds like earth's decaying leaves are shed,
Shook from the tangled boughs of Heaven and Ocean,

Angels of rain and lightning: there are spread
On the blue surface of thine aëry surge,
Like the bright hair uplifted from the head

Of some fierce Maenad, even from the dim verge
Of the horizon to the zenith's height,
The locks of the approaching storm. Thou dirge

Of the dying year, to which this closing night
Will be the dome of a vast sepulchre,
Vaulted with all thy congregated might

Of vapours, from whose solid atmosphere
Black rain, and fire, and hail will burst: oh, hear!

III

Thou who didst waken from his summer dreams
The blue Mediterranean, where he lay,
Lulled by the coil of his crystálline streams,

Beside a pumice isle in Baiae's bay,
And saw in sleep old palaces and towers
Quivering within the wave's intenser day,

All overgrown with azure moss and flowers
So sweet, the sense faints picturing them! Thou
For whose path the Atlantic's level powers

Cleave themselves into chasms, while far below
The sea-blooms and the oozy woods which wear
The sapless foliage of the ocean, know

Thy voice, and suddenly grow gray with fear,
And tremble and despoil themselves: oh, hear!

IV

If I were a dead leaf thou mightest bear;
If I were a swift cloud to fly with thee;
A wave to pant beneath thy power, and share

The impulse of thy strength, only less free
Than thou, O uncontrollable! If even
I were as in my boyhood, and could be

The comrade of thy wanderings over Heaven,
As then, when to outstrip thy skiey speed
Scarce seemed a vision; I would ne'er have striven

As thus with thee in prayer in my sore need.
Oh, lift me as a wave, a leaf, a cloud!
I fall upon the thorns of life! I bleed!

A heavy weight of hours has chained and bowed
One too like thee: tameless, and swift, and proud.

V

Make me thy lyre, even as the forest is;
What if my leaves are falling like its own!
The tumult of thy mighty harmonies

Will take from both a deep, autumnal tone,
Sweet though in sadness. Be thou, Spirit fierce,
My spirit! Be thou me, impetuous one!

Drive my dead thoughts over the universe
Like withered leaves to quicken a new birth!
And, by the incantation of this verse,

Scatter, as from an unextinguished hearth
Ashes and sparks, my words among mankind!
Be through my lips to unawakened earth

The trumpet of a prophecy! O, Wind,
If Winter comes, can Spring be far behind?

The Indian Serenade

I arise from dreams of thee
In the first sweet sleep of night.
When the winds are breathing low,
And the stars are shining bright:
I arise from dreams of thee,
And a spirit in my feet
Hath led me—who knows how?
To thy chamber window, Sweet!

The wandering airs they faint
On the dark, the silent stream—
The Champak odours fail
Like sweet thoughts in a dream;
The nightingale's complaint,
It dies upon her heart;—
As I must on thine,
Oh, belovéd as thou art!

Oh lift me from the grass!
I die! I faint! I fail!
Let thy love in kisses rain
On my lips and eyelids pale.
My cheek is cold and white, alas!
My heart beats loud and fast;—
Oh! press it to thine own again,
Where it will break at last.

Love's Philosophy

The fountains mingle with the river
    And the rivers with the Ocean,
The winds of Heaven mix for ever
    With a sweet emotion;
Nothing in the world is single;
    All things by a law divine
In one another's being mingle.
    Why not I with thine?—

See the mountains kiss high Heaven
    And the waves clasp one another;
No sister flower would be forgiven
    If it disdained its brother;
And the sunlight clasps the earth
    And the moonbeams kiss the sea:
What are all these kissings worth
    If thou kiss not me?

The Cloud

I bring fresh showers for the thirsting flowers,
    From the seas and the streams;
I bear light shade for the leaves when laid
    In their noonday dreams.
From my wings are shaken the dews that waken
    The sweet buds every one,
When rocked to rest on their mother's breast,
    As she dances about the sun.
I wield the flail of the lashing hail,
    And whiten the green plains under,
And then again I dissolve it in rain,
    And laugh as I pass in thunder.

I sift the snow on the mountains below,
    And their great pines groan aghast;
And all the night 'tis my pillow white,
    While I sleep in the arms of the blast.
Sublime on the towers of my skiey bowers,
    Lightning my pilot sits;
In a cavern under is fettered the thunder,
    It struggles and howls at fits;
Over earth and ocean, with gentle motion,
    This pilot is guiding me,
Lured by the love of the genii that move
    In the depths of the purple sea;
Over the rills, and the crags, and the hills,
    Over the lakes and the plains,

Wherever he dream, under mountain or stream,
    The Spirit he loves remains;
And I all the while bask in Heaven's blue smile,
    Whilst he is dissolving in rains.

The sanguine Sunrise, with his meteor eyes,
    And his burning plumes outspread,
Leaps on the back of my sailing rack,
    When the morning star shines dead;
As on the jag of a mountain crag,
    Which an earthquake rocks and swings,
An eagle alit one moment may sit
    In the light of its golden wings.
And when Sunset may breathe, from the lit sea beneath,
    Its ardours of rest and of love,
And the crimson pall of eve may fall
    From the depth of Heaven above,
With wings folded I rest, on mine aëry nest,
    As still as a brooding dove.

That orbéd maiden with white fire laden,
    Whom mortals call the Moon,
Glides glimmering o'er my fleece-like floor,
    By the midnight breezes strewn;
And whenever the beat of her unseen feet,
    Which only the angels hear,
May have broken the woof of my tent's thin roof,
    The stars peep behind her and peer;
And I laugh to see them whirl and flee,
    Like a swarm of golden bees,
When I widen the rent in my wind-built tent,
    Till the calm rivers, lakes, and seas,
Like strips of the sky fallen through me on high,
    Are each paved with the moon and these.

I bind the Sun's throne with a burning zone,
    And the Moon's with a girdle of pearl;
The volcanoes are dim, and the stars reel and swim,
    When the whirlwinds my banner unfurl.
From cape to cape, with a bridge-like shape,
    Over a torrent sea,

Sunbeam-proof, I hang like a roof,—
    The mountains its columns be.
The triumphal arch through which I march
    With hurricane, fire, and snow,
When the Powers of the air are chained to my chair,
    Is the million-coloured bow;
The sphere-fire above its soft colours wove,
    While the moist Earth was laughing below.

I am the daughter of Earth and Water,
    And the nursling of the Sky;
I pass through the pores of the ocean and shores;
    I change, but I cannot die.
For after the rain when with never a stain
    The pavilion of Heaven is bare,
And the winds and sunbeams with their convex gleams
    Build up the blue dome of air,
I silently laugh at my own cenotaph,
    And out of the caverns of rain,
Like a child from the womb, like a ghost from the tomb,
    I arise and unbuild it again.

To ——

I fear thy kisses, gentle maiden,
    Thou needest not fear mine;
My spirit is too deeply laden
    Ever to burthen thine.

I fear thy mien, thy tones, thy motion,
    Thou needest not fear mine;
Innocent is the heart's devotion
    With which I worship thine.

To the Moon

Art thou pale for weariness
Of climbing heaven and gazing on the earth,
    Wandering companionless
Among the stars that have a different birth,—
And ever changing, like a joyless eye
That finds no object worth its constancy?

The World's Wanderers

Tell me, thou Star, whose wings of light
Speed thee in thy fiery flight,
In what cavern of the night
       Will thy pinions close now?

Tell me, Moon, thou pale and gray
Pilgrim of Heaven's homeless way,
In what depth of night or day
       Seekest thou repose now?

Weary Wind, who wanderest
Like the world's rejected guest,
Hast thou still some secret nest
       On the tree or billow?

Good-Night

Good-night? ah! no; the hour is ill
  Which severs those it should unite;
Let us remain together still,
  Then it will be *good* night.

How can I call the lone night good,
  Though thy sweet wishes wing its flight?
Be it not said, thought, understood—
  Then it will be—*good* night.

To hearts which near each other move
  From evening close to morning light,
The night is good; because, my love,
  They never *say* good-night.

To Night

Swiftly walk o'er the western wave,
       Spirit of Night!
Out of the misty eastern cave
Where, all the long and lone daylight,

Thou wovest dreams of joy and fear,
Which make thee terrible and dear,—
     Swift be thy flight.

Wrap thy form in a mantle gray,
     Star-inwrought!
Blind with thine hair the eyes of Day;
Kiss her until she be wearied out,
Then wander o'er city, and sea, and land,
Touching all with thine opiate wand—
     Come, long-sought!

When I arose and saw the dawn,
     I sighed for thee;
When light rode high, and the dew was gone,
And noon lay heavy on flower and tree,
And the weary Day turned to his rest,
Lingering like an unloved guest,
     I sighed for thee.

Thy brother Death came, and cried,
     Wouldst thou me?
Thy sweet child Sleep, the filmy-eyed,
Murmured like a noontide bee,
Shall I nestle near thy side?
Wouldst thou me?—And I replied,
     No, not thee!

Death will come when thou art dead,
     Soon, too soon—
Sleep will come when thou art fled;
Of neither would I ask the boon
I ask of thee, belovéd Night—
Swift be thine approaching flight,
     Come soon, soon!

To ——

Music, when soft voices die,
Vibrates in the memory—
Odours, when sweet violets sicken,
Live within the sense they quicken.

Rose leaves, when the rose is dead,
Are heaped for the belovéd's bed;
And so thy thoughts, when thou art gone,
Love itself shall slumber on.

Mutability

The flower that smiles to-day
     To-morrow dies;
All that we wish to stay
     Tempts and then flies.
What is the world's delight?
Lightning that mocks the night,
     Brief even as bright.

Virtue, how frail it is!
     Friendship how rare!
Love, how it sells poor bliss
     For proud despair!
But we, though soon they fall,
Survive their joy, and all
     Which ours we call.

Whilst skies are blue and bright,
     Whilst flowers are gay,
Whilst eyes that change ere night
     Make glad the day;
Whilst yet the calm hours creep,
Dream thou—and from thy sleep
     Then wake to weep.

To ——

One word is too often profaned
　For me to profane it,
One feeling too falsely disdained
　For thee to disdain it;
One hope is too like despair
　For prudence to smother,
And pity from thee more dear
　Than that from another.

I can give not what men call love,
　But wilt thou accept not
The worship the heart lifts above
　And the heavens reject not,—
The desire of the moth for the star,
　Of the night for the morrow,
The devotion to something afar
　From the sphere of our sorrow?

Lines: "When the Lamp Is Shattered"

When the lamp is shattered
The light in the dust lies dead—
　When the cloud is scattered
The rainbow's glory is shed.
　When the lute is broken,
Sweet tones are remembered not;
　When the lips have spoken,
Loved accents are soon forgot.

　As music and splendour
Survive not the lamp and the lute,
　The heart's echoes render
No song when the spirit is mute:—
　No song but sad dirges,
Like the wind through a ruined cell,
　Or the mournful surges
That ring the dead seaman's knell.

When hearts have once mingled
Love leaves the well-built nest;
    The weak one is singled
To endure what it once possessed.
    O Love! who bewailest
The frailty of all things here,
    Why choose you the frailest
For your cradle, your home, and your bier?

    Its passions will rock thee
As the storms rock the ravens on high;
    Bright reason will mock thee,
Like the sun from a wintry sky.
    From thy nest every rafter
Will rot, and thine eagle home
    Leave thee naked to laughter,
When leaves fall and cold winds come.

To Stella

Thou wert the morning star among the living,
        Ere thy fair light had fled;
Now, having died, thou art as Hesperus, giving
        New splendour to the dead.

From the Greek of PLATO

FROM *Adonais*

I weep for Adonais—he is dead!
O, weep for Adonais! though our tears
Thaw not the frost which binds so dear a head!
And thou, sad Hour, selected from all years
To mourn our loss, rouse thy obscure compeers,
And teach them thine own sorrow, say: "With me
Died Adonais; till the Future dares
Forget the Past, his fate and fame shall be
An echo and a light unto eternity!"

Where wert thou, mighty Mother, when he lay,
When thy Son lay, pierced by the shaft which flies
In darkness? where was lorn Urania
When Adonais died? With veiléd eyes,
'Mid listening Echoes, in her Paradise
She sate, while one, with soft enamoured breath,
Rekindled all the fading melodies,
With which, like flowers that mock the corse beneath,
He had adorned and hid the coming bulk of Death.

Oh, weep for Adonais—he is dead!
Wake, melancholy Mother, wake and weep!
Yet wherefore? Quench within their burning bed
Thy fiery tears, and let thy loud heart keep
Like his, a mute and uncomplaining sleep;
For he is gone, where all things wise and fair
Descend;—oh, dream not that the amorous Deep
Will yet restore him to the vital air;
Death feeds on his mute voice, and laughs at our despair.

Most musical of mourners, weep again!
Lament anew, Urania!—He died,
Who was the Sire of an immortal strain,
Blind, old, and lonely, when his country's pride,
The priest, the slave, and the liberticide,
Trampled and mocked with many a loathéd rite
Of lust and blood; he went, unterrified,
Into the gulf of death; but his clear Sprite
Yet reigns o'er earth; the third among the sons of light.

Most musical of mourners, weep anew!
Not all to that bright station dared to climb;
And happier they their happiness who knew,
Whose tapers yet burn through that night of time
In which suns perished; others more sublime,
Struck by the envious wrath of man or god,
Have sunk, extinct in their refulgent prime;
And some yet live, treading the thorny road
Which leads, through toil and hate, to Fame's serene abode.

But now, thy youngest, dearest one, has perished—
The nursling of thy widowhood, who grew
Like a pale flower by some sad maiden cherished,
And fed with true-love tears, instead of dew;
Most musical of mourners, weep anew!
The extreme hope, the loveliest and the last,
The bloom, whose petals nipped before they blew
Died on the promise of the fruit, is waste;
The broken lily lies—the storm is overpast.

All he had loved, and moulded into thought,
From shape, and hue, and odour, and sweet sound,
Lamented Adonais. Morning sought
Her eastern watch-tower, and her hair unbound,
Wet with the tears which should adorn the ground,
Dimmed the aërial eyes that kindle day;
Afar the melancholy thunder moaned,
Pale Ocean in unquiet slumber lay,
And the wild Winds flew round, sobbing in their dismay.

Lost Echo sits amid the voiceless mountains,
And feeds her grief with his remembered lay,
And will no more reply to winds or fountains,
Or amorous birds perched on the young green spray,
Or herdsman's horn, or bell at closing day;
Since she can mimic not his lips, more dear
Than those for whose disdain she pined away
Into a shadow of all sounds:—a drear
Murmur, between their songs, is all the woodmen hear.

Grief made the young Spring wild, and she threw down
Her kindling buds, as if she Autumn were,
Or they dead leaves; since her delight is flown,
For whom should she have waked the sullen year?
To Phoebus was not Hyacinth so dear
Nor to himself Narcissus, as to both
Thou, Adonais: wan they stand and sere
Amid the faint companions of their youth,
With all dew turned to tears; odour, to sighing ruth.

Peace, peace! he is not dead, he doth not sleep—
He hath awakened from the dream of life—
'Tis we, who lost in stormy visions, keep
With phantoms and unprofitable strife,
And in mad trance, strike with our spirit's knife
Invulnerable nothings.—*We* decay
Like corpses in a charnel; fear and grief
Convulse us and consume us day by day,
And cold hopes swarm like worms within our living clay.

He has outsoared the shadow of our night;
Envy and calumny and hate and pain,
And that unrest which men miscall delight,
Can touch him not and torture not again;
From the contagion of the world's slow stain
He is secure, and now can never mourn
A heart grown cold, a head grown gray in vain;
Nor, when the spirit's self has ceased to burn,
With sparkless ashes load an unlamented urn.

He lives, he wakes—'tis Death is dead, not he;
Mourn not for Adonais.—Thou young Dawn,
Turn all thy dew to splendour, for from thee
The spirit thou lamentest is not gone;
Ye caverns and ye forests, cease to moan!
Cease, ye faint flowers and fountains, and thou Air,
Which like a mourning veil thy scarf hadst thrown
O'er the abandoned Earth, now leave it bare
Even to the joyous stars which smile on its despair!

He is made one with Nature: there is heard
His voice in all her music, from the moan
Of thunder, to the song of night's sweet bird;
He is a presence to be felt and known
In darkness and in light, from herb and stone,
Spreading itself where'er that Power may move
Which has withdrawn his being to its own;
Which wields the world with never-wearied love,
Sustains it from beneath, and kindles it above.

He is a portion of that loveliness
Which once he made more lovely: he doth bear
His part, while the one Spirit's plastic stress
Sweeps through the dull dense world, compelling there,
All new successions to the forms they wear;
Torturing th'unwilling dross that checks its flight
To its own likeness, as each mass may bear;
And bursting in its beauty and its might
From trees and beasts and men into the Heaven's light.

Go thou to Rome,—at once the Paradise,
The grave, the city, and the wilderness;
And where its wrecks like shattered mountains rise,
And flowering weeds, and fragrant copses dress
The bones of Desolation's nakedness
Pass, till the spirit of the spot shall lead
Thy footsteps to a slope of green access
Where, like an infant's smile, over the dead
A light of laughing flowers along the grass is spread;

And grey walls moulder round, on which dull Time
Feeds, like slow fire upon a hoary brand;
And one keen pyramid with wedge sublime,
Pavilioning the dust of him who planned
This refuge for his memory, doth stand
Like flame transformed to marble; and beneath,
A field is spread, on which a newer band
Have pitched in Heaven's smile their camp of death,
Welcoming him we lose with scarce extinguished breath.

Here pause: these graves are all too young as yet
To have outgrown the sorrow which consigned
Its charge to each; and if the seal is set,
Here, on one fountain of a mourning mind,
Break it not thou! too surely shalt thou find
Thine own well full, if thou returnest home,
Of tears and gall. From the world's bitter wind
Seek shelter in the shadow of the tomb.
What Adonais is, why fear we to become?

The One remains, the many change and pass;
Heaven's light forever shines, Earth's shadows fly;
Life, like a dome of many-coloured glass,
Stains the white radiance of Eternity,
Until Death tramples it to fragments.—Die,
If thou wouldst be with that which thou dost seek!
Follow, where all is fled!—Rome's azure sky,
Flowers, ruins, statues, music, words are weak
The glory they transfuse with fitting truth to speak.

The breath whose might I have invoked in song
Descends on me; my spirit's bark is driven,
Far from the shore, far from the trembling throng
Whose sails were never to the tempest given;
The massy earth and spheréd skies are riven!
I am borne darkly, fearfully afar;
Whilst, burning through the inmost veil of Heaven,
The soul of Adonais, like a star,
Beacons from the abode where the Eternal are.

JOHN CLARE

(1793–1864

Written in Northampton County Asylum

I am! yet what I am who cares, or knows?
    My friends forsake me like a memory lost.
I am the self-consumer of my woes;
    They rise and vanish, an oblivious host,
Shadows of life, whose very soul is lost.
And yet I am—I live—though I am tossed

Into the nothingness of scorn and noise,
    Into the living sea of waking dream,
Where there is neither sense of life, nor joys,
    But the huge shipwreck of my own esteem
And all that's dear. Even those I loved the best
Are strange—nay, they are stranger than the rest

I long for scenes where man has never trod—
   For scenes where woman never smiled or wept—
There to abide with my Creator, God,
   And sleep as I in childhood sweetly slept,
Full of high thoughts, unborn. So let me lie,—
The grass below; above, the vaulted sky.

WILLIAM CULLEN BRYANT
(1794–1878)

Thanatopsis

To him who in the love of Nature holds
Communion with her visible forms, she speaks
A various language; for his gayer hours
She has a voice of gladness, and a smile
And eloquence of beauty, and she glides
Into his darker musings, with a mild
And healing sympathy, that steals away
Their sharpness, ere he is aware. When thoughts
Of the last bitter hour come like a blight
Over thy spirit, and sad images
Of the stern agony, and shroud, and pall,
And breathless darkness, and the narrow house,
Make thee to shudder, and grow sick at heart;—
Go forth, under the open sky, and list
To Nature's teachings, while from all around—
Earth and her waters, and the depths of air—
Comes a still voice—Yet a few days, and thee
The all-beholding sun shall see no more
In all his course; nor yet in the cold ground,
Where thy pale form was laid, with many tears,
Nor in the embrace of ocean, shall exist
Thy image. Earth, that nourished thee, shall claim
Thy growth, to be resolved to earth again,
And, lost each human trace, surrendering up
Thine individual being, shalt thou go
To mix for ever with the elements,
To be a brother to the insensible rock
And to the sluggish clod, which the rude swain

Turns with his share, and treads upon. The oak
Shall send his roots abroad, and pierce thy mould.

Yet not to thine eternal resting-place
Shalt thou retire alone, nor couldst thou wish
Couch more magnificent. Thou shalt lie down
With patriarchs of the infant world—with kings,
The powerful of the earth—the wise, the good,
Fair forms, and hoary seers of ages past,
All in one mighty sepulchre. The hills
Rock-ribbed and ancient as the sun,—the vales
Stretching in pensive quietness between;
The venerable woods—rivers that move
In majesty, and the complaining brooks
That make the meadows green; and, poured round all,
Old Ocean's gray and melancholy waste,—
Are but the solemn decorations all
Of the great tomb of man. The golden sun,
The planets, all the infinite host of heaven,
Are shining on the sad abodes of death,
Through the still lapse of ages. All that tread
The globe are but a handful to the tribes
That slumber in its bosom.—Take the wings
Of morning, pierce the Barcan wilderness,
Or lose thyself in the contiguous woods
Where rolls the Oregon, and hears no sound,
Save his own dashings—yet the dead are there:
And millions in those solitudes, since first
The flight of years began, have laid them down
In their last sleep—the dead reign there alone.
So shalt thou rest, and what if thou withdraw
In silence from the living, and no friend
Take note of thy departure? All that breathe
Will share thy destiny. The gay will laugh
When thou art gone, the solemn brood of care
Plod on, and each one as before will chase
His favorite phantom; yet all these shall leave
Their mirth and their employments, and shall come
And make their bed with thee. As the long train
Of ages glide away, the sons of men,
The youth in life's green spring, and he who goes

In the full strength of years, matron and maid,
The speechless babe, and the gray-headed man—
Shall one by one be gathered to thy side,
By those, who in their turn shall follow them.

So live, that when thy summons comes to join
The innumerable caravan, which moves
To that mysterious realm, where each shall take
His chamber in the silent halls of death,
Thou go not, like the quarry-slave at night,
Scourged to his dungeon, but, sustained and soothed,
By an unfaltering trust, approach thy grave,
Like one who wraps the drapery of his couch
About him, and lies down to pleasant dreams.

"Oh Fairest of the Rural Maids!"

Oh fairest of the rural maids!
Thy birth was in the forest shades;
Green boughs, and glimpses of the sky,
Were all that met thine infant eye.

Thy sports, thy wanderings, when a child,
Were ever in the sylvan wild;
And all the beauty of the place
Is in thy heart and on thy face.

The twilight of the trees and rocks
Is in the light shade of thy locks;
Thy step is as the wind, that weaves
Its playful way among the leaves.

Thine eyes are springs, in whose serene
And silent waters heaven is seen;
Their lashes are the herbs that look
On their young figures in the brook.

The forest depths, by foot unpressed,
Are not more sinless than thy breast;
The holy peace, that fills the air
Of those calm solitudes, is there.

Dante

Who, mid the grasses of the field,
  That spring beneath our careless feet,
First found the shining stems that yield
  The grains of life-sustaining wheat:

Who first, upon the furrowed land,
  Strewed the bright grains to sprout, and grow
And ripen for the reaper's hand—
  We know not, and we cannot know.

But well we know the hand that brought
  And scattered, far as sight can reach,
The seeds of free and living thought
  On the broad field of modern speech.

Mid the white hills that round us lie,
  We cherish that Great Sower's fame,
And, as we pile the sheaves on high,
  With awe we utter Dante's name.

Six centuries, since the poet's birth,
  Have come and flitted o'er our sphere:
The richest harvest reaped on earth
  Crowns the last century's closing year.

JOHN KEATS

(1795–1821)

Dedication
(TO LEIGH HUNT, ESQ.)

Glory and Loveliness have passed away;
  For if we wander out in early morn,
  No wreathèd incense do we see upborne
Into the east to meet the smiling day:
No crowd of nymphs soft-voiced and young and gay,
  In woven baskets bringing ears of corn,
  Roses, and pinks, and violets, to adorn

The shrine of Flora in her early May.
But there are left delights as high as these,
    And I shall ever bless my destiny,
That in a time when under pleasant trees
    Pan is no longer sought, I feel a free,
A leafy luxury, seeing I could please,
    With these poor offerings, a man like thee.

On First Looking into Chapman's Homer

Much have I travelled in the realms of gold,
    And many goodly states and kingdoms seen;
    Round many western islands have I been
Which bards in fealty to Apollo hold.
Oft of one wide expanse had I been told,
    That deep-browed Homer ruled as his demesne:
    Yet did I never breathe its pure serene
Till I heard Chapman speak out loud and bold:
Then felt I like some watcher of the skies
    When a new planet swims into his ken;
Or like stout Cortez when with eagle eyes
    He stared at the Pacific—and all his men
Look'd at each other with a wild surmise—
    Silent, upon a peak in Darien.

To a Nightingale

My heart aches, and a drowsy numbness pains
    My sense, as though of hemlock I had drunk,
Or emptied some dull opiate to the drains
    One minute past, and Lethe-wards had sunk:
'Tis not through envy of thy happy lot,
    Being but too happy in thy happiness,—
        That thou, light-wingéd Dryad of the trees,
            In some melodious plot
    Of beechen green, and shadows numberless,
        Singest of summer in full-throated ease.

O for a draught of vintage, that hath been
 Cooled a long age in the deep-delvéd earth,
Tasting of Flora and the country-green,
 Dance, and Provençal song, and sun-burnt mirth!
O for a beaker full of the warm South,
 Full of the true, the blushful Hippocrene,
  With beaded bubbles winking at the brim,
   And purple-stainéd mouth;
 That I might drink and leave the world unseen,
 And with thee fade away into the forest dim:

Fade far away, dissolve, and quite forget
 What thou among the leaves hast never known,
The weariness, the fever, and the fret
 Here, where men sit and hear each other groan;
Where palsy shakes a few, sad, last grey hairs,
 Where youth grows pale, and spectre-thin, and dies;
  Where but to think is to be full of sorrow
   And leaden-eyed despairs;
 Where beauty cannot keep her lustrous eyes,
 Or new Love pine at them beyond to-morrow.

Away! away! for I will fly to thee,
 Not charioted by Bacchus and his pards,
But on the viewless wings of Poesy,
 Though the dull brain perplexes and retards:
Already with thee! tender is the night,
 And haply the Queen-Moon is on her throne,
  Clustered around by all her starry Fays;
   But here there is no light,
 Save what from heaven is with the breezes blown
  Through verdurous glooms and winding mossy ways.

I cannot see what flowers are at my feet,
 Nor what soft incense hangs upon the boughs,
But, in embalméd darkness, guess each sweet
 Wherewith the seasonable month endows
The grass, the thicket, and the fruit-tree wild;

White hawthorn, and the pastoral eglantine;
  Fast-fading violets covered up in leaves;
    And mid-May's eldest child,
The coming musk-rose, full of dewy wine,
  The murmurous haunt of flies on summer eves.

Darkling I listen; and for many a time
  I have been half in love with easeful Death,
Called him soft names in many a muséd rhyme,
  To take into the air my quiet breath;
Now more than ever seems it rich to die,
  To cease upon the midnight with no pain,
    While thou art pouring forth thy soul abroad
      In such an ecstasy!
  Still wouldst thou sing, and I have ears in vain—
    To thy high requiem become a sod.

Thou wast not born for death, immortal Bird!
  No hungry generations tread thee down;
The voice I hear this passing night was heard
  In ancient days by emperor and clown:
Perhaps the self-same song that found a path
  Through the sad heart of Ruth, when sick for home,
    She stood in tears amid the alien corn;
      The same that oft-times hath
  Charmed magic casements, opening on the foam
    Of perilous seas, in faery lands forlorn.

Forlorn! the very word is like a bell
  To toll me back from thee to my sole self.
Adieu! the fancy cannot cheat so well
  As she is famed to do, deceiving elf.
Adieu! adieu! thy plaintive anthem fades
  Past the near meadows, over the still stream,
    Up the hill-side; and now 'tis buried deep
      In the next valley-glades:
  Was it a vision, or a waking dream?
    Fled is that music:—do I wake or sleep?

On a Grecian Urn

Thou still unravished bride of quietness!
   Thou foster-child of Silence and slow Time,
Sylvan historian, who canst thus express
   A flowery tale more sweetly than our rhyme:
What leaf-fringed legend haunts about thy shape
   Of deities or mortals, or of both,
     In Tempe or the dales of Arcady?
    What men or gods are these? What maidens loath?
What mad pursuit? What struggle to escape?
    What pipes and timbrels? What wild ecstasy?

Heard melodies are sweet, but those unheard
   Are sweeter; therefore, ye soft pipes, play on;
Not to the sensual ear, but, more endeared,
   Pipe to the spirit ditties of no tone:
Fair youth, beneath the trees, thou canst not leave
   Thy song, nor ever can those trees be bare;
    Bold Lover, never, never canst thou kiss,
Though winning near the goal—yet, do not grieve;
    She cannot fade, though thou hast not thy bliss,
   For ever wilt thou love, and she be fair!

Ah, happy, happy boughs! that cannot shed
   Your leaves, nor ever bid the Spring adieu;
And, happy melodist, unweariéd,
   For ever piping songs for ever new;
More happy love! more happy, happy love!
   For ever warm and still to be enjoyed,
    For ever panting and for ever young;
All breathing human passion far above,
    That leaves a heart high sorrowful and cloyed,
   A burning forehead, and a parching tongue.

Who are these coming to the sacrifice?
   To what green altar, O mysterious priest,
Lead'st thou that heifer lowing at the skies,
   And all her silken flanks with garlands drest?

What little town by river or sea-shore,
    Or mountain-built with peaceful citadel,
      Is emptied of its folk, this pious morn?
And, little town, thy streets for evermore
    Will silent be; and not a soul to tell
      Why thou art desolate, can e'er return.

O Attic shape! Fair attitude! with brede
    Of marble men and maidens overwrought,
With forest branches and the trodden weed;
    Thou, silent form! dost tease us out of thought
As doth eternity: Cold Pastoral!
    When old age shall this generation waste,
      Thou shalt remain, in midst of other woe
Than ours, a friend to man, to whom thou ·say'st,
"Beauty is truth, truth beauty,"—that is all
      Ye know on earth, and all ye need to know.

To Psyche

O Goddess! hear these tuneless numbers, wrung
    By sweet enforcement and remembrance dear,
And pardon that thy secrets should be sung,
    Even into thy own soft-conchéd ear:
Surely I dreamt to-day, or did I see
    The wingéd Psyche with awakened eyes?
I wandered in a forest thoughtlessly,
    And, on the sudden, fainting with surprise,
Saw two fair creatures, couchéd side by side
    In deepest grass, beneath the whispering roof
    Of leaves and trembled blossoms, where there ran
      A brooklet, scarce espied:
'Mid hushed, cool-rooted flowers fragrant-eyed,
    Blue, silver-white, and budded Tyrian,
They lay calm-breathing on the bedded grass;
    Their arms embracéd, and their pinions too;
    Their lips touched not, but had not bade adieu
As if disjoinéd by soft-handed slumber,

And ready still past kisses to outnumber
   At tender eye-dawn of aurorean love:
      The wingéd boy I knew;
   But who wast thou, O happy, happy dove?
      His Psyche true!

O latest-born and loveliest vision far
   Of all Olympus' faded hierarchy!
Fairer than Phoebe's sapphire-regioned star,
   Or Vesper, amorous glow-worm of the sky;
Fairer than these, though temple thou hast none,
   Nor altar heaped with flowers;
Nor Virgin-choir to make delicious moan
   Upon the midnight hours;
No voice, no lute, no pipe, no incense sweet
   From chain-swung censer teeming;
No shrine, no grove, no oracle, no heat
   Of pale-mouthed prophet dreaming.
O brightest! though too late for antique vows,
   Too, too late for the fond believing lyre,
When holy were the haunted forest boughs,
   Holy the air, the water, and the fire;
Yet even in these days so far retired
   From happy pieties, thy lucent fans,
   Fluttering among the faint Olympians,
I see, and sing, by my own eyes inspired.
   So let me be thy choir, and make a moan
      Upon the midnight hours!
Thy voice, thy lute, thy pipe, thy incense sweet
   From swingéd censer teeming:
Thy shrine, thy grove, thy oracle, thy heat
   Of pale-mouthed prophet dreaming.

Yes, I will be thy priest, and build a fane
   In some untrodden region of my mind,
Where branchéd thoughts, new-grown with pleasant pain,
   Instead of pines shall murmur in the wind:
Far, far around shall those dark-clustered trees
   Fledge the wild-ridgéd mountains steep by steep;
And there by zephyrs, streams, and birds, and bees,
   The moss-lain Dryads shall be lulled to sleep;

And in the midst of this wide quietness
  A rosy sanctuary will I dress
With the wreathed trellis of a working brain,
  With buds, and bells, and stars without a name,
With all the gardener Fancy e'er could feign,
  Who breeding flowers, will never breed the same:
And there shall be for thee all soft delight
  That shadowy thought can win,
A bright torch, and a casement ope at night,
  To let the warm Love in!

To the Poets

Bards of Passion and of Mirth,
Ye have left your souls on earth!
Have ye souls in heaven too,
Double-lived in regions new?
Yes, and those of heaven commune
With the spheres of sun and moon;
With the noise of fountains wondrous,
And the parle of voices thund'rous;
With the whisper of heaven's trees
And one another, in soft ease
Seated on Elysian lawns
Browsed by none but Dian's fawns;
Underneath large blue-bells tented,
Where the daisies are rose-scented,
And the rose herself has got
Perfume which on earth is not;
Where the nightingale doth sing
Not a senseless, trancéd thing,
But divine, melodious truth,
Philosophic numbers smooth;
Tales and golden histories
Of heaven and its mysteries.

Thus ye live on high, and then
On the earth ye live again;
And the souls ye left behind you
Teach us, here, the way to find you,

Where your other souls are joying
Never slumbered, never cloying.
Here, your earth-born souls still speak
To mortals, of their little week;
Of their sorrows and delights;
Of their passions and their spites;
Of their glory and their shame;
What does strengthen, and what maim
Thus ye teach us, every day,
Wisdom, though fled far away.

Bards of Passion and of Mirth,
Ye have left your souls on earth!
Ye have souls in heaven too,
Double-lived in regions new!

Lines on the Mermaid Tavern

Souls of poets dead and gone,
What Elysium have ye known,
Happy field or mossy cavern,
Choicer than the Mermaid Tavern?
Have ye tippled drink more fine
Than mine host's Canary wine?
Or are fruits of Paradise
Sweeter than those dainty pies
Of venison? O generous food!
Drest as though bold Robin Hood
Would, with his maid Marian,
Sup and bowse from horn and can.

I have heard that on a day
Mine host's sign-board flew away,
Nobody knew whither, till
An Astrologer's old quill
To a sheepskin gave the story—
Said he saw you in your glory,
Underneath a new old-sign
Sipping beverage divine,
And pledging with contented smack
The Mermaid in the Zodiac.

Souls of poets dead and gone,
What Elysium have ye known,
Happy field or mossy cavern,
Choicer than the Mermaid Tavern?

To Autumn

Season of mists and mellow fruitfulness!
  Close bosom-friend of the maturing sun;
Conspiring with him how to load and bless
  With fruit the vines that round the thatch-eaves run;
To bend with apples the mossed cottage-trees,
  And fill all fruit with ripeness to the core;
    To swell the gourd, and plump the hazel shells
  With a sweet kernel; to set budding more,
And still more, later flowers for the bees,
Until they think warm days will never cease,
    For Summer has o'er-brimmed their clammy cells.

Who hath not seen thee oft amid thy store?
  Sometimes whoever seeks abroad may find
Thee sitting careless on a granary floor,
  Thy hair soft-lifted by the winnowing wind;
Or on a self-reaped furrow sound asleep,
  Drowsed with the fume of poppies, while thy hook
    Spares the next swath and all its twinéd flowers,
And sometimes like a gleaner thou dost keep
  Steady thy laden head across a brook;
  Or by a cider-press, with patient look,
    Thou watchest the last oozings, hours by hours

Where are the songs of Spring? Ay, where are they?
  Think not of them, thou hast thy music too,
    While barréd clouds bloom the soft-dying day,
And touch the stubble-plains with rosy hue;
  Then in a wailful choir, the small gnats mourn
  Among the river sallows, borne aloft
    Or sinking as the light wind lives or dies;
And full-grown lambs loud bleat from hilly bourn;
  Hedge-crickets sing; and now with.treble soft
  The red-breast whistles from a garden-croft,
    And gathering swallows twitter in the skies.

On Melancholy

No, no! go not to Lethe, neither twist
   Wolf's-bane, tight-rooted, for its poisonous wine;
Nor suffer thy pale forehead to be kissed
   By nightshade, ruby grape of Proserpine;
Make not your rosary of yew-berries,
   Nor let the beetle nor the death-moth be
     Your mournful Psyche, nor the downy owl
A partner in your sorrow's mysteries;
   For shade to shade will come too drowsily,
     And drown the wakeful anguish of the soul.

But when the melancholy fit shall fall
   Sudden from heaven like a weeping cloud,
That fosters the droop-headed flowers all,
   And hides the green hill in an April shroud;
Then glut thy sorrow on a morning rose,
   Or on the rainbow of the salt sand-wave,
     Or on the wealth of globéd peonies;
Or if thy mistress some rich anger shows,
   Emprison her soft hand, and let her rave,
     And feed deep, deep upon her peerless eyes.

She dwells with Beauty—Beauty that must die;
   And Joy, whose hand is ever at his lips
Bidding adieu; and aching Pleasure nigh,
   Turning to poison while the bee-mouth sips:
Ay, in the very temple of Delight
   Veiled Melancholy has her sovran shrine,
     Though seen of none save him whose strenuous tongue
     Can burst Joy's grape against his palate fine:
His soul shall taste the sadness of her might,
     And be among her cloudy trophies hung.

Sonnet on the Sea

It keeps eternal whispering around
   Desolate shores, and with its mighty swell
   Gluts twice ten thousand caverns, till the spell
Of Hecate leaves them their old shadowy sound.
Often 'tis in such gentle temper found,
   That scarcely will the very smallest shell
   Be moved for days from whence it sometime fell,
When last the winds of heaven were unbound.
Oh ye! who have your eye-balls vexed and tired,
   Feast them upon the wideness of the Sea;
Oh ye! whose ears are dinned with uproar rude,
   Or fed too much with cloying melody,—
Sit ye near some old cavern's mouth, and brood
Until ye start, as if the sea-nymphs quired!

Sonnet to Sleep

O soft embalmer of the still midnight!
   Shutting, with careful fingers and benign,
Our gloom-pleased eyes, embowered from the light,
   Enshaded in forgetfulness divine;
O soothest Sleep! if so it please thee, close,
   In midst of this thine hymn, my willing eyes,
Or wait the amen, ere thy poppy throws
   Around my bed its lulling charities;
   Then save me, or the passéd day will shine
Upon my pillow, breeding many woes;
   Save me from curious conscience, that still lord
Its strength, for darkness burrowing like a mole;
   Turn the key deftly in the oiléd wards,
And seal the hushéd casket of my soul.

Ballad: La Belle Dame sans Merci

   O what can ail thee, knight-at-arms,
      Alone and palely loitering?
   The sedge has withered from the lake,
      And no birds sing.

O what can ail thee, knight-at-arms,
  So haggard and so woe-begone?
The squirrel's granary is full,
  And the harvest's done.

I see a lily on thy brow
  With anguish moist and fever dew,
And on thy cheeks a fading rose
  Fast withereth too.

I met a lady in the meads,
  Full beautiful—a faery's child,
Her hair was long, her foot was light,
  And her eyes were wild.

I made a garland for her head,
  And bracelets too, and fragrant zone,
She looked at me as she did love,
  And made sweet moan.

I set her on my pacing steed,
  And nothing else saw all day long,
For sidelong would she bend, and sing
  A faery's song.

She found me roots of relish sweet,
  And honey wild, and manna dew,
And sure in language strange she said—
  "I love thee true!"

She took me to her elfin grot,
  And there she wept and sighed full sore,
And there I shut her wild, wild eyes
  With kisses four.

And there she lulléd me asleep,
  And there I dreamed—ah, woe betide!
The latest dream I ever dreamed
  On the cold hill's side.

I saw pale kings and princes too,
    Pale warriors, death-pale were they all;
They cried—"La Belle Dame sans Merci
    Hath thee in thrall!"

I saw their starved lips in the gloam,
    With horrid warning gapéd wide,
And I awoke and found me here,
    On the cold hill's side.

And this is why I sojourn here,
    Alone and palely loitering,
Though the sedge is withered from the lake,
    And no birds sing.

FROM *The Eve of St. Agnes*

Out went the taper as she hurried in;
Its little smoke in pallid moonshine died:
She closed the door, she panted, all akin
To spirits of the air, and visions wide:
No uttered syllable, or, woe betide!
But to her heart, her heart was voluble,
Paining with eloquence her balmy side;
As though a tongueless nightingale should swell
Her throat in vain, and die, heart-stifled, in her dell.

A casement high and triple-arched there was,
All garlanded with carven imageries,
Of fruits and flowers, and bunches of knot-grass,
And diamonded with panes of quaint device,
Innumerable of stains and splendid dyes,
As are the tiger-moth's deep-damasked wings;
And in the midst, 'mong thousand heraldries,
And twilight saints, and dim emblazonings,
A shielded scutcheon blushed with blood of queens and kings.

Full on this casement shone the wintry moon,
And threw warm gules on Madeline's fair breast,
As down she knelt for Heaven's grace and boon;
Rose-bloom fell on her hands, together prest,

And on her silver cross soft amethyst,
And on her hair a glory, like a saint:
She seemed a splendid angel, newly drest,
Save wings, for heaven:—Porphyro grew faint:
She knelt, so pure a thing, so free from mortal taint.

Anon his heart revives: her vespers done,
Of all its wreathéd pearls her hair she frees;
Unclasps her warméd jewels one by one;
Loosens her fragrant boddice; by degrees
Her rich attire creeps rustling to her knees:
Half-hidden, like a mermaid in sea-weed,
Pensive awhile she dreams awake, and sees,
In fancy, fair St. Agnes in her bed,
But dares not look behind, or all the charm is fled.

Soon, trembling in her soft and chilly nest,
In sort of wakeful swoon, perplexed she lay,
Until the poppied warmth of sleep oppressed
Her soothéd limbs, and soul fatigued away;
Flown, like a thought, until the morrow-day;
Blissfully havened both from joy and pain;
Clasped like a missal where swart Paynims pray;
Blinded alike from sunshine and from rain,
As though a rose should shut, and be a bud again.

Stolen to this paradise, and so entranced,
Porphyro gazed upon her empty dress,
And listened to her breathing, if it chanced
To wake into a slumberous tenderness;
Which when he heard, that minute did he bless,
And breathed himself: then from the closet crept,
Noiseless as fear in a wide wilderness,
And over the hushed carpet, silent, stept,
And 'tween the curtains peeped, where lo!—how fast she slept!

Then by the bed-side, where the faded moon
Made a dim, silver twilight, soft he set
A table, and, half anguished, threw thereon
A cloth of woven crimson, gold, and jet:—
O for some drowsy Morphean amulet!

The boisterous, midnight, festive clarion,
The kettle-drum, and far-heard clarionet,
Affray his ears, though but in dying tone:—
The hall-door shuts again, and all the noise is gone.

And still she slept an azure-lidded sleep,
In blanchéd linen, smooth, and lavendered,
While he from forth the closet brought a heap
Of candied apple, quince, and plum, and gourd;
With jellies soother than the creamy curd,
And lucent syrops, tinct with cinnamon;
Manna, and dates, in argosy transferred
From Fez; and spiced dainties, every one
From silken Samarcand to cedared Lebanon.

These delicates he heaped with glowing hand
On golden dishes and in baskets bright
Of wreathéd silver: sumptuous they stand
In the retiréd quiet of the night,
Filling the chilly room with perfume light.—
"And now, my love, my seraph fair, awake!
Thou art my heaven, and I thine eremite:
Open thine eyes, for meek St. Agnes' sake,
Or I shall drowse beside thee, so my soul doth ache."

Thus whispering, his warm unnervéd arm
Sank in her pillow. Shaded was her dream
By the dusk curtains:—'twas a midnight charm
Impossible to melt as iced stream:
The lustrous salvers in the moonlight gleam;
Broad golden fringe upon the carpet lies:
It seemed he never, never could redeem
From such a steadfast spell his lady's eyes;
So mused awhile, entoiled in wooféd phantasies.

FROM *Isabella or The Pot of Basil*

1.

Fair Isabel, poor simple Isabel!
    Lorenzo, a young palmer in Love's eye!
They could not in the self-same mansion dwell
    Without some stir of heart, some malady;

They could not sit at meals but feel how well
    It soothed each to be the other by;
They could not, sure, beneath the same roof sleep,
But to each other dream, and nightly weep.

With every morn their love grew tenderer,
    With every eve deeper and tenderer still;
He might not in house, field, or garden stir,
    But her full shape would all his seeing fill;
And his continual voice was pleasanter
    To her, than noise of trees or hidden rill;
Her lute-string gave an echo of his name,
She spoilt her half-done broidery with the same.

He knew whose gentle hand was at the latch,
    Before the door had given her to his eyes;
And from her chamber-window he would catch
    Her beauty farther than the falcon spies;
And constant as her vespers would he watch,
    Because her face was turned to the same skies;
And with sick longing all the night outwear,
To hear her morning-step upon the stair.

A whole long month of May in this sad plight
    Made their cheeks paler by the break of June:
"To-morrow will I bow to my delight,
    To-morrow will I ask my lady's boon."—
"O may I never see another night,
    Lorenzo, if thy lips breathe not love's tune."—
So spake they to their pillows; but, alas,
Honeyless days and nights did he let pass;

Until sweet Isabella's untouched cheek
    Fell sick within the rose's just domain,
Fell thin as a young mother's, who doth seek
    By every lull to cool her infant's pain:
"How ill she is!" said he, "I may not speak
    And yet I will, and tell my love all plain:
If looks speak love-laws, I will drink her tears,
And at the least 'twill startle off her cares."

So said he one fair morning, and all day
  His heart beat awfully against his side;
And to his heart he inwardly did pray
  For power to speak; but still the ruddy tide
Stifled his voice, and pulsed resolve away—
  Fevered his high conceit of such a bride,
Yet brought him to the meekness of a child:
Alas! when passion is both meek and wild!

So once more he had waked and anguished
  A dreary night of love and misery,
If Isabel's quick eye had not been wed
  To every symbol on his forehead high;
She saw it waxing very pale and dead,
  And straight all flushed; so, lisped tenderly,
"Lorenzo!"—here she ceased her timid quest,
But in her tone and look he read the rest.

"O Isabella! I can half perceive
  That I may speak my grief into thine ear;
If thou didst ever anything believe,
  Believe how I love thee, believe how near
My soul is to its doom: I would not grieve
  Thy hand by unwelcome pressing, would not fear
Thine eyes by gazing; but I cannot live
Another night, and not my passion shrive.

"Love: thou art leading me from wintry cold,
  Lady! thou leadest me to summer clime,
And I must taste the blossoms that unfold
  In its ripe warmth this gracious morning time."
So said, his erewhile timid lips grew bold,
  And poesied with hers in dewy rhyme:
Great bliss was with them, and great happiness
Grew, like a lusty flower in June's caress.

Parting they seemed to tread upon the air,
  Twin roses by the zephyr blown apart
Only to meet again more close, and share
  The inward fragrance of each other's heart.

She, to her chamber gone, a ditty fair
  Sang, of delicious love and honeyed dart;
He with light steps went up a western hill,
And bade the sun farewell, and joyed his fill.

All close they met again, before the dusk
  Had taken from the stars its pleasant veil,
All close they met, all eves, before the dusk
  Had taken from the stars its pleasant veil,
Close in a bower of hyacinth and musk,
  Unknown of any, free from whispering tale.
Ah! better had it been for ever so,
Than idle ears should pleasure in their woe.

Were they unhappy then?—It cannot be—
  Too many tears for lovers have been shed,
Too many sighs give we to them in fee,
  Too much of pity after they are dead,
Too many doleful stories do we see,
  Whose matter in bright gold were best be read;
Except in such a page where Theseus' spouse
Over the pathless waves towards him bows.

But for the general award of love,
  The little sweet doth kill much bitterness;
Though Dido silent is in under-grove,
  And Isabella's was a great distress,
Though young Lorenzo in warm Indian clove
  Was not embalmed, this truth is not the less—
Even bees, the little almsmen of spring-bowers,
Know there is richest juice in poison-flowers.

2.

O Melancholy, linger here awhile!
  O Music, Music, breathe despondingly!
O Echo, Echo, from some sombre isle,
  Unknown, Lethean, sigh to us—O sigh!
Spirits in grief, lift up your heads, and smile;
  Lift up your heads, sweet Spirits, heavily,
And make a pale light in your cypress glooms,
Tinting with silver wan your marble tombs.

Moan hither, all ye syllables of woe,
   From the deep throat of sad Melpomene!
Through bronzed lyre in tragic order go,
   And touch the strings into a mystery;
Sound mournfully upon the winds and low;
   For simple Isabel is soon to be
Among the dead: She withers, like a palm
Cut by an Indian for its juicy balm.

O leave the palm to wither by itself;
   Let not quick Winter chill its dying hour!—
It may not be—those Baälites of pelf,
   Her brethren, noted the continual shower
From her dead eyes; and many a curious elf,
   Among her kindred, wondered that such dower
Of youth and beauty should be thrown aside
By one marked out to be a Noble's bride.

And furthermore, her brethren wondered much
   Why she sat drooping by the Basil green,
And why it flourished, as by magic touch;
   Greatly they wondered what the thing might mean:
They could not surely give belief, that such
   A very nothing would have power to wean
Her from her own fair youth, and pleasures gay,
And even remembrance of her love's delay.

Therefore they watched a time when they might sift
   This hidden whim; and long they watched in vain;
For seldom did she go to chapel-shrift,
   And seldom felt she any hunger-pain:
And when she left, she hurried back, as swift
   As bird on wing to breast its eggs again:
And, patient as a hen-bird, sat her there
Beside her Basil, weeping through her hair.

Yet they contrived to steal the Basil-pot,
   And to examine it in secret place:
The thing was vile with green and livid spot,
   And yet they knew it was Lorenzo's face:

The guerdon of their murder they had got,
    And so left Florence in a moment's space,
Never to turn again.—Away they went,
With blood upon their heads, to banishment.

O Melancholy, turn thine eyes away!
    O Music, Music, breathe despondingly!
O Echo, Echo, on some other day,
    From isles Lethean, sigh to us—O sigh!
Spirits of grief, sing not your "Well-a-way!"
    For Isabel, sweet Isabel, will die;
Will die a death too lone and incomplete,
Now they have ta'en away her Basil sweet.

And so she pined, and so she died forlorn,
    Imploring for her Basil to the last.
No heart was there in Florence but did mourn
    In pity of her love, so overcast.
And a sad ditty of this story borne
    From mouth to mouth through all the country pass'd:
Still is the burthen sung—"O cruelty,
To steal my Basil-pot away from me!"

FROM *Endymion*

1.

A thing of beauty is a joy for ever:
Its loveliness increases; it will never
Pass into nothingness; but still will keep
A bower quiet for us, and a sleep
Full of sweet dreams, and health, and quiet breathing.
Therefore, on every morrow, are we wreathing
A flowery band to bind us to the earth,
Spite of despondence, of the inhuman dearth
Of noble natures, of the gloomy days,
Of all the unhealthy and o'er-darkened ways
Made for our searching: yes, in spite of all,
Some shape of beauty moves away the pall
From our dark spirits. Such the sun, the moon,
Trees old and young, sprouting a shady boon

For simple sheep; and such are daffodils
With the green world they live in; and clear rills
That for themselves a cooling covert make
'Gainst the hot season; the mid-forest brake,
Rich with a sprinkling of fair musk-rose blooms:
And such too is the grandeur of the dooms
We have imagined for the mighty dead;
All lovely tales that we have heard or read:
An endless fountain of immortal drink,
Pouring unto us from the heaven's brink.

Nor do we merely feel these essences
For one short hour; no, even as the trees
That whisper round a temple become soon
Dear as the temple's self, so does the moon,
The passion poesy, glories infinite,
Haunt us till they become a cheering light
Unto our souls, and bound to us so fast,
That, whether there be shine, or gloom o'ercast,
They always must be with us, or we die.

2.

And, truly, I would rather be struck dumb
Than speak against this ardent listlessness:
For I have ever thought that it might bless
The world with benefits unknowingly;
As does the nightingale, up-perchéd high,
And cloistered among cool and bunchéd leaves—
She sings but to her love, nor e'er conceives
How tiptoe Night holds back her dark-grey hood.
Just so may love, although 'tis understood
The mere commingling of passionate breath,
Produce more than our searching witnesseth:
What I know not: but who, of men, can tell
That flowers would bloom, or that green fruit would swell
To melting pulp, that fish would have bright mail,
The earth its dower of river, wood, and vale,
The meadows runnels, runnels pebble-stones,
The seed its harvest, or the lute its tones,
Tones ravishment, or ravishment its sweet,
If human souls did never kiss and greet?

3.

> O sovereign power of love! O grief! O balm!
> All records, saving thine, come cool, and calm,
> And shadowy, through the mist of passéd years:
> For others, good or bad, hatred and tears,
> Have become indolent; but touching thine,
> One sigh doth echo, one poor sob doth pine,
> One kiss brings honey-dew from buried days.
> The woes of Troy, towers smothering o'er their blaze,
> Stiff-holden shields, far-piercing spears, keen blades,
> Struggling, and blood, and shrieks—all dimly fades
> Into some backward corner of the brain;
> Yet, in our very souls, we feel amain
> The close of Troilus and Cressid sweet.
> Hence, pageant history! hence, gilded cheat!
> Swart planet in the universe of deeds!
> Wide sea, that one continuous murmur breeds
> Along the pebbled shore of memory!
> Many old rotten-timbered boats there be
> Upon thy vaporous bosom, magnified
> To goodly vessels; many a sail of pride,
> And golden-keeled, is left unlaunched and dry.
> But wherefore this? What care, though owl did fly
> About the great Athenian admiral's mast?
> What care, though striding Alexander past
> The Indus with his Macedonian numbers?
> Though old Ulysses tortured from his slumbers
> The glutted Cyclops, what care?—Juliet leaning
> Amid her window-flowers,—sighing,—weaning
> Tenderly her fancy from its maiden snow,
> Doth more avail than these: the silver flow
> Of Hero's tears, the swoon of Imogen,
> Fair Pastorella in the bandit's den,
> Are things to brood on with more ardency
> Than the death-day of empires.

4.

> Beneath my palm-trees, by the river side,
> I sat a-weeping: what enamoured bride

Cheated by shadowy wooer from the clouds,
   But hides and shrouds
Beneath dark palm-trees by a river side?

And as I sat, over the light blue hills
There came a noise of revellers: the rills
Into the wide stream came of purple hue—
   'Twas Bacchus and his crew!
The earnest trumpet spake, and silver thrills
From kissing cymbals made a merry din—
   'Twas Bacchus and his kind!
Like to a moving vintage down they came,
Crowned with green leaves, and faces all on flame;
All madly dancing through the pleasant valley,
   To scare thee, Melancholy!
O then, O then, thou wast a simple name!
And I forgot thee, as the berried holly
By shepherds is forgotten, when in June,
Tall chestnuts keep away the sun and moon:—
   I rushed into the folly!

Within his car, aloft, young Bacchus stood,
Trifling his ivy-dart, in dancing mood,
   With sidelong laughing;
And little rills of crimson wine imbrued
His plump white arms, and shoulders, enough white
   For Venus' pearly bite;
And near him rode Silenus on his ass,
Pelted with flowers as he on did pass
   Tipsily quaffing.

Whence came ye, merry Damsels, whence came ye,
So many, and so many, and such glee?
Why have ye left your forest haunts, why left
   Your nuts in oak-tree cleft?—
"For wine, for wine we left our kernel tree;
For wine we left our heath, and yellow brooms,
   And cold mushrooms;

For wine we follow Bacchus through the earth;
Great god of breathless cups and chirping mirth!
Come hither, fair lady, and joinéd be
    To our mad minstrelsy!"

Over wide streams and mountains great we went,
And, save when Bacchus kept his ivy tent,
Onward the tiger and the leopard pants,
    With Asian elephants:
Onward these myriads—with song and dance,
With zebras striped, and sleek Arabians' prance,
Web-footed alligators, crocodiles,
Bearing upon their scaly backs, in files,
Plump infant laughers mimicking the coil
Of seamen, and stout galley-rowers' toil:
With toying oars and silken sails they glide,
    Nor care for wind and tide.

Mounted on panthers' furs and lions' manes,
From rear to van they scour about the plains;
A three days' journey in a moment done;
And always, at the rising of the sun,
About the wilds they hunt with spear and horn,
    On spleenful unicorn.

I saw Osirian Egypt kneel adown
    Before the vine-wreath crown!
I saw parched Abyssinia rouse and sing
    To the silver cymbals' ring!
I saw the whelming vintage hotly pierce
    Old Tartary the fierce!

The kings of Ind their jewel-sceptres vail,
And from their treasures scatter pearléd hail;
Great Brahma from his mystic heaven groans,
    And all his priesthood moans,
Before young Bacchus' eye-wink turning pale.
Into these regions came I, following him,
Sick-hearted, weary—so I took a whim
To stray away into these forests drear,
    Alone, without a peer:
And I have told thee all thou mayest hear.

FROM *Hyperion*

1.

As when, upon a trancéd summer-night,
Those green-robed senators of mighty woods,
Tall oaks, branch-charméd by the earnest stars,
Dream, and so dream all night without a stir,
Save from one gradual solitary gust
Which comes upon the silence, and dies off,
As if the ebbing air had but one wave:
So came these words and went; the while in tears
She touched her fair large forehead to the ground,
Just where her falling hair might be outspread
A soft and silken mat for Saturn's feet.

2.

O leave them, Muse! O leave them to their woes
For thou art weak to sing such tumults dire:
A solitary sorrow best befits
Thy lips, and antheming a lonely grief.
Leave them, O Muse! for thou anon wilt find
Many a fallen old Divinity
Wandering in vain about bewildered shores.
Meantime touch piously the Delphic harp,
And not a wind of heaven but will breathe
In aid soft warble from the Dorian flute;
For lo! 'tis for the Father of all verse.
Flush everything that hath a vermeil hue,
Let the rose glow intense and warm the air,
And let the clouds of even and of morn
Float in voluptuous fleeces o'er the hills;
Let the red wine within the goblet boil,
Cold as a bubbling well; let faint-lipped shells,
On sands or in great deeps, vermilion turn
Through all their labyrinths; and let the maid
Blush keenly, as with some warm kiss surprised.
Chief isle of the embowered Cyclades,
Rejoice, O Delos, with thine olives green,
And poplars, and lawn-shading palms, and beech,
In which the Zephyr breathes the loudest song,
And hazels thick dark-stemmed beneath the shade:
Apollo is once more the golden theme!

"Bright Star! Would I Were Steadfast as Thou Art"

Bright star! would I were steadfast as thou art—
   Not in lone splendour hung aloft the night,
And watching, with eternal lids apart,
   Like Nature's patient, sleepless Eremite,
The moving waters at their priestlike task
   Of pure ablution round earth's human shores,
Or gazing on the new soft fallen mask
   Of snow upon the mountains and the moors—
No—yet still steadfast, still unchangeable,
   Pillowed upon my fair love's ripening breast,
To feel for ever its soft fall and swell,
   Awake for ever in a sweet unrest,
Still, still to hear her tender-taken breath,
And so live ever—or else swoon to death.

GEORGE DARLEY

(1795–1846)

Siren Chorus

Troop home to silent grots and caves,
   Troop home! and mimic as you go
The mournful winding of the waves
   Which to their dark abysses flow.

At this sweet hour all things beside
   In amorous pairs to covert creep,
The swans that brush the evening tide
   Homeward in snowy couples keep.

In his green den the murmuring seal
   Close by his sleek companion lies,
While singly we to bedward steal,
   And close in fruitless sleep our eyes.

In bowers of love men take their rest,
   In loveless bowers we sigh alone,
With bosom-friends are others blest,
   But we have none! but we have none!

HARTLEY COLERIDGE

(1796–1849)

Song

She is not fair to outward view
    As many maidens be,
Her loveliness I never knew
    Until she smiled on me;
Oh! then I saw her eye was bright,
A well of love, a spring of light.

But now her looks are coy and cold,
    To mine they ne'er reply,
And yet I cease not to behold
    The love-light in her eye:
Her very frowns are fairer far
Than smiles of other maidens are.

THOMAS HOOD

(1799–1845)

Autumn

I saw old Autumn in the misty morn
Stand shadowless like Silence, listening
To silence, for no lonely bird would sing
Into his hollow ear from woods forlorn,
Nor lowly hedge nor solitary thorn;
Shaking his languid locks all dewy bright
With tangled gossamer that fell by night,
    Pearling his coronet of golden corn.

Where are the songs of Summer? With the sun,
Oping the dusky eyelids of the south,
Till shade and silence waken up as one,
And Morning sings with a warm odorous mouth.
Where are the merry birds? Away, away,
On panting wings through the inclement skies,
    Lest owls should prey
    Undazzled at noonday,
And tear with horny beak their lustrous eyes.

Where are the blossoms of Summer? In the west,
Blushing their last to the last sunny hours,
When the mild Eve by sudden Night is prest
Like tearful Proserpine, snatched from her flowers
  To a most gloomy breast.
Where is the pride of Summer—the green prime—
The many, many leaves all twinkling? Three
  On the mossed elm; three on the naked lime
Trembling—and one upon the old oak tree.
  Where is the Dryads' immortality?
Gone into mournful cypress and dark yew,
Or wearing the long gloomy Winter through
  In the smooth holly's green eternity.

The squirrel gloats on his accomplished hoard,
The ants have brimmed their garners with ripe grain,
  And honey bees have stored
The sweets of Summer in their luscious cells;
The swallows all have winged across the main;
And here the Autumn melancholy dwells,
And sighs her tearful spells,
Amongst the sunless shadows of the plain.
  Alone, alone,
  Upon a mossy stone,
She sits and reckons up the dead and gone
With the last leaves for a love-rosary,
Whilst all the withered world looks drearily,
Like a dim picture of the drownéd past
In the hushed mind's mysterious far away,
Doubtful what ghostly thing will steal the last
Into that distance, grey upon the grey.

O go and sit with her, and be o'ershaded
Under the languid downfall of her hair:
She wears a coronal of flowers faded
Upon her forehead, and a face of care;
There is enough of withered everywhere
To make her bower—and enough of gloom;
There is enough of sadness to invite,
If only for the rose that died—whose doom
Is Beauty's—she that with the living bloom

Of conscious cheeks most beautifies the light;
There is enough of sorrowing, and quite
Enough of bitter fruits the earth doth bear—
Enough of chilly droppings for her bowl;
Enough of fear and shadowy despair,
To frame her cloudy prison for the soul.

The Water Lady

Alas, the moon should ever beam
To show what man should never see!
I saw a maiden on a stream,
And fair was she!

I stayed awhile, to see her throw
Her tresses back, that all beset
The fair horizon of her brow
With clouds of jet.

I stayed a little while to view
Her cheek, that wore in place of red
The bloom of water, tender blue,
Daintily spread.

I stayed to watch, a little space,
Her parted lips if she would sing;
The waters closed above her face
With many a ring.

And still I stayed a little more,
Alas! she never comes again;
I throw my flowers from the shore,
And watch in vain.

I know my life will fade away,
I know that I must vainly pine,
For I am made of mortal clay,
But she's divine.

Sonnet

It is not death, that sometime in a sigh
This eloquent breath shall take its speechless flight;
That sometime these bright stars, that now reply
In sunlight to the sun, shall set in night:
That this warm conscious flesh shall perish quite,
And all life's ruddy springs forget to flow;
That thoughts shall cease, and the immortal sprite
Be lapped in alien clay, and laid below;
It is not death to know this—but to know
That pious thoughts, which visit at new graves
In tender pilgrimage, will cease to go
So duly and so oft—and when grass waves
Over the past-away, there may be then
No resurrection in the minds of men.

Silence

There is a silence where hath been no sound,
There is a silence where no sound may be,
In the cold grave—under the deep, deep sea,
Or in wide desert where no life is found,
Which hath been mute, and still must sleep profound;
No voice is hushed—no life treads silently,
But clouds and cloudy shadows wander free,
That never spoke, over the idle ground:
But in green ruins, in the desolate walls
Of antique palaces, where Man hath been,
Though the dun fox, or wild hyena calls,
And owls, that flit continually between,
Shriek to the echo, and the low winds moan,
There the true Silence is, self-conscious and alone.

THOMAS BABINGTON MACAULAY, LORD MACAULAY
(1800–1859)

Epitaph on a Jacobite

To my true king I offered free from stain
Courage and faith; vain faith, and courage vain.
For him I threw lands, honours, wealth, away,
And one dear hope that was more prized than they.
For him I languished in a foreign clime,
Grey-haired with sorrow in my manhood's prime;
Heard on Lavernia Scargill's whispering trees,
And pined by Arno for my lovelier Tees;
Beheld each night my home in fevered sleep,
Each morning started from the dream to weep;
Till God, who saw me tried too sorely, gave
The resting place I asked, an early grave.
O thou, whom chance leads to this nameless stone,
From that proud country which was once mine own,
By those white cliffs I never more must see,
By that dear language which I spake like thee,
Forget all feuds, and shed one English tear
O'er English dust. A broken heart lies here.

WINTHROP MACKWORTH PRAED
(1802–1839)

FROM The Belle of the Ball-Room

Our love was like most other loves;—
    A little glow, a little shiver,
A rose-bud, and a pair of gloves,
    And "Fly not yet"—upon the river;
Some jealousy of some one's heir,
    Some hopes of dying broken-hearted,
A miniature, a lock of hair,
    The usual vows,—and then we parted.

We parted; months and years rolled by;
    We met again four summers after:
Our parting was all sob and sigh;
    Our meeting was all mirth and laughter:

For in my heart's most secret cell
  There had been many other lodgers;
And she was not the ball-room's Belle,
  But only—Mrs. Something Rogers!

RALPH WALDO EMERSON

(1803–1882)

"And When I Am Entombéd..."

And when I am entombéd in my place,
Be it remembered of a single man,
He never, though he dearly loved his race,
For fear of human eyes swerved from his plan.

FROM Ode Inscribed to W. H. Channing

The God who made New Hampshire
Taunted the lofty land
With little men;—
Small bat and wren
House in the oak:—
If earth-fire cleave
The upheaved land, and bury the folk,
The southern crocodile would grieve.
Virtue palters; Right is hence;
Freedom praised, but hid;
Funeral eloquence
Rattles the coffin-lid.

The horseman serves the horse,
The neatherd serves the neat,
The merchant serves the purse,
The eater serves his meat;
'Tis the day of the chattel,
Web to weave, and corn to grind;
Things are in the saddle,
And ride mankind.

There are two laws discrete,
Not reconciled,—
Law for man, and law for thing;
The last builds town and fleet,
But it runs wild,
And doth the man unking.

Let man serve law for man;
Live for friendship, live for love,
For truth's and harmony's behoof;
The state may follow how it can,
As Olympus follows Jove.

Yet do not I implore
The wrinkled shopman to my sounding woods,
Nor bid the unwilling senator
Ask votes of thrushes in the solitudes.
Every one to his chosen work;—
Foolish hands may mix and mar;
Wise and sure the issue are.
Round they roll till dark is light,
Sex to sex, and even to odd;—
The over-god
Who marries Right to Might
Who peoples, unpeoples,—
He who exterminates
Races by stronger races,
Black by white faces,—
Knows to bring honey
Out of the lion;
Grafts gentlest scion
On pirate and Turk.

Forbearance

Hast thou named all the birds without a gun?
Loved the wood-rose, and left it on its stalk?
At rich men's tables eaten bread and pulse?
Unarmed, faced danger with a heart of trust?

And loved so well a high behavior,
In man or maid, that thou from speech refrained,
Nobility more nobly to repay?
O, be my friend, and teach me to be thine!

Give All to Love

Give all to love;
Obey thy heart;
Friends, kindred, days,
Estate, good-fame,
Plans, credit and the Muse,—
Nothing refuse.

'Tis a brave master;
Let it have scope:
Follow it utterly,
Hope beyond hope:
High and more high
It dives into noon,
With wing unspent,
Untold intent;
But it is a god,
Knows its own path
And the outlets of the sky.

It was never for the mean;
It requireth courage stout.
Souls above doubt,
Valor unbending,
It will reward,—
They shall return
More than they were,
And ever ascending.

Leave all for love;
Yet, hear me, yet,
One word more thy heart behoved,
One pulse more of firm endeavor,—

Keep thee to-day,
To-morrow, forever,
Free as an Arab
Of thy beloved.

Cling with life to the maid;
But when the surprise,
First vague shadow of surmise,
Flits across her bosom young,
Of a joy apart from thee,
Free be she, fancy-free;
Nor thou detain her vesture's hem,
Nor the palest rose she flung
From her summer diadem.

Though thou loved her as thyself,
As a self of purer clay,
Though her parting dims the day,
Stealing grace from all alive;
Heartily know,
When half-gods go,
The gods arrive.

Bacchus

Bring me wine, but wine which never grew
In the belly of the grape,
Or grew on vine whose tap-roots, reaching through
Under the Andes to the Cape,
Suffer no savor of the earth to scape.

Let its grapes the morn salute
From a nocturnal root,
Which feels the acrid juice
Of Styx and Erebus;
And turns the woe of Night
By its own craft, to a more rich delight.

We buy ashes for bread;
We buy diluted wine;
Give me of the true,—
Whose ample leaves and tendrils curled
Among the silver hills of heaven
Draw everlasting dew;
Wine of wine,
Blood of the world,
Form of forms, and mould of statures,
That I intoxicated,
And by the draught assimilated,
May float at pleasure through all natures;
The bird-language rightly spell,
And that which roses say so well.

Wine that is shed
Like the torrents of the sun
Up the horizon walls,
Or like the Atlantic streams, which run
When the South Sea calls.
Water and bread,
Food which needs no transmuting,
Rainbow-flowering, wisdom-fruiting,
Wine which is already man,
Food which teach and reason can.

Wine which Music is,—
Music and wine are one,—
That I, drinking this,
Shall hear far Chaos talk with me;
Kings unborn shall walk with me;
And the poor grass shall plot and plan
What it will do when it is man.
Quickened so, will I unlock
Every crypt of every rock.

I thank the joyful juice
For all I know;—
Winds of remembering
Of the ancient being blow,
And seeming-solid walls of use
Open and flow.

Pour, Bacchus! the remembering wine;
Retrieve the loss of me and mine!
Vine for vine be antidote,
And the grape requite the lote!
Haste to cure the old despair,—
Reason in Nature's lotus drenched,
The memory of ages quenched;
Give them again to shine;
Let wine repair what this undid;
And where the infection slid,
A dazzling memory revive;
Refresh the faded tints,
Recut the aged prints,
And write my old adventures with the pen
Which on the first day drew,
Upon the tablets blue,
The dancing Pleiads and eternal men.

FROM *Concord Hymn*

By the rude bridge that arched the flood,
    Their flag to April's breeze unfurled,
Here once the embattled farmers stood
    And fired the shot heard round the world.

The foe long since in silence slept;
    Alike the conqueror silent sleeps;
And Time the ruined bridge has swept
    Down the dark stream which seaward creeps.

Days

Daughters of Time, the hypocritic Days,
Muffled and dumb like barefoot dervishes,
And marching single in an endless file,
Bring diadems and fagots in their hands.
To each they offer gifts after his will,

Bread, kingdoms, stars, and sky that holds them all.
I, in my pleached garden, watched the pomp,
Forgot my morning wishes, hastily
Took a few herbs and apples, and the Day
Turned and departed silently. I, too late,
Under her solemn fillet saw the scorn.

April

The April winds are magical
And thrill our tuneful frames;
The garden walks are passional
To bachelors and dames.
The hedge is gemmed with diamonds,
The air with Cupids full,
The cobweb clues of Rosamond
Guide lovers to the pool.
Each dimple in the water,
Each leaf that shades the rock
Can cozen, pique and flatter,
Can parley and provoke.
Goodfellow, Puck and goblins,
Know more than any book.
Down with your doleful problems,
And court the sunny brook.
The south-winds are quick-witted,
The schools are sad and slow,
The masters quite omitted
The lore we care to know.

Heroism

Ruby wine is drunk by knaves,
Sugar spends to fatten slaves,
Rose and vine-leaf deck buffoons;
Thunder-clouds are Jove's festoons,
Drooping oft in wreaths of dread,
Lightning-knotted round his head;

The hero is not fed on sweets,
Daily his own heart he eats;
Chambers of the great are jails,
And head-winds right for royal sails.

Brahma

If the red slayer think he slays,
    Or if the slain think he is slain,
They know not well the subtle ways
    I keep, and pass, and turn again.

Far or forgot to me is near;
    Shadow and sunlight are the same;
The vanished gods to me appear;
    And one to me are shame and fame.

They reckon ill who leave me out;
    When me they fly, I am the wings;
I am the doubter and the doubt,
    And I the hymn the Brahmin sings.

The strong gods pine for my abode,
    And pine in vain the sacred Seven;
But thou, meek lover of the good!
    Find me, and turn thy back on heaven.

THOMAS LOVELL BEDDOES
(1803–1849)

Song

How many times do I love thee, dear?
    Tell me how many thoughts there be
        In the atmosphere
        Of a new-fall'n year,
Whose white and sable hours appear
    The latest flake of Eternity:—
So many times do I love thee, dear.

How many times do I love again?
  Tell me how many beads there are
    In a silver chain
    Of evening rain,
Unravelled from the tumbling main,
  And threading the eye of a yellow star:—
So many times do I love again.

Torrismond

Dream-Pedlary

If there were dreams to sell
  What would you buy?
Some cost a passing bell;
  Some a light sigh,
That shakes from Life's fresh crown
Only a roseleaf down.
If there were dreams to sell,
Merry and sad to tell,
And the crier rung the bell,
  What would you buy?

A cottage lone and still,
  With bowers nigh,
Shadowy, my woes to still,
  Until I die.
Such pearl from Life's fresh crown
Fain would I shake me down.
Were dreams to have at will,
This would best heal my ill,
  This would I buy.

But there were dreams to sell,
  Ill didst thou buy;
Life is a dream, they tell,
  Waking, to die.
Dreaming a dream to prize,
Is wishing ghosts to rise;
  And, if I had the spell
  To call the buried, well,
    Which one would I?

If there are ghosts to raise,
  What shall I call,
Out of hell's murky haze,
  Heaven's blue hall?
Raise my loved longlost boy
To lead me to his joy.
    There are no ghosts to raise;
    Out of death lead no ways;
      Vain is the call.

Know'st thou not ghosts to sue?
  No love thou hast.
Else lie, as I will do,
  And breathe thy last.
So out of Life's fresh crown
Fall like a rose-leaf down.
    Thus are the ghosts to woo;
    Thus are all dreams made true,
      Ever to last!

Love-in-Idleness

He: "Shall I be your first love, lady, shall I be your first?
  Oh! then I'll fall before you down on my velvet knee
  And deeply bend my rosy head and press it upon thee,
And swear that there is nothing more for which my heart doth
      thirst,
    But a downy kiss and pink
    Between your lips' soft chink."

She: "Yes, you shall be my first love, boy, and you shall be my
      first,
  And I will raise you up again unto my bosom's fold;
  And when you kisses many a one on lip and cheek have told,
I'll let you loose upon the grass, to leave me if you durst;
    And so we'll toy away
    The night beside the day."

He: "But let me be your second love, but let me be your
      second,
  For then I'll tap so gently, dear, upon your window pane,

And creep between the curtains in, where never man has
    lain,
And never leave thy gentle side till the morning star hath
    beckoned,
      Within the silken lace
      Of thy young arms' embrace."

She: "Well thou shalt be my second love, yes, gentle boy, my
    second,
    And I will wait at eve for thee within my lonely bower,
    And yield unto thy kisses, like a bud to April's shower,
From moonset till the tower-clock the hour of dawn hath
    reckoned,
      And lock thee with my arms
      All silent up in charms."

He: "No, I will be thy third love, lady, aye, I will be the third,
    And break upon thee, bathing, in woody place alone,
    And catch thee to my saddle and ride o'er stream and stone,
And press thee well, and kiss thee well, and never speak a
    word,
      Till thou hast yielded up
      The first taste of love's cup."

She: "Then thou shalt not be my first love, boy, nor my sec-
    ond, nor my third;
    If thou'rt the first, I'll laugh at thee and pierce thy flesh
      with thorns;
    If the second, from my chamber pelt with jeering laugh and
      scorns;
And if thou darest be the third, I'll draw my dirk unheard
      And cut thy heart in two,—
      And then die, weeping you."

Song

Who tames the lion now?
Who smooths Jove's wrinkles now?
Who is the reckless wight
    That in the horrid middle

Of the deserted night
Doth play upon man's brain,
    As on a wanton fiddle,
The mad and magic strain,
The reeling tripping sound,
To which the world goes round?
    Sing heigh! ho! diddle!
            And then say—
Love, quotha, Love? Nay, nay!
It is a spirit fine
Of ale or ancient wine,
    Lord Alcohol, the drunken fay,
        Lord Alcohol alway!

Who maketh pipe-clay man
Think all that nature can?
Who dares the gods to flout,
    Lay fate beneath the table,
And make him stammer out
    A thousand monstrous things,
    For history a fable,
    Dish-clouts for kings?
And send the world along
Singing a ribald song
    Of heighho! Babel?
            Who, I pray—
Love, quotha, Love? Nay, nay!
It is a spirit fine
Of ale or ancient wine,
    Lord Alcohol, the drunken fay,
        Lord Alcohol alway!

The Phantom-Wooer

A ghost, that loved a lady fair,
Ever in the starry air
    Of midnight at her pillow stood;
And, with a sweetness skies above
The luring words of human love,
    Her soul the phantom wooed.

Sweet and sweet is their poisoned note,
The little snakes' of silver throat,
In mossy skulls that nest and lie,
Ever singing, "Die, oh! die."

Young soul put off your flesh, and come
With me into the quiet tomb,
    Our bed is lovely, dark, and sweet;
The earth will swing us, as she goes,
Beneath our coverlid of snows,
    And the warm leaden sheet.
Dear and dear is their poisoned note,
The little snakes' of silver throat,
In mossy skulls that nest and lie,
Ever singing, "Die, oh! die."

Song

Strew not earth with empty stars,
    Strew it not with roses,
Nor feathers from the crest of Mars,
    Nor summer's idle posies.
'Tis not the primrose-sandalled moon,
    Nor cold and silent morn,
Nor he that climbs the dusty noon,
Nor mower war with scythe that drops,
Stuck with helmed and turbanned tops
    Of enemies new shorn.

Ye cups, ye lyres, ye trumpets know,
Pour your music, let it flow,
'Tis Bacchus' son who walks below.

JAMES CLARENCE MANGAN

(1803–1849)

Dark Rosaleen

O my dark Rosaleen,
    Do not sigh, do not weep!
The priests are on the ocean green,
    They march along the deep.

There's wine from the royal Pope,
    Upon the ocean green;
And Spanish ale shall give you hope,
    My dark Rosaleen!
    My own Rosaleen!
Shall glad your heart, shall give you hope,
Shall give you health and help, and hope,
    My dark Rosaleen.

Over hills and through dales,
    Have I roamed for your sake;
All yesterday I sailed with sails
    On river and on lake.
The Erne, at its highest flood,
    I dashed across unseen,
For there was lightning in my blood,
    My dark Rosaleen!
    My own Rosaleen!
Oh! there was lightning in my blood,
Red lightning lightened through my blood,
    My dark Rosaleen!

All day long in unrest,
    To and fro do I move,
The very soul within my breast
    Is wasted for you, love!
The heart in my bosom faints
    To think of you, my Queen,
My life of life, my saint of saints,
    My dark Rosaleen!
    My own Rosaleen!
To hear your sweet and sad complaints,
My life, my love, my saint of saints,
    My dark Rosaleen!

Woe and pain, pain and woe,
    Are my lot, night and noon,
To see your bright face clouded so,
    Like to the mournful moon.
But yet will I rear your throne
    Again in golden sheen;

'Tis you shall reign, shall reign alone,
 My dark Rosaleen!
 My own Rosaleen!
'Tis you shall have the golden throne,
'Tis you shall reign, shall reign alone,
 My dark Rosaleen!

Over dews, over sands,
 Will I fly for your weal:
Your holy, delicate white hands
 Shall girdle me with steel.
At home in your emerald bowers,
 From morning's dawn till e'en,
You'll pray for me, my flower of flowers,
 My dark Rosaleen!
 My fond Rosaleen!
You'll think of me through daylight's hours,
My virgin flower, my flower of flowers,
 My dark Rosaleen!

I could scale the blue air,
 I could plough the high hills,
Oh, I could kneel all night in prayer,
 To heal your many ills!
And one beamy smile from you
 Would float like light between
My toils and me, my own, my true,
 My dark Rosaleen!
 My fond Rosaleen!
Would give me life and soul anew,
A second life, a soul anew,
 My dark Rosaleen!

O! the Erne shall run red
 With redundance of blood,
The earth shall rock beneath our tread,
 And flames wrap hill and wood,
And gun-peal, and slogan cry
 Wake many a glen serene,

Ere you shall fade, ere you shall die,
   My dark Rosaleen!
   My own Rosaleen!
The Judgment Hour must first be nigh
Ere you can fade, ere you can die,
   My dark Rosaleen!

ELIZABETH BARRETT BROWNING
(1806–1861)

Sonnets from the Portuguese

I

I thought once how Theocritus had sung
Of the sweet years, the dear and wished-for years,
Who each one in a gracious hand appears
To bear a gift for mortals, old or young:
And, as I mused it in his antique tongue,
I saw, in gradual vision through my tears,
The sweet, sad years, the melancholy years,
Those of my own life, who by turns had flung
A shadow across me. Straightway I was 'ware,
So weeping, how a mystic Shape did move
Behind me, and drew me backward by the hair;
And a voice said in mastery, while I strove,—
"Guess now who holds thee?"—"Death," I said. But, there,
The silver answer rang,—"Not Death, but Love."

VI

Go from me. Yet I feel that I shall stand
Henceforward in thy shadow. Nevermore
Alone upon the threshold of my door
Of individual life, I shall command
The uses of my soul, nor lift my hand
Serenely in the sunshine as before,
Without the sense of that which I forbore—
Thy touch upon the palm. The widest land
Doom takes to part us, leaves thy heart in mine
With pulses that beat double. What I do

And what I dream include thee, as the wine
Must taste of its own grapes. And when I sue
God for myself, He hears that name of thine,
And sees within my eyes the tears of two.

XIV

If thou must love me, let it be for nought
Except for love's sake only. Do not say
"I love her for her smile—her look—her way
Of speaking gently,—for a trick of thought
That falls in well with mine, and certes brought
A sense of pleasant ease on such a day"—
For these things in themselves, Belovéd, may
Be changed, or change for thee,—and love, so wrought,
May be unwrought so. Neither love me for
Thine own dear pity's wiping my cheeks dry,—
A creature might forget to weep, who bore
Thy comfort long, and lose thy love thereby!
But love me for love's sake, that evermore
Thou mayst love on, through love's eternity.

XXII

When our two souls stand up erect and strong,
Face to face, silent, drawing nigh and nigher,
Until the lengthening wings break into fire
At either curvéd point,—what bitter wrong
Can the earth do to us, that we should not long
Be here contented? Think. In mounting higher,
The angels would press on us and aspire
To drop some golden orb of perfect song
Into our deep, dear silence. Let us stay
Rather on earth, Belovéd,—where the unfit
Contrarious moods of men recoil away
And isolate pure spirits, and permit
A place to stand and love in for a day,
With darkness and the death-hour rounding it.

XXVIII

My letters! all dead paper, mute and white!
And yet they seem alive and quivering
Against my tremulous hands which loose the string

And let them drop down on my knee to-night.
This said,—he wished to have me in his sight
Once, as a friend: this fixed a day in spring
To come and touch my hand . . . a simple thing,
Yet I wept for it!—this, . . . the paper's light . . .
Said, *Dear, I love thee;* and I sank and quailed
As if God's future thundered on my past.
This said, *I am thine*—and so its ink has paled
With lying on my heart that beat too fast.
And this . . . O Love, thy words have ill availed
If, what this said, I dared repeat at last!

XXXII

The first time that the sun rose on thine oath
To love me, I looked forward to the moon
To slacken all those bonds which seemed too soon
And quickly tied to make a lasting troth.
Quick-loving hearts, I thought, may quickly loathe;
And, looking on myself, I seemed not one
For such man's love!—more like an out-of-tune
Worn viol, a good singer would be wroth
To spoil his song with, and which, snatched in haste,
Is laid down at the first ill-sounding note.
I did not wrong myself so, but I placed
A wrong on *thee.* For perfect strains may float
'Neath master-hands, from instruments defaced,—
And great souls, at one stroke, may do and doat.

XXXV

If I leave all for thee, wilt thou exchange
And be all to me? Shall I never miss
Home-talk and blessing and the common kiss
That comes to each in turn, nor count it strange,
When I look up, to drop on a new range
Of walls and floors, another home than this?
Nay, wilt thou fill that place by me which is
Filled by dead eyes too tender to know change?
That's hardest. If to conquer love, has tried,
To conquer grief, tries more, as all things prove;
For grief indeed is love and grief beside.

Alas, I have grieved so I am hard to love.
Yet love me—wilt thou? Open thine heart wide,
And fold within the wet wings of thy dove.

XXXVIII

First time he kissed me, he but only kissed
The fingers of this hand wherewith I write;
And ever since, it grew more clean and white,
Slow to world-greetings, quick with its "Oh, list,"
When the angels speak. A ring of amethyst
I could not wear here, plainer to my sight,
Than that first kiss. The second passed in height
The first, and sought the forehead, and half missed,
Half falling on the hair. O beyond meed!
That was the chrism of love, which love's own crown,
With sanctifying sweetness, did precede.
The third upon my lips was folded down
In perfect, purple state; since when, indeed,
I have been proud and said, "My love, my own."

XLIII

How do I love thee? Let me count the ways.
I love thee to the depth and breadth and height
My soul can reach, when feeling out of sight
For the ends of Being and ideal Grace.
I love thee to the level of everyday's
Most quiet need, by sun and candle-light.
I love thee freely, as men strive for Right;
I love thee purely, as they turn from Praise.
I love thee with the passion put to use
In my old griefs, and with my childhood's faith.
I love thee with a love I seemed to lose
With my lost saints,—I love thee with the breath,
Smiles, tears, of all my life!—and, if God choose,
I shall but love thee better after death.

The Cry of the Children

φεῦ, φεῦ· τί προσδέρκεσθε μ' ὄμμασιν, τέκνα;

Medea: Do ye hear the children weeping, O my brothers,
　　Ere the sorrow comes with years?
They are leaning their young heads against their
　　　mothers,
　　And *that* cannot stop their tears.
The young lambs are bleating in the meadows,
　　The young birds are chirping in the nest,
The young fawns are playing with the shadows,
　　The young flowers are blowing toward the west—
But the young, young children, O my brothers,
　　They are weeping bitterly!
They are weeping in the playtime of the others,
　　In the country of the free.

Do you question the young children in their sorrow,
　　Why their tears are falling so?
The old man may weep for his to-morrow
　　Which is lost in Long Ago;
The old tree is leafless in the forest,
　　The old year is ending in the frost,
The old wound, if stricken, is the sorest,
　　The old hope is hardest to be lost:
But the young, young children, O my brothers,
　　Do you ask them why they stand
Weeping sore before the bosoms of their mothers,
　　In our happy Fatherland?

They look up with their pale and sunken faces,
　　And their looks are sad to see,
For the man's hoary anguish draws and presses
　　Down the cheeks of infancy;
"Your old earth," they say, "is very dreary,
　　Our young feet," they say, "are very weak;
Few paces have we taken, yet are weary—
　　Our grave-rest is very far to seek:

Ask the aged why they weep, and not the children,
    For the outside earth is cold,
And we young ones stand without, in our bewilder-
    ing,
    And the graves are for the old."

"True," say the children, "it may happen
    That we die before our time:
Little Alice died last year, her grave is shapen
    Like a snowball, in the rime.
We looked into the pit prepared to take her:
    Was no room for any work in the close clay!
From the sleep wherein she lieth none will wake her,
    Crying, 'Get up, little Alice! it is day.'
If you listen by that grave, in sun and shower,
    With your ear down, little Alice never cries;
Could we see her face, be sure we should not know
    her,
    For the smile has time for growing in her eyes:
And merry go her moments, lulled and stilled in
    The shroud by the kirk-chime.
It is good when it happens," say the children,
    "That we die before our time."

Alas, alas, the children! They are seeking
    Death in life, as best to have:
They are binding up their hearts away from breaking,
    With a cerement from the grave.
Go out, children, from the mine and from the city,
    Sing out, children, as the little thrushes do;
Pluck you handfuls of the meadow-cowslips pretty,
    Laugh aloud, to feel your fingers let them through!
But they answer, "Are your cowslips of the meadows
    Like our weeds anear the mine?
Leave us quiet in the dark of the coal-shadows,
    From your pleasures fair and fine!

"For oh," say the children, "we are weary
    And we cannot run or leap;
If we cared for any meadows, it were merely
    To drop down in them and sleep.

Our knees tremble sorely in the stooping,
    We fall upon our faces, trying to go;
And, underneath our heavy eyelids drooping
    The reddest flower would look as pale as snow.
For, all day, we drag our burden tiring
    Through the coal-dark, underground;
Or, all day, we drive the wheels of iron
    In the factories, round and round.

"For all day the wheels are droning, turning;
    Their wind comes in our faces,
Till our hearts turn, our heads with pulses burning,
    And the walls turn in their places:
Turns the sky in the high window, blank and reeling,
    Turns the long light that drops adown the wall,
Turn the black flies that crawl along the ceiling:
    All are turning, all the day, and we with all.
And all day, the iron wheels are droning,
    And sometimes we could pray,
'O ye wheels' (breaking out in a mad moaning)
    'Stop! be silent for to-day!' "

Ay! be silent! Let them hear each other breathing
    For a moment, mouth to mouth!
Let them touch each other's hands, in a fresh wreath-
      ing
    Of their tender human youth!
Let them feel that this cold metallic motion
    Is not all the life God fashions or reveals:
Let them prove their living souls against the notion
    That they live in you, or under you, O wheels!
Still, all day, the iron wheels go onward,
    Grinding life down from its mark;
And the children's souls, which God is calling sun-
      ward,
    Spin on blindly in the dark.

Now tell the poor young children, O my brothers,
    To look up to Him, and pray;
So the blesséd One who blesseth all the others,
    Will bless them another day.

They answer, "Who is God that He should hear us,
   While the rushing of the iron wheels is stirred?
When we sob aloud, the human creatures near us
   Pass by, hearing not, or answer not a word.
And *we* hear not (for the wheels in their resounding)
   Strangers speaking at the door:
Is it likely God, with angels singing round Him,
   Hears our weeping any more?

"Two words, indeed, of praying we remember,
   And at midnight's hour of harm,
'Our Father', looking upward in the chamber,
   We say softly for a charm.
We know no other words except 'Our Father',
   And we think that, in some pause of angels' song,
God may pluck them with the silence sweet to gather,
   And hold both within His right hand which is
         strong.
'Our Father!' If He heard us, He would surely
   (For they call Him good and mild)
Answer, smiling down the steep world very purely,
   'Come and rest with me, my child.'

"But, no!" say the children, weeping faster,
   "He is speechless as a stone:
And they tell us, of His image is the master
   Who commands us to work on.
Go to!" say the children,—"up in Heaven,
   Dark, wheel-like, turning clouds are all we find.
Do not mock us; grief has made us unbelieving:
   We look up for God; but tears have made us
         blind."
Do you hear the children weeping and disproving,
   O my brothers, what ye preach?
For God's possible is taught by His world's loving,
   And the children doubt of each.

And well may the children weep before you!
   They are weary ere they run;
They have never seen the sunshine, nor the glory
   Which is brighter than the sun.

They know the grief of man, without its wisdom;
  They sink in man's despair, without its calm;
Are slaves, without the liberty in Christdom,
  Are martyrs, by the pang without the palm:
Are worn as if with age, yet unretrievingly
  The harvest of its memories cannot reap,—
Are orphans of the earthly love and heavenly.
  Let them weep! let them weep!

They look up with their pale and sunken faces,
  And their look is dread to see,
For they mind you of their angels in high places,
  With eyes turned on Deity.
"How long," they say, "how long, O cruel nation,
  Will you stand, to move the world, on a child's
      heart,—
Stifle down with a mailed heel its palpitation,
  And tread onward to your throne amid the mart?
Our blood splashes upward, O gold-heaper,
  And your purple shows your path!
But the child's sob in the silence curses deeper
  Than the strong man in his wrath."

HENRY WADSWORTH LONGFELLOW
(1807–1882)

Hymn to the Night

I heard the trailing garments of the Night
  Sweep through her marble halls!
I saw her sable skirts all fringed with light
  From the celestial walls!

I felt her presence, by its spell of might,
  Stoop o'er me from above;
The calm, majestic presence of the Night,
  As of the one I love.

I heard the sounds of sorrow and delight,
  The manifold soft chimes,
That fill the haunted chambers of the Night,
  Like some old poet's rhymes.

From the cool cisterns of the midnight air
   My spirit drank repose;
The fountain of perpetual peace flows there,—
   From those deep cisterns flows.

O holy Night! from thee I learn to bear
   What man has borne before!
Thou layest thy finger on the lips of Care,
   And they complain no more.

Peace! Peace! Orestes-like I breathe this prayer!
   Descend with broad-winged flight,
The welcome, the thrice-prayed for, the most fair,
   The best-belovéd Night!

Serenade

Stars of the summer night!
   Far in yon azure deeps,
Hide, hide your golden light!
   She sleeps!
My lady sleeps!
   Sleeps!

Moon of the summer night!
   Far down yon western steeps,
Sink, sink in silver light!
   She sleeps!
My lady sleeps!
   Sleeps!

Wind of the summer night!
   Where yonder woodbine creeps,
Fold, fold thy pinions light!
   She sleeps!
My lady sleeps!
   Sleeps!

Dreams of the summer night!
Tell her, her lover keeps
Watch! while in slumbers light
She sleeps!
My lady sleeps!
Sleeps!

The Spanish Student

Suspiria

Take them, O Death! and bear away
Whatever thou canst call thine own!
Thine image, stamped upon this clay,
Doth give thee that, but that alone!

Take them, O Grave! and let them lie
Folded upon thy narrow shelves,
As garments by the soul laid by,
And precious only to ourselves!

Take them, O great Eternity!
Our little life is but a gust
That bends the branches of thy tree,
And trails its blossoms in the dust!

My Lost Youth

Often I think of the beautiful town
That is seated by the sea;
Often in thought go up and down
The pleasant streets of that dear old town,
And my youth comes back to me.
And a verse of a Lapland song
Is haunting my memory still:
"A boy's will is the wind's will,
And the thoughts of youth are long, long thoughts."

I can see the shadowy lines of its trees,
   And catch, in sudden gleams,
The sheen of the far-surrounding seas,
And islands that were the Hesperides
   Of all my boyish dreams.
     And the burden of that old song,
     It murmurs and whispers still:
     "A boy's will is the wind's will,
And the thoughts of youth are long, long thoughts."

I remember the black wharves and the slips,
   And the sea-tides tossing free;
And Spanish sailors with bearded lips,
And the beauty and mystery of the ships,
   And the magic of the sea.
     And the voice of the wayward song
     Is singing and saying still:
     "A boy's will is the wind's will,
And the thoughts of youth are long, long thoughts."

I remember the bulwarks by the shore,
   And the fort upon the hill;
The sunrise gun, with its hollow roar,
The drum-beat repeated o'er and o'er,
   And the bugle wild and shrill.
     And the music of that old song
     Throbs in my memory still:
     "A boy's will is the wind's will,
And the thoughts of youth are long, long thoughts."

I remember the sea-fight far away,
   How it thundered o'er the tide!
And the dead captains, as they lay
In their graves, o'erlooking the tranquil bay,
   Where they in battle died.
     And the sound of that mournful song
     Goes through me with a thrill:
     "A boy's will is the wind's will,
And the thoughts of youth are long, long thoughts."

I can see the breezy dome of groves,
   The shadows of Deering's Woods;
And the friendships old and the early loves
Come back with a Sabbath sound, as of doves
   In quiet neighborhoods.
      And the verse of that sweet old song,
      It flutters and murmurs still:
      "A boy's will is the wind's will,
And the thoughts of youth are long, long thoughts."

I remember the gleams and glooms that dart
   Across the school-boy's brain;
The song and the silence in the heart,
That in part are prophecies, and in part
   Are longings wild and vain.
      And the voice of that fitful song
      Sings on, and is never still:
      "A boy's will is the wind's will,
And the thoughts of youth are long, long thoughts."

There are things of which I may not speak;
   There are dreams that cannot die;
There are thoughts that make the strong heart weak,
And bring a pallor into the cheek,
   And a mist before the eye.
      And the words of that fatal song
      Come over me like a chill:
      "A boy's will is the wind's will,
And the thoughts of youth are long, long thoughts."

Strange to me now are the forms I meet
   When I visit the dear old town;
But the native air is pure and sweet,
And the trees that o'ershadow each well-known street,
   As they balance up and down,
      Are singing the beautiful song,
      Are sighing and whispering still:
      "A boy's will is the wind's will,
And the thoughts of youth are long, long thoughts."

And Deering's Woods are fresh and fair,
 And with joy that is almost pain
My heart goes back to wander there,
And among the dreams of the days that were,
 I find my lost youth again.
  And the strange and beautiful song,
  The groves are repeating it still:
  "A boy's will is the wind's will,
And the thoughts of youth are long, long thoughts."

"Some Day, Some Day"

Some day, some day,
O troubled breast,
Shalt thou find rest.

If Love in thee
To grief give birth,
Six feet of earth
Can more than he;
There calm and free
And unoppressed
Shalt thou find rest.

The unattained
In life at last,
When life is passed,
Shall all be gained;
And no more pained,
No more distressed,
Shalt thou find rest.

Divina Commedia

Oft have I seen at some cathedral door
 A laborer, pausing in the dust and heat,
 Lay down his burden, and with reverent feet
Enter, and cross himself, and on the floor
Kneel to repeat his paternoster o'er;
 Far off the noises of the world retreat;
 The loud vociferations of the street

Become an undistinguishable roar.
So, as I enter here from day to day,
    And leave my burden at this minster gate,
Kneeling in prayer, and not ashamed to pray,
    The tumult of the time disconsolate
To inarticulate murmurs dies away,
    While the eternal ages watch and wait.

Ultima Thule
(DEDICATION)

With favoring winds o'er sunlit seas,
We sailed for the Hesperides,
The land where the golden apples grow;
But that, ah! that was long ago.

How far, since then, the ocean streams
Have swept us from that land of dreams,
That land of fiction and of truth,
The lost Atlantis of our youth!

Whither, ah, whither? Are not these
The tempest-haunted Hebrides,
Where sea-gulls scream, and breakers roar,
And wreck and sea-weed line the shore?

Ultima Thule! Utmost Isle!
Here in thy harbors for a while
We lower our sails; a while we rest
From the unending, endless quest.

JOHN GREENLEAF WHITTIER
(1807–1892)
"I Call the Old Time Back..."

I call the old time back: I bring these lays
To thee, in memory of the summer days
When, by our native streams and forest ways,

We dreamed them over; while the rivulets made
Songs of their own, and the great pine-trees laid
On warm noon-lights the masses of their shade.

And *she* was with us, living o'er again
Her life in ours, despite of years and pain,—
The autumn's brightness after latter rain.

Beautiful in her holy peace as one
Who stands, at evening, when the work is done,
Glorified in the setting of the sun!

Her memory makes our common landscape seem
Fairer than any of which painters dream,
Lights the brown hills and sings in every stream;

For she whose speech was always truth's pure gold
Heard, not unpleased, its simple legends told,
And loved with us the beautiful and old.

OLIVER WENDELL HOLMES

(1809–1894)

The Voiceless

We count the broken lyres that rest
   Where the sweet wailing singers slumber,
But o'er their silent sister's breast
   The wild-flowers who will stoop to number?
A few can touch the magic string,
   And noisy Fame is proud to win them:—
Alas for those that never sing,
   But die with all their music in them!

Nay, grieve not for the dead alone
   Whose song has told their hearts' sad story,—
Weep for the voiceless, who have known
   The cross without the crown of glory!
Not where Leucadian breezes sweep
   O'er Sappho's memory-haunted billow,
But where the glistening night-dews weep
   On nameless sorrow's churchyard pillow.

O hearts that break and give no sign
   Save whitening lip and fading tresses,
Till Death pours out his longed-for wine
   Slow-dropped from Misery's crushing presses,—
If singing breath or echoing chord
   To every hidden pang were given,
What endless melodies were poured,
   As sad as earth, as sweet as heaven!

After a Lecture on Keats

The wreath that star-crowned Shelley gave
Is lying on thy Roman grave,
Yet on its turf young April sets
Her store of slender violets;
Though all the Gods their garlands shower,
I too may bring one purple flower.
Alas! what blossom shall I bring,
That opens in my Northern spring?
The garden beds have all run wild,
So trim when I was yet a child;
Flat plantains and unseemly stalks
Have crept across the gravel walks;
The vines are dead, long, long ago,
The almond buds no longer blow.
No more upon its mound I see
The azure, plume-bound fleur-de-lis;
Where once the tulips used to show,
In straggling tufts the pansies grow;
The grass has quenched my white-rayed gem,
The flowering "Star of Bethlehem",
Though its long blade of glossy green
And pallid stripe may still be seen.
Nature, who treads her nobles down,
And gives their birthright to the clown,
Has sown her base-born weedy things
About the garden's queens and kings.
Yet one sweet flower of ancient race
Springs in the old familiar place.
When snows were melting down the vale,

And Earth unlaced her icy mail,
And March his stormy trumpet blew,
And tender green came peeping through,
I loved the earliest one to seek
That broke the soil with emerald beak,
And watch the trembling bells so blue
Spread on the column as it grew.
Meek child of earth! thou wilt not shame
The sweet, dead poet's holy name;
The God of music gave thee birth,
Called from the crimson-spotted earth,
Where, sobbing his young life away,
His own fair Hyacinthus lay.
The hyacinth my garden gave
Shall lie upon that Roman grave!

EDWARD FITZGERALD

(1809–1883)

Rubáiyát of Omar Khayyám of Naishápúr

Wake! For the Sun, who scattered into flight
The Stars before him from the Field of Night,
    Drives Night along with them from Heav'n, and strikes
The Sultán's Turret with a Shaft of Light.

Before the phantom of False morning died,
Methought a Voice within the Tavern cried,
    "When all the Temple is prepared within,
Why nods the drowsy Worshipper outside?"

And, as the Cock crew, those who stood before
The Tavern shouted—"Open then the door!
    You know how little while we have to stay,
And, once departed, may return no more."

Now the New Year reviving old Desires,
The thoughtful Soul to Solitude retires,
    Where the White Hand of Moses on the Bough
Puts out, and Jesus from the Ground suspires.

Iram indeed is gone with all his Rose,
And Jamshyd's Sev'n-ring'd Cup where no one knows;
　　But still a Ruby gushes from the Vine,
And many a Garden by the Water blows.

And David's lips are lockt; but in divine
High-piping Péhleví, with "Wine! Wine! Wine!
　　Red Wine!"—the Nightingale cries to the Rose
That sallow cheek of hers t' incarnadine.

Come, fill the Cup, and in the fire of Spring
Your Winter-garment of Repentance fling;
　　The Bird of Time has but a little way
To flutter—and the Bird is on the Wing.

Whether at Naishápúr or Babylon,
Whether the Cup with sweet or bitter run,
　　The Wine of Life keeps oozing drop by drop,
The Leaves of Life keep falling one by one.

Each Morn a thousand Roses brings, you say;
Yes, but where leaves the Rose of Yesterday?
　　And this first Summer month that brings the Rose
Shall take Jamshyd and Kaikobád away.

Well, let it take them! What have we to do
With Kaikobád the Great, or Kaikhosrú?
　　Let Zál and Rustum thunder as they will,
Or Hátim call to Supper—heed not you.

With me along the strip of Herbage strown
That just divides the desert from the sown,
　　Where name of Slave and Sultán is forgot—
And Peace to Máhmúd on his golden Throne!

A Book of Verses underneath the Bough,
A Jug of Wine, a Loaf of Bread—and Thou
　　Beside me singing in the Wilderness—
Oh, Wilderness were Paradise enow!

Some for the Glories of This World; and some
Sigh for the Prophet's Paradise to come;
   Ah, take the Cash, and let the Credit go,
Nor heed the rumble of a distant Drum!

Look to the blowing Rose about us—Lo,
"Laughing," she says, "into the world I blow,
   At once the silken tassel of my Purse
Tear, and its Treasure on the Garden throw."

And those who husbanded the Golden grain,
And those who flung it to the winds like Rain,
   Alike to no such aureate Earth are turn'd
As, buried once, Men want dug up again.

The Worldly Hope men set their Hearts upon
Turns Ashes—or it prospers; and anon,
   Like Snow upon the Desert's dusty Face
Lighting a little hour or two—was gone.

Think, in this batter d Caravanserai
Whose portals are alternate Night and Day,
   How Sultán after Sultán with his Pomp
Abode his destin'd Hour, and went his way.

They say the Lion and the Lizard keep
The Courts where Jamshyd gloried and drank deep;
   And Bahrám, that great Hunter—the Wild Ass
Stamps o'er his Head, but cannot break his Sleep.

I sometimes think that never blows so red
The Rose as where some buried Caesar bled;
   That every Hyacinth the Garden wears
Dropt in her Lap from some once lovely Head.

And this reviving Herb whose tender Green
Fledges the River-Lip on which we lean—
   Ah, lean upon it lightly! for who knows
From what once lovely lip it springs unseen!

Ah, my Belovéd, fill the Cup that clears
To-Day of past Regret and future Fears:
   To-morrow!—Why, To-morrow I may be
Myself with Yesterday's Sev'n thousand Years.

For some we loved, the loveliest and the best
That from his Vintage rolling Time has prest,
   Have drunk their Cup a Round or two before,
And one by one crept silently to rest.

And we, that now make merry in the Room
They left, and Summer dresses in new bloom,
   Ourselves must we beneath the Couch of Earth
Descend—ourselves to make a Couch—for whom!

Ah, make the most of what we yet may spend,
Before we too into the Dust descend;
   Dust into Dust, and under Dust, to lie,
Sans Wine, sans Song, sans Singer, and—sans End!

Alike for those who for To-Day prepare,
And those that after some To-Morrow stare,
   A Muezzín from the Tower of Darkness cries,
"Fools! your reward is neither Here nor There."

Why, all the Saints and Sages who discuss'd
Of the Two Worlds so learnedly are thrust
   Like foolish Prophets forth; their Words to Scorn
Are scatter'd, and their Mouths are stopt with Dust.

Myself when young did eagerly frequent
Doctor and Saint, and heard great argument
   About it and about: but evermore
Came out by that same door where in I went.

With them the seed of Wisdom did I sow,
And with my own hand wrought to make it grow;
   And this was all the Harvest that I reap'd—
"I came like Water, and like Wind I go."

Into this Universe, and *Why* not knowing,
Nor *Whence*, like Water willy-nilly flowing;
   And out of it, as Wind along the Waste,
I know not *Whither*, willy-nilly blowing.

What, without asking, hither hurried *Whence?*
And, without asking, *Whither* hurried hence!
   Oh, many a Cup of this forbidden Wine
Must drown the memory of that insolence!

Up from Earth's Centre through the Seventh Gate
I rose, and on the Throne of Saturn sate,
   And many a Knot unravel'd by the Road;
But not the Master-knot of Human Fate.

There was the Door to which I found no Key;
There was the Veil through which I could not see:
   Some little talk awhile of Me and Thee
There was—and then no more of Thee and Me.

Earth could not answer; nor the Seas that mourn
In flowing Purple, of their Lord forlorn;
   Nor rolling Heaven, with all his Signs reveal'd
And hidden by the sleeve of Night and Morn.

Then of the Thee in Me who works behind
The Veil, I lifted up my hands to find
   A Lamp amid the Darkness; and I heard,
As from Without—"The Me Within Thee Blind!"

Then, to the Lip of this poor earthen Urn
I lean'd, the Secret of my Life to learn:
   And Lip to Lip it murmur'd—"While you live,
Drink!—for, once dead, you never shall return."

I think the Vessel, that with fugitive
Articulation answer'd, once did live
   And drink: and Ah! the passive Lip I kiss'd
How many Kisses might it take—and give!

For I remember stopping by the way
To watch a Potter thumping his wet Clay,
   And with its all-obliterated Tongue
It murmur'd—"Gently, Brother, gently, pray!"

And has not such a Story from of Old
Down Man's successive generations roll'd
   Of such a clod of saturated Earth
Cast by the Maker into Human Mould?

And not a drop that from our Cups we throw
For Earth to drink of, but may steal below
   To quench the fire of Anguish in some Eye
There hidden—far beneath, and long ago.

As then the Tulip for her morning sup
Of Heav'nly Vintage from the soil looks up,
   Do you devoutly do the like, till Heav'n
To Earth invert you—like an empty Cup.

Perplext no more with Human or Divine,
To-morrow's tangle to the winds resign,
   And lose your fingers in the tresses of
The Cypress-slender Minister of Wine.

And if the Wine you drink, the Lip you press,
End in what All begins and ends in—Yes:
   Think then you are To-Day what Yesterday
You were—To-Morrow you shall not be less.

So when that Angel of the darker Drink
At last shall find you by the river-brink,
   And, offering his Cup, invite your Soul
Forth to your Lips to quaff—you shall not shrink.

Why, if the Soul can fling the Dust aside,
And naked on the Air of Heaven ride,
   Were't not a Shame—were't not a Shame for him
In this clay carcase crippled to abide?

'Tis but a Tent where takes his one day's rest
A Sultán to the realm of Death addrest;
    The Sultán rises, and the dark Ferrásh
Strikes, and prepares it for another Guest.

And fear not lest Existence closing your
Account, and mine, should know the like no more;
    The Eternal Sáki from that Bowl has pour'd
Millions of Bubbles like us, and will pour.

When You and I behind the Veil are past,
Oh, but the long, long while the World shall last,
    Which of our Coming and Departure heeds
As the Sea's self should heed a pebble-cast.

A Moment's Halt—a momentary taste
Of Being from the Well amid the Waste—
    And Lo!—the phantom Caravan has reach'd
The Nothing it set out from—Oh, make haste!

Would you that spangle of Existence spend
About The Secret—quick about it, Friend!
    A Hair perhaps divides the False and True—
And upon what, prithee, may life depend?

A Hair perhaps divides the False and True-
Yes; and a single Alif were the clue—
    Could you but find it—to the Treasure-house,
And peradventure to The Master too;

Whose secret Presence, through Creation's veins
Running Quicksilver-like eludes your pains;
    Taking all shapes from Máh to Máhi; and
They change and perish all—but He remains;

A moment guess'd—then back behind the Fold
Immerst of Darkness round the Drama roll'd
    Which, for the Pastime of Eternity,
He doth Himself contrive, enact, behold.

But if in vain, down on the stubborn floor
Of Earth, and up to Heav'n's unopening Door,
   You gaze To-Day, while You are You—how then
To-Morrow, You when shall be You no more?

Waste not your hour, nor in the vain pursuit
Of This and That endeavour and dispute;
   Better be jocund with the fruitful Grape
Than sadden after none, or bitter, Fruit.

You know, my Friends, with what a brave Carouse
I made a Second Marriage in my house;
   Divorced old barren Reason from my Bed,
And took the Daughter of the Vine to Spouse.

For "Is" and "Is-Not" though with Rule and Line
And "Up-And-Down" by Logic I define,
   Of all that one should care to fathom, I
Was never deep in anything but—Wine.

Ah, but my Computations, People say,
Reduced the Year to better Reckoning? Nay,
   'Twas only striking from the Calendar
Unborn To-morrow and dead Yesterday.

And lately, by the Tavern Door agape,
Came shining through the Dusk an Angel Shape
   Bearing a Vessel on his Shoulder; and
He bid me taste of it; and 'twas—the Grape!

The Grape that can with Logic absolute
The Two-and-Seventy jarring Sects confute:
   The Sovereign Alchemist that in a trice
Life's leaden metal into Gold transmute:

The mighty Mahmúd, Allah-breathing Lord,
That all the misbelieving and black Horde
   Of Fears and Sorrows that infest the Soul
Scatters before him with his whirlwind Sword.

Why, be this Juice the Growth of God, who dare
Blaspheme the twisted tendril as a Snare?
   A Blessing, we should use it, should we not?
And if a Curse—why, then, Who set it there?

I must abjure the Balm of Life, I must,
Scared by some After-reckoning ta'en on trust,
   Or lured with Hope of some Diviner Drink,
To fill the Cup—when crumbled into Dust!

Oh threats of Hell and Hopes of Paradise!
One thing at least is certain—*This* Life flies;
   One thing is certain and the rest is Lies;
The Flower that once has blown for ever dies.

Strange, is it not? that of the myriads who
Before us pass'd the door of Darkness through,
   Not one returns to tell us of the Road,
Which to discover we must travel too.

The Revelations of Devout and Learn'd
Who rose before us, and as Prophets burn'd,
   Are all but Stories, which, awoke from Sleep
They told their comrades, and to Sleep return'd.

I sent my Soul through the Invisible.
Some letter of the After-life to spell:
   And by and by my Soul return'd to me,
And answer'd "I Myself am Heav'n and Hell:"

Heav'n but the Vision of fulfill'd Desire,
And Hell the Shadow from a Soul on fire,
   Cast on the Darkness into which Ourselves,
So late emerged from, shall so soon expire.

We are no other than a moving row
Of Magic Shadow-shapes that come and go
   Round with the Sun-illumined Lantern held
In Midnight by the Master of the Show;

But helpless Pieces of the Game He plays
Upon this Chequer-board of Nights and Days;
    Hither and thither moves, and checks, and slays,
And one by one back in the Closet lays.

The Ball no question makes of Ayes and Noes,
But Here or There as strikes the Player goes;
    And He that toss'd you down into the Field,
He knows about it all—HE knows—HE knows!

The Moving Finger writes; and, having writ,
Moves on: nor all your Piety nor Wit
    Shall lure it back to cancel half a Line,
Nor all your Tears wash out a Word of it.

And that inverted Bowl they call the Sky,
Whereunder crawling coop'd we live and die,
    Lift not your hands to *It* for help—for It
As impotently moves as you or I.

With Earth's first Clay They did the Last Man knead,
And there of the Last Harvest sow'd the Seed:
    And the first Morning of Creation wrote
What the Last Dawn of Reckoning shall read.

Yesterday *This* Day's Madness did prepare;
To-Morrow's Silence, Triumph, or Despair:
    Drink! for you know not whence you came, nor why:
Drink! for you know not why you go, nor where.

I tell you this—When, started from the Goal,
Over the flaming shoulders of the Foal
    Of Heav'n Parwín and Mushtarí they flung,
In my predestined Plot of Dust and Soul

The Vine had struck a fibre: which about
If clings my being—let the Dervish flout;
    Of my Base metal may be filed a Key
That shall unlock the Door he howls without.

And this I know: whether the one True Light
Kindle to Love, or Wrath-consume me quite,
　　One Flash of It within the Tavern caught
Better than in the Temple lost outright.

What! out of Senseless Nothing to provoke
A conscious Something to resent the yoke
　　Of unpermitted Pleasure, under pain
Of Everlasting Penalties, if broke!

What! from his helpless Creature be repaid
Pure Gold for what he lent him dross-allay'd—
　　Sue for a Debt he never did contract,
And cannot answer—Oh the sorry trade!

Oh Thou, who didst with pitfall and with gin
Beset the Road I was to wander in,
　　Thou wilt not with Predestined Evil round
Enmesh, and then impute my Fall to Sin!

Oh Thou, who Man of baser Earth didst make,
And ev'n with Paradise devise the Snake:
　　For all the Sin wherewith the Face of Man
Is blacken'd—Man's forgiveness give—and take!

＊　　＊　　＊　　＊　　＊　　＊

As under cover of departing Day
Slunk hunger-stricken Ramazán away,
　　Once more within the Potter's house alone
I stood, surrounded by the Shapes of Clay.

Shapes of all Sorts and Sizes, great and small,
That stood along the floor and by the wall;
　　And some loquacious Vessels were; and some
Listen'd perhaps, but never talk'd at all.

Said one among them—"Surely not in vain
My substance of the common Earth was ta'en
　　And to this Figure moulded, to be broke,
Or trampled back to shapeless Earth again."

Then said a Second—"Ne'er a peevish Boy
Would break the Bowl from which he drank in joy;
    And He that with his hand the Vessel made
Will surely not in after Wrath destroy."

After a momentary silence spake
Some Vessel of a more ungainly Make;
    "They sneer at me for leaning all awry;
What! did the Hand then of the Potter shake?"

Whereat some one of the loquacious Lot—
I think a Súfi pipkin—waxing hot—
    "All this of Pot and Potter—Tell me then,
Who is the Potter, pray, and who the Pot?"

"Why," said another, "Some there are who tell
Of one who threatens he will toss to Hell
    The luckless Pots he marr'd in making—Pish!
He's a Good Fellow, and 'twill all be well."

"Well," murmur'd one, "Let whoso make or buy,
My Clay with long Oblivion is gone dry:
    But fill me with the old familiar Juice,
Methinks I might recover by and by."

So while the Vessels one by one were speaking,
The little Moon look'd in that all were seeking:
    And then they jogg'd each other, "Brother, Brother!
Now for the Porter's shoulder-knot a-creaking!"

*   *   *   *   *   *

Ah, with the Grape my fading Life provide,
And wash the Body whence the Life has died,
    And lay me, shrouded in the living Leaf,
By some not unfrequented Garden-side.

That ev'n my buried Ashes such a snare
Of Vintage shall fling up into the Air
    As not a True-believer passing by
But shall be overtaken unaware.

Indeed the Idols I have loved so long
Have done my credit in this World much wrong:
   Have drown'd my Glory in a shallow Cup,
And sold my Reputation for a Song.

Indeed, indeed, Repentance oft before
I swore—but was I sober when I swore?
   And then and then came Spring, and Rose-in-hand
My thread-bare Penitence apieces tore.

And much as Wine has played the Infidel,
And robb'd me of my Robe of Honour—Well,
   I wonder often what the Vintners buy
One half so precious as the stuff they sell.

Yet Ah, that Spring should vanish with the Rose!
That Youth's sweet-scented manuscript should close!
   The Nightingale that in the branches sang,
Ah whence, and whither flown again, who knows!

Would but the Desert of the Fountain yield
One glimpse—if dimly, yet indeed, reveal'd,
   To which the fainting Traveller might spring,
As springs the trampled herbage of the field!

Would but some wingéd Angel ere too late
Arrest the yet unfolded Roll of Fate,
   And make the stern Recorder otherwise
Enregister, or quite obliterate!

Ah Love! could you and I with Him conspire
To grasp this sorry Scheme of Things entire,
   Would not we shatter it to bits—and then
Re-mould it nearer to the Heart's Desire!

      ❋   ❋   ❋   ❋   ❋   ❋

Yon rising Moon that looks for us again—
How oft hereafter will she wax and wane;
   How oft hereafter rising look for us
Through this same Garden—and for *one* in vain!

And when like her, oh Sáki, you shall pass
Among the Guests Star-scatter'd on the Grass,
   And in your joyous errand reach the spot
Where I made One—turn down an empty Glass!

Tamám

ALFRED TENNYSON, Lord Tennyson
(1809–1892)

Mariana

> Mariana in the moated grange.
> —Measure for Measure

With blackest moss the flower-plots
   Were thickly crusted, one and all:
The rusted nails fell from the knots
   That held the pear to the gable-wall.
The broken sheds looked sad and strange:
   Unlifted was the clinking latch;
   Weeded and worn the ancient thatch
Upon the lonely moated grange.
   She only said, "My life is dreary,
     He cometh not," she said;
   She said, "I am aweary, aweary,
     I would that I were dead!"

Her tears fell with the dews at even;
   Her tears fell ere the dews were dried;
She could not look on the sweet heaven,
   Either at morn or eventide.
After the flitting of the bats,
   When thickest dark did trance the sky,
   She drew her casement-curtain by,
And glanced athwart the glooming flats.
   She only said, "The night is dreary,
     He cometh not," she said;
   She said, "I am aweary, aweary,
     I would that I were dead!"

Upon the middle of the night,
   Waking she heard the night-fowl crow;
The cock sung out an hour ere light:
   From the dark fen the oxen's low
Came to her: without hope of change,
   In sleep she seemed to walk forlorn,
   Till cold winds woke the gray-eyed morn
About the lonely moated grange.
   She only said, "The day is dreary,
      He cometh not," she said;
   She said, "I am aweary, aweary,
      I would that I were dead!"

About a stone-cast from the wall
   A sluice with blackened waters slept,
And o'er it many, round and small,
   The clustered marish-mosses crept.
Hard by a poplar shook alway,
   All silver-green with gnarléd bark:
   For leagues no other tree did mark
The level waste, the rounding gray.
   She only said, "My life is dreary,
      He cometh not," she said;
   She said, "I am aweary, aweary,
      I would that I were dead!"

And ever when the moon was low,
   And the shrill winds were up and away,
In the white curtain, to and fro,
   She saw the gusty shadow sway.
But when the moon was very low,
   And wild winds bound within their cell,
   The shadow of the poplar fell
Upon her bed, across her brow.
   She only said, "The night is dreary,
      He cometh not," she said;
   She said, "I am aweary, aweary,
      I would that I were dead!"

All day within the dreamy house,
   The doors upon their hinges creaked;

The blue fly sung in the pane; the mouse
　　Behind the mouldering wainscot shrieked,
Or from the crevice peered about.
　　Old faces glimmered thro' the doors,
　　Old footsteps trod the upper floors,
Old voices called her from without.
　　She only said, "My life is dreary,
　　　　He cometh not," she said;
　　She said, "I am aweary, aweary,
　　　　I would that I were dead!"

The sparrow's chirrup on the roof,
　　The slow clock ticking, and the sound
Which to the wooing wind aloof
　　The poplar made, did all confound
Her sense; but most she loathed the hour
　　When the thick-moted sunbeam lay
　　Athwart the chamber, and the day
Was sloping toward his western bower.
　　Then, said she, "I am very dreary,
　　　　He will not come," she said;
　　She wept, "I am aweary, aweary,
　　　　Oh God, that I were dead!"

Choric Song of the Lotos-Eaters

There is sweet music here that softer falls
Than petals from blown roses on the grass,
Or night-dews on still waters between walls
Of shadowy granite, in a gleaming pass;
Music that gentlier on the spirit lies
Than tired eyelids upon tired eyes;
Music that brings sweet sleep down from the blissful skies.
Here are cool mosses deep,
And through the moss the ivies creep,
And in the stream the long-leaved flowers weep,
And from the craggy ledge the poppy hangs in sleep.

Why are we weighed upon with heaviness,
And utterly consumed with sharp distress,
While all things else have rest from weariness?
All things have rest: why should we toil alone,
We only toil, who are the first of things,
And make perpetual moan,
Still from one sorrow to another thrown;
Nor ever fold our wings,
And cease from wanderings,
Nor steep our brows in slumber's holy balm;
Nor hearken what the inner spirit sings,
"There is no joy but calm!"—
Why should we only toil, the roof and crown of things?

Lo! in the middle of the wood,
The folded leaf is wooed from out the bud
With winds upon the branch, and there
Grows green and broad, and takes no care,
Sun-steeped at noon, and in the moon
Nightly dew-fed; and turning yellow
Falls, and floats adown the air.
Lo! sweetened with the summer light,
The full-juiced apple, waxing over-mellow,
Drops in a silent autumn night.
All its allotted length of days
The flower ripens in its place,
Ripens and fades, and falls, and hath no toil,
Fast-rooted in the fruitful soil.

Hateful is the dark-blue sky,
Vaulted o'er the dark-blue sea.
Death is the end of life; ah, why
Should life all labour be?
Let us alone. Time driveth onward fast,
And in a little while our lips are dumb.
Let us alone. What is it that will last?
All things are taken from us, and become
Portions and parcels of the dreadful past.
Let us alone. What pleasure can we have
To war with evil? Is there any peace
In ever climbing up the climbing wave?

All things have rest, and ripen toward the grave
In silence—ripen, fall, and cease:
Give us long rest or death, dark death, or dreamful ease.

How sweet it were, hearing the downward stream,
With half-shut eyes ever to seem
Falling asleep in a half-dream!
To dream and dream, like yonder amber light,
Which will not leave the myrrh-bush on the height;
To hear each other's whispered speech;
Eating the Lotos day by day,
To watch the crisping ripples on the beach,
And tender curving lines of creamy spray;
To lend our hearts and spirits wholly
To the influence of mild-minded melancholy;
To muse and brood and live again in memory,
With those old faces of our infancy
Heaped over with a mound of grass,
Two handfuls of white dust, shut in an urn of brass!

Dear is the memory of our wedded lives,
And dear the last embraces of our wives
And their warm tears; but all hath suffered change;
For surely now our household hearths are cold,
Our sons inherit us, our looks are strange,
And we should come like ghosts to trouble joy.
Or else the island princes over-bold
Have eat our substance, and the minstrel sings
Before them of the ten years' war in Troy,
And our great deeds, as half-forgotten things.
Is there confusion in the little isle?
Let what is broken so remain.
The Gods are hard to reconcile;
'Tis hard to settle order once again.
There *is* confusion worse than death,
Trouble on trouble, pain on pain,
Long labour unto aged breath,
Sore task to hearts worn out by many wars
And eyes grown dim with gazing on the pilot-stars.

But, propt on beds of amaranth and moly,
How sweet—while warm airs lull us, blowing lowly—
With half-dropt eyelid still,
Beneath a heaven dark and holy,
To watch the long bright river drawing slowly
His waters from the purple hill—
To hear the dewy echoes calling
From cave to cave through the thick-twined vine—
To watch the emerald-coloured water falling
Through many a woven acanthus-wreath divine!
Only to hear and see the far-off sparkling brine,
Only to hear were sweet, stretched out beneath the pine.

The Lotos blooms below the barren peak,
The Lotos blows by every winding creek;
All day the wind breathes low with mellower tone;
Through every hollow cave and alley lone
Round and round the spicy downs the yellow Lotos-dust is
        blown.
We have had enough of action, and of motion we,
Rolled to starboard, rolled to larboard, when the surge was
        seething free,
Where the wallowing monster spouted his foam-fountains
        in the sea.

Let us swear an oath, and keep it with an equal mind,
In the hollow Lotos-land to live and lie reclined
On the hills like Gods together, careless of mankind.
For they lie beside their nectar, and the bolts are hurled
Far below them in the valleys, and the clouds are lightly
        curled
Round their golden houses, girdled with the gleaming world;
Where they smile in secret, looking over wasted lands,
Blight and famine, plague and earthquake, roaring deeps and
        fiery sands,
Clanging fights, and flaming towns, and sinking ships and
        praying hands.
But they smile, they find a music centred in a doleful song
Steaming up, a lamentation and an ancient tale of wrong,
Like a tale of little meaning though the words are strong;
Chanted from an ill-used race of men that cleave the soil,

Sow the seed, and reap the harvest with enduring toil,
Storing yearly little dues of wheat, and wine and oil;
Till they perish and they suffer—some, 'tis whispered—down
    in hell
Suffer endless anguish, others in Elysian valleys dwell,
Resting weary limbs at last on beds of asphodel.
Surely, surely, slumber is more sweet than toil, the shore
Than labour in the deep mid-ocean, wind and wave and oar;
O, rest, brother mariners, we will not wander more.

Œnone

There lies a vale in Ida, lovelier
Than all the valleys of Ionian hills.
The swimming vapour slopes athwart the glen,
Puts forth an arm, and creeps from pine to pine,
And loiters, slowly drawn. On either hand
The lawns and meadow-ledges midway down
Hang rich in flowers, and far below them roars
The long brook falling thro' the clov'n ravine
In cataract after cataract to the sea.
Behind the valley topmost Gargarus
Stands up and takes the morning: but in front
The gorges, opening wide apart, reveal
Troas and Ilion's column'd citadel,
The crown of Troas.
          Hither came at noon
Mournful Œnone, wandering forlorn
Of Paris, once her playmate on the hills.
Her cheek had lost the rose, and round her neck
Floated her hair or seemed to float in rest.
She, leaning on a fragment twined with vine,
Sang to the stillness, till the mountain-shade
Sloped downward to her seat from the upper cliff.

"O mother Ida, many-fountained Ida,
Dear mother Ida, harken ere I die.
For now the noonday quiet holds the hill:
The grasshopper is silent in the grass:
The lizard, with his shadow on the stone,

Rests like a shadow, and the winds are dead.
The purple flower droops: the golden bee
Is lily-cradled: I alone awake.
My eyes are full of tears, my heart of love,
My heart is breaking, and my eyes are dim,
And I am all aweary of my life.

"O mother Ida, many-fountained Ida,
Dear mother Ida, harken ere I die.
Hear me, O Earth, hear me, O Hills, O Caves
That house the cold crowned snake! O mountain brooks,
I am the daughter of a River-God,
Hear me, for I will speak, and build up all
My sorrow with my song, as yonder walls
Rose slowly to a music slowly breathed,
A cloud that gathered shape: for it may be
That, while I speak of it, a little while
My heart may wander from its deeper woe.

"O mother Ida, many-fountained Ida,
Dear mother Ida, harken ere I die.
I waited underneath the dawning hills,
Aloft the mountain lawn was dewy-dark,
And dewy-dark aloft the mountain-pine:
Beautiful Paris, evil-hearted Paris,
Leading a jet-black goat white-horned, white-hooved,
Came up from reedy Simois all alone.

"O mother Ida, harken ere I die.
Far off the torrent called me from the cleft:
Far up the solitary morning smote
The streaks of virgin snow. With down-dropt eyes
I sat alone: white-breasted like a star
Fronting the dawn he moved; a leopard skin
Drooped from his shoulder but his sunny hair
Clustered about his temples like a God's:
And his cheeks brightened as the foam-bow brightens
When the wind blows the foam, and all my heart
Went forth to embrace him coming ere he came.

"Dear mother Ida, harken ere I die.
He smiled, and opening out his milk-white palm
Disclosed a fruit of pure Hesperian gold,
That smelt ambrosially, and while I looked
And listened, the full-flowing river of speech
Came down upon my heart.
                              " 'My own Œnone,
Beautiful-browed Œnone, my own soul,
Behold this fruit, whose gleaming rind ingrav'n
"For the most fair," would seem to award it thine,
As lovelier than whatever Oread haunt
The knolls of Ida, loveliest in all grace
Of movement, and the charm of married brows.'

"Dear mother Ida, harken ere I die.
He prest the blossom of his lips to mine,
And added 'This was cast upon the board,
When all the full-faced presence of the Gods
Ranged in the halls of Peleus; whereupon
Rose feud, with question unto whom 'twere due:
But light-foot Iris brought it yester-eve,
Delivering, that to me, by common voice
Elected umpire, Heré comes to-day,
Pallas and Aphrodité, claiming each
This meed of fairest. Thou, within the cave
Behind yon whispering tuft of oldest pine,
Mayst well behold them unbeheld, unheard
Hear all, and see thy Paris judge of Gods.'

"Dear mother Ida, harken ere I die.
It was the deep midnoon: one silvery cloud
Had lost his way between the piney sides
Of this long glen. Then to the bower they came,
Naked they came to that smooth-swarded bower,
And at their feet the crocus brake like fire,
Violet, amaracus, and asphodel,
Lotos and lilies: and a wind arose,
And overhead the wandering ivy and vine,
This way and that, in many a wild festoon
Ran riot, garlanding the gnarléd boughs
With bunch and berry and flower thro' and thro'.

"O mother Ida, harken ere I die.
On the tree-tops a crested peacock lit,
And o'er him flowed a golden cloud, and leaned
Upon him, slowly dropping fragrant dew.
Then first I heard the voice of her, to whom
Coming thro' Heaven, like a light that grows
Larger and clearer, with one mind the Gods
Rise up for reverence. She to Paris made
Proffer of royal power, ample rule
Unquestioned, overflowing revenue
Wherewith to embellish state, 'from many a vale
And river-sundered champaign clothed with corn,
Or laboured mine undrainable of ore.
Honour,' she said, 'and homage, tax and toll,
From many an inland town and haven large,
Mast-thronged beneath her shadowing citadel
In glassy bays among her tallest towers.'

"O mother Ida, harken ere I die.
Still she spake on and still she spake of power,
'Which in all action is the end of all;
Power fitted to the season; wisdom-bred
And throned of wisdom—from all neighbour crowns
Alliance and allegiance, till thy hand
Fail from the sceptre-staff. Such boon from me,
From me, Heaven's Queen, Paris, to thee king-born,
A shepherd all thy life but yet king-born,
Should come most welcome, seeing men, in power
Only, are likest gods, who have attained
Rest in a happy place and quiet seats
Above the thunder, with undying bliss
In knowledge of their own supremacy.'

"Dear mother Ida, harken ere I die.
She ceased, and Paris held the costly fruit
Out at arm's-length, so much the thought of power
Flattered his spirit; but Pallas where she stood
Somewhat apart, her clear and bared limbs
O'erthwarted with the brazen-headed spear
Upon her pearly shoulder leaning cold,

The while, above, her full and earnest eye
Over her snow-cold breast and angry cheek
Kept watch, waiting decision, made reply.

" 'Self-reverence, self-knowledge, self-control,
These three alone lead life to sovereign power.
Yet not for power (power of herself
Would come uncalled for) but to live by law,
Acting the law we live by without fear;
And, because right is right, to follow right
Were wisdom in the scorn of consequence.'

"Dear mother Ida, harken ere I die.
Again she said: 'I woo thee not with gifts.
Sequel of guerdon could not alter me
To fairer. Judge thou me by what I am
So shalt thou find me fairest.
               Yet, indeed,
If gazing on divinity disrobed
Thy mortal eyes are frail to judge of fair,
Unbias'd by self-profit, oh! rest thee sure
That I shall love thee well and cleave to thee,
So that my vigour, wedded to thy blood,
Shall strike within thy pulses, like a God's,
To push thee forward thro' a life of shocks,
Dangers, and deeds, until endurance grow
Sinewed with action, and the full-grown will,
Circled thro' all experiences, pure law,
Commeasure perfect freedom.'
          "Here she ceased,
And Paris pondered, and I cried, 'O Paris,
Give it to Pallas!' but he heard me not,
Or hearing would not hear me, woe is me!

"Oh mother Ida, many-fountained Ida,
Dear mother Ida, harken ere I die.
Idalian Aphrodité beautiful,
Fresh as the foam, new-bathed in Paphian wells,
With rosy slender fingers backward drew
From her warm brows and bosom her deep hair
Ambrosial, golden round her lucid throat

And shoulder: from the violets her light foot
Shone rosy-white, and o'er her rounded form
Between the shadows of the vine-bunches
Floated the glowing sunlights, as she moved.

"Dear mother Ida, harken ere I die.
She with a subtle smile in her mild eyes,
The herald of her triumph, drawing nigh
Half-whispered in his ear, 'I promise thee
The fairest and most loving wife in Greece.'
She spoke and laughed: I shut my sight for fear:
But when I looked, Paris had raised his arm,
And I beheld great Heré's angry eyes,
As she withdrew into the golden cloud,
And I was left alone within the bower;
And from that time to this I am alone,
And I shall be alone until I die.

"Yet, mother Ida, harken ere I die.
Fairest—why fairest wife? am I not fair?
My love hath told me so a thousand times.
Methinks I must be fair, for yesterday,
When I past by, a wild and wanton pard,
Eyed like the evening star, with playful tail
Crouched fawning in the weed. Most loving is she?
Ah me, my mountain shepherd, that my arms
Were wound about thee, and my hot lips prest
Close, close to thine in that quick-fallen dew
Of fruitful kisses, thick as Autumn rains
Flash in the pools of whirling Simois.

"O mother, hear me yet before I die.
They came, they cut away my tallest pines,
My tall dark pines, that plumed the craggy ledge
High over the blue gorge, and all between
The snowy peak and snow-white cataract
Fostered the callow eaglet—from beneath
Whose thick mysterious boughs in the dark morn
The panther's roar came muffled, while I sat
Low in the valley. Never, never more
Shall lone Œnone see the morning mist

Sweep thro' them; never see them overlaid
With narrow moon-lit slips of silver cloud,
Between the loud stream and the trembling stars.

"O mother, hear me yet before I die.
I wish that somewhere in the ruined folds,
Among the fragments tumbled from the glens,
Or the dry thickets, I could meet with her
The Abominable, that uninvited came
Into the fair Peleïan banquet-hall,
And cast the golden fruit upon the board,
And bred this change; that I might speak my mind,
And tell her to her face how much I hate
Her presence, hated both of Gods and men.

"O mother, hear me yet before I die.
Hath he not sworn his love a thousand times,
In this green valley, under this green hill,
Ev'n on this hand, and sitting on this stone?
Sealed it with kisses? watered it with tears?
O happy tears, and how unlike to these!
O happy Heaven, how canst thou see my face?
O happy earth, how canst thou bear my weight?
O death, death, death, thou ever-floating cloud,
There are enough unhappy on this earth,
Pass by the happy souls, that love to live:
I pray thee, pass before my light of life,
And shadow all my soul, that I may die.
Thou weighest heavy on the heart within,
Weigh heavy on my eyelids: let me die.

"O mother, hear me yet before I die.
I will not die alone, for fiery thoughts
Do shape themselves within me, more and more,
Whereof I catch the issue, as I hear
Dead sounds at night come from the inmost hills,
Like footsteps upon wool. I dimly see
My far-off doubtful purpose, as a mother
Conjectures of the features of her child
Ere it is born: her child!—a shudder comes
Across me: never child be born of me,
Unblest, to vex me with his father's eyes!

"O mother, hear me yet before I die.
Hear me, O earth. I will not die alone,
Lest their shrill happy laughter come to me
Walking the cold and starless road of death
Uncomforted, leaving my ancient love
With the Greek woman. I will rise and go
Down into Troy, and ere the stars come forth
Talk with the wild Cassandra, for she says
A fire dances before her, and a sound
Rings ever in her ears of armed men.
What this may be I know not, but I know
That, whatsoe'er I am by night and day,
All earth and air seem only burning fire."

FROM *The Princess*

1.

The splendour falls on castle walls
    And snowy summits old in story;
The long light shakes across the lakes,
    And the wild cataract leaps in glory,
Blow, bugle, blow, set the wild echoes flying,
Blow, bugle; answer, echoes, dying, dying, dying.

O hark, O hear! how thin and clear,
    And thinner, clearer, farther going!
O, sweet and far from cliff and scar
    The horns of Elfland faintly blowing!
Blow, let us hear the purple glens replying,
Blow, bugle; answer, echoes, dying, dying, dying.

O love, they die in yon rich sky,
    They faint on hill or field or river;
Our echoes roll from soul to soul,
    And grow for ever and for ever.
Blow, bugle, blow, set the wild echoes flying,
And answer, echoes, answer, dying, dying, dying.

2.

Tears, idle tears, I know not what they mean,
Tears from the depth of some divine despair
Rise in the heart, and gather to the eyes,
In looking on the happy autumn-fields,
And thinking of the days that are no more.

Fresh as the first beam glittering on a sail,
That brings our friends up from the under-world,
Sad as the last which reddens over one
That sinks with all we love below the verge;
So sad, so fresh, the days that are no more.

Ah, sad and strange as in dark summer dawns
The earliest pipe of half-awakened birds
To dying ears, when unto dying eyes
The casement slowly grows a glimmering square;
So sad, so strange, the days that are no more.

Dear as remembered kisses after death,
And sweet as those by hopeless fancy feigned
On lips that are for others; deep as love,
Deep as first love, and wild with all regret;
O Death in Life, the days that are no more!

3.

Now sleeps the crimson petal, now the white;
Nor waves the cypress in the palace walk;
Nor winks the gold fin in the porphyry font.
The fire-fly wakens; waken thou with me.

Now droops the milk-white peacock like a ghost,
And like a ghost she glimmers on to me.

Now lies the Earth all Danaë to the stars,
And all thy heart lies open unto me.

Now slides the silent meteor on, and leaves
A shining furrow, as thy thoughts in me.

Now folds the lily all her sweetness up,
And slips into the bosom of the lake.
So fold thyself, my dearest, thou, and slip
Into my bosom and be lost in me.

4.

Come down, O maid, from yonder mountain height.
What pleasure lives in height (the shepherd sang)
In height and cold, the splendour of the hills?
But cease to move so near the heavens, and cease
To glide a sunbeam by the blasted pine,
To sit a star upon the sparkling spire;
And come, for Love is of the valley, come,
For Love is of the valley, come thou down
And find him; by the happy threshold, he,
Or hand in hand with Plenty in the maize,
Or red with spirted purple of the vats,
Or foxlike in the vine; nor cares to walk
With Death and Morning on the Silver Horns,
Nor wilt thou snare him in the white ravine,
Nor find him dropt upon the firths of ice,
That huddling slant in furrow-cloven falls
To roll the torrent out of dusky doors.
But follow; let the torrent dance thee down
To find him in the valley; let the wild
Lean-headed eagles yelp alone, and leave
The monstrous ledges there to slope, and spill
Their thousand wreaths of dangling water-smoke,
That like a broken purpose waste in air.
So waste not thou, but come; for all the vales
Await thee; azure pillars of the hearth
Arise to thee; the children call, and I
Thy shepherd pipe, and sweet is every sound,
Sweeter thy voice, but every sound is sweet;
Myriads of rivulets hurrying through the lawn,
The moan of doves in immemorial elms,
And murmuring of innumerable bees.

FROM *In Memoriam*

XXXV

Yet if some voice that man could trust
   Should murmur from the narrow house,
   "The cheeks drop in, the body bows;
Man dies, nor is there hope in dust;"

Might I not say? "Yet even here
   But for one hour, O Love, I strive
   To keep so sweet a thing alive."
But I should turn mine ears and hear

The moanings of the homeless sea,
   The sound of streams that swift or slow
   Draw down Æonian hills, and sow
The dust of continents to be;

And Love would answer with a sigh,
   "The sound of that forgetful shore
   Will change my sweetness more and more,
Half-dead to know that I shall die."

LXXXII

Dip down upon the northern shore,
   O sweet new-year delaying long;
   Thou doest expectant Nature wrong;
Delaying long, delay no more.

What stays thee from the clouded noons,
   Thy sweetness from its proper place?
   Can trouble live with April days,
Or sadness in the summer moons?

Bring orchis, bring the foxglove spire,
   The little speedwell's darling blue,
   Deep tulips dashed with fiery dew,
Laburnums, dropping-wells of fire.

O thou, new-year, delaying long,
  Delayest the sorrow in my blood,
  That longs to burst a frozen bud
And flood a fresher throat with song.

XC

When rosy plumelets tuft the larch,
  And rarely pipes the mounted thrush,
  Or underneath the barren bush
Flits by the sea-blue bird of March;

Come, wear the form by which I knew
  Thy spirit in time among thy peers;
  The hope of unaccomplished years
Be large and lucid round thy brow.

When summer's hourly-mellowing change
  May breathe, with many roses sweet,
  Upon the thousand waves of wheat
That rippled round the lowly grange.

Come; not in watches of the night,
  But where the sunbeam broodeth warm,
  Come, beauteous in thine after form,
And like a finer light in light.

CXIV

Now fades the last long streak of snow,
  Now burgeons every maze of quick
  About the flowering squares, and thick
By ashen roots the violets blow.

Now rings the woodland loud and long,
  The distance takes a lovelier hue,
  And drowned in yonder living blue
The lark becomes a sightless song.

Now dance the lights on lawn and lea,
  The flocks are whiter down the vale,
  And milkier every milky sail
On winding stream or distant sea;

Where now the seamew pipes, or dives
  In yonder greening gleam, and fly
  The happy birds, that change their sky
To build and brood, that live their lives

From land to land; and in my breast
  Spring wakens too, and my regret
  Becomes an April violet,
And buds and blossoms like the rest.

Ulysses

It little profits that an idle king,
By this still hearth, among these barren crags,
Matched with an aged wife, I mete and dole
Unequal laws unto a savage race,
That hoard, and sleep, and feed, and know not me.
I cannot rest from travel; I will drink
Life to the lees. All times I have enjoyed
Greatly, have suffered greatly, both with those
That loved me, and alone; on shore, and when
Through scudding drifts the rainy Hyades
Vext the dim sea. I am become a name;
For always roaming with a hungry heart
Much have I seen and known,—cities of men
And manners, climates, councils, governments,
Myself not least, but honoured of them all,—
And drunk delight of battle with my peers,
Far on the ringing plains of windy Troy.
I am a part of all that I have met;
Yet all experience is an arch wherethrough
Gleams that untravelled world whose margin fades
For ever and for ever when I move.
How dull it is to pause, to make an end,
To rust unburnished, not to shine in use!
As though to breathe were life! Life piled on life
Were all too little, and of one to me
Little remains; but every hour is saved
From that eternal silence, something more,

A bringer of new things; and vile it were
For some three suns to store and hoard myself,
And this gray spirit yearning in desire
To follow knowledge like a sinking star,
Beyond the utmost bound of human thought.

This is my son, mine own Telemachus,
To whom I leave the sceptre and the isle,—
Well-loved of me, discerning to fulfill
This labour, by slow prudence to make mild
A rugged people, and through soft degrees
Subdue them to the useful and the good.
Most blameless is he, centred in the sphere
Of common duties, decent not to fail
In offices of tenderness, and pay
Meet adoration to my household gods,
When I am gone. He works his work, I mine.
There lies the port; the vessel puffs her sail;
There gloom the dark, broad seas. My mariners,
Souls that have toiled and wrought, and thought with me,—
That ever with a frolic welcome took
The thunder and the sunshine, and opposed
Free hearts, free foreheads,—you and I are old;
Old age hath yet his honour and his toil.
Death closes all; but something ere the end,
Some work of noble note, may yet be done,
Not unbecoming men that strove with Gods.
The lights begin to twinkle from the rocks;
The long day wanes; the slow moon climbs; the deep
Moans round with many voices. Come, my friends,
'Tis not too late to seek a newer world.
Push off, and sitting well in order smite
The sounding furrows; for my purpose holds
To sail beyond the sunset, and the baths
Of all the western stars, until I die.
It may be that the gulfs will wash us down;
It may be we shall touch the Happy Isles,
And see the great Achilles, whom we knew.
Though much is taken, much abides; and though
We are not now that strength which in old days
Moved earth and heaven, that which we are, we are,—

One equal temper of heroic hearts,
Made weak by time and fate, but strong in will
To strive, to seek, to find, and not to yield.

Crossing the Bar

Sunset and evening star,
    And one clear call for me!
And may there be no moaning of the bar,
    When I put out to sea,

But such a tide as moving seems asleep,
    Too full for sound and foam,
When that which drew from out the boundless deep
    Turns again home.

Twilight and evening bell,
    And after that the dark!
And may there be no sadness of farewell,
    When I embark;

For though from out our bourne of Time and Place
    The flood may bear me far,
I hope to see my Pilot face to face
    When I have crost the bar.

EDGAR ALLAN POE

(1809–1849)

The Raven

Once upon a midnight dreary, while I pondered weak and
        weary,
Over many a quaint and curious volume of forgotten lore,
While I nodded, nearly napping, suddenly there came a
        tapping,
As of someone gently rapping, rapping at my chamber door.
" 'Tis some visitor," I muttered, "tapping at my chamber door—
        Only this, and nothing more."

Ah, distinctly I remember it was in the bleak December,
And each separate dying ember wrought its ghost upon the
    floor.
Eagerly I wished the morrow;—vainly I had sought to borrow
From my books surcease of sorrow—sorrow for the lost
    Lenore—
For the rare and radiant maiden whom the angels name
    Lenore—
        Nameless here for evermore.

And the silken sad uncertain rustling of each purple curtain
Thrilled me—filled me with fantastic terrors never felt before;
So that now, to still the beating of my heart, I stood repeating,
" 'Tis some visitor entreating entrance at my chamber door—
Some late visitor entreating entrance at my chamber door;—
        This it is, and nothing more."

Presently my soul grew stronger; hesitating then no longer,
"Sir," said I, "or Madam, truly your forgiveness I implore;
But the fact is I was napping, and so gently you came rapping,
And so faintly you came tapping, tapping at my chamber door,
That I scarce was sure I heard you"—here I opened wide the
    door;—
        Darkness there, and nothing more.

Deep into the darkness peering, long I stood there, wonder-
    ing, fearing,
Doubting, dreaming dreams no mortals ever dared to dream
    before;
But the silence was unbroken, and the stillness gave no token,
And the only word there spoken was the whispered word,
    "Lenore!"
This I whispered, and an echo murmured back the word,
    "Lenore!"—
        Merely this, and nothing more.

Back into the chamber turning, all my soul within me burning,
Soon again I heard a tapping somewhat louder than before.
"Surely," said I, "surely that is something at my window
    lattice:

Let me see, then, what thereat is, and this mystery explore—
Let my heart be still a moment and this mystery explore;—
      'Tis the wind and nothing more."

Open here I flung the shutter, when, with many a flirt and
    flutter,
In there stepped a stately raven of the saintly days of yore;
Not the least obeisance made he; not a minute stopped or
    stayed he;
But, with mien of lord or lady, perched above my chamber
    door—
Perched upon a bust of Pallas just above my chamber door—
      Perched and sat, and nothing more.

Then this ebony bird beguiling my sad fancy into smiling,
By the grave and stern decorum of the countenance it wore.
"Though thy crest be shorn and shaven, thou," I said, "art
    sure no craven,
Ghastly grim and ancient raven wandering from the Nightly
    shore—
Tell me what thy lordly name is on the Night's Plutonian
    shore!"
      Quoth the Raven, "Nevermore."

Much I marvelled this ungainly fowl to hear discourse so
    plainly,
Though its answer little meaning—little relevancy bore;
For we cannot help agreeing that no living human being
Ever yet was blest with seeing bird above his chamber door—
Bird or beast upon the sculptured bust above his chamber
    door,
      With such name as "Nevermore."

But the raven, sitting lonely on the placid bust, spoke only
That one word, as if his soul in that one word he did outpour.
Nothing further then he uttered—not a feather then he
    fluttered—
Till I scarcely more than muttered, "Other friends have flown
    before,
On the morrow *he* will leave me, as my hopes have flown
    before."
      Then the bird said, "Nevermore."

Startled at the stillness broken by reply so aptly spoken,
"Doubtless," said I, "what it utters is its only stock and store,
Caught from some unhappy master whom unmerciful Disaster
Followed fast and followed faster till his songs one burden
    bore—
Till the dirges of his Hope that melancholy burden bore
        Of 'Never—nevermore'."

But the Raven still beguiling all my fancy into smiling,
Straight I wheeled a cushioned seat in front of bird, and bust
    and door;
Then upon the velvet sinking, I betook myself to linking
Fancy unto fancy, thinking what this ominous bird of yore—
What this grim, ungainly, ghastly, gaunt and ominous bird
    of yore
        Meant in croaking, "Nevermore."

This I sat engaged in guessing, but no syllable expressing
To the fowl whose fiery eyes now burned into my bosom's
    core;
This and more I sat divining, with my head at ease reclining
On the cushion's velvet lining that the lamplight gloated o'er,
But whose velvet violet lining with the lamplight gloating o'er,
        She shall press, ah, nevermore!

Then methought the air grew denser, perfumed from an
    unseen censer
Swung by Seraphim whose footfalls tinkled on the tufted
    floor.
"Wretch," I cried, "thy God hath lent thee—by these angels he
    hath sent thee
Respite—respite and nepenthe, from the memories of Lenore!
Quaff, oh quaff this kind nepenthe and forget this lost Lenore!"
        Quoth the Raven, "Nevermore."

"Prophet!" said I, "thing of evil!—prophet still, if bird or
    devil!—
Whether Tempter sent, or whether tempest tossed thee here
    ashore,
Desolate yet all undaunted, on this desert land enchanted—
On this home by horror haunted—tell me truly, I implore—

Is there—*is* there balm in Gilead?—tell me—tell me, I implore!"
        Quoth the Raven, "Nevermore."

"Prophet!" said I, "thing of evil!—prophet still, if bird or devil!
By that Heaven that bends above us—by that God we both
      adore—
Tell this soul with sorrow laden if, within the distant Aidenn,
It shall clasp a sainted maiden whom the angels name Lenore—
Clasp a rare and radiant maiden whom the angels name
      Lenore."
        Quoth the Raven, "Nevermore."

"Be that word our sign in parting, bird or fiend," I shrieked,
      upstarting—
"Get thee back into the tempest and the Night's Plutonian
      shore!
Leave no black plume as a token of that lie thy soul hath
      spoken!
Leave my loneliness unbroken! quit the bust above my door!
Take thy beak from out my heart, and thy form from off my
      door!"
        Quoth the Raven, "Nevermore."

And the Raven, never flitting, still is sitting, still is sitting
On the pallid bust of Pallas just above my chamber door;
And his eyes have all the seeming of a demon's that is
      dreaming,
And the lamplight o'er him streaming throws his shadow on
      the floor;
And my soul from out that shadow that lies floating on the
      floor
        Shall be lifted—nevermore!

Ulalume

    The skies they were ashen and sober;
      The leaves they were crispéd and sere—
      The leaves they were withering and sere;
    It was night in the lonesome October
      Of my most immemorial year;

It was hard by the dim lake of Auber,
   In the misty mid region of Weir—
It was down by the dark tarn of Auber,
   In the ghoul-haunted woodland of Weir.

Here once, through an alley Titanic,
   Of cypress, I roamed with my Soul—
   Of cypress, with Psyche, my Soul.
These were days when my heart was volcanic
   As the scoriac rivers that roll—
   As the lavas that restlessly roll
Their sulphurous currents down Yaanek
   In the ultimate climes of the pole—
That groan as they roll down Mount Yaanek
   In the realms of the boreal pole.

Our talk had been serious and sober,
   But our thoughts they were palsied and sere—
   Our memories were treacherous and sere—
For we knew not the month was October,
   And we marked not the night of the year—
   (Ah, night of all nights in the year!)
We noted not the dim lake of Auber—
   (Though once we had journeyed down here),
Remembered not the dark tarn of Auber,
   Nor the ghoul-haunted woodland of Weir.

And now, as the night was senescent,
   And star-dials pointed to morn—
   As the star-dials hinted of morn—
At the end of our path a liquescent
   And nebulous lustre was born,
Out of which a miraculous crescent
   Arose with a duplicate horn—
Astarte's bediamonded crescent
   Distinct with its duplicate horn.

And I said—"She is warmer than Dian:
   She rolls through an ether of sighs—
   She revels in a region of sighs:

She has seen that the tears are not dry on
   These cheeks, where the worm never dies,
And has come past the stars of the Lion
   To point out the path to the skies—
   To the Lethean peace of the skies—
Come up, in despite of the Lion,
   To shine on us with her bright eyes—
Come up through the lair of the Lion,
   With love in her luminous eyes."

But Psyche, uplifting her finger,
   Said—"Sadly this star I mistrust—
   Her pallor I strangely mistrust:—
Oh hasten!—oh, let us not linger!
   Oh, fly!—let us fly!—for we must."
In terror she spoke, letting sink her
   Wings until they trailed in the dust—
In agony sobbed, letting sink her
   Plumes till they trailed in the dust—
   Till they sorrowfully trailed in the dust.

I replied—"This is nothing but dreaming:
   Let us on by this tremulous light!
   Let us bathe in this crystalline light!
Its Sibyllic splendour is beaming
   With Hope and in Beauty to-night:—
   See!—it flickers up the sky through the night!
Ah, we safely may trust to its gleaming,
   And be sure it will lead us aright—
We safely may trust to a gleaming
   That cannot but guide us aright,
   Since it flickers up to Heaven through the night."

Thus I pacified Psyche and kissed her,
   And tempted her out of her gloom—
   And conquered her scruples and gloom;
And we passed to the end of the vista,
   But were stopped by the door of a tomb—
   By the door of a legended tomb;

And I said—"What is written, sweet sister,
   On the door of this legended tomb?"
She replied—"Ulalume—Ulalume—
   'Tis the vault of thy lost Ulalume!"

Then my heart it grew ashen and sober
   As the leaves that were crispéd and sere—
   As the leaves that were withering and sere,
And I cried—"It was surely October
   On *this* very night of last year
   That I journeyed—I journeyed down here—
   That I brought a dread burden down here—
   On this night of all nights in the year,
   Ah, what demon has tempted me here?
Well I know, now, this dim lake of Auber—
   This misty mid region of Weir—
Well I know, now, this dank tarn of Auber,
   This ghoul-haunted woodland of Weir."

The Valley of Unrest

Once it smiled a silent dell
Where the people did not dwell;
They had gone unto the wars,
Trusting to the mild-eyed stars,
Nightly, from their azure towers,
To keep watch above the flowers,
In the midst of which all day
The red sunlight lazily lay.
Now each visitor shall confess
The sad valley's restlessness.
Nothing there is motionless—
Nothing save the airs that brood
Over the magic solitude.
Ah, by no wind are stirred those trees
That palpitate like the chill seas
Around the misty Hebrides!
Ah, by no wind those clouds are driven
That rustle through the unquiet Heaven
Uneasily, from morn till even,

Over the violets there that lie
In myriad types of the human eye—
Over the lilies there that wave
And weep above a nameless grave!
They wave:—from out their fragrant tops
Eternal dews come down in drops.
They weep:—from off their delicate stems
Perennial tears descend in gems.

The City in the Sea

Lo! Death has reared himself a throne
In a strange city lying alone
Far down within the dim West,
Where the good and the bad and the worst and the best
Have gone to their eternal rest.
There shrines and palaces and towers
(Time-eaten towers that tremble not!)
Resemble nothing that is ours.
Around, by lifting winds forgot,
Resignedly beneath the sky
The melancholy waters lie.

No rays from the holy heaven come down
On the long night-time of that town;
But light from out the lurid sea
Streams up the turrets silently—
Gleams up the pinnacles far and free—
Up domes—up spires—up kingly halls—
Up fanes—up Babylon-like walls—
Up shadowy long-forgotten bowers
Of sculptured ivy and stone flowers—
Up many and many a marvellous shrine
Whose wreathèd friezes intertwine
The viol, the violet, and the vine.
Resignedly beneath the sky
The melancholy waters lie.
So blend the turrets and shadows there
That all seem pendulous in air,
While from a proud tower in the town
Death looks gigantically down.

There open fanes and gaping graves
Yawn level with the luminous waves;
But not the riches there that lie
In each idol's diamond eye—
Not the gaily-jewelled dead
Tempt the waters from their bed;
For no ripples curl, alas!
Along that wilderness of glass—
No swellings tell that winds may be
Upon some far-off happier sea—
No heavings hint that winds have been
On seas less hideously serene.

But lo, a stir is in the air!
The wave—there is a movement there!
As if the towers had thrust aside,
In slightly sinking, the dull tide—
As if their tops had feebly given
A void within the filmy Heaven.
The waves have now a redder glow—
The hours are breathing faint and low—
And when, amid no earthly moans,
Down, down that town shall settle hence,
Hell, rising from a thousand thrones,
Shall do it reverence.

To One in Paradise

Thou wast all that to me, love,
    For which my soul did pine—
A green isle in the sea, love,
    A fountain and a shrine,
All wreathed with fairy fruits and flowers,
    And all the flowers were mine.

Ah, dream too bright to last!
    Ah, starry Hope! that didst arise
But to be overcast!

A voice from out the Future cries,
"On! on!"—but o'er the Past
  (Dim gulf!) my spirit hovering lies
Mute, motionless, aghast!

For, alas! alas! with me
  The light of Life is o'er!
  "No more—no more—no more—"
(Such language holds the solemn sea
  To the sands upon the shore)
Shall bloom the thunder-blasted tree
  Or the stricken eagle soar!

And all my days are trances,
  And all my nightly dreams
Are where thy grey eye glances,
  And where thy footstep gleams—
In what ethereal dances,
  By what eternal streams.

The Haunted Palace

In the greenest of our valleys
  By good angels tenanted,
Once a fair and stately palace—
  Radiant palace—reared its head.
In the monarch Thought's dominion—
  It stood there!
Never seraph spread a pinion
  Over fabric half so fair!

Banners yellow, glorious, golden,
  On its roof did float and flow,
(This—all this—was in the olden
  Time long ago,)

And every gentle air that dallied,
   In that sweet day,
Along the ramparts plumed and pallid,
   A wingéd odour went away.

Wanderers in that happy valley,
   Through two luminous windows, saw
Spirits moving musically,
   To a lute's well-tunéd law,
Round about a throne where, sitting
   (Porphyrogene!)
In state his glory well-befitting,
   The ruler of the realm was seen.

And all with pearl and ruby glowing
   Was the fair palace door,
Through which came flowing, flowing, flowing,
   And sparkling evermore,
A troop of Echoes, whose sweet duty
   Was but to sing,
In voices of surpassing beauty,
   The wit and wisdom of their king.

But evil things, in robes of sorrow,
   Assailed the monarch's high estate.
(Ah, let us mourn!—for never morrow
   Shall dawn upon him desolate!)
And round about his home the glory
   That blushed and bloomed,
Is but a dim-remembered story
   Of the old time entombed.

And travellers, now, within that valley,
   Through the red-litten windows see
Vast forms, that move fantastically
   To a discordant melody,
While, like a ghastly rapid river,
   Through the pale door
A hideous throng rush out forever
   And laugh—but smile no more.

Annabel Lee

It was many and many a year ago,
　In a kingdom by the sea,
That a maiden there lived whom you may know
　By the name of ANNABEL LEE;
And this maiden she lived with no other thought
　Than to love and be loved by me.

I was a child and *she* was a child,
　In this kingdom by the sea;
But we loved with a love which was more than love—
　I and my Annabel Lee;
With a love that the wingéd seraphs of heaven
　Coveted her and me.

And this was the reason that, long ago,
　In this kingdom by the sea,
A wind blew out of a cloud, chilling
　My beautiful Annabel Lee;
So that her highborn kinsmen came
　And bore her away from me,
To shut her up in a sepulchre
　In this kingdom by the sea.

The angels, not half so happy in heaven,
　Went envying her and me—
Yes!—that was the reason (as all men know,
　In this kingdom by the sea)
That the wind came out of the cloud by night,
　Chilling and killing my Annabel Lee.

But our love it was stronger by far than the love
　Of those who were older than we—
　Of many far wiser than we—
And neither the angels in heaven above,
　Nor the demons down under the sea,
Can ever dissever my soul from the soul
　Of the beautiful Annabel Lee.

For the moon never beams without bringing me dreams
    Of the beautiful Annabel Lee;
And the stars never rise but I feel the bright eyes
    Of the beautiful Annabel Lee;
And so, all the night-tide, I lie down by the side
Of my darling—my darling—my life and my bride,
    In the sepulchre there by the sea,
    In her tomb by the sounding sea.

To Helen

Helen, thy beauty is to me
    Like those Nicaean barks of yore,
That gently o'er a perfumed sea,
    The weary, wayworn wanderer bore
    To his own native shore.

On desperate seas long wont to roam,
    Thy hyacinth hair, thy classic face,
Thy Naiad airs have brought me home
    To the glory that was Greece
    And the grandeur that was Rome.

Lo! in yon brilliant window-niche
    How statue-like I see thee stand,
The agate lamp within thy hand!
    Ah, Psyche, from the regions which
    Are Holy Land!

WILLIAM MAKEPEACE THACKERAY

(1811–1863)

FROM *The Chronicle of the Drum*

Ah, gentle, tender lady mine!
    The winter wind blows cold and shrill;
Come, fill me one more glass of wine,
    And give the silly fools their will.

And what care we for war and wrack,
   And kings and heroes rise and fall?
Look yonder, in his coffin black,
   There lies the greatest of them all.

To pluck him down, and keep him up,
   Died many million human souls.—
'Tis twelve o'clock and time to sup:
   Bid Mary heap the fire with coals.

He captured many thousand guns;
   He wrote "The Great" before his name;
And dying, only left his sons
   The recollection of his shame.

Though more than half the world was his,
   He died without a rood his own;
And borrowed from his enemies
   Six foot of ground to lie upon.

He fought a thousand glorious wars,
   And more than half the world was his,
And somewhere now, in yonder stars,
   Can tell, mayhap, what greatness is.

The Ballad of Bouillabaisse

A street there is in Paris famous,
   For which no rhyme our language yields,
Rue Neuve des Petits Champs its name is—
   The New Street of the Little Fields.
And here's an inn, not rich and splendid,
   But still in comfortable case;
The which in youth I oft attended,
   To eat a bowl of Bouillabaisse.

This Bouillabaisse a noble dish is—
   A sort of soup or broth, or brew,
Or hotchpotch of all sorts of fishes,
   That Greenwich never could outdo;

Green herbs, red peppers, mussels, saffron,
  Soles, onions, garlic, roach, and dace:
All these you eat at TERRÉ's tavern,
  In that one dish of Bouillabaisse.

Indeed, a rich and savoury stew 'tis;
  And true philosophers, methinks,
Who love all sorts of natural beauties,
  Should love good victuals and good drinks.
And Cordelier or Benedictine
  Might gladly, sure, his lot embrace,
Nor find a fast-day too afflicting,
  Which served him up a Bouillabaisse.

I wonder if the house still there is?
  Yes, here the lamp is, as before;
The smiling red-cheeked *écaillère* is
  Still opening oysters at the door.
Is TERRÉ still alive and able?
  I recollect his droll grimace:
He'd come and sit before your table,
  And hope you liked your Bouillabaisse.

We enter—nothing's changed or older.
  "How's Monsieur TERRÉ, waiter, pray?"
The waiter stares and shrugs his shoulder—
  "Monsieur is dead this many a day."
"It is the lot of saint and sinner,
  So honest TERRÉ's run his race."
"What will Monsieur require for dinner?"
  "Say, do you still cook Bouillabaisse?"

"Oh, oui, Monsieur," 's the waiter's answer;
  "Quel vin Monsieur désire-t-il?"
"Tell me a good one."—"That I can, Sir;
  The Chambertin with yellow seal."
"So TERRÉ's gone," I say, and sink in
  My old accustomed corner-place;
"He's done with feasting and with drinking,
  With Burgundy and Bouillabaisse."

My old accustomed corner here is,
    The table still is in the nook;
Ah! vanished many a busy year is
    This well-known chair since last I took.
When first I saw ye, *cari luoghi,*
    I'd scarce a beard upon my face,
And now a grizzled, grim old fogy,
    I sit and wait for Bouillabaisse.

Where are you, old companions trusty
    Of early days here met to dine?
Come, waiter! quick, a flagon crusty—
    I'll pledge them in the good old wine.
The kind old voices and old faces
    My memory can quick retrace;
Around the board they take their places,
    And share the wine and Bouillabaisse.

There's Jack has made a wondrous marriage;
    There's laughing Tom is laughing yet;
There's brave Augustus drives his carriage;
    There's poor old Fred in the *Gazette;*
On James's head the grass is growing:
    Good Lord! the world has wagged apace
Since here we set the claret flowing,
    And drank, and ate the Bouillabaisse.

Ah me! how quick the days are flitting!
    I mind me of a time that's gone,
When here I'd sit, as now I'm sitting,
    In this same place—but not alone.
A fair young form was nestled near me,
    A dear, dear face looked fondly up,
And sweetly spoke and smiled to cheer me
    —There's no one now to share my cup.

I drink it as the Fates ordain it.
    Come, fill it, and have done with rhymes:
Fill up the lonely glass, and drain it
    In memory of dear old times.

Welcome the wine, whate'er the seal is;
  And sit you down, and say your grace
With thankful heart, whate'er the meal is.
  Here comes the smoking Bouillabaisse!

ROBERT HINCKLEY MESSINGER

(1811–1874)

A Winter Wish

Old wine to drink!
  Ay, give the slippery juice
That drippeth from the grape thrown loose
  Within the tun;
Plucked from beneath the cliff
Of sunny-sided Teneriffe,
  And ripened 'neath the blink
    Of India's sun!
Tempered with well-boiled water!
  Peat whiskey hot,
These make the long night shorter—
  Forgetting not
Good stout old English porter.

Old wood to burn!
Ay, bring the hill-side beech
From where the owlets meet and screech,
  And ravens croak;
The crackling pine, and cedar sweet;
Bring too a clump of fragrant peat,
  Dug 'neath the fern;
    The knotted oak,
      A fagot too, perhaps,
Whose bright flame, dancing, winking,
Shall light us at our drinking;
  While the oozing sap
Shall make sweet music to our thinking.

Old books to read!
Ay, bring those nodes of wit,
The brazen-clasped, the vellum writ,
  Time-honored tomes!

The same my sire scanned before,
The same my grandsire thumbéd o'er,
The same his sire from college bore,
   The well-earned meed
      Of Oxford's domes:
      Old Homer blind,
Old Horace, rake Anacreon, by
Old Tully, Plautus, Terence lie;
Mort Arthur's olden minstrelsie,
Quaint Burton, quainter Spenser, ay!
And Gervase Markham's venerie—
   Nor leave behind
The holye Book by which we live and die.

Old friends to talk!
Ay, bring those chosen few,
The wise, the courtly, and the true,
   So rarely found;
Him for my wine, him for my stud,
Him for my easel, distich, bud
   In mountain walk!
      Bring Walter good,
With soulful Fred, and learned Will,
And thee, my alter ego (dearer still
   For every mood).

These add a bouquet to my wine!
These add a sparkle to my pine!
   If these I tine,
Can books, or fire, or wine be good?

ROBERT BROWNING

(1812–1889)

Song

Give her but a least excuse to love me!
When—where—
How—can this arm establish her above me,
If fortune fixed her as my lady there,

There already, to eternally reprove me?
    ("Hist!"—said Kate the Queen;
    But "Oh!"—cried the maiden, binding her tresses,
    " 'Tis only a page that carols unseen,
    Crumbling your hounds their messes!")

Is she wronged?—To the rescue of her honour,
My heart!
Is she poor?—What costs it to be styled a donor?
Merely an earth to cleave, a sea to part.
But that fortune should have thrust all this upon her!
    ("Nay, list!"—bade Kate the Queen;
    And still cried the maiden, binding her tresses,
    " 'Tis only a page that carols unseen,
    Fitting your hawks their jesses!")

Pippa Passes

The Lost Leader

Just for a handful of silver he left us,
    Just for a riband to stick in his coat—
Found the one gift of which fortune bereft us,
    Lost all the others she lets us devote;
They, with the gold to give, doled him out silver,
    So much was theirs who so little allowed:
How all our copper had gone for his service!
    Rags—were they purple, his heart had been proud!
We that had loved him so, followed him, honoured him,
    Lived in his mild and magnificent eye,
Learned his great language, caught his clear accents,
    Made him our pattern to live and to die!
Shakespeare was of us, Milton was for us,
    Burns, Shelley, were with us,—they watch from their graves!
He alone breaks from the van and the freemen,
    —He alone sinks to the rear and the slaves!

We shall march prospering,—not through his presence;
    Songs may inspirit us,—not from his lyre;
Deeds will be done,—while he boasts his quiescence,
    Still bidding crouch whom the rest bade aspire:

Blot out his name, then, record one lost soul more,
    One task more declined, one more foot-path untrod,
One more devils'-triumph and sorrow for angels,
    One wrong more to man, one more insult to God!
Life's night begins: let him never come back to us!
    There would be doubt, hesitation, and pain,
Forced praise on our part—the glimmer of twilight,
    Never glad confident morning again!
Best fight on well, for we taught him—strike gallantly,
    Menace our heart ere we master his own;
Then let him receive the new knowledge and wait us
    Pardoned in heaven, the first by the throne!

The Confessional
(SPAIN)

It is a lie—their Priests, their Pope,
    Their Saints, their . . . all they fear or hope
Are lies, and lies—there! through my door
And ceiling, there! and walls and floor,
There, lies, they lie—shall still be hurled
Till spite of them I reach the world!

You think Priests just and holy men!
Before they put me in this den
I was a human creature too,
With flesh and blood like one of you,
A girl that laughed in beauty's pride
Like lilies in your world outside.

I had a lover—shame avaunt!
This poor wrenched body, grim and gaunt,
Was kissed all over till it burned,
By lips the truest, love e'er turned
His heart's own tint: one night they kissed
My soul out in a burning mist.

So, next day when the accustomed train
Of things grew round my sense again,
"That is a sin," I said: and slow

With downcast eyes to church I go,
And pass to the confession-chair,
And tell the old mild father there.

But when I falter Beltran's name,
"Ha?" quoth the father; "much I blame
The sin; yet wherefore idly grieve?
Despair not—strenuously retrieve!
Nay I will turn this love of thine
To lawful love, almost divine;

"For he is young, and led astray,
This Beltran, and he schemes, men say,
To change the laws of church and state;
So, thine shall be an angel's fate,
Who, ere the thunder breaks, should roll
Its cloud away and save his soul.

"For, when he lies upon thy breast,
Thou mayst demand and be possessed
Of all his plans, and next day steal
To me, and all those plans reveal,
That I and every priest, to purge
His soul, may fast and use the scourge."

That father's beard was long and white,
With love and truth his brow seemed bright;
I went back, all on fire with joy,
And, that same evening, bade the boy
Tell me, as lovers should, heart-free,
Something to prove his love of me.

He told me what he would not tell
For hope of heaven or fear of hell;
And I lay listening in such pride!
And, soon as he had left my side,
Tripped to the church by morning-light
To save his soul in his despite.

I told the father all his schemes,
Who were his comrades, what their dreams;
"And now make haste," I said, "to pray
The one spot from his soul away;
To-night he comes, but not the same
Will look!" At night he never came.

Nor next night; and the after-morn,
I went forth with a strength new-born.
The church was empty; something drew
My steps into the street; I knew
It led me to the market-place:
Where, lo, on high, the father's face!

That horrible black scaffold dressed,
That stapled block . . . God sink the rest!
That head strapped back, that blinding vest,
Those knotted hands and naked breast,
Till near one busy hangman pressed,
And, on the neck these arms caressed . . .

No part in aught they hope or fear!
No heaven with them, no hell!—and here,
No earth, not so much space as pens
My body in their worst of dens
But shall bear God and man my cry,
Lies—lies, again—and still, they lie!

Meeting at Night

The grey sea and the long black land;
And the yellow half-moon large and low;
And the startled little waves that leap
In fiery ringlets from their sleep,
As I gain the cove with pushing prow,
And quench its speed i' the slushy sand.

Then a mile of warm sea-scented beach;
Three fields to cross till a farm appears;
A tap at the pane, the quick sharp scratch

And blue spurt of a lighted match,
And a voice less loud, through its joys and fears,
Than the two hearts beating each to each!

A Woman's Last Word

Let's contend no more, Love,
  Strive nor weep:
All be as before, Love,
  —Only sleep!

What so wild as words are?
  I and thou
In debate, as birds are,
  Hawk on bough!

See the creature stalking
  While we speak!
Hush and hide the talking,
  Cheek on cheek!

What so false as truth is,
  False to thee?
Where the serpent's tooth is
  Shun the tree—

Where the apple reddens
  Never pry—
Lest we lose our Edens,
  Eve and I.

Be a god and hold me
  With a charm!
Be a man and fold me
  With thine arm!

Teach me, only teach, Love!
  As I ought
I will speak thy speech, Love,
  Think thy thought—

Meet, if thou require it,
    Both demands,
Laying flesh and spirit
    In thy hands.

That shall be to-morrow
    Not to-night:
I must bury sorrow
    Out of sight:

—Must a little weep, Love,
    (Foolish me!)
And so fall asleep, Love,
    Loved by thee.

Respectability

Dear, had the world in its caprice
    Deigned to proclaim "I know you both,
    Have recognised your plighted troth,
Am sponsor for you: live in peace."
How many precious months and years
    Of youth had passed, that sped so fast,
    Before we found it out at last,
The world, and what it fears?

How much of priceless life were spent
    With men that every virtue decks,
    And women models of their sex,
Society's true ornament,—
Ere we dared wander, nights like this,
    Through wind and rain, and watch the Seine,
    And feel the Boulevart break again
To warmth and light and bliss?

I know! the world proscribes not love;
    Allows my finger to caress
    Your lips' contour and downiness,
Provided it supply a glove.

The world's good word!—the Institute!
　Guizot receives Montalembert!
　　Eh? Down the court three lampions flare:
Put forward your best foot!

Women and Roses

I dream of a rose-red tree.
And which of its roses three
Is the dearest rose to me?

Round and round, like a dance of snow
In a dazzling drift, as its guardians, go
Floating the women faded for ages,
Sculptured in stone, on the poet's pages.
Then follow women fresh and gay,
Living and loving and loved to-day.
Last, in the rear, flee the multitude of maidens,
Beauties yet unborn. And all, to one cadence,
They circle their rose on my rose tree.

Dear rose, thy term is reached,
Thy leaf hangs loose and bleached:
Bees pass it unimpeached.

Stay then, stoop, since I cannot climb,
You, great shapes of the antique time!
How shall I fix you, fire you, freeze you,
Break my heart at your feet to please you?
Oh, to possess and be possessed!
Hearts that beat 'neath each pallid breast!
Once but of love, the poesy, the passion,
Drink but once and die!—In vain, the same fashion,
They circle their rose on my rose tree.

Dear rose, thy joy's undimmed,
Thy cup is ruby-rimmed,
Thy cup's heart nectar-brimmed.

Deep, as drops from a statue's plinth
The bee sucked in by the hyacinth,
So will I bury me while burning,
Quench like him at a plunge my yearning,
Eyes in your eyes, lips on your lips!
Fold me fast where the cincture slips,
Prison all my soul in eternities of pleasure,
Girdle me for once! But no—the old measure,
They circle their rose on my rose tree.

Dear rose without a thorn,
Thy bud's the babe unborn:
First streak of a new morn.

Wings, lend wings for the cold, the clear!
What is far conquers what is near.
Roses will bloom nor want beholders,
Sprung from the dust where our flesh moulders.
What shall arrive with the cycle's change?
A novel grace and a beauty strange.
I will make an Eve, be the artist that began her,
Shaped her to his mind!—Alas! in like manner
They circle their rose on my rose tree.

FROM *In a Gondola*

He sings

I send my heart up to thee, all my heart
  In this my singing.
For the stars help me, and the sea bears part;
  The very night is clinging
Closer to Venice' streets to leave one space
  Above me, whence thy face
May light my joyous heart to thee its dwelling-place.

She speaks

Say after me, and try to say
My very words, as if each word
Came from you of your own accord,

In your own voice, in your own way:
"This woman's heart and soul and brain
Are mine as much as this gold chain
She bids me wear; which" (say again)
"I choose to make by cherishing
A precious thing, or choose to fling
Over the boat-side, ring by ring."
And yet once more say . . . no word more!
Since words are only words. Give o'er!

Unless you call me, all the same,
Familiarly by my pet name,
Which if the Three should hear you call,
And me reply to, would proclaim
At once our secret to them all.
Ask of me, too, command me, blame—
Do, break down the partition-wall
'Twixt us, the daylight world beholds
Curtained in dusk and splendid folds!
What's left but—all of me to take?
I am the Three's: prevent them, slake
Your thirst! 'Tis said, the Arab sage,
In practising with gems, can loose
Their subtle spirit in his cruce
And leave but ashes: so, sweet mage,
Leave them my ashes when thy use
Sucks out my soul, thy heritage!

He sings

Past we glide, and past and past!
    What's that poor Agnese doing
Where they make the shutters fast?
    Grey Zanobi's just a-wooing
To his couch the purchased bride:
    Past we glide!

Past we glide, and past, and past!
    Why's the Pucci Palace flaring
Like a beacon to the blast?
    Guests by hundreds, not one caring
If the dear host's neck were wried:
    Past we glide!

She sings

The moth's kiss, first!
Kiss me as if you made believe
You were not sure, this eve,
How my face, your flower, had pursed
Its petals up; so, here and there
You brush it, till I grow aware
Who wants me, and wide ope I burst.

The bee's kiss, now!
Kiss me as if you entered gay
My heart at some noonday,
A bud that dares not disallow
The claim, so all is rendered up,
And passively its shattered cup
Over your head to sleep I bow.

He muses

Oh, which were best, to roam or rest?
The land's lap or the water's breast?
To sleep on yellow millet-sheaves,
Or swim in lucid shallows just
Eluding water-lily leaves,
An inch from Death's black fingers, thrust
To lock you, whom release he must;
Which life were best on Summer eves?

Still he muses

What if the Three should catch at last
Thy serenader? While there's cast
Paul's cloak about my head, and fast
Gian pinions me, Himself has past
His stylet through my back; I reel;
And . . . is it thou I feel?

They trail me, these three godless knaves,
Past every church that sains and saves,
Nor stop till, where the cold sea raves
By Lido's wet accursed graves,
They scoop mine, roll me to its brink,
And . . . on thy breast I sink!

She speaks

To-morrow, if a harp-string, say,
Is used to tie the jasmine back
That overfloods my room with sweets,
Contrive your Zorzi somehow meets
My Zanze! If the ribbon's black,
The Three are watching: keep away!

Your gondola—let Zorzi wreathe
A mesh of water-weeds about
Its prow, as if he unaware
Had struck some quay or bridge-foot stair!
That I may throw a paper out
As you and he go underneath.

There's Zanze's vigilant taper; safe are we.
Only one minute more to-night with me?
Resume your past self of a month ago!
Be you the bashful gallant, I will be
The lady with the colder breast than snow.
Now bow you, as becomes, nor touch my hand
More than I touch yours when I step to land,
And say, "All thanks, Siora!"—
                                   Heart to heart
And lips to lips! Yet once more, ere we part,
Clasp me and make me thine, as mine thou art!

He is surprised, and stabbed

It was ordained to be so, sweet!—and best
Comes now, beneath thine eyes, upon thy breast.
Still kiss me! Care not for the cowards! Care
Only to put aside thy beauteous hair
My blood will hurt! The Three, I do not scorn
To death, because they never lived: but I
Have lived indeed, and so—(yet one more kiss)—can die!

The Bishop Orders His Tomb
at Saint Praxed's Church

(ROME, 15—)

Vanity, saith the preacher, vanity!
Draw round my bed: is Anselm keeping back?
Nephews—sons mine . . . ah God, I know not! Well—
She, men would have to be your mother once,
Old Gandolf envied me, so fair she was!
What's done is done, and she is dead beside,
Dead long ago, and I am Bishop since,
And as she died so must we die ourselves,
And thence ye may perceive the world's a dream.
Life, how and what is it? As here I lie
In this state-chamber, dying by degrees,
Hours and long hours in the dead night, I ask
"Do I live, am I dead?" Peace, peace seems all.
Saint Praxed's ever was the church for peace;
And so, about this tomb of mine. I fought
With tooth and nail to save my niche, ye know:
—Old Gandolf cozened me, despite my care;
Shrewd was the snatch from out the corner South
He graced his carrion with, God curse the same!
Yet still my niche is not so cramped but thence
One sees the pulpit o' the epistle-side,
And somewhat of the choir, those silent seats,
And up into the aery dome where live
The angels, and a sunbeam's sure to lurk:
And I shall fill my slab of basalt there,
And 'neath my tabernacle take my rest,
With those nine columns round me, two and two,
The odd one at my feet where Anselm stands:
Peach-blossom marble all, the rare, the ripe
As fresh-poured red wine of a mighty pulse.
—Old Gandolf with his paltry onion-stone,
Put me where I may look at him! True peach,
Rosy and flawless: how I earned the prize!
Draw close: that conflagration of my church
—What then? So much was saved if aught were missed!
My sons, ye would not be my death? Go dig

The white-grape vineyard where the oil-press stood,
Drop water gently till the surface sink,
And if ye find . . . Ah God, I know not, I! . . .
Bedded in store of rotten fig-leaves soft,
And corded up in a tight olive-frail,
Some lump, ah God, of *lapis lazuli*,
Big as a Jew's head cut off at the nape,
Blue as a vein o'er the Madonna's breast . . .
Sons, all have I bequeathed you, villas, all,
That brave Frascati villa with its bath,
So, let the blue lump poise between my knees,
Like God the Father's globe on both his hands
Ye worship in the Jesu Church so gay,
For Gandolf shall not choose but see and burst!
Swift as a weaver's shuttle fleet our years:
Man goeth to the grave, and where is he?
Did I say basalt for my slab, sons? Black—
'Twas ever antique-black I meant! How else
Shall ye contrast my frieze to come beneath?
The bas-relief in bronze ye promised me,
Those Pans and Nymphs ye wot of, and perchance
Some tripod, thyrsus, with a vase or so,
The Saviour at his sermon on the mount,
Saint Praxed in a glory, and one Pan
Ready to twitch the Nymph's last garment off,
And Moses with the tables . . . but I know
Ye mark me not! What do they whisper thee,
Child of my bowels, Anselm? Ah, ye hope
To revel down my villas while I gasp
Bricked o'er with beggar's mouldy travertine
Which Gandolf from his tomb-top chuckles at!
Nay, boys, ye love me—all of jasper, then!
'Tis jasper ye stand pledged to, lest I grieve.
My bath must needs be left behind, alas!
One block, pure green as a pistachio-nut,
There's plenty jasper somewhere in the world—
And have I not Saint Praxed's ear to pray
Horses for ye, and brown Greek manuscripts,
And mistresses with great smooth marbly limbs?
—That's if ye carve my epitaph aright,
Choice Latin, picked phrase, Tully's every word,

No gaudy ware like Gandolf's second line—
Tully, my masters? Ulpian serves his need!
And then how I shall lie through centuries,
And hear the blessed mutter of the mass,
And see God made and eaten all day long,
And feel the steady candle-flame, and taste
Good strong thick stupefying incense-smoke!
For as I lie here, hours of the dead night,
Dying in state and by such slow degrees,
I fold my arms as if they clasped a crook,
And stretch my feet forth straight as stone can point,
And let the bedclothes, for a mortcloth, drop
Into great laps and folds of sculptor's-work:
And as yon tapers dwindle, and strange thoughts
Grow, with a certain humming in my ears,
About the life before I lived this life,
And this life too, popes, cardinals, and priests,
Saint Praxed at his sermon on the mount,
Your tall pale mother with her talking eyes,
And new-found agate urns as fresh as day,
And marble's language, Latin pure, discreet,
—Aha, ELUCESCEBAT quoth our friend?
No Tully, said I, Ulpian at the best!
Evil and brief hath been my pilgrimage.
All *lapis*, all, sons! Else I give the Pope
My villas! Will ye ever eat my heart?
Ever your eyes were as a lizard's quick,
They glitter like your mother's for my soul,
Or ye would heighten my impoverished frieze,
Piece out its starved design, and fill my vase
With grapes, and add a vizor and a Term,
And to the tripod ye would tie a lynx
That in his struggle throws the thyrsus down,
Whereon I am to lie till I must ask
"Do I live, am I dead?" There, leave me, there!
For ye have stabbed me with ingratitude
To death—ye wish it—God, ye wish it! Stone—
Gritstone, a-crumble! Clammy squares which sweat
As if the corpse they keep were oozing through—
And no more *lapis* to delight the world!
Well, go! I bless ye. Fewer tapers there,

But in a row: and, going, turn your backs
—Ay, like departing altar-ministrants,
And leave me in my church, the church for peace,
That I may watch at leisure if he leers—
Old Gandolf, at me, from his onion-stone,
As still he envied me, so fair she was!

Fra Lippo Lippi

I am poor brother Lippo, by your leave!
You need not clap your torches to my face.
Zooks, what's to blame? you think you see a monk!
What, 'tis past midnight, and you go the rounds,
And here you catch me at an alley's end
Where sportive ladies leave their doors ajar?
The Carmine's my cloister: hunt it up,
Do,—harry out, if you must show your zeal,
Whatever rat, there, haps on his wrong hole,
And nip each softling of a wee white mouse,
Weke, weke, that's crept to keep him company!
Aha, you know your betters? Then, you'll take
Your hand away that's fiddling on my throat,
And please to know me likewise. Who am I?
Why, one, sir, who is lodging with a friend
Three streets off—he's a certain . . . how d'ye call?
Master—a . . . Cosimo of the Medici,
In the house that caps the corner. Boh! you were best!
Remember and tell me, the day you're hanged,
How you affected such a gullet's-gripe!
But you, sir, it concerns you that your knaves
Pick up a manner nor discredit you:
Zooks, are we pilchards, that they sweep the streets
And count fair prize what comes into their net?
He's Judas to a tittle, that man is!
Just such a face! Why, sir, you make amends.
Lord, I'm not angry! Bid your hangdogs go
Drink out this quarter-florin to the health
Of the munificent House that harbours me
(And many more beside, lads! more beside!)

And all's come square again. I'd like his face—
His, elbowing on his comrade in the door
With the pike and lantern,—for the slave that holds
John Baptist's head a-dangle by the hair
With one hand ("look you, now," as who should say)
And his weapon in the other, yet unwiped!
It's not your chance to have a bit of chalk,
A wood-coal or the like? or you should see!
Yes, I'm the painter, since you style me so.
What, brother Lippo's doings, up and down,
You know them and they take you? like enough!
I saw the proper twinkle in your eye—
'Tell you, I liked your looks at very first.
Let's sit and set things straight now, hip to haunch.
Here's spring come, and the nights one makes up bands
To roam the town and sing out carnival,
And I've been three weeks shut within my mew,
A-painting for the great man, saints and saints
And saints again. I could not paint all night—
Ouf! I leaned out of window for fresh air.
There came a hurry of feet and little feet,
A sweep of lute-strings, laughs, and whiffs of song,—
Flower o' the broom,
Take away love, and our earth is a tomb!
Flower o' the quince,
I let Lisa go, and what good's in life since?
Flower o' the thyme—and so on. Round they went.
Scarce had they turned the corner when a titter
Like the skipping of rabbits by moonlight,—three slim shapes—
And a face that looked up . . . zooks, sir, flesh and blood,
That's all I'm made of! Into shreds it went,
Curtain and counterpane and coverlet,
All the bed-furniture—a dozen knots,
There was a ladder! down I let myself,
Hands and feet, scrambling somehow, and so dropped,
And after them. I came up with the fun
Hard by Saint Laurence, hail fellow, well met,—
Flower o' the rose,
If I've been merry, what matter who knows?
And so as I was stealing back again
To get to bed and have a bit of sleep

Ere I rise up to-morrow and go work
On Jerome knocking at his poor old breast
With his great round stone to subdue the flesh,
You snap me of the sudden. Ah, I see!
Though your eye twinkles still, you shake your head—
Mine's shaved,—a monk, you say—the sting's in that!
If Master Cosimo announced himself,
Mum's the word naturally; but a monk!
Come, what am I a beast for? tell us, now!
I was a baby when my mother died
And father died and left me in the street.
I starved there, God knows how, a year or two
On fig skins, melon-parings, rinds and shucks,
Refuse and rubbish. One fine frosty day,
My stomach being empty as your hat,
The wind doubled me up and down I went.
Old Aunt Lapaccia trussed me with one hand,
(Its fellow was a stinger as I knew)
And so along the wall, over the bridge,
By the straight cut to the convent. Six words, there,
While I stood munching my first bread that month:
"So, boy, you're minded," quoth the good fat father
Wiping his own mouth, 'twas refection-time,—
"To quit this very miserable world?
Will you renounce" . . . The mouthful of bread? thought I;
By no means! Brief, they made a monk of me;
I did renounce the world, its pride and greed,
Palace, farm, villa, shop, and banking-house,
Trash, such as these poor devils of Medici
Have given their hearts to—all at eight years old.
Well, sir, I found in time, you may be sure,
'Twas not for nothing—the good bellyful,
The warm serge and the rope that goes all round,
And day-long blessed idleness beside!
"Let's see what the urchin's fit for"—that came next.
Not overmuch their way, I must confess.
Such a to-do! They tried me with their books.
Lord, they'd have taught me Latin in pure waste!
Flower o' the clove,
All the Latin I construe is, "amo" I love!

But, mind you, when a boy starves in the streets
Eight years together, as my fortune was,
Watching folk's faces to know who will fling
The bit of half-stripped grape-bunch he desires,
And who will curse or kick him for his pains—
Which gentleman processional and fine,
Holding a candle to the Sacrament,
Will wink and let him lift a plate and catch
The droppings of the wax to sell again,
Or holla for the Eight and have him whipped,—
How say I?—nay, which dog bites, which lets drop
His bone from the heap of offal in the street,—
Why, soul and sense of him grow sharp alike,
He learns the look of things, and none the less
For admonition from the hunger-pinch.
I had a store of such remarks, be sure,
Which, after I found leisure, turned to use.
I drew men's faces on my copy-books,
Scrawled them within the antiphonary's marge,
Joined legs and arms to the long music-notes,
Found nose and eyes and chin for A's and B's,
And made a string of pictures of the world
Betwixt the ins and outs of verb and noun,
On the wall, the bench, the door. The monks looked black.
"Nay," quoth the Prior, "turn him out, d'ye say?
In no wise. Lose a crow and catch a lark.
What if at last we get our man of parts,
We Carmelites, like those Camaldolese
And Preaching Friars, to do our church up fine
And put the front on it that ought to be!"
And hereupon he bade me daub away.
Thank you! my head being crammed, their walls a blank,
Never was such prompt disemburdening.
First, every sort of monk, the black and white,
I drew them, fat and lean: then, folks at church,
From good old gossips waiting to confess
Their cribs of barrel-droppings, candle-ends,—
To the breathless fellow at the altar-foot,
Fresh from his murder, safe and sitting there
With the little children round him in a row

Of admiration, half for his beard and half
For that white anger of his victim's son
Shaking a fist at him with one fierce arm,
Signing himself with the other because of Christ
(Whose sad face on the cross sees only this
After the passion of a thousand years)
Till some poor girl, her apron o'er her head
Which the intense eyes looked through, came at eve
On tip-toe, said a word, dropped in a loaf,
Her pair of earrings and a bunch of flowers
The brute took growling, prayed, and then was gone.
I painted all, then cried " 'tis ask and have—
Choose, for more's ready!"—laid the ladder flat,
And showed my covered bit of cloister-wall.
The monks closed in a circle and praised loud
Till checked,—taught what to see and not to see,
Being simple bodies,—"that's the very man!
Look at the boy who stoops to pat the dog!
That woman's like the Prior's niece who comes
To care about his asthma: it's the life!"
But there my triumph's straw-fire flared and funked—
Their betters took their turn to see and say:
The Prior and the learned pulled a face
And stopped all that in no time. "How? what's here?
Quite from the mark of painting, bless us all!
Faces, arms, legs and bodies like the true
As much as pea and pea! it's devil's-game!
Your business is not to catch men with show,
With homage to the perishable clay,
But lift them over it, ignore it all,
Make them forget there's such a thing as flesh.
Your business is to paint the souls of men—
Man's soul, and it's a fire, smoke . . . no it's not . .
It's vapour done up like a new-born babe—
(In that shape when you die it leaves your mouth)
It's . . . well, what matters talking, it's the soul!
Give us no more of body than shows soul!
Here's Giotto, with his Saint a-praising God,
That sets us praising,—why not stop with him?
Why put all thoughts of praise out of our heads
With wonder at lines, colours, and what not?

Paint the soul, never mind the legs and arms!
Rub all out, try at it a second time.
Oh, that white smallish female with the breasts,
She's just my niece . . . Herodias, I would say,—
Who went and danced and got men's heads cut off—
Have it all out!" Now, is this sense, I ask?
A fine way to paint soul, by painting body
So ill, the eye can't stop there, must go further
And can't fare worse! Thus, yellow does for white
When what you put for yellow's simply black,
And any sort of meaning looks intense
When all beside itself means and looks nought.
Why can't a painter lift each foot in turn,
Left foot and right foot, go a double step,
Make his flesh liker and his soul more like,
Both in their order? Take the prettiest face,
The Prior's niece . . . patron-saint—is it so pretty
You can't discover if it means hope, fear,
Sorrow or joy? won't beauty go with these?
Suppose I've made her eyes all right and blue,
Can't I take breath and try to add life's flash,
And then add soul and heighten them threefold?
Or say there's beauty with no soul at all—
(I never saw it—put the case the same—)
If you get simple beauty and nought else,
You get about the best thing God invents,—
That's somewhat. And you'll find the soul you have missed,
Within yourself, when you return Him thanks.
"Rub all out!" Well, well, there's my life, in short,
And so the thing has gone on ever since.
I've grown a man no doubt, I've broken bounds—
You should not take a fellow eight years old
And make him swear to never kiss the girls.
I'm my own master, paint now as I please—
Having a friend, you see, in the Corner-house!
Lord, it's fast holding by the rings in front—
Those great rings serve more purposes than just
To plant a flag in, or tie up a horse!
And yet the old schooling sticks, the old grave eyes
Are peeping o'er my shoulder as I work,
The heads shake still—"It's Art's decline, my son!

You're not of the true painters, great and old;
Brother Angelico's the man, you'll find;
Brother Lorenzo stands his single peer:
Fag on at flesh, you'll never make the third!"
Flower o' the pine,
You keep your mistr . . . manners, and I'll stick to mine!
I'm not the third, then: bless us, they must know!
Don't you think they're the likeliest to know,
They with their Latin? so, I swallow my rage,
Clench my teeth, suck my lips in tight, and paint
To please them—sometimes do and sometimes don't,
For, doing most, there's pretty sure to come
A turn, some warm eve finds me at my saints—
A laugh, a cry, the business of the world—
(*Flower o' the peach,*
Death for us all, and his own life for each!)
And my whole soul revolves, the cup runs over,
The world and life's too big to pass for a dream,
And I do these wild things in sheer despite,
And play the fooleries you catch me at,
In pure rage! The old mill-horse, out at grass
After hard years, throws up his stiff heels so,
Although the miller does not preach to him
The only good of grass is to make chaff.
What would men have? Do they like grass or no—
May they or mayn't they? all I want's the thing
Settled for ever one way: as it is,
You tell too many lies and hurt yourself.
You don't like what you only like too much,
You do like what, if given you at your word,
You find abundantly detestable.
For me, I think I speak as I was taught—
I always see the Garden and God there
A-making man's wife—and, my lesson learned,
The value and significance of flesh,
I can't unlearn ten minutes afterwards.

You understand me: I'm a beast, I know.
But see, now—why, I see as certainly
As that the morning-star's about to shine,
What will hap some day. We've a youngster here

Comes to our convent, studies what I do,
Slouches and stares and lets no atom drop—
His name is Guidi—he'll not mind the monks—
They call him Hulking Tom, he lets them talk—
He picks my practice up—he'll paint apace,
I hope so—though I never live so long,
I know what's sure to follow. You be judge!
You speak no Latin more than I, belike—
However, you're my man, you've seen the world
—The beauty and the wonder and the power,
The shapes of things, their colours, lights and shades,
Changes, surprises,—and God made it all!
—For what? Do you feel thankful, ay or no,
For this fair town's face, yonder river's line,
The mountain round it and the sky above,
Much more the figures of man, woman, child,
These are the frame to? What's it all about?
To be passed over, despised? or dwelt upon,
Wondered at? oh, this last of course!—you say.
But why not do as well as say,—paint these
Just as they are, careless what comes of it?
God's works—paint anyone, and count it crime
To let a truth slip. Don't object, "His works
Are here already—nature is complete:
Suppose you reproduce her—(which you can't)
There's no advantage! you must beat her, then."
For, don't you mark? we're made so that we love
First when we see them painted, things we have passed
Perhaps a hundred times nor cared to see;
And so they are better, painted—better to us,
Which is the same thing. Art was given for that—
God uses us to help each other so,
Lending our minds out. Have you noticed, now,
Yon cullion's hanging face? A bit of chalk,
And trust me but you should, though! How much more,
If I drew higher things with the same truth!
That were to take the Prior's pulpit-place,
Interpret God to all of you! oh, oh,
It makes me mad to see what men shall do
And we in our graves! This world's no blot for us,
Nor blank—it means intensely, and means good:

To find its meaning is my meat and drink.
"Ay, but you don't so instigate to prayer!"
Strikes in the Prior: "when your meaning's plain
It does not say to folk—remember matins,
Or, mind you fast next Friday!" Why, for this
What need of art at all? A skull and bones,
Two bits of stick nailed cross-wise, or, what's best,
A bell to chime the hour with, does as well.
I painted a Saint Laurence six months since
At Prato, splashed the fresco in fine style:
"How looks my painting, now the scaffold's down?"
I ask a brother: "Hugely," he returns—
"Already not one phiz of your three slaves
Who turn the Deacon off his toasted side,
But's scratched and prodded to our heart's content,
The pious people have so eased their own
When coming to say prayers there in a rage:
We get on fast to see the bricks beneath.
Expect another job this time next year,
For pity and religion grow i' the crowd—
Your painting serves its purpose!" Hang the fools!

—That is—you'll not mistake an idle word
Spoke in a huff by a poor monk, God wot,
Tasting the air in this spicy night which turns
The unaccustomed head like Chianti wine!
Oh, the church knows! don't misreport me, now!
It's natural a poor monk out of bounds
Should have his apt word to excuse himself:
And hearken how I plot to make amends.
I have bethought me: I shall paint a piece
. . . There's for you! Give me six months, then go, see
Something in Sant' Ambrogio's! Bless the nuns!
They want a cast of my office. I shall paint
God in the midst, Madonna and her babe,
Ringed by a bowery, flowery angel-brood,
Lilies and vestments and white faces, sweet
As puff on puff of grated orris-root
When ladies crowd to church at midsummer.

And then in the front, of course a saint or two—
Saint John, because he saves the Florentines,
Saint Ambrose, who puts down in black and white
The convent's friends and gives them a long day,
And Job, I must have him there past mistake,
The man of Uz, (and Us without the z,
Painters who need his patience.) Well, all these
Secured at their devotions, up shall come
Out of a corner when you least expect,
As one by a dark stair into a great light,
Music and talking, who but Lippo! I!—
Mazed, motionless and moonstruck—I'm the man!
Back I shrink—what is this I see and hear?
I, caught up with my monk's things by mistake,
My old serge gown and rope that goes all round,
I, in this presence, this pure company!
Where's a hole, where's a corner for escape?
Then steps a sweet angelic slip of a thing
Forward, puts out a soft palm—"Not so fast!"
—Addresses the celestial presence, "nay—
He made you and devised you, after all,
Though he's none of you! Could Saint John there, draw—
His camel-hair make up a painting-brush?
We come to brother Lippo for all that,
Iste perfecit opus!" So, all smile—
I shuttle sideways with my blushing face
Under the cover of a hundred wings
Thrown like a spread of kirtles when you're gay
And play hot cockles, all the doors being shut,
Till, wholly unexpected, in there pops
The hothead husband! Thus I scuttle off
To some safe bench behind, not letting go
The palm of her, the little lily thing
That spoke the good word for me in the nick,
Like the Prior's niece . . . Saint Lucy, I would say.
And so all's saved for me, and for the church
A pretty picture gained. Go, six months hence!
Your hand, sir, and good-bye: no lights, no lights!
The street's hushed, and I know my own way back,
Don't fear me! There's the grey beginning. Zooks!

Song

Nay but you, who do not love her,
 Is she not pure gold, my mistress?
Holds earth aught—speak truth—above her?
 Aught like this tress, see, and this tress,
And this last fairest tress of all,
So fair, see, ere I let it fall?

Because, you spend your lives in praising;
 To praise, you search the wide world over:
Then why not witness, calmly gazing,
 If earth holds aught—speak truth—above her?
Above this tress, and this, I touch
But cannot praise, I love so much!

Confessions

What is he buzzing in my ears?
 "Now that I come to die,
Do I view the world as a vale of tears?"
 Ah, reverend sir, not I!

What I viewed there once, what I view again
 Where the physic bottles stand
On the table's edge,—is a suburb lane,
 With a wall to my bedside hand.

That lane sloped, much as the bottles do,
 From a house you could descry
O'er the garden-wall: is the curtain blue
 Or green to a healthy eye?

To mine, it serves for the old June weather
 Blue above lane and wall;
And that farthest bottle labelled "Ether"
 Is the house o'ertopping all.

At a terrace, somewhere near the stopper,
    There watched for me, one June,
A girl; I know, sir, it's improper,
    My poor mind's out of tune.

Only, there was a way . . . you crept
    Close by the side, to dodge
Eyes in the house, two eyes except:
    They styled their house "The Lodge".

What right had a lounger up their lane?
    But, by creeping very close,
With the good wall's help—their eyes might strain
    And stretch themselves to Oes,

Yet never catch her and me together,
    As she left the attic, there,
By the rim of the bottle labelled "Ether",
    And stole from stair to stair,

And stood by the rose-wreathed gate. Alas,
    We loved, sir—used to meet:
How sad and bad and mad it was—
    But then, how it was sweet!

Youth and Art

It once might have been, once only:
    We lodged in a street together,
You, a sparrow on the housetop lonely,
    I, a lone she-bird of his feather.

Your trade was with sticks and clay,
    You thumbed, thrust, patted and polished,
Then laughed "They will see some day
    "Smith made, and Gibson demolished."

My business was song, song, song;
    I chirped, cheeped, trilled and twittered,
"Kate Brown's on the boards ere long,
    And Grisi's existence embittered!"

I earned no more by a warble
    That you by a sketch in plaster;
You wanted a piece of marble,
    I needed a music-master.

We studied hard in our styles,
    Chipped each at a crust like Hindoos,
For air looked out on the tiles,
    For fun watched each other's windows.

You lounged, like a boy of the South,
    Cap and blouse—nay, a bit of a beard too;
Or you got it, rubbing your mouth
    With fingers the clay adhered to.

And I—soon managed to find
    Weak points in the flower-fence facing,
Was forced to put up a blind
    And be safe in my corset-lacing.

No harm! It was not my fault
    If you never turned your eye's tail up
As I shook upon E *in alt*,
    Or ran the chromatic scale up:

For spring bade the sparrows pair,
    And the boys and girls gave guesses,
And stalls in our street looked rare
    With bulrush and watercresses.

Why did not you pinch a flower
    In a pellet of clay and fling it?
Why did not I put a power
    Of thanks in a look, or sing it?

I did look, sharp as a lynx,
    (And yet the memory rankles)
When models arrived, some minx
    Tripped up-stairs, she and her ankles.

But I think I gave you as good!
 "That foreign fellow—who can know
How she pays, in a playful mood,
 For his tuning her that piano?"

Could you say so, and never say
 "Suppose we join hands and fortunes,
And I fetch her from over the way,
 Her, piano, and long tunes and short tunes?"

No, no: you would not be rash,
 Nor I rasher and something over:
You've to settle yet Gibson's hash,
 And Grisi yet lives in clover.

But you meet the Prince at the Board,
 I'm queen myself at *bals-paré*,
I've married a rich old lord,
 And you're dubbed knight and an R.A.

Each life's unfulfilled, you see;
 It hangs still, patchy and scrappy:
We have not sighed deep, laughed free,
 Starved, feasted, despaired—been happy.

And nobody calls you a dunce,
 And people suppose me clever:
This could have happened but once,
 And we missed it, lost it for ever.

FROM *One Word More*
(TO E.B.B.)

There they are, my fifty men and women
Naming me the fifty poems finished!
Take them, Love, the book and me together:
Where the heart lies, let the brain lie also.

Rafael made a century of sonnets,
Made and wrote them in a certain volume
Dinted with the silver-pointed pencil
Else he only used to draw Madonnas:
These, the world might view—but one, the volume.

Who that one, you ask? Your heart instructs you.
Did she live and love it all her life-time?
Did she drop, his lady of the sonnets,
Die, and let it drop beside her pillow
Where it lay in place of Rafael's glory,
Rafael's cheek so duteous and so loving—
Cheek, the world was wont to hail a painter's,
Rafael's cheek, her love had turned a poet's?

You and I would rather read that volume,
(Taken to his beating bosom by it)
Lean and list the bosom-beats of Rafael,
Would we not? than wonder at Madonnas—
Her, San Sisto names, and Her, Foligno,
Her, that visits Florence in a vision,
Her, that's left with lilies in the Louvre—
Seen by us and all the world in circle.

You and I will never read that volume.
Guido Reni, like his own eye's apple
Guarded long the treasure-book and loved it.
Guido Reni dying, all Bologna
Cried, and the world cried too, "Ours, the treasure!"
Suddenly, as rare things will, it vanished.

Dante once prepared to paint an angel:
Whom to please? You whisper "Beatrice."
While he mused and traced it and retraced it,
(Peradventure with a pen corroded
Still by drops of that hot ink he dipped for,
When, his left-hand i' the hair o' the wicked,
Back he held the brow and pricked its stigma,
Bit into the live man's flesh for parchment,
Loosed him, laughed to see the writing rankle,
Let the wretch go festering through Florence)—
Dante, who loved well because he hated,
Hated wickedness that hinders loving,
Dante standing, studying his angel—
In there broke the folk of his Inferno.
Says he—"Certain people of importance"

(Such he gave his daily dreadful line to)
"Entered and would seize, forsooth, the poet."
Says the poet—"Then I stopped my painting."

You and I would rather see that angel,
Painted by the tenderness of Dante,
Would we not?—than read a fresh Inferno.

You and I will never see that picture.
While he mused on love and Beatrice,
While he softened o'er his outlined angel,
In they broke, those "people of importance":
We and Bice bear the loss for ever.

What of Rafael's sonnets, Dante's picture?
This: no artist lives and loves, that longs not
Once, and only once, and for one only,
(Ah, the prize!) to find his love a language
Fit and fair and simple and sufficient—
Using nature that's an art to others,
Not, this one time, art that's turned his nature.
Ay, of all the artists living, loving,
None but would forego his proper dowry,—
Does he paint? he fain would write a poem,—
Does he write? he fain would paint a picture,
Put to proof art alien to the artist's,
Once, and only once, and for one only,
So to be the man and leave the artist,
Gain the man's joy, miss the artist's sorrow.

I shall never, in the years remaining,
Paint you pictures, no, nor carve you statues,
Make you music that should all-express me;
So it seems: I stand on my attainment.
This of verse alone, one life allows me;
Verse and nothing else have I to give you.
Other heights in other lives, God willing:
All the gifts from all the heights, your own, Love!

Yet a semblance of resource avails us—
Shade so finely touched, love's sense must seize it.
Take these lines, look lovingly and nearly,
Lines I write the first time and the last time.
He who works in fresco, steals a hair-brush,
Curbs the liberal hand, subservient proudly,
Cramps his spirit, crowds its all in little,
Makes a strange art of an art familiar,
Fills his lady's missal-marge with flowerets.
He who blows through bronze, may breathe through silver,
Fitly serenade a slumbrous princess.
He who writes, may write for once as I do.

Love, you saw me gather men and women,
Live or dead or fashioned by my fancy,
Enter each and all, and use their service,
Speak from every mouth,—the speech, a poem.
Hardly shall I tell my joys and sorrows,
Hopes and fears, belief and disbelieving:
I am mine and yours—the rest be all men's,
Karshish, Cleon, Norbert and the fifty.
Let me speak this once in my true person,
Not as Lippo, Roland or Andrea,
Though the fruit of speech be just this sentence:
Pray you, look on these my men and women,
Take and keep my fifty poems finished;
Where my heart lies, let my brain lie also!
Poor the speech; be how I speak, for all things.

Not but that you know me! Lo, the moon's self!
Here in London, yonder late in Florence,
Still we find her face, the thrice-transfigured.
Curving on a sky imbrued with colour,
Drifted over Fiesole by twilight,
Came she, our new crescent of a hair's-breadth.
Full she flared it, lamping Samminiato,
Rounder 'twixt the cypresses and rounder,
Perfect till the nightingales applauded.
Now, a piece of her old self, impoverished,
Hard to greet, she traverses the houseroofs,
Hurries with unhandsome thrift of silver,
Goes dispiritedly, glad to finish.

What, there's nothing in the moon noteworthy?
Nay: for if that moon could love a mortal,
Use, to charm him (so to fit a fancy),
All her magic ('tis the old sweet mythos),
She would turn a new side to her mortal,
Side unseen of herdsman, huntsman, steersman—
Blank to Zoroaster on his terrace,
Blind to Galileo on his turret,
Dumb to Homer, dumb to Keats—him, even!
Think, the wonder of the moonstruck mortal—
When she turns round, comes again in heaven,
Opens out anew for worse or better!
Proves she like some portent of an iceberg
Swimming full upon the ship it founders,
Hungry with huge teeth of splintered crystals?
Proves she as the paved work of a sapphire
Seen by Moses when he climbed the mountain?

What were seen? None knows, none ever shall know.
Only this is sure—the sight were other,
Not the moon's same side, born late in Florence,
Dying now impoverished here in London.
God be thanked, the meanest of his creatures
Boasts two soul-sides, one to face the world with,
One to show a woman when he loves her!

This I say of me, but think of you, Love!
This to you—yourself my moon of poets!
Ah, but that's the world's side, there's the wonder,
Thus they see you, praise you, think they know you!
There, in turn I stand with them and praise you—
Out of my own self, I dare to phrase it.
But the best is when I glide from out them,
Cross a step or two of dubious twilight,
Come out on the other side, the novel
Silent silver lights and darks undreamed of,
Where I hush and bless myself with silence.

Oh, their Rafael of the dear Madonnas,
Oh, their Dante of the dread Inferno,
Wrote one song—and in my brain I sing it,
Drew one angel—borne, see, on my bosom!

Epilogue

At the midnight in the silence of the sleep-time,
 When you set your fancies free,
Will they pass to where—by death, fools think, imprisoned
 Low he lies who once so loved you, whom you loved so,
  —Pity me?

Oh to love so, be so loved, yet so mistaken!
 What had I on earth to do
With the slothful, with the mawkish, the unmanly?
 Like the aimless, helpless, hopeless, did I drivel
  —Being—who?

One who never turned his back but marched breast forward,
 Never doubted clouds would break,
Never dreamed, though right were worsted, wrong would
   triumph,
 Held we fall to rise, are baffled to fight better,
  Sleep to wake.

No, at noonday in the bustle of man's work-time,
 Greet the unseen with a cheer!
Bid him forward, breast and back as either should be,
 "Strive and thrive!" cry "Speed,—fight on, fare ever
  There as here!"

CHARLOTTE BRONTË

(1816–1855)

On the Death of Anne Brontë

There's little joy in life for me,
 And little terror in the grave;
I've lived the parting hour to see
 Of one I would have died to save.

Calmly to watch the failing breath,
 Wishing each sigh might be the last;
Longing to see the shade of death
 O'er those belovéd features cast;

The cloud, the stillness that must part
  The darling of my life from me;
And then to thank God from my heart,
  To thank him well and fervently;

Although I knew that we had lost
  The hope and glory of our life;
And now, benighted, tempest-tossed,
  Must bear alone the weary strife.

HENRY DAVID THOREAU

(1817–1862)

"Low-Anchored Cloud"

Low-anchored cloud,
Newfoundland air,
Fountain-head and source of rivers,
Dew-cloth, dream drapery,
And napkin spread by fays;
Drifting meadow of the air,
Where bloom the daisied banks and violets,
And in whose fenny labyrinth
The bittern booms and heron wades;
Spirit of lakes and seas and rivers,
Bear only perfumes and the scent
Of healing herbs to just men's fields!

A Week on the Concord and Merrimack Rivers

"Woof of the Sun..."

Woof of the sun, ethereal gauze,
Woven of Nature's richest stuffs,
Visible heat, air-water, and dry sea,
Last conquest of the eye;
Toil of the day displayed, sun-dust,
Aerial surf upon the shores of earth,
Ethereal estuary, frith of light,

Breakers of air, billows of heat,
Fine summer spray on inland seas;
Bird of the sun, transparent-winged
Owlet of noon, soft-pinioned,
From heat or stubble rising without song;
Establish thy serenity o'er the fields.

A Week on the Concord and Merrimack Rivers

The Atlantides

The smothered streams of love, which flow
More bright than Phlegethon, more low,
Island us ever, like the sea,
In an Atlantic mystery.
Our fabled shores none ever reach,
No mariner has found our beach,
Surely our mirage now is seen,
And neighbouring waves with floating green,
Yet still the oldest charts contain
Some dotted outline of our main;
In ancient times midsummer days
Unto the western islands' gaze,
To Teneriffe and the Azores,
Have shown our faint and cloud-like shores.

But sink not yet, ye desolate isles,
Anon your coast with commerce smiles,
And richer freights ye'll furnish far
Than Africa or Malabar.
Be fair, be fertile evermore,
Ye rumored but untrodden shore,
Princes and monarchs will contend
Who first unto your land shall send,
And pawn the jewels of their crown
To call your distant soil their own.

A Week on the Concord and Merrimack Rivers

"All Things Are Current Found"

All things are current found
On earthly ground,
Spirits, and elements
Have their descents.

Night and day, year on year,
High and low, far and near,
These are our own aspects,
These are our own regrets.

Ye gods of the shore,
Who abide evermore,
I see your far headland,
Stretching on either hand;

I hear the sweet evening sounds
From your undecaying grounds;
Cheat me no more with time,
Take me to your clime.

A Week on the Concord and Merrimack Rivers

"Light-Winged Smoke..."

Light-winged Smoke, Icarian bird,
Melting thy pinions in thy upward flight,
Lark without song, and messenger of dawn,
Circling above the hamlets as thy nest;
Or else, departing dream, and shadowy form
Of midnight vision, gathering up thy skirts;
By night star-veiling, and by day
Darkening the light and blotting out the sun;
Go thou my incense upward from this hearth,
And ask the gods to pardon this clear flame.

Walden

EMILY JANE BRONTË

(1818–1848)

The Old Stoic

Riches I hold in light esteem,
    And love I laugh to scorn;
And lust of fame was but a dream,
    That vanished with the morn:

And if I pray, the only prayer
    That moves my lips for me
Is, "Leave the heart that now I bear,
    And give me liberty!"

Yes, as my swift days near their goal,
    'Tis all that I implore;—
In life and death a chainless soul,
    With courage to endure.

"Tell Me, Tell Me..."

Tell me, tell me, smiling child,
    What the past is like to thee?
"An autumn evening, soft and mild,
    With a wind that sighs mournfully."

Tell me, what is the present hour?
    "A green and flowery spray,
Where a young bird sits gathering its power
    To mount and fly away."

And what is the future, happy one?
    "A sea beneath a cloudless sun—
A mighty, glorious, dazzling sea,
    Stretching into infinity."

"The Sun Has Set..."

The sun has set, and the long grass now
  Waves dreamily in the evening wind;
And the wild bird has flown from that old grey stone
  In some warm nook a couch to find.

In all the lonely landscape round
I see no light and hear no sound,
Except the wind that far away
Comes sighing o'er the heathy sea.

"Sleep Brings No Joy..."

Sleep brings no joy to me,
  Remembrance never dies;
My soul is given to misery,
  And lives in sighs.

Sleep brings no rest to me;
  The shadows of the dead,
My wakening eyes may never see,
  Surround my bed.

Sleep brings no hope to me;
  In soundest sleep they come,
And with their doleful imagery
  Deepen the gloom.

Sleep brings no strength to me,
  No power renewed to brave:
I only sail a wilder sea,
  A darker wave.

Sleep brings no friend to me
  To soothe and aid to bear;
They all gaze on—how scornfully!
  And I despair.

Sleep brings no wish to fret
  My harassed heart beneath:
My only wish is to forget
  In endless sleep of death.

"A Little While, a Little While"

A little while, a little while,
  The noisy crowd are barred away;
And I can sing and smile—
  A little while I've holiday!

Where wilt thou go, my harassed heart?
  Full many a land invites thee now;
And places near, and far apart
  Have rest for thee, my weary brow—

There is a spot mid barren hills,
  Where winter howls and driving rain,
But if the dreary tempest chills,
  There is a light that warms again.

The house is old, the trees are bare,
  And moonless bends the misty dome,
But what on earth is half so dear—
  So longed for as the hearth of home?

The mute bird sitting on the stone,
  The dank moss dripping from the wall,
The garden-walk with weeds o'er grown,
  I love them—how I love them all!

Shall I go there? or shall I seek
  Another clime, another sky,
Where tongues familiar music speak
  In accents dear t' memory?

Yes, as I mused, the naked room,
  The flickering firelight died away,
And from the midst of cheerless gloom
  I passed to bright, unclouded day.

A little and a lone green lane,
   That opened on a common wide;
A distant, dreamy, dim blue chain
   Of mountains circling every side;

A heaven so clear, an earth so calm,
   So sweet, so soft, so hushed an air;
And, deepening still the dream-like charm,
   Wild moor-sheep feeding everywhere.

That was the scene—I knew it well;
   I knew the path-ways far and near,
That, winding o'er each billowy swell,
   Marked out the tracks of wandering deer.

Could I have lingered but an hour,
   It had well paid a week of toil;
But truth has banished fancy's power,
   I hear my dungeon bars recoil.

Even as I stood with raptured eye,
   Absorbed in bliss so deep and dear,
My hour of rest had fleeted by,
   And given me back to weary care.

FROM "I Am the Only Being..."

I am the only being whose doom
   No tongue would ask, no eye would mourn;
I've never caused a thought of gloom,
   A smile of joy, since I was born.

In secret pleasure, secret tears,
   This changeful life has slipped away,
As friendless after eighteen years,
   As lone as on my natal day.

"I Gazed Within..."

I gazed within thy earnest eyes,
    And read the sorrow brooding there;
I heard thy young breast torn with sighs,
    And envied such despair.

Go to the grave in youth's bare woel
That dream was written long ago.

At Castle Wood

The day is done, the winter sun
    Is setting in its sullen sky;
And drear the course that has been run,
    And dim the hearts that slowly die.

No star will light my coming night;
    No morn of hope for me will shine;
I mourn not heaven would blast my sight,
    And I ne'er longed for joys divine.

Through life's hard task I did not ask
    Celestial aid, celestial cheer:
I saw my fate without its mask,
    And met it too without a tear.

The grief that pressed my aching breast
    Was heavier far than earth can be;
And who would dread eternal rest
    When labour's hour was agony?

Dark falls the fear of this despair
    On spirits born of happiness;
But I was bred the mate of care,
    The foster-child of sore distress.

No sighs for me, no sympathy,
  No wish to keep my soul below;
The heart is dead in infancy,
  Unwept for let the body go.

"No Coward Soul..."

No coward soul is mine,
No trembler in the world's storm-troubled sphere:
  I see Heaven's glories shine,
And Faith shines equal, arming me from Fear.

O God within my breast,
Almighty, ever-present Deity!
  Life, that in me hast rest
As I, undying Life, have power in Thee!

Vain are the thousand creeds
That move men's hearts: unutterably vain;
  Worthless as withered weeds,
Or idlest froth amid the boundless main,

To waken doubt in one
Holding so fast by Thy infinity,
  So surely anchored on
The steadfast rock of Immortality.

With wide-embracing love
Thy Spirit animates eternal years,
  Pervades and broods above,
Changes, sustains, dissolves, creates, and rears.

Though earth and moon were gone,
And suns and universes ceased to be,
  And Thou wert left alone,
Every existence would exist in Thee.

There is not room for Death,
Nor atom that his might could render void:
  Since Thou art Being and Breath
And what Thou art may never be destroyed.

ARTHUR HUGH CLOUGH

(1819–1861)

The Latest Decalogue

Thou shalt have one God only; who
Would be at the expense of two?
No graven images may be
Worshipped, except the currency:
Swear not at all; for, for thy curse
Thine enemy is none the worse:
At church on Sunday to attend
Will serve to keep the world thy friend:
Honour thy parents; that is, all
From whom advancement may befall:
Thou shalt not kill; but needst not strive
Officiously to keep alive:
Do not adultery commit;
Advantage rarely comes of it:
Thou shalt not steal; an empty feat,
When it's so lucrative to cheat:
Bear not false witness; let the lie
Have time on its own wings to fly:
Thou shalt not covet; but tradition
Approves all forms of competition.
The sum of all is, thou shalt love,
If any body, God above:
At any rate shall never labour
More than thyself to love thy neighbour.

"Say Not the Struggle..."

Say not the struggle nought availeth,
  The labour and the wounds are vain,
The enemy faints not, nor faileth,
  And as things have been, things remain.

If hopes were dupes, fears may be liars;
  It may be, in yon smoke concealed,

Your comrades chase e'en now the fliers,
  And, but for you, possess the field.

For while the tired waves, vainly breaking,
  Seem here no painful inch to gain,
Far back, through creeks and inlets making,
  Comes silent, flooding in, the main.

And not by eastern windows only,
  When daylight comes, comes in the light,
In front, the sun climbs slow, how slowly,
  But westward, look, the land is bright.

WALT WHITMAN

(1819–1892)

FROM *Starting from Paumanok*

Starting from fish-shape Paumanok where I was born,
Well-begotten, and rais'd by a perfect mother,
After roaming many lands, lover of populous pavements,
Dweller in Mannahatta my city, or on southern savannas,
Or a soldier camp'd or carrying my knapsack and gun, or a
    miner in California,
Or rude in my home in Dakota's woods, my diet meat, my
    drink from the spring,
Or withdrawn to muse and meditate in some deep recess,
Far from the clank of crowds intervals passing rapt and happy,
Aware of the fresh free giver the flowing Missouri, aware of
    mighty Niagara,
Aware of the buffalo herds grazing the plains, the hirsute
    and strong-breasted bull,
Of earth, rocks, Fifth-month flowers experienced, stars, rain,
    snow, my amaze,
Having studied the mocking-bird's tones and the flight of the
    mountain-hawk,
And heard at dawn the unrivall'd one, the hermit thrush from
    the swamp-cedars,
Solitary, singing in the West, I strike up for a New World . . .

FROM *Song of Myself*

I celebrate myself, and sing myself,
And what I assume you shall assume,
For every atom belonging to me as good belongs to you.

I loafe and invite my soul,
I lean and loafe at my ease observing a spear of summer grass.

My tongue, every atom of my blood, form'd from this soil,
    this air,
Born here of parents born here from parents the same, and
    their parents the same,
I, now thirty-seven years old in perfect health begin,
Hoping to cease not till death.

Creeds and schools in abeyance,
Retiring back a while sufficed at what they are, but never
    forgotten,
I harbor for good or bad, I permit to speak at every hazard,
Nature without check with original energy.

    .   .   .   .   .

A child said *What is the grass?* fetching it to me with full
    hands;
How could I answer the child? I do not know what it is any
    more than he.
I guess it must be the flag of my disposition, out of hopeful
    green stuff woven.

Or I guess it is the handkerchief of the Lord,
A scented gift and remembrancer designedly dropt,
Bearing the owner's name someway in the corners, that we
    may see and remark, and say *Whose?*

Or I guess it is a uniform hieroglyphic,
And it means, Sprouting alike in broad zones and narrow
    zones,
Growing among black folks as among white,
Kanuck, Tuckahoe, Congressman, Cuff, I give them the same,
    I receive them the same.

And now it seems to me the beautiful uncut hair of graves.

Tenderly will I use you curling grass,
It may be you transpire from the breasts of young men,
It may be if I had known them I would have loved them,
It may be you are from old people, or from offspring taken
     soon out of their mothers' laps,
And here you are the mothers' laps.

This grass is very dark to be from the white heads of old
     mothers,
Darker than the colorless beards of old men,
Dark to come from under the faint red roofs of mouths.

O I perceive after all so many uttering tongues,
And I perceive they do not come from the roofs of mouths
     for nothing.

I wish I could translate the hints about the dead young men
     and women,
And the hints about old men and mothers, and the offspring
     taken soon out of their laps.

What do you think has become of the young and old men?
And what do you think has become of the women and chil-
     dren?

They are alive and well somewhere,
The smallest sprout shows there is really no death,
And if ever there was it led forward life, and does not wait
     at the end to arrest it,
And ceas'd the moment life appear'd.

All goes onward and outward, nothing collapses,
And to die is different from what any one supposed, and
     luckier.

.   .   .   .   .

Walt Whitman, a kosmos, of Manhattan the son,
Turbulent, fleshy, sensual, eating, drinking and breeding,
No sentimentalist, no stander above men and women or apart
     from them,
No more modest than immodest.

Unscrew the locks from the doors!
Unscrew the doors themselves from their jambs!

Whoever degrades another degrades me,
And whatever is done or said returns at last to me.

Through me the afflatus surging and surging, through me the
          current and index.

I speak the pass-word primeval, I give the sign of democracy,
By God! I will accept nothing which all cannot have their
          counterpart of on the same terms.

Through me many long dumb voices,
Voices of the interminable generations of prisoners and slaves,
Voices of the diseas'd and despairing and of thieves and
          dwarfs,
Voices of cycles of preparation and accretion,
And of the threads that connect the stars, and of wombs and
          of the father-stuff,
And of the rights of them the others are down upon,
And of the deform'd, trivial, flat, foolish, despised,
Fog in the air, beetles rolling balls of dung.

Through me forbidden voices,
Voices of sexes and lusts, voices veil'd and I remove the veil,
Voices indecent by me clarified and transfigur'd.

.   .   .   .   .   .

I think I could turn and live with animals, they are so placid
          and self-contain'd,
I stand and look at them long and long.

They do not sweat and whine about their condition,
They do not lie awake in the dark and weep for their sins,
They do not make me sick discussing their duty to God,
Not one is dissatisfied, not one is demented with the mania of
          owning things,
Not one kneels to another, nor to his kind that lived thou-
          sands of years ago,
Not one is respectable or unhappy over the whole earth.

. . . . . .

I have said that the soul is not more than the body,
And I have said that the body is not more than the soul,
And nothing, not God, is greater to one than one's self is,
And whoever walks a furlong without sympathy walks to his
     own funeral dressed in his own shroud,
And I or you pocketless of a dime may purchase the pick of
     the earth,
And to glance with an eye or show a bean in its pod confounds
     the learning of all times,
And there is no trade or employment but the young man fol-
     lowing it may become a hero,
And there is no object so soft but it makes a hub for the
     wheel'd universe,
And I say to any man or woman, Let your soul stand cool
     and composed before a million universes.

And I say to mankind, Be not curious about God,
For I who am curious about each am not curious about God,
(No array of terms can say how much I am at peace about
     God and about death.)

I hear and behold God in every object, yet understand God
     not in the least,
Nor do I understand who there can be more wonderful than
     myself.

From Pent-Up Aching Rivers

From pent-up aching rivers,
From that of myself without which I were nothing,
From what I am determin'd to make illustrious, even if I stand
     sole among men,
From my own voice resonant, singing the phallus,
Singing the song of procreation,
Singing the need of superb children and therein superb
     grown people,
Singing the muscular urge and the blending,
Singing the bedfellow's song, (O resistless yearning!
O for any and each the body correlative attracting!

O for you whoever you are your correlative body! O it, more
      than all else, you delighting!)
From the hungry gnaw that eats me night and day,
From native moments, from bashful pains, singing them,
Seeking something yet unfound though I have diligently
      sought it many a long year,
Singing the true song of the soul fitful at random,
Renascent with grossest Nature or among animals,
Of that, of them and what goes with them my poems inform-
      ing,
Of the smell of apples and lemons, of the pairing of birds,
Of the wet of woods, of the lapping of waves,
Of the mad pushes of waves upon the land, I them chanting,
The overture lightly sounding, the strain anticipating,
The welcome nearness, the sight of the perfect body,
The swimmer swimming naked in the bath, or motionless on
      his back lying and floating,
The female form approaching, I pensive, love-flesh tremulous
      aching,
The divine list for myself or you or for any one making,
The face, the limbs, the index from head to foot, and what
      it arouses,
The mystic deliria, the madness amorous, the utter abandon-
      ment,
(Hark close and still what I now whisper to you,
I love you, O you entirely possess me,
O that you and I could escape from the rest and go utterly off,
      free and lawless,
Two hawks in the air, two fishes swimming in the sea not
      more lawless than we;)
The furious storm through me careering, I passionately trem-
      bling,
The oath of the inseparableness of two together, of the
      woman that loves me and whom I love more than my
      life, that oath swearing,
(O I willingly stake all for you,
O let me be lost if it must be so!
O you and I! what is it to us what the rest do or think?
What is all else to us? only that we enjoy each other and
      exhaust each other if it must be so;)
From the master, the pilot I yield the vessel to,

The general commanding me, commanding all, from him per-
    mission taking,
From time the programme hastening (I have loiter'd too long
    as it is)
From sex, from the warp and from the woof,
From privacy, from frequent repinings alone,
From plenty of persons near and yet the right person not near,
From the soft sliding of hands over me and thrusting of fin-
    gers through my hair and beard,
From the long sustain'd kiss upon the mouth or bosom,
From the close pressure that makes me or any man drunk,
    fainting with excess,
From what the divine husband knows, from the work of
    fatherhood,
From exultation, victory and relief, from the bedfellow's em-
    brace in the night,
From the act-poems of eyes, hands, hips and bosoms,
From the cling of the trembling arm,
From the bending curve and the clinch,
From side by side the pliant coverlet off-throwing,
From the one so unwilling to have me leave, and me just as
    unwilling to leave,
(Yet a moment O tender waiter, and I return,)
From the hour of shining stars and dropping dews,
From the night a moment I emerging flitting out,
Celebrate you act divine and you children prepared for,
And you stalwart loins.

Out of the Rolling Ocean the Crowd

Out of the rolling ocean the crowd came a drop gently to me,
Whispering *I love you, before long I die,*
I have travel'd a long way merely to look on you to touch you,
For I could not die till I once look'd on you,
For I fear'd I might afterwards lose you.

Now we have met, we have look'd, we are safe,
Return in peace to the ocean my love,
I too am part of that ocean my love, we are not so much
    separated,

Behold the great rondure, the cohesion of all, how perfect!
But as for me, for you, the irresistible sea is to separate us,
As for an hour carrying us diverse, yet cannot carry us diverse
    forever;
Be not impatient—a little space—know you I salute the air,
    the ocean and the land,
Every day at sundown for your dear sake my love.

FROM *Song of the Open Road*

Afoot and light-hearted I take to the open road,
Healthy, free, the world before me,
The long brown path before me leading wherever I choose.
Henceforth I ask not good-fortune, I myself am good-fortune,
Henceforth I whimper no more, postpone no more, need noth-
    ing,
Done with indoor complaints, libraries, querulous criticisms,
Strong and content I travel the open road.

The earth, that is sufficient,
I do not want the constellations any nearer,
I know they are very well where they are,
I know they suffice for those who belong to them.

    .   .   .   .   .

I think heroic deeds were all conceiv'd in the open air, and
    all free poems also,
I think I could stop here myself and do miracles,
I think whatever I shall meet on the road I shall like, and
    whoever beholds me shall like me,
I think whoever I see must be happy.

From this hour I ordain myself loos'd of limits and imaginary
    lines,
Going where I list, my own master total and absolute,
Listening to others, considering well what they say,
Pausing, searching, receiving, contemplating,
Gently, but with undeniable will, divesting myself of the holds
    that would hold me.

I inhale great draughts of space,
The east and the west are mine, and the north and the south
      are mine.

I am larger, better than I thought,
I did not know I held so much goodness.

.   .   .   .   .

Now if a thousand perfect men were to appear it would not
      amaze me,
Now if a thousand beautiful forms of women appear'd it
      would not astonish me.

Now I see the secret of the making of the best persons,
It is to grow in the open air and to eat and sleep with the
      earth.

.   .   .   .   .

Listen! I will be honest with you,
I do not offer the old smooth prizes, but offer rough new
      prizes,
These are the days that must happen to you:
You shall not heap up what is call'd riches,
You shall scatter with lavish hand all that you earn or achieve,
You but arrive at the city to which you were destined, you
          hardly settle yourself to satisfaction before you are
          call'd by an irresistible call to depart,
You shall be treated to the ironical smiles and mockings of
          those who remain behind you,
What beckonings of love you receive you shall only answer
          with passionate kisses of parting,
You shall not allow the hold of those who spread their reach'd
          hands toward you.

.   .   .   .   .

Allons! the road is before us!
It is safe—I have tried it—my own feet have tried it well—be
      not detain'd!
Let the paper remain on the desk unwritten, and the book
      on the shelf unopen'd!

Let the tools remain in the workshop! let the money remain
    unearn'd!
Let the school stand! mind not the cry of the teacher!
Let the preacher preach in his pulpit! let the lawyer plead
    in the court, and the judge expound the law.

Camerado, I give you my hand!
I give you my love more precious than money,
I give you myself before preaching or law;
Will you give me yourself? will you come travel with me?
Shall we stick by each other as long as we live?

FROM *Out of the Cradle Endlessly Rocking*

Out of the cradle endlessly rocking,
Out of the mocking-bird's throat, the musical shuttle,
Out of the Ninth-month midnight,
Over the sterile sands and the fields beyond, where the child
    leaving his bed wander'd alone, bareheaded, barefoot,
Down from the shower'd halo,
Up from the mystic play of shadows, twining and twisting as
    if they were alive,
Out from the patches of briers and blackberries,
From the memories of the bird that chanted to me,
From your memories sad brother, from the fitful risings and
    fallings I heard,
From under that yellow half-moon late-risen and swollen as if
    with tears,
From those beginning notes of yearning and love there in the
    mist.
From the thousand responses of my heart never to cease,
From the myriad thence-arous'd words,
From the word stronger and more delicious than any,
From such as now they start the scene revisiting,
As a flock, twittering, rising, or overhead passing,
Borne hither, ere all eludes me, hurriedly,
A man, yet by these tears a little boy again,
Throwing myself on the sand, confronting the waves,
I, chanter of pains and joys, uniter of here and hereafter,
Taking all hints to use them, but swiftly leaping beyond them,
A reminiscence sing.

As Toilsome I Wander'd Virginia's Woods

As toilsome I wander'd Virginia's woods,
To the music of rustling leaves kick'd by my feet (for 'twas
    autumn)
I mark'd at the foot of a tree the grave of a soldier;
Mortally wounded he and buried on the retreat, (easily all
    could I understand,)
The halt of a mid-day hour, when up! no time to lose—yet this
    sign left,
On a tablet scrawl'd and nail'd on the tree by the grave,
Bold, cautious, true, and my loving comrade.

Long, long I muse, then on my way go wandering,
Many a changeful season to follow, and many a scene of life,
Yet at times through changeful season and scene, abrupt,
    alone, or in the crowded street,
Comes before me the unknown soldier's grave, comes the
    inscription rude in Virginia's woods,
Bold, cautious, true, and my loving comrade.

The Wound-Dresser

An old man bending I come among new faces,
Years looking backward resuming in answer to children,
Come tell us old man, as from young men and maidens that
    love me,
(Arous'd and angry, I'd thought to beat the alarum, and urge
    relentless war,
But soon my fingers fail'd me, my face droop'd and I resign'd
    myself
To sit by the wounded and soothe them, or silently watch the
    dead;)
Years hence of these scenes, of these furious passions, these
    chances,
Of unsurpass'd heroes, (was one side so brave? the other was
    equally brave;)
Now be witness again, paint the mightiest armies of earth,
Of those armies so rapid so wondrous what saw you to tell
    us?

What stays with you latest and deepest? of curious panics,
Of hard-fought engagements or sieges tremendous what deep-
    est remains?

O maidens and young men I love and that love me,
What you ask of my days those the strangest and sudden your
    talking recalls,
Soldier alert I arrive after a long march cover'd with sweat
    and dust,
In the nick of time I come, plunge in the fight, loudly shout in
    the rush of successful charge,
Enter the captur'd works—yet lo, like a swift-running river
    they fade,
Pass and are gone they fade—I dwell not on soldiers' perils or
    soldiers' joys,
(Both I remember well—many the hardships, few the joys,
    yet I was content.)

But in silence, in dreams' projections,
While the world of gain and appearance and mirth goes on,
So soon what is over forgotten, and waves wash the imprints
    off the sand,
With hinged knees returning I enter the doors (while for you
    up there,
Whoever you are, follow without noise and be of strong
    heart.)

Bearing the bandages, water and sponge,
Straight and swift to my wounded I go,
Where they lie on the ground after the battle brought in,
Where their priceless blood reddens the grass the ground,
Or to the rows of the hospital tent, or under the roof'd hospi-
    tal,
To the long row of cots up and down each side I return,
To each and all one after another I draw near, not one do I
    miss,
An attendant follows holding a tray, he carries a refuse pail,
Soon to be filled with clotted rags and blood, emptied, and
    fill'd again.

I onward go, I stop,
With hinged knees and steady hand to dress wounds,
I am firm with each, the pangs are sharp but unavoidable,

One turns to me his appealing eyes—poor boy! I never knew
    you,
Yet I think I could not refuse this moment to die for you, if
    that would save you.

On, on I go, (open doors of time! open hospital doors!)
The crush'd head I dress, (poor crazed hand tear not the
    bandage away)
The neck of the cavalry-man with the bullet through and
    through I examine,
Hard the breathing rattles, quite glazed already the eye, yet
    life struggles hard,
(Come sweet death! be persuaded O beautiful death! In
    mercy come quickly.)

From the stump of the arm, the amputated hand,
I undo the clotted lint, remove the slough, wash off the mat-
    ter and blood,
Back on the pillow the soldier bends with curv'd neck and
    side-falling head,
His eyes are closed, his face is pale, he dares not look on the
    bloody stump,
And has not yet look'd on it.

I dress a wound in the side, deep, deep,
But a day or two more, for see the frame all wasted and sink-
    ing,
And the yellow-blue countenance see.

I dress the perforated shoulder, the foot with the bullet-
    wound,
Cleanse the one with a gnawing and putrid gangrene, so sick-
    ening, so offensive,
While the attendant stands behind aside me holding the tray
    and pail.
I am faithful, I do not give out,
The fractur'd thigh, the knee, the wound in the abdomen,
These and more I dress with impassive hand, (yet deep in
    my breast a fire, a burning flame.)

Thus in silence in dreams' projections,
Returning, resuming, I thread my way through the hospitals,
The hurt and wounded I pacify with soothing hand,

I sit by the restless all the dark night, some are so young,
Some suffer so much, I recall the experience sweet and sad,
(Many a soldier's loving arms about this neck have cross'd
          and rested,
Many a soldier's kiss dwells on these bearded lips.)

When Lilacs Last in the Dooryard Bloom'd

When lilacs last in the dooryard bloom'd,
And the great star early droop'd in the western sky in the
          night,
I mourn'd, and yet shall mourn with ever-returning spring.

Ever-returning spring, trinity sure to me you bring,
Lilac blooming perennial and drooping star in the west,
And thought of him I love.

O powerful western fallen star!
O shades of night—O moody, tearful night!
O great star disappear'd—O the black murk that hides the
          star!
O cruel hands that hold me powerless—O helpless soul of me!
O harsh surrounding cloud that will not free my soul.

In the dooryard fronting an old farm-house near the white-
          wash'd palings,
Stands the lilac-bush tall-growing with heart-shaped leaves
          of rich green,
With many a pointed blossom rising delicate, with the per-
          fume strong I love,
With every leaf a miracle—and from this bush in the door-
          yard,
With delicate-color'd blossoms and heart-shaped leaves of
          rich green,
A sprig with its flowers I break.

In the swamp in secluded recesses,
A shy and hidden bird is warbling a song.

Solitary the thrush,
The hermit withdrawn to himself, avoiding the settlements,
Sings by himself a song.

Song of the bleeding throat,
Death's outlet song of life, (for well dear brother I know,
If thou wast not granted to sing thou would'st surely die.)

Over the breast of the spring, the land, amid cities,
Amid lanes and through old woods, where lately the violets
      peep'd from the ground, spotting the gray debris,
Amid the grass in the fields each side of the lanes, passing the
      endless grass,
Passing the yellow-speared wheat, every grain from its shroud
      in the dark-brown fields uprisen,
Passing the apple-tree blows of white and pink in the orchards,
Carrying a corpse to where it shall rest in the grave,
Night and day journeys a coffin.

Coffin that passes through lanes and streets,
Through day and night with the great cloud darkening the
      land,
With the pomp of the inloop'd flags with the cities draped
      in black,
With the show of the States themselves as of crape-veil'd
      women standing,
With processions long and winding and the flambeaus of the
      night,
With the countless torches lit, with the silent sea of faces
      and the unbared heads,
With the waiting depot, the arriving coffin, and the sombre
      faces,
With dirges through the night, with the thousand voices ris-
      ing strong and solemn,
With all the mournful voices of the dirges pour'd around the
      coffin,
The dim-lit churches and the shuddering organs—where amid
      these you journey,
With the tolling tolling bells' perpetual clang,
Here, coffin that slowly passes,
I give you my sprig of lilac.

(Nor for you, for one alone,
Blossoms and branches green to coffins all I bring,
For fresh as the morning, thus would I chant a song for you
   O sane and sacred death.

All over bouquets of roses,
O death, I cover you over with roses and early lilies,
But mostly and now the lilac that blooms the first,
Copious I break, I break the sprigs from the bushes,
With loaded arms I come, pouring for you,
For you and the coffins of all of you O death.)

O western orb sailing the heaven,
Now I know what you must have meant as a month since I
   walk'd,
As I walk'd in silence the transparent shadowy night,
As I saw you had something to tell as you bent to me night
   after night,
As you droop'd from the sky low down as if to my side,
   (while the other stars all look'd on,)
As we wander'd together the solemn night, (for something I
   know not what kept me from sleep,)
As the night advanced, and I saw on the rim of the west how
   full you were of woe,
As I stood on the rising ground in the breeze in the cool
   transparent night,
As I watch'd where you pass'd and was lost in the netherward
   black of the night,
As my soul in its trouble dissatisfied sank, as where you, sad
   orb,
Concluded, dropt in the night, and was gone.

Sing on there in the swamp,
O singer bashful and tender, I hear your notes, I hear your
   call,
I hear, I come presently, I understand you,
But a moment I linger, for the lustrous star has detain'd me,
The star my departing comrade holds and detains me.

O how shall I warble myself for the dead one there I
   loved?

And how shall I deck my song for the large sweet soul that
has gone?
And what shall my perfume be for the grave of him I love?

Sea-winds blown from east and west,
Blown from the Eastern sea and blown from the Western
sea, till there on the prairies meeting,
These and with these and the breath of my chant,
I'll perfume the grave of him I love.

O what shall I hang on the chamber walls?
And what shall the pictures be that I hang on the walls,
To adorn the burial-house of him I love?

Pictures of growing spring and farms and homes,
With the Fourth-month eve at sundown, and the gray smoke
lucid and bright,
With floods of the yellow gold of the gorgeous, indolent,
sinking sun, burning, expanding the air,
With the fresh sweet herbage under foot, and the pale
green leaves of the trees prolific,
In the distance the flowing glaze, the breast of the river, with
a wind-dapple here and there,
With ranging hills on the banks, with many a line against the
sky, and shadows,
And the city at hand with dwellings so dense, and stacks of
chimneys,
And all the scenes of life and the workshops, and the workmen
homeward returning.

Lo, body and soul—this land,
My own Manhattan with spires, and the sparkling and hurry-
ing tides, and the ships,
The varied and ample land, the South and the North in the
light, Ohio's shores and flashing Missouri,
And ever the far-spreading prairies cover'd with grass and
corn.

Lo, the most excellent sun so calm and haughty,
The violet and purple morn with just-felt breezes,
The gentle soft-born measureless light,

The miracles spreading bathing all, the fulfill'd noon,
The coming eve delicious, the welcome night and the stars,
Over my cities shining all, enveloping man and land.

Sing on, sing on, you gray-brown bird,
Sing from the swamps, the recesses, pour your chant from
          the bushes,
Limitless out of the dusk, out of the cedars and pines.

Sing on dearest brother, warble your reedy song,
Loud human song, with voice of uttermost woe.

O liquid and free and tender!
O wild and loose to my soul—O wondrous singer!
You only I hear—yet the star holds me, (but will soon depart)
Yet the lilac with mastering odor holds me.

Now while I sat in the day and look'd forth,
In the close of the day with its light and the fields of spring,
          and the farmers preparing their crops,
In the large unconscious scenery of my land with its lakes
          and forests,
In the heavenly aerial beauty, (after the perturb'd winds
          and the storms,)
Under the arching heavens of the afternoon swift passing,
          and the voices of children and women,
The many-moving sea-tides, and I saw the ships how they
          sail'd,
And the summer approaching with richness, and the fields all
          busy with labor,
And the infinite separate houses, how they all went on, each
          with its meals and minutia of daily usages,
And the streets how their throbbings throbb'd, and the
          cities pent—lo, then and there,
Falling upon them all and among them all, enveloping me
          with the rest,
Appear'd the cloud, appear'd the long black trail,
And I knew death, its thought, and the sacred knowledge of
          death.

Then with the knowledge of death as walking one side of me,
And the thought of death close-walking the other side of
     me,
And I in the middle as with companions, and as holding the
     hands of companions,
I fled forth to the hiding receiving night that talks not,
Down to the shores of the water, the path by the swamp in
     the dimness,
To the solemn shadowy cedars and ghostly pines so still.

And the singer so shy to the rest receiv'd me,
The gray-brown bird I know receiv'd us comrades three,
And he sang the carol of death, and a verse for him I love.

From deep secluded recesses,
From the fragrant cedars and the ghostly pines so still,
Came the carol of the bird.

And the charm of the carol rapt me,
As I held as if by their hands my comrades in the night,
And the voice of my spirit tallied the song of the bird.

Come lovely and soothing death,
Undulate round the world, serenely arriving, arriving,
In the day, in the night, to all, to each,
Sooner or later delicate death.

Prais'd be the fathomless universe,
For life and joy, and for objects and knowledge curious,
And for love, sweet love—but praise! praise! praise!
For the sure-enwinding arms of cool-enfolding death!

Dark mother always gliding near with soft feet,
Have none chanted for thee a chant of fullest welcome?
Then I chant it for thee, I glorify thee above all,
I bring thee a song that when thou must indeed come, come
     unfalteringly.

Approach strong deliveress,
When it is so, when thou hast taken them I joyously sing the
     dead,

Lost in the loving floating ocean of thee,
Laved in the flood of thy bliss O death.

From me to thee glad serenades,
Dances for thee I propose saluting thee, adornments and
*   feastings for thee,*
And the sights of the open landscape and the high-spread sky
*   are fitting,*
And life and the fields, and the huge and thoughtful night.

The night in silence under many a star,
The ocean shore and the husky whispering wave whose voice
*   I know,*
And the soul turning to thee O vast and well-veil'd death,
And the body gratefully nestling close to thee.

Over the tree-tops I float thee a song,
Over the rising and sinking waves, over the myriad fields and
*   the prairies wide,*
Over the dense-pack'd cities all and the teeming wharves and
*   ways,*
I float this carol with joy, with joy to thee O death.

To the tally of my soul,
Loud and strong kept up the gray-brown bird,
With pure deliberate notes spreading filling the night.

Loud in the pines and cedars dim,
Clear in the freshness moist and the swamp-perfume,
And I with my comrades there in the night.

While my sight that was bound in my eyes unclosed,
As to long panoramas of visions.

And I saw askant the armies,
I saw as in noiseless dreams hundreds of battle-flags,
Borne through the smoke of the battles and pierc'd with
        missiles I saw them,
And carried hither and yon through the smoke, and torn
        and bloody,

And at last but a few shreds left on the staffs, (and all in
    silence,)
And the staffs all splinter'd and broken.

I saw battle-corpses, myriads of them,
And the white skeletons of young men, I saw them,
I saw the debris and debris of all the slain soldiers of the
    war,
But I saw they were not as was thought,
They themselves were fully at rest, they suffer'd not,
The living remain'd and suffer'd, the mother suffer'd,
And the wife and the child and the musing comrade suffer'd,
And the armies that remain'd suffer'd.

Passing the visions, passing the night,
Passing unloosing the hold of my comrades' hands,
Passing the song of the hermit bird and the tallying song of
    my soul,
Victorious song, death's outlet song, yet varying ever-altering
    song,
As low and wailing, yet clear the notes, rising and falling,
    flooding the night,
Sadly sinking and fainting, as warning and warning, and yet
    again bursting with joy,
Covering the earth and filling the spread of the heaven,
As that powerful psalm in the night I heard from recesses,
Passing, I leave thee lilac with heart-shaped leaves,
I leave thee there in the door-yard, blooming, returning with
    spring.

I cease from my song for thee,
From my gaze on thee in the west, fronting the west, com-
    muning with thee,
O comrade lustrous with silver face in the night.

Yet each to keep and all, retrievements out of the night,
The song, the wondrous chant of the gray-brown bird,
And the tallying chant, the echo arous'd in my soul,
With the lustrous and drooping star with the countenance
    full of woe,

With the holders holding my hand nearing the call of the
   bird,
Comrades mine and I in the midst, and their memory ever to
   keep, for the dead I loved so well,
For the sweetest, wisest soul of all my days and lands—and
   this for his dear sake,
Lilac and star and bird twined with the chant of my soul,
There in the fragrant pines and cedars dusk and dim.

To a Common Prostitute

Be composed—be at ease with me—I am Walt Whitman,
   liberal and lusty as Nature,
Not till the sun excludes you do I exclude you,
Not till the waters refuse to glisten for you and the leaves to
   rustle for you, do my words refuse to glisten and
   rustle for you.
My girl I appoint with you an appointment, and I charge
   you that you make preparation to be worthy to meet
   me,
And I charge you that you be patient and perfect till I come.

Till then I salute you with a significant look that you do not
   forget me.

Darest Thou Now O Soul

Darest thou now O soul,
Walk out with me toward the unknown region,
Where neither ground is for the feet nor any path to follow?

No map there, nor guide,
Nor voice sounding, nor touch of human hand,
Nor face with blooming flesh, nor lips, nor eyes, are in that
   land.

I know it not O soul,
Nor dost thou, all is a blank before us,
All waits undream'd of in that region, that inaccessible land.

Till when the ties loosen,
All but the ties eternal, Time and Space,
Nor darkness, gravitation, sense, nor any bounds bounding us.

Then we burst forth, we float,
In Time and Space O soul, prepared for them,
Equal, equipt at last, (O joy, O fruit of all) them to fulfil
     O soul.

CHARLES KINGSLEY

(1819–1875)

"When All the World..."

When all the world is young, lad,
   And all the trees are green;
And every goose a swan, lad,
   And every lass a queen;
Then hey for boot and horse, lad,
   And round the world away:
Young blood must have its course, lad,
   And every dog his day.

When all the world is old, lad,
   And all the trees are brown;
And all the sport is stale, lad,
   And all the wheels run down;
Creep home, and take your place there,
   The spent and maimed among:
God grant you find one face there,
   You loved when all was young.

The Water Babies

JAMES RUSSELL LOWELL

(1819–1891)

She Came and Went

As a twig trembles, which a bird
   Lights on to sing, then leaves unbent,
So is my memory thrilled and stirred;—
   I only know she came and went.

As clasps some lake, by gusts unriven,
   The blue dome's measureless content,
So my soul held that moment's heaven;—
   I only know she came and went.

As, at one bound, our swift spring heaps
   The orchard full of bloom and scent,
So clove her May my wintry sleeps;—
   I only know she came and went.

An angel stood and met my gaze,
   Through the low doorway of my tent;
The tent is struck, the vision stays;—
   I only know she came and went.

Oh, when the room grows slowly dim,
   And life's last oil is nearly spent,
One gush of light these eyes will brim,
   Only to think she came and went.

HERMAN MELVILLE

(1819–1891)

"The Ribs and Terrors..."

The ribs and terrors in the whale,
   Arched over me a dismal gloom,
While all God's sun-lit waves rolled by,
   And lift* me deepening down to doom.

I saw the opening maw of hell,
   With endless pains and sorrows there;
Which none but they that feel can tell—
   Oh, I was plunging to despair.

In black distress, I called my God,
   When I could scarce believe Him mine,
He bowed His ear to my complaints—
   No more the whale did me confine.

With speed He flew to my relief,
   As on a radiant dolphin borne;
Awful, yet bright, as lightning shone
   The face of my Deliverer God.

* Left (?)

My song for ever shall record
   That terrible, that joyful hour;
I give the glory to my God,
   His all the mercy and the power.

Moby-Dick

The March into Virginia
(JULY 1861)

Did all the lets and bars appear
   To every just or larger end,
Whence should come the trust and cheer?
   Youth must its ignorant impulse lend—
Age finds place in the rear.
   All wars are boyish, and are fought by boys,
The champions and enthusiasts of the state:
   Turbid ardours and vain joys
     Not barrenly abate—
   Stimulants to the power mature,
     Preparatives of fate.

Who here forecasteth the event?
What heart but spurns at precedent
And warnings of the wise,
Contemned foreclosures of surprise?
The banners play, the bugles call,
The air is blue and prodigal.
   No berrying party, pleasure-wooed,
No picnic party in the May,
Ever went less loth than they
   Into that leafy neighborhood.
In Bacchic glee they file toward Fate,
Moloch's uninitiate;
Expectancy, and glad surmise
Of battle's unknown mysteries.
All they feel is this: 'tis glory,
A rapture sharp, though transitory,
Yet lasting in belaurelled story.
So they gaily go to fight,
Chatting left and laughing right.

But some who this blithe mood present,
  As on in lightsome files they fare,
Shall die experienced ere three days are spent—
  Perish, enlightened by the volleyed glare;
Or shame survive, and like to adamant,
  The throe of Second Manassas share.

Shiloh, a Requiem
(APRIL 1862)

Skimming lightly, wheeling still,
  The swallows fly low
Over the field in clouded days,
  The forest-field of Shiloh—
Over the field where April rain
Solaced the parched one stretched in pain
Through the pause of night
That followed the Sunday fight
  Around the church of Shiloh—
The church so lone, the log-built one,
That echoed to many a parting groan
    And natural prayer
  Of dying foemen mingled there—
Foemen at morn, but friends at eve—
  Fame or country least their care:
(What like a bullet can undeceive!)
  But now they lie low,
While over them the swallows skim
  And all is hushed at Shiloh.

FROM *John Marr*

Since as in night's deck-watch ye show,
Why, lads, so silent here to me,
Your watchmate of times long ago?

Once, for all the darkling sea,
You your voices raised how clearly,
Striking in when tempest sung;

Hoisting up the storm-sail cheerly,
Life is storm—let storm! you rung.
Taking things as fated merely,
Childlike though the world ye spanned;
Nor holding unto life too dearly,
Ye who held your lives in hand—
Skimmers, who on oceans four
Petrels were, and larks ashore.

O, not from memory lightly flung,
Forgot, like strains no more availing,
The heart to music haughtier strung;
Nay, frequent near me, never staling,
Whose good feeling kept ye young.
Like tides that enter creek or stream,
Ye come, ye visit me, or seem
Swimming out from seas of faces,
Alien myriads memory traces,
To enfold me in a dream!

I yearn as ye. But rafts that strain,
Parted, shall they lock again?
Twined we were, entwined, then riven,
Ever to new embracements driven,
Shifting gulf-weed of the main!
And how if one here shift no more,
Lodged by the flinging surge ashore?
Nor less, as now, in eve's decline,
Your shadowy fellowship is mine.
Ye float around me, form and feature:—
Tattooings, ear-rings, love-locks curled;
Barbarians of man's simpler nature,
Unworldly servers of the world.
Yea, present all, and dear to me,
Though shades, or scouring China's sea.

Whither, whither, merchant-sailors,
Witherward now in roaring gales?
Competing still, ye huntsman-whalers,
In leviathan's wake what boat prevails?
And man-of-war's men, whereaway?

If now no dinned drum beat to quarters
On the wilds of midnight waters—
Foemen looming through the spray;
Do yet your gangway lanterns, streaming,
Vainly strive to pierce below,
When tilted from the slant plank gleaming,
A brother you see to darkness go?

But, gunmates lashed in shotted canvas,
If where long watch-below ye keep,
Never the shrill *"All hands up hammocks!"*
Breaks the spell that charms your sleep,
And summoning trumps might vainly call,
And booming guns implore—
A beat, a heart-beat musters all,
One heart-beat at heart-core.
It musters. But to clasp, retain;
To see you at the halyards main—
To hear your chorus once again!

To Ned

Where is the world we roved, Ned Bunn?
    Hollows thereof lay rich in shade
By voyagers old inviolate thrown
    Ere Paul Pry cruised with Pelf and Trade.
To us old lads some thoughts come home
Who roamed a world young lads no more shall roam.

Nor less the satiate year impends
    When, wearying of routine-resorts,
The pleasure-hunter shall break loose,
    Ned, for our Pantheistic ports:—
Marquesas and glenned isles that be
Authentic Edens in a Pagan sea.

The charm of scenes untried shall lure,
    And, Ned, a legend urge the flight—
The Typee-truants under stars
    Unknown to Shakespeare's *Midsummer-Night;*

And man, if lost to Saturn's Age,
Yet feeling life no Syrian pilgrimage.

But, tell, shall he, the tourist, find
    Our isles the same in violet-glow
Enamouring us what years and years—
    Ah, Ned, what years and years ago!
Well, Adam advances, smart in pace,
But scarce by violets that advance you trace.

But we, in anchor-watches calm,
    The Indian Psyche's languor won,
And, musing, breathed primeval balm
    From Edens ere yet overrun;
Marvelling mild if mortal twice,
Here and hereafter, touch a Paradise.

Lone Founts

Though fast youth's glorious fable flies,
View not the world with worldling's eyes;
Nor turn with weather of the time.
Foreclose the coming of surprise:
Stand where Posterity shall stand;
Stand where the Ancients stood before,
And, dipping in lone founts thy hand,
Drink of the never-varying lore:
Wise once, and wise thence evermore.

Art

In placid hours well pleased we dream
Of many a brave unbodied scheme.
But form to lend, pulsed life create,
What unlike things must meet and mate:
A flame to melt—a wind to freeze;
Sad patience—joyous energies;

Humility—yet pride and scorn;
Instinct and study; love and hate;
Audacity—reverence. These must mate
And fuse with Jacob's mystic heart,
To wrestle with the angel—Art.

Fragments of a Lost Gnostic Poem
of the Twelfth Century

Found a family, build a state,
The pledged event is still the same:
Matter in end will never abate
His ancient brutal claim.

Indolence is heaven's ally here,
And energy the child of hell:
The Good Man pouring from his pitcher clear
But brims the poisoned well.

L'Envoi: The Return of the Sire de Nesle
(A.D. 16—)

My towers at last! These rovings end,
Their thirst is slaked in larger dearth:
The yearning infinite recoils,
    For terrible is earth.

Kaf thrusts his snouted crags through fog:
Araxes swells beyond his span,
And knowledge poured by pilgrimage
    Overflows the banks of man.

But thou, my stay, thy lasting love
One lonely good, let this but be!
Weary to view the wide world's swarm,
    But blest to fold but thee.

Immolated

Children of my happier prime,
When One yet lived with me, and threw
Her rainbow over life and time,
Even Hope, my bride, and mother to you!
O, nurtured in sweet pastoral air,
And fed on flowers and light and dew
Of morning meadows—spare, ah, spare
Reproach; spare, and upbraid me not
That, yielding scarce to reckless mood,
But jealous of your future lot,
I sealed you in a fate subdued.
Have I not saved you from the dread
Theft, and ignoring which need be
The triumph of the insincere
Unanimous Mediocrity?
Rest therefore, free from all despite,
Snugged in the arms of comfortable night.

Camoens

(BEFORE)

And ever must I fan this fire?
Thus ever in flame on flame aspire?
Ever restless, restless, craving rest—
The Imperfect toward Perfection pressed!
Yea, for the God demands thy best.
The world with endless beauty teems,
And thought evokes new worlds of dreams:
Hunt then the flying herds of themes!
And fan, still fan, thy fervid fire,
Until thy crucibled gold shall show
That fire can purge as well as glow.
In ordered ardour, nobly strong,
Flame to the height of epic song.

(AFTER)
Camoens in the Hospital

What now avails the pageant verse,
Trophies and arms with music borne?
Base is the world; and some rehearse
Now noblest meet ignoble scorn,
Vain now thy ardour, vain thy fire,
Delirium mere, unsound desire;
Fate's knife hath ripped thy corded lyre.
Exhausted by the exacting lay,
Thou dost but fall a surer prey
To wile and guile ill understood;
While they who work them, fair in face,
Still keep their strength in prudent place,
And claim they worthier run life's race,
Serving high God with useful good.

Falstaff's Lament over Prince Hal Become Henry V

One that I cherished,
Yea, loved as a son—
Up early, up late with,
My promising one:
No use in good nurture,
None, lads, none!

Here on this settle
He wore the true crown,
King of good fellows,
And Fat Jack was one—
Now, Beadle of England
In formal array—
Best fellow alive
On a throne flung away!

Companions and cronies
Keep fast and lament;—
Come drawer, more sack here
To drown discontent;

For now intuitions
Shall wither to codes,
Pragmatised morals
Shall libel the gods.

One I instructed,
Yea, talked to—alone:
Precept—example
Clean away thrown!

Sorrow makes thirsty:
Sack, drawer, more sack!—
One that I prayed for,
I, Honest Jack!

To bring down these gray hairs—
To cut his old pal!
But, I'll be magnanimous—
Here's to thee, Hal!

MATTHEW ARNOLD

(1822–1888)

Shakespeare

Others abide our question. Thou art free.
We ask and ask: Thou smilest and art still,
Out-topping knowledge. For the loftiest hill
That to the stars uncrowns his majesty,
Planting his steadfast footsteps in the sea,
Making the Heaven of Heavens his dwelling-place,
Spares but the cloudy border of his base
To the foil'd searching of mortality:
And thou, who didst the stars and sunbeams know,
Self-school'd, self-scann'd, self-honour'd, self-secure,
Didst walk on earth unguess'd at. Better so!
All pains the immortal spirit must endure,
All weakness that impairs, all griefs that bow,
Find their sole voice in that victorious brow.

The Forsaken Merman

Come, dear children, let us away;
Down and away below.
Now my brothers call from the bay;
Now the great winds shoreward blow;
Now the salt tides seaward flow;
Now the wild white horses play,
Champ and chafe and toss in the spray.
Children dear, let us away.
This way, this way.

Call her once before you go.
Call once yet.
In a voice that she will know:
"Margaret! Margaret!"
Children's voices should be dear
(Call once more) to a mother's ear:
Children's voices, wild with pain.
Surely she will come again.
Call her once and come away.
This way, this way.
"Mother dear, we cannot stay."
The wild white horses foam and fret.
Margaret! Margaret!

Come, dear children, come away down.
Call no more.
One last look at the white-wall'd town,
And the little grey church on the windy shore.
Then come down.
She will not come though you call all day.
Come away, come away.

Children dear, was it yesterday
We heard the sweet bells over the bay?
In the caverns where we lay,
Through the surf and through the swell,
The far-off sound of a silver bell?
Sand-strewn caverns, cool and deep,

Where the winds are all asleep;
Where the spent lights quiver and gleam;
Where the salt weed sways in the stream;
Where the sea-beasts rang'd all round
Feed in the ooze of their pasture-ground;
Where the sea-snakes coil and twine,
Dry their mail and bask in the brine;
Where great whales come sailing by,
Sail and sail, with unshut eye,
Round the world for ever and aye?
When did music come this way?
Children dear, was it yesterday?

Children dear, was it yesterday
(Call yet once) that she went away?
Once she sate with you and me,
On a red gold throne in the heart of the sea,
And the youngest sate on her knee.
She comb'd its bright hair, and she tended it well,
When down swung the sound of the far-off bell.
She sigh'd, she look'd up through the clear green sea.
She said: "I must go, for my kinsfolk pray
In the little grey church on the shore to-day.
'Twill be Easter-time in the world—ah me!
And I lose my poor soul, Merman, here with thee."
I said: "Go up, dear heart, through the waves;
Say thy prayer, and come back to the kind sea-caves."
She smil'd, she went up through the surf in the bay.
Children dear, was it yesterday?

Children dear, were we long alone?
"The sea grows stormy, the little ones moan.
Long prayers," I said, "in the world they say.
Come," I said, and we rose through the surf in the bay.
We went up the beach, by the sandy down
Where the sea-stocks bloom, to the white-wall'd town.
Through the narrow pav'd streets, where all was still,
To the little grey church on the windy hill.
From the church came a murmur of folk at their prayers,
For we stood without in the cold blowing airs.
We climb'd on the graves, on the stones, worn with rains,

And we gaz'd up the aisle through the small leaded panes.
She sate by the pillar; we saw her clear:
"Margaret, hist! come quick, we are here.
Dear heart," I said, "we are long alone.
The sea grows stormy, the little ones moan."
But, ah, she gave me never a look,
For her eyes were seal'd to the holy book.
Loud prays the priest; shut stands the door.
Come away, children, call no more.
Come away, come down, call no more.

Down, down, down.
Down to the depths of the sea.
She sits at her wheel in the humming town,
Singing most joyfully.
Hark, what she sings: "O joy, O joy,
For the humming street, and the child with its toy.
For the priest, and the bell, and the holy well.
For the wheel where I spun,
And the blessed light of the sun."
And so she sings her fill,
Singing most joyfully,
Till the shuttle falls from her hand,
And the whizzing wheel stands still.
She steals to the window, and looks at the sand;
And over the sand at the sea;
And her eyes are set in a stare;
And anon there breaks a sigh,
And anon there drops a tear,
From a sorrow-clouded eye,
And a heart sorrow-laden,
A long, long sigh,
For the cold strange eyes of a little Mermaiden,
And the gleam of her golden hair.

Come away, away children.
Come children, come down.
The hoarse wind blows colder;
Lights shine in the town.
She will start from her slumber
When gusts shake the door;

She will hear the winds howling,
Will hear the waves roar.
We shall see, while above us
The waves roar and whirl,
A ceiling of amber,
A pavement of pearl.
Singing, "Here came a mortal,
But faithless was she.
And alone dwell for ever
The kings of the sea."

But, children, at midnight,
When soft the winds blow;
When clear falls the moonlight;
When spring-tides are low:
When sweet airs come seaward
From heaths starr'd with broom;
And high rocks throw mildly
On the blanch'd sands a gloom:
Up the still, glistening beaches,
Up the creeks we will hie;
Over banks of bright seaweed
The ebb-tide leaves dry.
We will gaze, from the sand-hills,
At the white sleeping town;
At the church on the hill-side—
    And then come back down.
Singing, "There dwells a lov'd one,
But cruel is she.
She left lonely for ever
The kings of the sea."

Requiescat

Strew on her roses, roses,
    And never a spray of yew.
In quiet she reposes:
    Ah! would that I did too.

Her mirth the world required:
    She bathed it in smiles of glee.
But her heart was tired, tired,
    And now they let her be.

Her life was turning, turning,
    In mazes of heat and sound.
But for peace her soul was yearning,
    And now peace laps her round.

Her cabin'd, ample Spirit,
    It flutter'd, and fail'd for breath.
To-night it doth inherit
    The vasty Hall of Death.

The Scholar Gipsy

Go, for they call you, Shepherd, from the hill;
    Go, Shepherd, and untie the wattled cotes:
    No longer leave thy wistful flock unfed,
Nor let thy bawling fellows rack their throats,
    Nor the cropp'd grasses shoot another head.
        But when the fields are still,
And the tired men and dogs all gone to rest,
    And only the white sheep are sometimes seen
    Cross and recross the strips of moon-blanch'd green;
        Come, Shepherd, and again renew the quest.

Here, where the reaper was at work of late,
    In this high field's dark corner, where he leaves
        His coat, his basket, and his earthen cruse,
    And in the sun all morning binds the sheaves,
        Then here, at noon, comes back his stores to use;
            Here will I sit and wait,
    While to my ear from uplands far away
        The bleating of the folded flocks is borne,
        With distant cries of reapers in the corn—
            All the live murmur of a summer's day.

Screen'd in this nook o'er the high, half-reap'd field,
  And here till sun-down, Shepherd, will I be.
    Through the thick corn the scarlet poppies peep,
  And round green roots and yellowing stalks I see
    Pale blue convolvulus in tendrils creep:
      And air-swept lindens yield
Their scent, and rustle down their perfum'd showers
  Of bloom on the bent grass where I am laid,
  And bower me from the August sun with shade;
    And the eye travels down to Oxford's towers:

And near me on the grass lies Glanvil's book—
  Come, let me read the oft-read tale again,
    The story of the Oxford scholar poor
  Of pregnant parts and quick inventive brain,
    Who, tir'd of knocking at Preferment's door,
      One summer morn forsook
His friends, and went to learn the Gipsy lore,
  And roamed the world with that wild brotherhood,
  And came, as most men deem'd, to little good,
    But came to Oxford and his friends no more.

But once, years after, in the country lanes,
  Two scholars whom at college erst he knew
    Met him, and of his way of life inquir'd.
  Whereat he answered that the Gipsy crew,
    His mates, had arts to rule as they desir'd
      The workings of men's brains;
And they can bind them to what thoughts they will:
  "And I," he said, "the secret of their art,
  When fully learned, will to the world impart:
    But it needs heaven-sent moments for this skill."

This said, he left them, and return'd no more,
  But rumours hung about the country side
    That the lost Scholar long was seen to stray,
  Seen by rare glimpses, pensive and tongue-tied,
    In hat of antique shape, and cloak of grey,
      The same the Gipsies wore.

Shepherds had met him on the Hurst in spring;
  At some lone alehouse in the Berkshire moors,
    On the warm ingle bench, the smock-frock'd boors
      Had found him seated at their entering.

But, mid their drink and clatter, he would fly:
  And I myself seem half to know thy looks,
    And put the shepherds, Wanderer, on thy trace;
  And boys who in lone wheatfields scare the rooks
    I ask if thou hast passed their quiet place;
      Or in my boat I lie
  Moor'd to the cool bank in the summer heats,
    Mid wide grass meadows which the sunshine fills,
    And watch the warm green-muffled Cumner hills,
      And wonder if thou haunt'st their shy retreats.

For most, I know, thou lov'st retired ground.
  Thee, at the ferry, Oxford riders blithe,
    Returning home on summer nights, have met
  Crossing the stripling Thames at Bab-lock-hithe,
    Trailing in the cool stream thy fingers wet,
      As the slow punt swings round:
  And leaning backwards in a pensive dream,
    And fostering in thy lap a heap of flowers
    Pluck'd in shy fields and distant Wychwood bowers,
      And thine eyes resting on the moonlit stream:

And then they land, and thou art seen no more.
  Maidens who from the distant hamlet come
    To dance around the Fyfield elm in May,
  Oft through the darkening fields have seen thee roam,
    Or cross a stile into the public way.
      Oft thou hast given them store
  Of flowers—the frail-leaf'd, white anemone—
    Dark bluebells drench'd with dews of summer eves—
    And purple orchises with spotted leaves—
      But none has words she can report of thee.

And, above Godstow Bridge, when hay-time's here
  In June, and many a scythe in sunshine flames,
    Men who through those wild fields of breezy grass

Where black-wing'd swallows haunt the glittering Thames,
  To bathe in the abandon'd lasher pass,
    Have often pass'd thee near
Sitting upon the river bank o'ergrown:
    Mark'd thy outlandish garb, thy figure spare,
    Thy dark vague eyes, and soft abstracted air;
      But, when they came from bathing, thou wert gone.

At some lone homestead in the Cumner hills,
  Where at her open door the housewife darns,
    Thou hast been seen, or hanging on a gate
To watch the threshers in the mossy barns.
    Children, who early range these slopes and late
      For cresses from the rills,
Have known thee watching, all an April day,
    The springing pastures and the feeding kine;
    And mark'd thee, when the stars come out and shine,
      Through the long dewy grass move slow away.

In autumn, on the skirts of Bagley wood,
  Where most the Gipsies by the turf-edg'd way
    Pitch their smok'd tents, and every bush you see
With scarlet patches tagged and shreds of grey,
    Above the forest ground call'd Thessaly—
      The blackbird picking food
Sees thee, nor stops his meal, nor fears at all;
    So often has he known thee past him stray
    Rapt, twirling in thy hand a wither'd spray,
      And waiting for the spark from Heaven to fall.

And once, in winter, on the causeway chill
  Where home through flooded fields foot-travellers go,
    Have I not pass'd thee on the wooden bridge
Wrapt in thy cloak and battling with the snow,
    Thy face towards Hinksey and its wintry ridge?
      And thou hast climb'd the hill
And gain'd the white brow of the Cumner range,
    Turn'd once to watch, while thick the snowflakes fall,
    The line of festal light in Christ-Church hall—
      Then sought thy straw in some sequester'd grange.

But what—I dream! Two hundred years are flown
   Since first thy story ran through Oxford halls,
      And the grave Glanvil did the tale inscribe
   That thou wert wander'd from the studious walls
      To learn strange arts, and join a Gipsy tribe:
         And thou from earth art gone
      Long since, and in some quiet churchyard laid;
         Some country nook, where o'er thy unknown grave
         Tall grasses and white flowering nettles wave—
           Under a dark red-fruited yew-tree's shade.

No, no, thou hast not felt the lapse of hours.
   For what wears out the life of mortal men?
      'Tis that from change to change their being rolls:
   'Tis that repeated shocks, again, again,
      Exhaust the energy of strongest souls,
         And numb the elastic powers.
   Till having us'd our nerves with bliss and teen,
      And tir'd upon a thousand schemes our wit,
      To the just-pausing Genius we remit
         Our worn-out life, and are—what we have been.

Thou hast not liv'd, why should'st thou perish, so?
   Thou hadst *one* aim, *one* business, *one* desire:
      Else wert thou long since number'd with the dead—
   Else hadst thou spent like other men thy fire.
      The generations of thy peers are fled,
         And we ourselves shall go;
   But thou possessest an immortal lot,
      And we imagine thee exempt from age
      And living as thou liv'st on Glanvil's page,
         Because thou hadst—what we, alas, have not!

For early didst thou leave the world, with powers
   Fresh, undiverted to the world without,
      Firm to their mark, not spent on other things;
   Free from the sick fatigue, the languid doubt,
      Which much to have tried, in much been baffled, brings.
        O Life unlike to ours!

Who fluctuate idly without term or scope,
　Of whom each strives, nor knows for what he strives,
　　And each half lives a hundred different lives;
　　　Who wait like thee, but not, like thee, in hope.

Thou waitest for the spark from Heaven: and we,
　Vague half-believers of our casual creeds,
　　Who never deeply felt, nor clearly will'd,
　Whose insight never has borne fruit in deeds,
　　Whose weak resolves never have been fulfill'd;
　　　For whom each year we see
　Breeds new beginnings, disappointments new;
　　Who hesitate and falter life away,
　　And lose to-morrow the ground won to-day—
　　　Ah, do not we, Wanderer, await it too?

Yes, we await it, but it still delays,
　And then we suffer; and amongst us One,
　　Who most has suffer'd, takes dejectedly
　His seat upon the intellectual throne;
　　And all his store of sad experience he
　　　Lays bare of wretched days;
　Tells us his misery's birth and growth and signs,
　　And how the dying spark of hope was fed,
　　And how the breast was sooth'd, and how the head,
　　　And all his hourly varied anodynes.

This for our wisest: and we others pine,
　And wish the long unhappy dream would end,
　　And waive all claim to bliss, and try to bear,
　With close-lipp'd Patience for our only friend,
　　Sad Patience, too near neighbour to Despair:
　　　But none has hope like thine.
　Thou through the fields and through the woods dost stray,
　　Roaming the country side, a truant boy,
　　Nursing thy project in unclouded joy,
　　　And every doubt long blown by time away.

O born in days when wits were fresh and clear,
　And life ran gaily as the sparkling Thames;
　　Before this strange disease of modern life,

With its sick hurry, its divided aims,
  Its heads o'ertax'd, its palsied hearts, was rife—
    Fly hence, our contact fear!
Still fly, plunge deeper in the bowering wood!
  Averse, as Dido did with gesture stern
  From her false friend's approach in Hades turn,
    Wave us away, and keep thy solitude.

Still nursing the unconquerable hope,
  Still clutching the inviolable shade,
    With a free onward impulse brushing through,
  By night, the silver'd branches of the glade—
    Far on the forest skirts, where none pursue,
      On some mild pastoral slope
  Emerge, and resting on the moonlit pales,
    Freshen thy flowers, as in former years,
    With dew, or listen with enchanted ears,
      From the dark dingles, to the nightingales.

But fly our paths, our feverish contact fly!
  For strong the infection of our mental strife,
    Which, though it gives no bliss, yet spoils for rest;
  And we should win thee from thy own fair life,
    Like us distracted, and like us unblest.
      Soon, soon thy cheer would die,
  Thy hopes grow timorous, and unfix'd thy powers,
    And thy clear aims be cross and shifting made:
    And then thy glad perennial youth would fade,
      Fade, and grow old at last, and die like ours.

They fly our greetings, fly our speech and smiles!
  As some grave Tyrian trader, from the sea,
    Descried at sunrise an emerging prow
  Lifting the cool-hair'd creepers stealthily,
    The fringes of a southward-facing brow
      Among the Aegean isles;
  And saw the merry Grecian coaster come,
    Freighted with amber grapes, and Chian wine,
    Green bursting figs, and tunnies steeped in brine;
      And knew the intruders on his ancient home,

The young light-hearted Masters of the waves;
    And snatch'd his rudder, and shook out more sail,
    And day and night held on indignantly
O'er the blue Midland waters with the gale,
    Betwixt the Syrtes and soft Sicily,
        To where the Atlantic raves
Outside the Western Straits, and unbent sails
    There, where down cloudy cliffs, through sheets of foam,
    Shy traffickers, the dark Iberians come;
        And on the beach undid his corded bales.

FROM *Stanzas from the Grande Chartreuse*

For rigorous teachers seized my youth,
And purged its faith, and trimm'd its fire,
Show'd me the high white star of Truth,
There bade me gaze, and there aspire;
Even now their whispers pierce the gloom:
What dost thou in this living tomb?

Forgive me, masters of the mind!
At whose behest I long ago
So much unlearnt, so much resign'd!
I come not here to be your foe.
I seek these anchorites, not in ruth,
To curse and to deny your truth;

Not as their friend or child I speak!
But as on some far northern strand,
Thinking of his own gods, a Greek
In pity and mournful awe might stand
Before some fallen Runic stone—
For both were faiths, and both are gone.

Wandering between two worlds, one dead,
The other powerless to be born,
With nowhere yet to rest my head,
Like these, on earth I wait forlorn.
Their faith, my tears, the world deride;
I come to shed them at their side.

Dover Beach

The sea is calm to-night.
The tide is full, the moon lies fair
Upon the straits;—on the French coast the light
Gleams and is gone; the cliffs of England stand
Glimmering and vast, out in the tranquil bay.
Come to the window, sweet is the night-air!
Only, from the long line of spray
Where the sea meets the moon-blanch'd land,
Listen! you hear the grating roar
Of pebbles which the waves draw back, and fling,
At their return, up the high strand,
Begin, and cease, and then again begin,
With tremulous cadence slow, and bring
The eternal note of sadness in.

Sophocles long ago
Heard it on the Ægean, and it brought
Into his mind the turbid ebb and flow
Of human misery; we
Find also in the sound a thought,
Hearing it by this distant northern sea.

The Sea of Faith
Was once, too, at the full, and round earth's shore
Lay like the folds of a bright girdle furl'd.
But now I only hear
Its melancholy, long, withdrawing roar,
Retreating, to the breath
Of the night-wind, down the vast edges drear
And naked shingles of the world.

Ah, love, let us be true
To one another! for the world, which seems
To lie before us like a land of dreams,
So various, so beautiful, so new,
Hath really neither joy, nor love, nor light,
Nor certitude, nor peace, nor help for pain;
And we are here as on a darkling plain
Swept with confused alarms of struggle and flight,
Where ignorant armies clash by night.

WILLIAM JOHNSON CORY
(1823–1892)

Heraclitus

They told me, Heraclitus, they told me you were dead,
They brought me bitter news to hear and bitter tears to shed.
I wept as I remembered how often you and I
Had tired the sun with talking and sent him down the sky.

And now that thou art lying, my dear old Carian guest,
A handful of grey ashes, long, long ago at rest,
Still are thy pleasant voices, thy nightingales, awake;
For Death, he taketh all away, but them he cannot take.

From the Greek

COVENTRY KERSEY DIGHTON PATMORE
(1823–1896)

FROM *The Angel in the House*

An idle poet, here and there,
Looks round him; but, for all the rest
The world, unfathomably fair,
Is duller than a witling's jest.

Love wakes men, once a lifetime each;
They lift their heavy lids and look;
And, lo, what one sweet page can teach
They read with joy, then shut the book:

And some give thanks, and some blaspheme,
And most forget; but, either way,
That and the child's unheeded dream
Is all the light of all their day.

The Toys

My little Son, who looked from thoughtful eyes,
And moved and spoke in quiet grown-up wise,
Having my law the seventh time disobeyed,

I struck him, and dismissed
With hard words and unkissed,
—His Mother, who was patient, being dead.
Then, fearing lest his grief should hinder sleep,
I visited his bed,
But found him slumbering deep,
With darkened eyelids, and their lashes yet
From his late sobbing wet.
And I, with moan,
Kissing away his tears, left others of my own;
For, on a table drawn beside his head,
He had put, within his reach,
A box of counters and a red-veined stone,
A piece of glass abraded by the beach,
And six or seven shells,
A bottle with bluebells,
And two French copper coins, ranged there with careful art,
To comfort his sad heart.
So when that night I prayed
To God, I wept, and said:
Ah, when at last we lie with trancéd breath,
Not vexing Thee in death,
And Thou rememberest of what toys
We made our joys,
How weakly understood
Thy great commanded good,
Then fatherly not less
Than I whom Thou hast moulded from the clay,
Thou'lt leave Thy wrath, and say,
"I will be sorry for their childishness."

WILLIAM ALLINGHAM

(1824–1889)

The Fairies

Up the airy mountain,
  Down the rushy glen,
We daren't go a-hunting
  For fear of little men.

Wee folk, good folk,
    Trooping all together;
Green jacket, red cap,
    And white owl's feather!

Down along the rocky shore
    Some make their home—
They live on crispy pancakes
    Of yellow tide-foam;
Some in the reeds
    Of the black mountain-lake,
With frogs for their watch-dogs,
    All night awake.

High on the hill-top
    The old King sits;
He is now so old and grey,
    He's nigh lost his wits.
With a bridge of white mist
    Columbkill he crosses,
On his stately journeys
    From Slieveleague to Rosses;
Or going up with music
    On cold starry nights,
To sup with the Queen
    Of the gay Northern Lights.

They stole little Bridget
    For seven years long;
When she came down again,
    Her friends were all gone.
They took her lightly back,
    Between the night and morrow;
They thought that she was fast asleep,
    But she was dead with sorrow.
They have kept her ever since
    Deep within the lake,
On a bed of flag-leaves,
    Watching till she wake.

By the craggy hill-side,
    Through the mosses bare,
They have planted thorn-trees,
    For pleasure here and there.
Is any man so daring
    As dig them up in spite,
He shall find their sharpest thorns
    In his bed at night.

Up the airy mountain,
    Down the rushy glen,
We daren't go a-hunting
    For fear of little men.
Wee folk, good folk,
    Trooping all together;
Green jacket, red cap,
    And white owl's feather!

GEORGE MEREDITH

(1828–1909)

Love in the Valley

Under yonder beech-tree single on the green-sward,
    Couched with her arms behind her golden head,
Knees and tresses folded to slip and ripple idly,
    Lies my young love sleeping in the shade.
Had I the heart to slide an arm beneath her,
    Press her parting lips as her waist I gather slow,
Waking in amazement she could not but embrace me:
    Then would she hold me and never let me go?

Shy as the squirrel and wayward as the swallow,
    Swift as the swallow along the river's light
Circleting the surface to meet his mirrored winglets,
    Fleeter she seems in her stay than in her flight.
Shy as the squirrel that leaps among the pine-tops,
    Wayward as the swallow overhead at set of sun,
She whom I love is hard to catch and conquer,
    Hard, but O the glory of the winning were she won!

When her mother tends her before the laughing mirror,
   Tying up her laces, looping up her hair,
Often she thinks, were this wild thing wedded,
   More love should I have, and much less care.
When her mother tends her before the lighted mirror,
   Loosening her laces, combing down her curls,
Often she thinks, were this wild thing wedded,
   I should miss but one for many boys and girls.

Heartless she is as the shadow in the meadows
   Flying to the hills on a blue and breezy noon.
No, she is athirst and drinking up her wonder:
   Earth to her is young as the slip of the new moon.
Deals she an unkindness, 'tis but her rapid measure,
   Even as in a dance; and her smile can heal no less:
Like the swinging May-cloud that pelts the flowers with
      hailstones
   Off a sunny border, she was made to bruise and bless.

Lovely are the curves of the white owl sweeping
   Wavy in the dusk lit by one large star.
Lone on the fir-branch, his rattle-note unvaried,
   Brooding o'er the gloom, spins the brown eve-jar.
Darker grows the valley, more and more forgetting:
   So were it with me if forgetting could be willed.
Tell the grassy hollow that holds the bubbling well-spring,
   Tell it to forget the source that keeps it filled.

Stepping down the hill with her fair companions,
   Arm in arm, all against the raying West,
Boldly she sings, to the merry tune she marches,
   Brave is her shape, and sweeter unpossessed.
Sweeter, for she is what my heart first awaking
   Whispered the world was; morning light is she.
Love that so desires would fain keep her changeless;
   Fain would fling the net, and fain have her free.

Happy, happy time, when the white star hovers
   Low over dim fields fresh with bloomy dew,
Near the face of dawn, that draws athwart the darkness,
   Threading it with colour, like yewberries the yew.

Thicker crowd the shades as the grave East deepens
  Glowing, and with crimson a long cloud swells.
Maiden still the morn is; and strange she is, and secret;
  Strange her eyes; her cheeks are cold as cold sea-shells.

Sunrays, leaning on our southern hills and lighting
  Wild cloud-mountains that drag the hills along,
Oft ends the day of your shifting brilliant laughter
  Chill as a dull face frowning on a song.
Ay, but shows the South-West a ripple-feathered bosom
  Blown to silver while the clouds are shaken and ascend,
Scaling the mid-heavens as they stream, there comes a sunset
  Rich, deep like love in beauty without end.

When at dawn she sighs, and like an infant to the window
  Turns grave eyes craving light, released from dreams,
Beautiful she looks, like a white water-lily
  Bursting out of bud in havens of the streams.
When from bed she rises clothed from neck to ankle
  In her long nightgown sweet as boughs of May,
Beautiful she looks, like a tall garden lily
  Pure from the night, and splendid for the day.

Mother of the dews, dark eye-lashed twilight,
  Low-lidded twilight, o'er the valley's brim,
Rounding on thy breast sings the dew-delighted sky-lark,
  Clear as though the dewdrops had their voice in him.
Hidden where the rose-flush drinks the rayless planet,
  Fountain-full he pours the spraying fountain-showers.
Let me hear her laughter, I would have her ever
  Cool as dew in twilight, the lark above the flowers.

All the girls are out with their baskets for the primrose;
  Up lanes, woods through, they troop in joyful bands.
My sweet leads: she knows not why, but now she loiters,
  Eyes the bent anemones, and hangs her hands.
Such a look will tell that the violets are peeping,
  Coming the rose: and unaware a cry
Springs in her bosom for odours and for colour,
  Covert and the nightingale; she knows not why.

Kerchiefed head and chin she darts between her tulips,
    Streaming like a willow grey in arrowy rain:
Some bend beaten cheek to gravel, and their angel
    She will be; she lifts them, and on she speeds again.
Black the driving raincloud breasts the iron gateway:
    She is forth to cheer a neighbour lacking mirth.
So when sky and grass met rolling dumb for thunder
    Saw I once a white dove, sole light of earth.

Prim little scholars are the flowers of her garden,
    Trained to stand in rows, and asking if they please.
I might love them well but for loving more the wild ones:
    O my wild ones! they tell me more than these.
You, my wild one, you tell of honied field-rose,
    Violet, blushing eglantine in life; and even as they,
They by the wayside are earnest of your goodness,
    You are of life's, on the banks that line the way.

Peering at her chamber the white crowns the red rose,
    Jasmine winds the porch with stars two and three.
Parted is the window; she sleeps; the starry jasmine
    Breathes a falling breath that carries thoughts of me.
Sweeter unpossessed, have I said of her my sweetest?
    Not while she sleeps: while she sleeps the jasmine breathes,
Luring her to love; she sleeps; the starry jasmine
    Bears me to her pillow under white rose-wreaths.

Yellow with birdfoot-trefoil are the grass-glades;
    Yellow with cinquefoil of the dew-grey leaf;
Yellow with stone-crop; the moss-mounds are yellow;
    Blue-necked the wheat sways, yellowing to the sheaf.
Green-yellow bursts from the copse the laughing yaffle;
    Sharp as a sickle is the edge of shade and shine:
Earth in her heart laughs looking at the heavens,
    Thinking of the harvest: I look and think of mine.

This I may know: her dressing and undressing
    Such a change of light shows as when the skies in sport
Shift from cloud to moonlight; or edging over thunder
    Slips a ray of sun; or sweeping into port

White sails furl; or on the ocean borders
   White sails lean along the waves leaping green.
Visions of her shower before me, but from eyesight
   Guarded she would be like the sun were she seen.

Front door and back of the mossed old farmhouse
   Open with the morn, and in a breezy link
Freshly sparkles garden to stripe-shadowed orchard,
   Green across a rill where on sand the minnows wink.
Busy in the grass the early sun of summer
   Swarms, and the blackbird's mellow fluting notes
Call my darling up with round and roguish challenge:
   Quaintest, richest carol of all the singing throats!

Cool was the woodside; cool as her white dairy
   Keeping sweet the cream-pan; and there the boys from
      school,
Cricketing below, rushed brown and red with sunshine;
   O the dark translucence of the deep-eyed cool!
Spying from the farm, herself she fetched a pitcher
   Full of milk, and tilted for each in turn the beak.
Then a little fellow, mouth up and on tiptoe,
   Said "I will kiss you": she laughed and leaned her cheek.

Doves of the fir-wood walling high our red roof
   Through the long noon coo, crooning through the coo.
Loose droop the leaves, and down the sleepy roadway
   Sometimes pipes a chaffinch; loose droops the blue.
Cows flap a slow tail knee-deep in the river,
   Breathless, given up to sun and gnat and fly.
Nowhere is she seen; and if I see her nowhere,
   Lightning may come, straight rains and tiger sky.

O the golden sheaf, the rustling treasure-armful!
   O the nutbrown tresses nodding interlaced!
O the treasure-tresses one another over
   Nodding! O the girdle slack about the waist!
Slain are the poppies that shot their random scarlet
   Quick amid the wheatears: wound about the waist,
Gathered, see these brides of Earth one blush of ripeness!
   O the nutbrown tresses nodding interlaced!

Large and smoky red the sun's cold disk drops,
    Clipped by naked hills, on violet shaded snow:
Eastward large and still lights up a bower of moonrise,
    Whence at her leisure steps the moon aglow.
Nightlong on black print-branches our beech-tree
    Gazes in this whiteness: nightlong could I.
Here may life on death or death on life be painted.
    Let me clasp her soul to know she cannot die!

Gossips count her faults; they scour a narrow chamber
    Where there is no window, read not heaven or her.
"When she was a tiny," one aged woman quavers,
    Plucks at my heart and leads me by the ear.
Faults she had once as she learnt to run and tumbled:
    Faults of feature some see, beauty not complete.
Yet, good gossips, beauty that makes holy
    Earth and air, may have faults from head to feet.

Hither she comes; she comes to me; she lingers,
    Deepens her brown eyebrows, while in new surprise
High rise the lashes in wonder of a stranger;
    Yet am I the light and living of her eyes.
Something friends have told her fills her heart to brimming,
    Nets her in her blushes, and wounds her, and tames.—
Sure of her haven, O like a dove alighting,
    Arms up, she dropped: our souls were in our names.

Soon will she lie like a white-frost sunrise.
    Yellow oats and brown wheat, barley pale as rye,
Long since your sheaves have yielded to the thresher,
    Felt the girdle loosened, seen the tresses fly.
Soon will she lie like a blood-red sunset.
    Swift with the to-morrow, green-winged Spring!
Sing from the South-West, bring her back the truants,
    Nightingale and swallow, song and dipping wing.

Soft new beech-leaves, up to beamy April
    Spreading bough on bough a primrose mountain, you
Lucid in the moon, raise lilies to the skyfields,
    Youngest green transfused in silver shining through:

Fairer than the lily, than the wild white cherry:
   Fair as in image my seraph love appears
Borne to me by dreams when dawn is at my eyelids:
   Fair as in the flesh she swims to me on tears.

Could I find a place to be alone with heaven,
   I would speak my heart out: heaven is my need.
Every woodland tree is flushing like the dogwood,
   Flashing like the whitebeam, swaying like the reed.
Flushing like the dogwood crimson in October;
   Streaming like the flag-reed South-West blown;
Flashing as in gusts the sudden-lighted whitebeam:
   All seem to know what is for heaven alone.

FROM *Modern Love*

VI

It chanced his lips did meet her forehead cool.
She had no blush, but slanted down her eye.
Shamed nature, then, confesses love can die:
And most she punishes the tender fool
Who will believe what honours her the most!
Dead! Is it dead? She has a pulse, and flow
Of tears, the price of blood-drops, as I know,
For whom the midnight sobs around Love's ghost,
Since then I heard her, and so will sob on.
The love is here; it has but changed its aim.
O bitter barren woman! what's the name?
The name, the name, the new name thou hast won?
Behold me striking the world's coward stroke!
That will I not do, though the sting is dire.
—Beneath the surface this, while by the fire
They sat, she laughing at a quiet joke.

XII

Not solely that the Future she destroys,
And the fair life which in the distance lies
For all men, beckoning out from dim rich skies:
Nor that the passing hour's supporting joys

Have lost the keen-edged flavour, which begat
Distinction in old times, and still should breed
Sweet Memory, and Hope,—earth's modest seed,
And heaven's high-prompting: not that the world is flat
Since that soft-luring creature I embraced,
Among the children of Illusion went:
Methinks with all this loss I were content,
If the mad Past, on which my foot is based,
Were firm, or might be blotted: but the whole
Of life is mixed: the mocking Past will stay:
And if I drink oblivion of a day,
So shorten I the stature of my soul.

XXX

What are we first? First, animals; and next
Intelligences at a leap; on whom
Pale lies the distant shadow of the tomb,
And all that draweth on the tomb for text.
Into which state comes Love, the crowning sun:
Beneath whose light the shadow loses form.
We are the lords of life, and life is warm.
Intelligence and instinct now are one.
But nature says: "My children most they seem
When they least know me: therefore I decree
That they shall suffer." Swift doth young Love flee,
And we stand wakened, shivering from our dream.
Then if we study Nature we are wise,
Thus do the few who live but with the day:
The scientific animals are they.—
Lady, this is my sonnet to your eyes.

XLII

I am to follow her. There is much grace
In women when thus bent on martyrdom.
They think that dignity of soul may come,
Perchance, with dignity of body. Base!
But I was taken by that air of cold
And statuesque sedateness, when she said
"I'm going"; lit a taper, bowed her head,
And went, as with the stride of Pallas bold.
Fleshly indifference horrible! The hands

Of Time now signal: O, she's safe from me!
Within those secret walls what do I see?
Where first she set the taper down she stands:
Not Pallas: Hebe shamed! Thoughts black as death,
Like a stirred pool in sunshine break. Her wrists
I catch: she faltering, as she half resists,
"You love . . . ? love . . . ? love . . . ?" all on
        an indrawn breath.

XLVII

We saw the swallows gathering in the sky,
And in the osier-isle we heard them noise.
We had not to look back on summer joys,
Or forward to a summer of bright dye:
But in the largeness of the evening earth
Our spirits grew as we went side by side.
The hour became her husband and my bride.
Love that had robbed us so, thus blessed our dearth!
The pilgrims of the year waxed very loud
In multitudinous chatterings, as the flood
Full brown came from the West, and like pale blood
Expanded to the upper crimson cloud.
Love that had robbed us of immortal things,
This little moment mercifully gave,
Where I have seen across the twilight wave
The swan sail with her young beneath her wings.

L

Thus piteously Love closed what he begat:
The union of this ever-diverse pair!
These two were rapid falcons in a snare,
Condemned to do the flitting of the bat.
Lovers beneath the singing sky of May,
They wandered once; clear as the dew on flowers:
But they fed not on the advancing hours:
Their hearts held cravings for the buried day.
Then each applied to each that fatal knife,
Deep questioning, which probes to endless dole.
Ah, what a dusty answer gets the soul
When hot for certainties in this our life!—
In tragic hints here see what evermore

Moves dark as yonder midnight ocean's force,
Thundering like ramping hosts of warrior horse,
To throw that faint thin line upon the shore!

Appreciation

Earth was not Earth before her sons appeared,
Nor Beauty Beauty ere young Love was born:
And thou when I lay hidden wast as morn
At city-windows, touching eyelids bleared;
To none by her fresh wingedness endeared;
Unwelcome unto revellers outworn.
I the last echoes of Diana's horn
In woodland heard, and saw thee come, and cheered.
No longer wast thou then mere light, fair soul!
And more than simple duty moved thy feet.
New colours rose in thee, from fear, from shame,
From hope, effused: though not less pure a scroll
May men read on the heart I taught to beat:
That change in thee, if not thyself, I claim.

Lucifer in Starlight

On a starred night Prince Lucifer uprose.
Tired of his dark dominion swung the fiend
Above the rolling ball in cloud part screened,
Where sinners hugged their spectre of repose.
Poor prey to his hot fit of pride were those.
And now upon his western wing he leaned,
Now his huge bulk o'er Afric's sands careened,
Now the black planet shadowed Arctic snows.
Soaring through wider zones that pricked his scars
With memory of the old revolt from Awe,
He reached a middle height, and at the stars,
Which are the brain of heaven, he looked, and sank.
Around the ancient track marched, rank on rank,
The army of unalterable law.

DANTE GABRIEL ROSSETTI
(1828–1882)

A Little While

A little while a little love
  The hour yet bears for thee and me
  Who have not drawn the veil to see
If still our heaven be lit above.
Thou merely, at the day's last sigh,
  Hast felt thy soul prolong the tone;
And I have heard the night-wind cry
  And deemed its speech mine own.

A little while a little love
  The scattering autumn hoards for us
  Whose bower is not yet ruinous
Nor quite unleaved our songless grove.
Only across the shaken boughs
  We hear the flood-tides seek the sea,
And deep in both our hearts they rouse
  One wail for thee and me.

A little while a little love
  May yet be ours who have not said
  The word it makes our eyes afraid
To know that each is thinking of.
Not yet the end: be our lips dumb
  In smiles a little season yet:
I'll tell thee, when the end is come,
  How we may best forget.

Three Shadows

I looked and saw your eyes
  In the shadow of your hair,
As a traveller sees the stream
  In the shadow of the wood;

And I said, "My faint heart sighs,
   Ah me! to linger there,
To drink deep and to dream
   In that sweet solitude."

I looked and saw your heart
   In the shadow of your eyes,
As a seeker sees the gold
   In the shadow of the stream;
And I said, "Ah me! what art
   Should win the immortal prize,
Whose want must make life cold
   And Heaven a hollow dream?"

I looked and saw your love
   In the shadow of your heart,
As a diver sees the pearl
   In the shadow of the sea;
And I murmured, not above
   My breath, but all apart,—
"Ah! you can love, true girl,
   And is your love for me?"

Autumn Song

Know'st thou not at the fall of the leaf
How the heart feels a languid grief
   Laid on it for a covering,
   And how sleep seems a goodly thing
In Autumn at the fall of the leaf?

And how the swift beat of the brain
Falters because it is in vain,
   In Autumn at the fall of the leaf
   Knowest thou not? and how the chief
Of joys seems—not to suffer pain?

Know'st thou not at the fall of the leaf
How the soul feels like a dried sheaf
   Bound up at length for harvesting,
   And how death seems a comely thing
In Autumn at the fall of the leaf?

For a Venetian Pastoral by Giorgione

Water, for anguish of the solstice:—nay,
  But dip the vessel slowly,—nay, but lean
  And hark how at its verge the wave sighs in
Reluctant. Hush! beyond all depth away
The heat lies silent at the brink of day:
  Now the hand trails upon the viol-string
  That sobs, and the brown faces cease to sing,
Sad with the whole of pleasure. Whither stray
Her eyes now, from whose mouth the slim pipes creep
  And leave it pouting, while the shadowed grass
  Is cool against her naked side? Let be:—
Say nothing now unto her lest she weep,
  Nor name this ever. Be it as it was,—
  Life touching lips with immortality.

FROM *The House of Life*

1.

A Sonnet is a moment's monument,—
  Memorial from the Soul's eternity
  To one dead deathless hour. Look that it be,
Whether for lustral rite or dire portent,
Of its own arduous fullness reverent:
  Carve it in ivory or in ebony,
  As Night or Day may rule; and let Time see
Its flowering crest impearled and orient.

A Sonnet is a coin: its face reveals
  The soul,—its converse, to what Power 'tis due:—
Whether for tribute to the august appeals
  Of Life, or dower in Love's high retinue,
It serve; or, mid the dark wharf's cavernous breath,
In Charon's palm it pay the toll to Death.

2.   **LOVESIGHT**

When do I see thee most, beloved one?
  When in the light the spirits of mine eyes
  Before thy face, their altar, solemnize

The worship of that Love through thee made known?
Or when in the dusk hours (we two alone),
    Close-kissed and eloquent of still replies
    Thy twilight-hidden glimmering visage lies,
And my soul only sees thy soul its own?

O love, my love! if I no more should see
Thyself, nor on the earth the shadow of thee,
    Nor image of thine eyes in any spring,—
How then should sound upon Life's darkening slope
The ground-whirl of the perished leaves of Hope,
    The wind of Death's imperishable wing?

3.   WITHOUT HER

What of her glass without her? The blank grey
    There where the pool is blind of the moon's face.
    Her dress without her? The tossed empty space
Of cloud-rack whence the moon has passed away.
Her paths without her? Day's appointed sway
    Usurped by desolate night. Her pillowed place
    Without her? Tears, ah me! for love's good grace,
And cold forgetfulness of night or day.

What of the heart without her? Nay, poor heart,
    Of thee what word remains ere speech be still?
    A wayfarer by barren ways and chill,
Steep ways and weary, without her thou art,
Where the long cloud, the long wood's counterpart,
    Sheds doubled darkness up the labouring hill.

4.   THE CHOICE

I

Eat thou and drink; to-morrow thou shalt die.
    Surely the earth, that's wise being very old,
    Needs not our help. Then loose me, love, and hold
Thy sultry hair up from my face; that I

May pour for thee this golden wine, brim-high,
   Till round the glass thy fingers glow like gold.
   We'll drown all hours: thy song, while hours are toll'd,
Shall leap, as fountains veil the changing sky.

Now kiss, and think that there are really those,
   My own high-bosomed beauty, who increase
      Vain gold, vain lore, and yet might choose our way!
      Through many years they toil; then on a day
   They die not,—for their life was death,—but cease;
And round their narrow lips the mould falls close.

II

Watch thou and fear; to-morrow thou shalt die.
   Or art thou sure thou shalt have time for death?
   Is not the day which God's word promiseth
To come man knows not when? In yonder sky
Now while we speak, the sun speeds forth: can I
   Or thou assure him of his goal? God's breath
   Even at this moment haply quickeneth
The air to a flame; till spirits, always nigh
Though screened and hid, shall walk the daylight here.
   And dost thou prate of all that men shall do?
      Canst thou, who hast but plagues, presume to be
      Glad in his gladness that comes after thee?
   Will *his* strength slay *thy* worm in Hell? Go to:
Cover thy countenance, and watch, and fear.

III

Think thou and act; to-morrow thou shalt die.
   Outstretched in the sun's warmth upon the shore,
   Thou say'st: "Man's measured path is all gone o'er:
Up all his years, steeply, with strain and sigh,
Man clomb until he touched the truth; and I,
   Even I, am he whom it was destined for."
   How should this be? Art thou then so much more
Than they who sowed, that thou shouldst reap thereby?

Nay, come up hither. From this wave-washed mound
   Unto the furthest flood-brim look with me;

Then reach on with thy thought till it be drowned.
  Miles and miles distant though the last line be,
And though thy soul sail leagues and leagues beyond,—
  Still, leagues beyond those leagues, there is more sea.

The Ballad of Dead Ladies

Tell me now in what hidden way is
  Lady Flora the hidden Roman?
Where's Hipparchia, and where is Thais,
  Neither of them the fairer woman?
  Where is Echo, beheld of no man,
Only heard in river and mere,—
  She whose beauty was more than human? . . .
But where are the snows of yester-year?

Where's Héloïse, the learned nun,
  For whose sake Abeillard, I ween,
Lost manhood and put priesthood on?
  (From Love he won such dule and teen!)
  And where, I pray you, is the Queen
Who willed that Buridan should steer
  Sewed in a sack's mouth down the Seine? . . .
But where are the snows of yester-year?

White Queen Blanche, like a queen of lilies,
  With a voice like any mermaiden,—
Bertha Broadfoot, Beatrice, Alice,
  And Ermengarde the lady of Maine,—
  And that good Joan whom Englishmen
At Rouen doomed and burned her there,—
  Mother of God, where are they then? . . .
But where are the snows of yester-year?

Nay, never ask this week, fair lord,
  Where they are gone, nor yet this year,
Save with thus much for an overword,—
  But where are the snows of yester-year?

From the French of FRANÇOIS VILLON, 1450

Beauty
(A COMBINATION FROM SAPPHO)

Like the sweet apple which reddens upon the topmost bough,
A-top on the topmost twig,—which the pluckers forgot some-
how,—
Forgot it not, nay, but got it not, for none could get it till now.

Like the wild hyacinth which on the hills is found,
Which the passing feet of the shepherds for ever tear and
wound,
Until the purple blossom is trodden into the ground.

SILAS WEIR MITCHELL
(1829–1914)

A Decanter of Madeira, Aged 86,
to George Bancroft, Aged 86

Good master, you and I were born
    In "Teacup days" of hoop and hood,
And when the silver cue hung down,
    And toasts were drunk, and wine was good;

When kin of mine (a jolly brood)
    From sideboards looked, and knew full well
What courage they had given the beau,
    How generous made the blushing belle.

Ah me! what gossip could I prate
    Of days when doors were locked at dinners!
Believe me, I have kissed the lips
    Of many pretty saints—or sinners.

Lip service have I done, alack!
    I don't repent, but come what may,
What ready lips, sir, I have kissed,
    Be sure at least I shall not say.

Two honest gentlemen are we,—
    I Demi John, whole George are you;
When Nature grew us one in years
    She meant to make a generous brew.

She bade me store for festal hours
    The sun our south-side vineyard knew;
To sterner tasks she set your life,
    As statesman, writer, scholar, grew.

Years eighty-six have come and gone;
    At last we meet. Your health to-night.
Take from this board of friendly hearts
    The memory of a proud delight.

The days that went have made you wise.
    There's wisdom in my rare bouquet.
I'm rather paler than I was;
    And on my soul, you're growing gray.

I like to think, when Toper Time
    Has drained the last of me and you,
Some here shall say, They both were good,—
    The wine we drank, the man we knew.

CHRISTINA GEORGINA ROSSETTI

(1830–1894)

FROM *Monna Innominata*

XI

Many in after times will say of you
"He loved her"—while of me what will they say?
Not that I loved you more than just in play,
For fashion's sake as idle women do.
Even let them prate; who know not what we knew
Of love and parting in exceeding pain,
Of parting hopeless here to meet again,
Hopeless on earth, and heaven is out of view.
But by my heart of love laid bare to you,

My love that you can make not void nor vain,
Love that foregoes you but to claim anew
Beyond this passage of the gate of death,
I charge you at the Judgment make it plain
My love of you was life and not a breath.

XIV

Youth gone, and beauty gone if ever there
Dwelt beauty in so poor a face as this;
Youth gone and beauty, what remains of bliss?
I will not bind fresh roses in my hair,
To shame a cheek at best but little fair,—
Leave youth his roses, who can bear a thorn,—
I will not seek for blossoms anywhere,
Except such common flowers as blow with corn.
Youth gone and beauty gone, what doth remain?
The longing of a heart pent up forlorn,
A silent heart whose silence loves and longs;
The silence of a heart which sang its songs
While youth and beauty made a summer morn,
Silence of love that cannot sing again.

Song

When I am dead, my dearest,
    Sing no sad songs for me;
Plant thou no roses at my head,
    Nor shady cypress tree:
Be the green grass above me
    With showers and dewdrops wet:
And if thou wilt, remember,
    And if thou wilt, forget.

I shall not see the shadows,
    I shall not feel the rain;
I shall not hear the nightingale
    Sing on as if in pain:
And dreaming through the twilight
    That doth not rise nor set,
Haply I may remember,
    And haply may forget.

Song

Oh roses for the flush of youth,
    And laurel for the perfect prime;
But pluck an ivy branch for me
    Grown old before my time.

Oh violets for the grave of youth,
    And bay for those dead in their prime;
Give me the withered leaves I chose
    Before in the old time.

Remember

Remember me when I am gone away,
Gone far away into the silent land;
When you can no more hold me by the hand,
Nor I half turn to go yet turning stay.
Remember me when no more day by day
You tell me of our future that you plann'd:
Only remember me; you understand
It will be late to counsel then or pray.
Yet if you should forget me for a while
And afterwards remember, do not grieve:
For if the darkness and corruption leave
A vestige of the thoughts that once I had,
Better by far you should forget and smile
Than that you should remember and be sad.

FROM *The Prince's Progress*

Too late for love, too late for joy,
    Too late, too late!
You loitered on the road too long,
    You trifled at the gate:
The enchanted dove upon her branch
    Died without a mate;
The enchanted princess in her tower
    Slept, died, behind the grate;
Her heart was starving all this while
    You made it wait.

Ten years ago, five years ago,
  One year ago,
Even then you had arrived in time,
  Though somewhat slow;
Then you had known her living face
  Which now you cannot know:
The frozen fountain would have leaped,
  The buds gone on to blow,
The warm south wind would have awaked
  To melt the snow.

Is she fair now as she lies?
  Once she was fair;
Meet queen for any kindly king,
  With gold-dust on her hair.
Now these are poppies in her locks,
  White poppies she must wear;
Must wear a veil to shroud her face
  And the want graven there:
Or is the hunger fed at length,
  Cast off the care?

We never saw her with a smile
  Or with a frown;
Her bed seemed never soft to her,
  Though tossed of down;
She little heeded what she wore,
  Kirtle, or wreath, or gown;
We think her white brows often ached
  Beneath her crown,
Till silvery hairs showed in her locks
  That used to be so brown.

We never heard her speak in haste;
  Her tones were sweet,
And modulated just so much
  As it was meet:
Her heart sat silent through the noise
  And concourse of the street.

There was no hurry in her hands,
    No hurry in her feet;
There was no bliss drew nigh to her,
    That she might run to greet.

You should have wept her yesterday,
    Wasting upon her bed:
But wherefore should you weep to-day
    That she is dead?
Lo, we who love weep not to-day,
    But crown her royal head.
Let be these poppies that we strew,
    Your roses are too red:
Let these be poppies, not for you
    Cut down and spread.

A Birthday

My heart is like a singing bird
    Whose nest is in a watered shoot:
My heart is like an apple-tree
    Whose boughs are bent with thickset fruit;
My heart is like a rainbow shell
    That paddles in a halcyon sea;
My heart is gladder than all these
    Because my love is come to me.

Raise me a dais of silk and down;
    Hang it with vair and purple dyes;
Carve it in doves and pomegranates,
    And peacocks with a hundred eyes;
Work it in gold and silver grapes,
    In leaves and silver fleurs-de-lys;
Because the birthday of my life
    Is come, my love is come to me.

Echo

Come to me in the silence of the night;
  Come in the speaking silence of a dream;
Come with soft rounded cheeks and eyes as bright
    As sunlight on a stream;
      Come back in tears,
O memory, hope, love of finished years.

O dream how sweet, too sweet, too bitter sweet,
  Whose wakening should have been in Paradise,
Where souls brimfull of love abide and meet;
    Where thirsty longing eyes
      Watch the slow door
That opening, letting in, lets out no more.

Yet come to me in dreams, that I may live
  My very life again though cold in death:
Come back to me in dreams, that I may give
    Pulse for pulse, breath for breath:
      Speak low, lean low,
As long ago, my love, how long ago.

Up-Hill

Does the road wind up-hill all the way?
  Yes, to the very end.
Will the day's journey take the whole long day?
  From morn to night, my friend.

But is there for the night a resting-place?
  A roof for when the slow dark hours begin.
May not the darkness hide it from my face?
  You cannot miss that inn.

Shall I meet other wayfarers at night?
  Those who have gone before.
Then must I knock, or call when just in sight?
  They will not keep you standing at that door.

Shall I find comfort, travel-sore and weak?
    Of labour you shall find the sum.
Will there be beds for me and all who seek?
    Yea, beds for all who come.

Twice

I took my heart in my hand,
    (O my love, O my love),
I said: Let me fall or stand,
    Let me live or die,
But this once hear me speak—
    (O my love, O my love)—
Yet a woman's words are weak;
    You should speak, not I.

You took my heart in your hand
    With a friendly smile,
With a critical eye you scanned,
    Then set it down,
And said: It is still unripe
    Better wait awhile;
Wait while the skylarks pipe,
    Till the corn grows brown.

As you set it down it broke—
    Broke, but did not wince;
I smiled at the speech you spoke,
    At your judgment that I heard:
But I have not often smiled
    Since then, nor questioned since,
Nor cared for corn-flowers wild,
    Nor sung with the singing bird.

I take my heart in my hand,
    O my God, O my God,
My broken heart in my hand:
    Thou hast seen, judge Thou.

My hope was written on sand,
    O my God, O my God:
Now let Thy judgment stand—
    Yea, judge me now.

This contemned of a man,
    This marred one heedless day,
This heart take Thou to scan
    Both within and without:
Refine with fire its gold,
    Purge Thou its dross away—
Yea hold it in Thy hold,
    Whence none can pluck it out.

I take my heart in my hand—
    I shall not die, but live—
Before Thy face I stand;
    I, for Thou callest such:
All that I have I bring,
    All that I am I give;
Smile Thou and I shall sing,
    But shall not question much.

EMILY DICKINSON

(1830–1886)

"My Life Closed Twice..."

My life closed twice before its close;
    It yet remains to see
If Immortality unveil
    A third event to me,

So huge, so hopeless to conceive,
    As these that twice befell.
Parting is all we know of heaven,
    And all we need of hell.

"Doubt Me..."

Doubt me, my dim companion!
Why, God would be content
With but a fraction of the love
Poured thee without a stint.
The whole of me, forever,
What more the woman can,—
Say quick, that I may dower thee
With last delight I own!

It cannot be my spirit,
For that was thine before;
I ceded all of dust I knew,—
What opulence the more
Had I, a humble maiden,
Whose farthest of degree
Was that she might
Some distant heaven,
Dwell timidly with thee!

"I'm Ceded..."

I'm ceded, I've stopped being theirs;
The name they dropped upon my face
With water, in the country church,
Is finished using now,
And they can put it with my dolls,
My childhood, and the string of spools
I've finished threading too.

Baptized before without the choice,
But this time consciously, of grace
Unto supremest name,
Called to my full, the crescent dropped,
Existence's whole arc filled up
With one small diadem.

My second rank, too small the first,
Crowned, crowing on my father's breast,
A half unconscious queen;
But this time, adequate, erect,
With will to choose or to reject,
And I choose—just a throne.

"I'm Wife..."

I'm wife; I've finished that,
That other state;
I'm Czar, I'm woman now:
It's safer so.

How odd the girl's life looks
Behind this soft eclipse!
I think that earth seems so
To those in heaven now.

This being comfort, then
That other kind was pain;
But why compare?
I'm wife! stop there!

"Proud of My Broken Heart..."

Proud of my broken heart since thou didst break it,
    Proud of the pain I did not feel till thee.
Proud of my night since thou with moons dost slake it,
    Not to partake thy passion, my humility.

"Heart, We Will Forget Him!"

Heart, we will forget him!
   You and I, to-night!
You may forget the warmth he gave,
   I will forget the light.

When you have done, pray tell me,
   That I my thoughts may dim;
Haste! lest while you're lagging,
   I may remember him!

"Title Divine Is Mine"

Title divine is mine
The Wife without
The Sign.
Acute degree
Conferred on me—
Empress of Calvary.
Royal all but the
Crown—
Betrothed, without the swoon
God gives us women
When two hold
Garnet to garnet,
Gold to gold—
Born—Bridalled—
Shrouded—
In a day
Tri-Victory—
"My Husband"
Women say
Stroking the melody,
Is this the way?

"This Quiet Dust..."

This quiet dust was Gentlemen and Ladies,
   And Lads and Girls;
Was laughter and ability and sighing,
   And frocks and curls.
This passive place a Summer's nimble mansion,
   Where Bloom and Bees
Fulfilled their Oriental Circuit,
   Then ceased like these.

JAMES THOMSON

(1834–1882)

FROM *The City of Dreadful Night*

PROEM

Lo, thus, as prostrate, "In the dust I write
  My heart's deep languor and my soul's sad tears."
Yet why evoke the spectres of black night
  To blot the sunshine of exultant years?
Why disinter dead faith from mouldering hidden?
Why break the seals of mute despair unbidden,
  And wail life's discords into careless ears?

Because a cold rage seizes one at whiles
  To show their bitter old and wrinkled truth
Stripped naked of all vesture that beguiles,
  False dreams, false hopes, false masks and modes of youth;
Because it gives some sense of power and passion
In helpless impotence to try to fashion
  Our woe in living words howe'er uncouth.

Surely I write not for the hopeful young,
  Or those who deem their happiness of worth,
Or such as pasture and grow fat among
  The shows of life and feel not doubt nor dearth,
Or pious spirits with a God above them
To sanctify and glorify and love them,
  Or sages who foresee a heaven on earth.

For none of these I write, and none of these
  Could read the writing if they deigned to try:
So may they flourish in their due degrees,
  On our sweet earth and in their unplaced sky.
If any cares for the weak words here written,
It must be some one desolate, Fate-smitten,
  Whose faith and hope are dead, and who would die.

Yes, here and there some weary wanderer
  In that same city of tremendous night
Will understand the speech, and feel a stir
  Of fellowship in all-disastrous fight;

"I suffer mute and lonely, yet another
Uplifts his voice to let me know a brother
    Travels the same wild paths though out of sight."

O sad Fraternity, do I unfold
    Your dolorous mysteries shrouded from of yore?
Nay, be assured; no secret can be told
    To any who divined it not before:
None uninitiate by many a presage
Will comprehend the language of the message,
    Although proclaimed aloud for evermore.

I

The City is of Night; perchance of Death,
    But certainly of Night; for never there
Can come the lucid morning's fragrant breath
    After the dewy dawning's cold grey air;
The moon and stars may shine with scorn or pity;
The sun has never visited that city,
    For it dissolveth in the daylight fair.

Dissolveth like a dream of night away;
    Though present in distempered gloom of thought
And deadly weariness of heart all day.
    But when a dream night after night is brought
Throughout a week, and such weeks few or many
Recur each year for several years, can any
    Discern that dream from real life in aught?

For life is but a dream whose shapes return,
    Some frequently, some seldom, some by night
And some by day, some night and day: we learn,
    The while all change and many vanish quite,
In their recurrence with recurrent changes
A certain seeming order; where this ranges
    We count things real; such is memory's might.

A river girds the city west and south,
    The main north channel of a broad lagoon,
Regurging with the salt tides from the mouth;
    Waste marshes shine and glister to the moon

For leagues, then moorland black, then stony ridges;
Great piers and causeways, many noble bridges,
  Connect the town and islet suburbs strewn.

Upon an easy slope it lies at large,
  And scarcely overlaps the long curved crest
Which swells out two leagues from the river marge.
  A trackless wilderness rolls north and west,
Savannahs, savage woods, enormous mountains,
Bleak uplands, black ravines with torrent fountains;
  And eastward rolls the shipless sea's unrest.

The city is not ruinous, although
  Great ruins of an unremembered past,
With others of a few short years ago
  More sad, are found within its precincts vast.
The street-lamps always burn; but scarce a casement
In house or palace front from roof to basement
  Doth glow or gleam athwart the mirk air cast.

The street-lamps burn amidst the baleful glooms,
  Amidst the soundless solitudes immense
Of rangéd mansions dark and still as tombs.
  The silence which benumbs or strains the sense
Fulfils with awe the soul's despair unweeping:
Myriads of habitants are ever sleeping,
  Or dead, or fled from nameless pestilence!

Yet as in some necropolis you find
  Perchance one mourner to a thousand dead,
So there; worn faces that look deaf and blind
  Like tragic masks of stone. With weary tread,
Each wrapt in his own doom, they wander, wander,
Or sit foredone and desolately ponder
  Through sleepless hours with heavy drooping head.

Mature men chiefly, few in age or youth,
  A woman rarely, now and then a child:
A child! If here the heart turns sick with ruth
  To see a little one from birth defiled,

Or lame or blind, as preordained to languish
Through youthless life, think how it bleeds with anguish
    To meet one erring in that homeless wild.

They often murmur to themselves, they speak
    To one another seldom, for their woe
Broods maddening inwardly, and scorns to wreak
    Itself abroad; and if at whiles it grow
To frenzy which must rave, none heeds the clamour,
Unless there waits some victim of like glamour,
    To rave in turn, who lends attentive show.

The City is of Night, but not of Sleep;
    There sweet sleep is not for the weary brain;
The pitiless hours like years and ages creep,
    A night seems termless hell. This dreadful strain
Of thought and consciousness which never ceases,
Or which some moments' stupor but increases,
    This, worse than woe, makes wretches there insane.

They leave all hope behind who enter there:
    One certitude while sane they cannot leave,
One anodyne for torture and despair;
    The certitude of Death, which no reprieve
Can put off long; and which, divinely tender,
But waits the outstretched hand to promptly render
    That draught whose slumber nothing can bereave.

XIII

Of all things human which are strange and wild
    This is perchance the wildest and most strange,
And showeth man most utterly beguiled,
    To those who haunt that sunless City's range;
That he bemoans himself for aye, repeating
How time is deadly swift, how life is fleeting,
    How naught is constant on the earth but change.

The hours are heavy on him and the days;
    The burden of the months he scarce can bear;
And often in his secret soul he prays
    To sleep through barren periods unaware,

Arousing at some longed-for date of pleasure;
Which having passed and yielded him small treasure,
   He would outsleep another term of care.

Yet in his marvellous fancy he must make
   Quick wings for Time, and see it fly from us;
This Time that crawleth like a monstrous snake,
   Wounded and slow and very venomous;
Which creeps blindwormlike round the earth and ocean,
Distilling poison at each painful motion,
   And seems condemned to circle ever thus.

And since he cannot spend and use aright
   The little time here given him in trust,
But wasteth it in weary undelight
   Of foolish toil and trouble, strife and lust,
He naturally claimeth to inherit
The everlasting Future, that his merit
   May have full scope; as surely is most just.

O length of the intolerable hours,
   O nights that are as aeons of slow pain,
O Time, too ample for our vital powers,
   O Life, whose woeful vanities remain
Immutable for all of all our legions
Through all the centuries and in all the regions,
   Not of your speed and variance *we* complain.

We do not ask a longer term of strife,
   Weakness and weariness and nameless woes;
We do not claim renewed and endless life
   When this which is our torment here shall close,
An everlasting conscious inanition!
We yearn for speedy death in full fruition,
   Dateless oblivion and divine repose.

FROM *Sunday up the River*

I

I looked out into the morning,
　I looked out into the west:
The soft blue eye of the quiet sky
　Still drooped in dreamy rest;

The trees were still like clouds there,
　The clouds like mountains dim;
The broad mist lay, a silver bay
　Whose tide was at the brim.

I looked out into the morning,
　I looked out into the east:
The flood of light upon the night
　Had silently increased;

The sky was pale with fervour,
　The distant trees were grey,
The hill-lines drawn like waves of dawn
　Dissolving in the day.

I looked out into the morning;
　Looked east, looked west, with glee:
O richest day of happy May,
　My love will spend with me!

XVIII

The wine of Love is music,
　And the feast of Love is song:
And when Love sits down to the banquet,
　　Love sits long;

Sits long and ariseth drunken,
　But not with the feast and the wine;
He reeleth with his own heart,
　　That great rich Vine.

FROM *Sunday at Hampstead*

x

As we rush, as we rush in the Train,
  The trees and the houses go wheeling back,
But the starry heavens above the plain
  Come flying on our track.

All the beautiful stars of the sky,
  The silver doves of the forest of Night,
Over the dull earth swarm and fly,
  Companions of our flight.

We will rush ever on without fear;
  Let the goal be far, the flight be fleet!
For we carry the Heavens with us, Dear,
  While the Earth slips from our feet!

WILLIAM MORRIS

(1834–1896)

Summer Dawn

Pray but one prayer for me 'twixt thy closed lips,
  Think but one thought of me up in the stars.
  The summer night waneth, the morning light slips,
Faint and grey 'twixt the leaves of the aspen, betwixt the
    cloud-bars,
That are patiently waiting there for the dawn:
  Patient and colourless, though Heaven's gold
Waits to float through them along with the sun.
Far out in the meadows, above the young corn,
  The heavy elms wait, and restless and cold
The uneasy wind rises; the roses are dun;
Through the long twilight they pray for the dawn.
Round the lone house in the midst of the corn.
  Speak but one word to me over the corn,
  Over the tender, bowed locks of the corn.

FROM *The Life and Death of Jason*

1.

I know a little garden-close,
Set thick with lily and red rose,
Where I would wander if I might
From dewy dawn to dewy night,
And have one with me wandering.

And though within it no birds sing,
And though no pillared house is there,
And though the apple boughs are bare
Of fruit and blossom, would to God,
Her feet upon the green grass trod,
And I beheld them as before.

There comes a murmur from the shore,
And in the place two fair streams are,
Drawn from the purple hills afar,
Drawn down unto the restless sea;
The hills whose flowers ne'er fed the bee,
The shore no ship has ever seen,
Still beaten by the billows green,
Whose murmur comes unceasingly
Unto the place for which I cry.

For which I cry both day and night,
For which I let slip all delight,
That maketh me both deaf and blind,
Careless to win, unskilled to find,
And quick to lose what all men seek.

Yet tottering as I am and weak,
Still have I left a little breath
To seek within the jaws of death
An entrance to that happy place,
To seek the unforgotten face
Once seen, once kissed, once reft from me
Anigh the murmuring of the sea.

2.

The Sirens: O happy seafarers are ye,
And surely all your ills are past,

And toil upon the land and sea,
   Since ye are brought to us at last.

To you the fashion of the world,
   Wide lands laid waste, fair cities burned,
And plagues, and kings from kingdoms hurled,
   Are nought, since hither ye have turned.

For as upon this beach we stand,
   And o'er our heads the sea-fowl flit,
Our eyes behold a glorious land,
   And soon shall ye be kings of it.

Orpheus: A little more, a little more,
   O carriers of the Golden Fleece,
A little labour with the oar,
   Before we reach the land of Greece.

E'en now perchance faint rumours reach
   Men's ears of this our victory,
And draw them down unto the beach
   To gaze across the empty sea.

But since the longed-for day is nigh,
   And scarce a God could stay us now,
Why do ye hang your heads and sigh,
   Hindering for nought our eager prow?

The Sirens: Ah, had ye chanced to reach the home
   On which your fond desires were set,
Into what troubles had ye come?
   Short love and joy and long regret.

But now, but now, when ye have lain
   Asleep with us a little while
Beneath the washing of the main,
   How calm shall be your waking smile!

For ye shall smile to think of life
   That knows no troublous change or fear,

No unavailing bitter strife,
    That ere its time brings trouble near.

Orpheus: Is there some murmur in your ears,
        That all that we have done is nought,
And nothing ends our cares and fears,
        Till the last fear on us is brought?

The Sirens: Alas! and will ye stop your ears,
        In vain desire to do aught,
And wish to live 'mid cares and fears,
        Until the last fear makes you nought?

Orpheus: Is not the May-time now on earth,
        When close against the city wall
The folks are singing in their mirth,
        While on their heads the May-flowers fall?

The Sirens: Yes, May is come, and its sweet breath
        Shall well-nigh make you weep to-day,
And pensive with swift-coming death,
        Shall ye be satiate of the May.

Orpheus: Shall not July bring fresh delight,
        As underneath green trees ye sit,
And o'er some damsel's body white
        The noontide shadows change and flit?

The Sirens: No new delight July shall bring
        But ancient fear and fresh desire,
And, spite of every lovely thing,
        Of July surely shall ye tire.

Orpheus: And now, when August comes on thee,
        And 'mid the golden sea of corn
The merry reapers thou mayst see,
        Wilt thou still think the earth forlorn?

The Sirens: Set flowers upon thy short-lived head,
            And in thine heart forgetfulness
          Of man's hard toil, and scanty bread,
            And weary of those days no less.

Orpheus: Or wilt thou climb the sunny hill,
            In the October afternoon,
          To watch the purple earth's blood fill
            The grey vat to the maiden's tune?

The Sirens: When thou beginnest to grow old,
            Bring back remembrance of thy bliss
          With that the shining cup doth hold,
            And weary helplessly of this.

Orpheus: Or pleasureless shall we pass by
            The long cold night and leaden day,
          That song and tale and minstrelsy
            Shall make as merry as the May?

The Sirens: List then, to-night, to some old tale
            Until the tears o'erflow thine eyes;
          But what shall all these things avail
            When sad to-morrow comes and dies?

Orpheus: And when the world is born again,
            And with some fair love, side by side,
          Thou wanderest 'twixt the sun and rain,
            In that fresh love-begetting tide;

          Then, when the world is born again,
            And the sweet year before thee lies,
          Shall thy heart think of coming pain,
            Or vex itself with memories?

The Sirens: Ah! then the world is born again
            With burning love unsatisfied,
          And new desires fond and vain,
            And weary days from tide to tide.

Ah! when the world is born again,
  A little day is soon gone by,
When thou, unmoved by sun or rain,
  Within a cold straight house shall lie.

FROM *The Earthly Paradise*

1.

Of Heaven or Hell I have no power to sing,
I cannot ease the burden of your fears,
Or make quick-coming death a little thing,
Or bring again the pleasure of past years,
Nor for my words shall ye forget your tears,
Or hope again for aught that I can say,
The idle singer of an empty day.

But rather, when aweary of your mirth,
From full hearts still unsatisfied ye sigh,
And, feeling kindly unto all the earth,
Grudge every minute as it passes by,
Made the more mindful that the sweet days die—
Remember me a little then I pray,
The idle singer of an empty day.

The heavy trouble, the bewildering care
That weighs us down who live and earn our bread,
These idle verses have no power to bear;
So let me sing of names remember'd,
Because they, living not, can ne'er be dead,
Or long time take their memory quite away
From us poor singers of an empty day.

Dreamer of dreams, born out of my due time,
Why should I strive to set the crooked straight?
Let it suffice me that my murmuring rhyme
Beats with light wing against the ivory gate,
Telling a tale not too importunate
To those who in the sleepy region stay,
Lulled by the singer of an empty day.

2.

O June, O June, that we desired so,
Wilt thou not make us happy on this day?
Across the river thy soft breezes blow
Sweet with the scent of beanfields far away,
Above our heads rustle the aspens grey,
Calm is the sky with harmless clouds beset,
No thought of storm the morning vexes yet.

See, we have left our hopes and fears behind
To give our very hearts up unto thee;
What better place than this then could we find
By this sweet stream that knows not of the sea,
That guesses not the city's misery,
This little stream whose hamlets scarce have names
This far-off, lonely mother of the Thames?

Here then, O June, thy kindness will we take;
And if indeed but pensive men we seem,
What should we do? thou wouldst not have us wake
From out the arms of this rare happy dream
And wish to leave the murmur of the stream,
The rustling boughs, the twitter of the birds,
And all thy thousand peaceful happy words.

FROM *Ogier the Dane*

Haec: In the white-flowered hawthorn brake,
Love, be merry for my sake;
Twine the blossoms in my hair,
Kiss me where I am most fair—
Kiss me, love! for who knoweth
What thing cometh after death?

Ille: Nay, the garlanded gold hair
Hides thee where thou art most fair;
Hides the rose-tinged hills of snow—
Ay, sweet love, I have thee now!
Kiss me, love! for who knoweth
What thing cometh after death?

Haec: Shall we weep for a dead day,
        Or set Sorrow in our way?
        Hidden by my golden hair,
        Wilt thou weep that sweet days wear?
        Kiss me, love! for who knoweth
        What thing cometh after death?

Ille: Weep, O Love, the days that flit,
          Now, while I can feel thy breath;
        Then may I remember it
          Sad and old, and near my death.
        Kiss me, love! for who knoweth
        What thing cometh after death?

FROM *Love Is Enough*

Love is Enough: though the World be a-waning
And the woods have no voice but the voice of complaining,
   Though the sky be too dark for dim eyes to discover
The gold-cups and daisies fair blooming thereunder,
Though the hills be held shadows, and the sea a dark wonder,
   And this day draw a veil over all deeds passed over,
Yet their hands shall not tremble, their feet shall not falter;
The void shall not weary, the fear shall not alter
   These lips and these eyes of the loved and the lover.

ALGERNON CHARLES SWINBURNE
(1837–1909)
FROM *The Triumph of Time*

I have put my days and dreams out of mind
   Days that are over, dreams that are done.
Though we seek life through, we shall surely find
   There is none of them clear to us now, not one.
But clear are these things; the grass and the sand,
Where, sure as the eyes reach, ever at hand,
With lips wide open and face burnt blind,
   The strong sea-daisies feast on the sun.

The low downs lean to the sea; the stream,
    One loose thin pulseless tremulous vein,
Rapid and vivid and dumb as a dream,
    Works downward, sick of the sun and the rain;
No wind is rough with the rank rare flowers;
The sweet sea, mother of loves and hours,
Shudders and shines as the grey winds gleam,
    Turning her smile to a fugitive pain.

Mother of loves that are swift to fade,
    Mother of mutable winds and hours.
A barren mother, a mother-maid,
    Cold and clean as her faint salt flowers.
I would we twain were even as she,
Lost in the night and the light of the sea,
Where faint sounds falter and wan beams wade,
    Break, and are broken, and shed into showers.

The loves and hours of the life of a man,
    They are swift and sad, being born of the sea.
Hours that rejoice and regret for a span,
    Born with a man's breath, mortal as he;
Loves that are lost ere they come to birth,
Weeds of the wave, without fruit upon earth.
I lose what I long for, save what I can,
    My love, my love, and no love for me!

It is not much that a man can save
    On the sands of life, in the straits of time,
Who swims in sight of the great third wave
    That never a swimmer shall cross or climb.
Some waif washed up with the strays and spars
That ebb-tide shows to the shore and the stars;
Weed from the water, grass from a grave,
    A broken blossom, a ruined rhyme.

There will no man do for your sake, I think,
    What I would have done for the least word said.
I had wrung life dry for your lips to drink,
    Broken it up for your daily bread:

Body for body and blood for blood,
As the flow of the full sea risen to flood
That yearns and trembles before it sink,
　　I had given, and lain down for you, glad and dead.

Yea, hope at highest and all her fruit,
　　And time at fullest and all his dower,
I had given you surely, and life to boot,
　　Were we once made one for a single hour.
But now, you are twain, you are cloven apart,
Flesh of his flesh, but heart of my heart;
And deep in one is the bitter root,
　　And sweet for one is the lifelong flower.

I will go back to the great sweet mother,
　　Mother and lover of men, the sea.
I will go down to her, I and none other,
　　Close with her, kiss her and mix her with me;
Cling to her, strive with her, hold her fast:
O fair white mother, in days long past
Born without sister, born without brother,
　　Set free my soul as thy soul is free.

O fair green-girdled mother of mine,
　　Sea, that art clothed with the sun and the rain,
Thy sweet hard kisses are strong like wine,
　　Thy large embraces are keen like pain.
Save me and hide me with all thy waves,
Find me one grave of thy thousand graves,
Those pure cold populous graves of thine
　　Wrought without hand in a world without stain.

I shall sleep, and move with the moving ships,
　　Change as the winds change, veer in the tide;
My lips will feast on the foam of thy lips,
　　I shall rise with thy rising, with thee subside;
Sleep, and not know if she be, if she were,
Filled full with life to the eyes and hair,
As a rose is fulfilled to the roseleaf tips
　　With splendid summer and perfume and pride.

This woven raiment of nights and days,
  Were it once cast off and unwound from me,
Naked and glad would I walk in thy ways,
  Alive and aware of thy ways and thee;
Clear of the whole world, hidden at home,
Clothed with the green and crowned with the foam
A pulse of the life of thy straits and bays,
  A vein in the heart of the streams of the sea.

There lived a singer in France of old
  By the tideless dolorous midland sea.
In a land of sand and ruin and gold
  There shone one woman, and none but she.
And finding life for her love's sake fail,
Being fain to see her, he bade set sail,
Touched land, and saw her as life grew cold,
  And praised God, seeing; and so died he.

Died, praising God for his gift and grace:
  For she bowed down to him weeping, and said
"Live"; and her tears were shed on his face
  Or ever the life in his face was shed.
The sharp tears fell through her hair, and stung
Once, and her close lips touched him and clung
Once, and grew one with his lips for a space;
  And so drew back, and the man was dead.

O brother, the gods were good to you.
  Sleep, and be glad while the world endures.
Be well content as the years wear through;
  Give thanks for life, and the loves and lures;
Give thanks for life, O brother, and death,
For the sweet last sound of her feet, her breath,
For gifts she gave you, gracious and few,
  Tears and kisses, that lady of yours.

Rest, and be glad of the gods; but I,
  How shall I praise them, or how take rest?
There is not room under all the sky
  For me that know not of worst or best,

Dream or desire of the days before,
Sweet things or bitterness, any more.
Love will not come to me now though I die,
    As love came close to you, breast to breast.

I shall never be friends again with roses;
    I shall loathe sweet tunes, where a note grown strong
Relents and recoils, and climbs and closes,
    As a wave of the sea turned back by song.
There are sounds where the soul's delight takes fire,
Face to face with its own desire;
A delight that rebels, a desire that reposes;
I shall hate sweet music my whole life long.

A Leave-Taking

Let us go hence, my songs; she will not hear.
Let us go hence together without fear;
Keep silence now, for singing time is over,
And over all old things and all things dear.
She loves not you nor me as all we love her.
Yea, though we sang as angels in her ear,
        She would not hear.

Let us rise up and part; she will not know.
Let us go seaward as the great winds go,
Full of blown sand and foam; what help is here?
There is no help, for all these things are so,
And all the world is bitter as a tear.
And how these things are, though ye strove to show,
        She would not know.

Let us go home and hence; she will not weep.
We gave love many dreams and days to keep,
Flowers without scent, and fruits that would not grow,
Saying "If thou wilt, thrust in thy sickle and reap".
All is reaped now; no grass is left to mow;
And we that sowed, though all we fell on sleep,
        She would not weep.

Let us go hence and rest; she will not love.
She shall not hear us if we sing hereof,
Nor see love's ways, how sore they are and steep.
Come hence, let be, lie still; it is enough.
Love is a barren sea, bitter and deep;
And though she saw all heaven in flower above,
     She would not love.

Let us give up, go down; she will not care.
Though all the stars made gold of all the air,
And the sea moving saw before it move
One moon-flower making all the foam-flowers fair;
Though all those waves went over us, and drove
Deep down the stifling lips and drowning hair,
     She would not care.

Let us go hence, go hence; she will not see.
Sing all once more together; surely she,
She too, remembering days and words that were,
Will turn a little toward us, sighing; but we,
We are hence, we are gone, as though we had not been there.
Nay, and though all men seeing had pity on me,
     She would not see.

FROM *Anactoria*

Thee too the years shall cover; thou shalt be
As the rose born of one same blood with thee,
As a song sung, as a word said, and fall
Flower-wise, and be not any more at all,
Nor any memory of thee anywhere;
For never Muse has bound above thine hair
The high Pierian flower whose graft outgrows
All summer kinship of the mortal rose
And colour of deciduous days, nor shed
Reflux and flush of heaven about thine head,
Nor reddened brows made pale by floral grief
With splendid shadow from that lordlier leaf.
Yea, thou shalt be forgotten like spilt wine,
Except these kisses of my lips on thine

Brand them with immortality; but me—
Men shall not see bright fire nor hear the sea,
Nor mix their hearts with music, nor behold
Cast forth of heaven, with feet of awful gold
And plumeless wings, that make the bright air blind,
Lightning, with thunder for a hound behind
Hunting through fields unfurrowed and unsown,
But in the light and laughter, in the moan
And music, and in grasp of lip and hand
And shudder of water that makes felt on land
The immeasurable tremor of all the sea,
Memories shall mix and metaphors of me.
Like me shall be the shuddering calm of night,
When all the winds of the world for pure delight
Close lips that quiver and fold up wings that ache;
When nightingales are louder for love's sake,
And leaves tremble like lute-strings or like fire;
Like me the one star swooning with desire
Even at the cold lips of the sleepless moon,
As I at thine; like me the waste white noon,
Burnt through with barren sunlight; and like me
The land-stream and the tide-stream in the sea.
I am sick with time as these with ebb and flow,
And by the yearning in my veins I know
The yearning sound of waters; and mine eyes
Burn as that beamless fire which fills the skies
With troubled stars and travailing things of flame;
And in my heart the grief consuming them
Labours, and in my veins the thirst of these,
And all the summer travail of the trees
And all the winter sickness; and the earth,
Filled full with deadly works of death and birth,
Sore spent with hungry lusts of birth and death,
Has pain like mine in her divided breath;
Her spring of leaves is barren, and her fruit
Ashes; her boughs are burdened, and her root
Fibrous and gnarled with poison; underneath
Serpents have gnawn it through with tortuous teeth
Made sharp upon the bones of all the dead,
And wild birds rend her branches overhead.
These, woven as raiment for his word and thought,

These hath God made, and me as these, and wrought
Song, and hath lit it at my lips; and me
Earth shall not gather though she feed on thee.
As a tear shed shalt thou be shed; but I—
Lo, earth may labour, men live long and die,
Years change and stars, and the high God devise
New things, and old things wane before his eyes
Who wields and wrecks them, being more strong than they—
But, having made me, me he shall not slay.
Nor slay nor satiate, like those herds of his
Who laugh and live a little, and their kiss
Contents them, and their loves are swift and sweet,
And sure death grasps and gains them with slow feet,
Love they or hate they, strive or bow the knees—
And all these end; he hath his will of these.
Yea, but albeit he slay me, hating me—
Albeit he hide me in the deep dear sea
And cover me with cool wan foam, and ease
This soul of mine as any soul of these,
And give me water and great sweet waves, and make
The very sea's name lordlier for my sake,
The whole sea sweeter—albeit I die indeed
And hide myself and sleep and no man heed,
Of me the high God hath not all his will.
Blossom of branches, and on each high hill
Clear air and wind, and under in clamorous vales
Fierce noises of the fiery nightingales,
Buds burning in the sudden spring like fire,
The wan washed sand and the waves' vain desire,
Sails seen like blown white flowers at sea, and words
That bring tears swiftest, and long notes of birds
Violently singing till the whole world sings—
I Sappho shall be one with all these things,
With all high things for ever; and my face
Seen once, my songs once heard in a strange place,
Cleave to men's lives, and waste the days thereof
With gladness and much sadness and long love.
Yea, they shall say, earth's womb has borne in vain
New things, and never this best thing again;
Borne days and men, borne fruits and wars and wine,
Seasons and songs, but no song more like mine.

And they shall know me as ye who have known me here,
Last year when I loved Atthis, and this year
When I love thee; and they shall praise me and say:
"She hath all time as all we have our day,
Shall she not live and have her will"—even I?
For these shall give me of their souls, shall give
Life, and the days and loves wherewith I live,
Shall quicken me with loving, fill with breath,
Save me and serve me, strive for me with death.
Alas, that neither moon nor snow nor dew
Nor all cold things can purge me wholly through,
Assuage me nor allay me nor appease,
Till supreme sleep shall bring me bloodless ease;
Till time wax faint in all his periods;
Till fate undo the bondage of the gods,
And lay, to slake and satiate me all through,
Lotus and Lethe on my lips like dew,
And shed around and over and under me
Thick darkness and the insuperable sea.

Rococo

Take hands and part with laughter;
   Touch lips and part with tears;
Once more and no more after,
   Whatever comes with years.
We twain shall not remeasure
   The ways that left us twain;
Nor crush the lees of pleasure
   From sanguine grapes of pain.

We twain once well in sunder,
   What will the mad gods do
For hate with me, I wonder,
   Or what for love with you?
Forget them till November,
   And dream there's April yet;
Forget that I remember,
   And dream that I forget.

Time found our tired love sleeping,
  And kissed away his breath;
But what should we do weeping,
  Though light love sleep to death?
We have drained his lips at leisure,
  Till there's not left to drain
A single sob of pleasure,
  A single pulse of pain.

Dream that the lips once breathless
  Might quicken if they would;
Say that the soul is deathless;
  Dream that the gods are good;
Say March may wed September,
  And time divorce regret;
But not that you remember,
  And not that I forget.

We have heard from hidden places
  What love scarce lives and hears:
We have seen on fervent faces
  The pallor of strange tears:
We have trod the wine-vat's treasure,
  Whence, ripe to steam and stain,
Foams round the feet of pleasure
  The blood-red must of pain.

Remembrance may recover
  And time bring back to time
The name of your first lover,
  The ring of my first rhyme;
But rose-leaves of December
  The frosts of June shall fret,
The day that you remember,
  The day that I forget.

The snake that hides and hisses
  In heaven we twain have known;
The grief of cruel kisses,
  The joy whose mouth makes moan;

The pulse's pause and measure,
  Where in one furtive vein
Throbs through the heart of pleasure
  The purpler blood of pain.

We have done with tears and treasons
  And love for treason's sake;
Room for the swift new seasons,
  The years that burn and break,
Dismantle and dismember
  Men's days and dreams, Juliette;
For love may not remember,
  But time will not forget.

Life treads down love in flying,
  Time withers him at root;
Bring all dead things and dying,
  Reaped sheaf and ruined fruit,
Where, crushed by three days' pressure,
  Our three days' love lies slain;
And earlier leaf of pleasure,
  And latter flower of pain.

Breathe close upon the ashes,
  It may be flame will leap;
Unclose the soft close lashes,
  Lift up the lids, and weep.
Light love's extinguished ember,
  Let one tear leave it wet
For one that you remember
  And ten that you forget.

Rondel

Kissing her hair I sat against her feet,
Wove and unwove it, wound and found it sweet;
Made fast therewith her hands, drew down her eyes,
Deep as deep flowers and dreamy like dim skies;
With her own tresses bound and found her fair,
    Kissing her hair.

Sleep were no sweeter than her face to me,
Sleep of cold sea-bloom under the cold sea;
What pain could get between my face and hers?
What new sweet thing would love not relish worse?
Unless, perhaps, white death had kissed me there,
    Kissing her hair?

The Garden of Proserpine

Here, where the world is quiet;
    Here, where all trouble seems
Dead winds' and spent waves' riot
    In doubtful dreams of dreams;
I watch the green field growing
For reaping folk and sowing,
For harvest-time and mowing,
    A sleepy world of streams.

I am tired of tears and laughter,
    And men that laugh and weep;
Of what may come hereafter
    For men that sow to reap:
I am weary of days and hours,
Blown buds of barren flowers,
Desires and dreams and powers
    And everything but sleep.

Here night has death for neighbour,
    And far from eye or ear
Wan waves and wet winds labour,
    Weak ships and spirits steer;
They drive adrift, and whither
They wot not who make thither;
But no such winds blow hither,
    And no such things grow here.

No growth of moor or coppice,
    No heather-flower or vine,
But bloomless buds of poppies,
    Green grapes of Proserpine,

Pale beds of blowing rushes
Where no leaf blooms or blushes
Save this whereout she crushes
    For dead men deadly wine.

Pale, without name or number,
    In fruitless fields of corn,
They bow themselves and slumber
    All night till light is born;
And like a soul belated,
In hell and heaven unmated,
By cloud and mist abated,
    Comes out of darkness morn.

Though one were strong as seven,
    He too with death shall dwell,
Nor wake with wings in heaven,
    Nor weep for pains in hell;
Though one were fair as roses,
His beauty clouds and closes;
And well though love reposes,
    In the end it is not well.

Pale, beyond porch and portal,
    Crowned with calm leaves, she stands,
Who gathers all things mortal
    With cold immortal hands;
Her languid lips are sweeter
Than love's who fears to greet her
To men that mix and meet her
    From many times and lands.

She waits for each and other,
    She waits for all men born;
Forgets the earth her mother,
    The life of fruits and corn;
And spring and seed and swallow
Take wing for her and follow
Where summer song rings hollow,
    And flowers are put to scorn.

There go the old loves that wither,
   The old loves with wearier wings;
And all dead years draw thither,
   And all disastrous things;
Dead dreams of days forsaken,
Blind buds that snows have shaken,
Wild leaves that winds have taken,
   Red strays of ruined springs.

We are not sure of sorrow,
   And joy was never sure;
To-day will die to-morrow;
   Time stoops to no man's lure;
And love, grown faint and fretful,
With lips but half regretful
Sighs, and with eyes forgetful
   Weeps that no loves endure.

From too much love of living,
   From hope and fear set free,
We thank with brief thanksgiving
   Whatever gods may be
That no life lives for ever;
That dead men rise up never;
That even the weariest river
   Winds somewhere safe to sea.

An Interlude

In the greenest growth of the Maytime,
   I rode where the woods were wet,
Between the dawn and the daytime;
   The spring was glad that we met.

There was something the season wanted,
   Though the ways and the woods smelt sweet;
The breath of your lips that panted,
   The pulse of the grass at your feet.

You came, and the sun came after,
  And the green grew golden above;
And the flag-flowers lightened with laughter,
  And the meadow-sweet shook with love.

Your feet in the full-grown grasses,
  Moved soft as a weak wind blows;
You passed me as April passes,
  With face made out of a rose.

By the stream where the stems were slender,
  Your bright foot paused at the sedge;
It might be to watch the tender
  Light leaves in the springtime hedge,

On boughs that the sweet month blanches
  With flowery frost of May:
It might be a bird in the branches,
  It might be a thorn in the way.

I waited to watch you linger
  With foot drawn back from the dew,
Till a sunbeam straight like a finger
  Struck sharp through the leaves at you.

And a bird overhead sang *Follow*,
  And a bird to the right sang *Here;*
And the arch of the leaves was hollow,
  And the meaning of May was clear.

I saw where the sun's hand pointed,
  I knew what the bird's note said;
By the dawn and the dewfall anointed,
  You were queen by the gold on your head.

As the glimpse of a burnt-out ember
  Recalls a regret of the sun,
I remember, forget, and remember
  What Love saw done and undone.

I remember the way we parted,
  The day and the way we met;
You hoped we were both broken-hearted,
  And knew we should both forget.

And May with her world in flower
  Seemed still to murmur and smile
As you murmured and smiled for an hour;
  I saw you turn at the stile.

A hand like a white wood-blossom
  You lifted, and waved, and passed,
With head hung down to the bosom,
  And pale, as it seemed, at last.

And the best and the worst of this is
  That neither is most to blame
If you've forgotten my kisses
  And I've forgotten your name.

At Parting

For a day and a night Love sang to us, played with us,
  Folded us round from the dark and the light;
And our hearts were fulfilled of the music he made with us,
Made with our hearts and our lips while he stayed with us,
  Stayed in mid passage his pinions from flight
      For a day and a night.

From his foes that kept watch with his wings had he hidden
      us,
  Covered us close from the eyes that would smite,
From the feet that had tracked and the tongues that had chid-
      den us
Sheltering in shade of the myrtles forbidden us
  Spirit and flesh growing one with delight
      For a day and a night.

But his wings will not rest and his feet will not stay for us:
   Morning is here in the joy of its might;
With his breath has he sweetened a night and a day for us;
Now let him pass, and the myrtles make way for us;
   Love can but last in us here at his height
      For a day and a night.

Ave atque Vale
(IN MEMORY OF CHARLES BAUDELAIRE)

> Nous devrions pourtant lui porter quelques fleurs;
> Les morts, les pauvres morts, ont de grandes douleurs,
> Et quand Octobre souffle, émondeur des vieux arbres,
> Son vent mélancolique à l'entour de leurs marbres,
> Certe, ils doivent trouver les vivants bien ingrats.
>   —Les Fleurs du Mal

Shall I strew on thee rose or rue or laurel,
     Brother, on this that was the veil of thee?
     Or quiet sea-flower moulded by the sea,
Or simplest growth of meadow-sweet or sorrel,
     Such as the summer-sleepy Dryads weave,
     Waked up by snow-soft sudden rains at eve?
Or wilt thou rather, as on earth before,
     Half-faded fiery blossoms, pale with heat
     And full of bitter summer, but more sweet
To thee than gleanings of a northern shore
     Trod by no tropic feet?

For always thee the fervid languid glories
     Allured of heavier suns in mightier skies;
     Thine ears knew all the wandering watery sighs
Where the sea sobs round Lesbian promontories,
     The barren kiss of piteous wave to wave
     That knows not where is that Leucadian grave
Which hides too deep the supreme head of song.
     Ah, salt and sterile as her kisses were,
     The wild sea winds her and the green gulfs bear
Hither and thither, and vex and work her wrong,
     Blind gods that cannot spare.

Thou sawest, in thine old singing season, brother,
        Secrets and sorrows unbeheld of us:
Fierce loves, and lovely leaf-buds poisonous,
Bare to thy subtler eye, but for none other
        Blowing by night in some unbreathed-in clime;
        The hidden harvest of luxurious time,
Sin without shape, and pleasure without speech;
        And where strange dreams in a tumultuous sleep
        Make the shut eyes of stricken spirits weep;
And with each face thou sawest the shadow of each,
        Seeing as men sow men reap.

O sleepless heart and sombre soul unsleeping,
        That were athirst for sleep and no more life
        And no more love, for peace and no more strife!
Now the dim gods of death have in their keeping
        Spirit and body and all the springs of song,
        Is it well now where love can do no wrong,
Where stingless pleasure has no foam or fang
        Behind the unopening closure of her lips?
        Is it well now where soul from body slips
And flesh from bone divides without a pang
        As dew from flower-bell drips?

It is enough; the end and the beginning
        Are one thing to thee, who art past the end.
        O hand unclasped of unbeholden friend,
For thee no fruits to pluck, no palms for winning,
        No triumph and no labour and no lust,
        Only dead yew-leaves and a little dust.
O quiet eyes wherein the light saith nought,
        Whereto the day is dumb, nor any night
        With obscure finger silences your sight,
Nor in your speech the sudden soul speaks thought,
        Sleep, and have sleep for light.

Now all strange hours and all strange loves are over,
        Dreams and desires and sombre songs and sweet,
        Hast thou found place at the great knees and feet
Of some pale Titan-woman like a lover,
        Such as thy vision here solicited,
        Under the shadow of her fair vast head,

The deep division of prodigious breasts,
    The solemn slope of mighty limbs asleep,
    The weight of awful tresses that still keep
The savour and shade of old-world pine-forests
    Where the wet hill-winds weep?

Hast thou found any likeness for thy vision?
    O gardener of strange flowers, what bud, what bloom,
    Hast thou found sown, what gathered in the gloom?
What of despair, of rapture, of derision,
    What of life is there, what of ill or good?
    Are the fruits grey like dust or bright like blood?
Does the dim ground grow any seed of ours,
    The faint fields quicken any terrene root,
    In low lands where the sun and moon are mute
And all the stars keep silence? Are there flowers
    At all, or any fruit?

Alas, but though my flying song flies after,
    O sweet strange elder singer, thy more fleet
    Singing, and footprints of thy fleeter feet,
Some dim derision of mysterious laughter
    From the blind tongue-less warders of the dead,
    Some gainless glimpse of Proserpine's veiled head,
Some little sound of unregarded tears
    Wept by effaced unprofitable eyes,
    And from pale mouths some cadence of dead sighs—
These only, these the hearkening spirit hears,
    Sees only such things rise.

Thou art far too far for wings of words to follow,
    Far too far off for thought or any prayer.
    What ails us with thee, who art wind and air?
What ails us gazing where all seen is hollow?
    Yet with some fancy, yet with some desire,
    Dreams pursue death as winds a flying fire,
Our dreams pursue our dead and do not find.
    Still, and more swift than they, the thin flame flies,
    The low light fails us in elusive skies,
Still the foiled earnest ear is deaf, and blind
    Are still the eluded eyes.

Not thee, O never thee, in all time's changes,
      Not thee, but this the sound of thy sad soul,
      The shadow of thy swift spirit, this shut scroll
I lay my hand on, and not death estranges
      My spirit from communion of thy song—
      These memories and these melodies that throng
Veiled porches of a Muse funereal—
      These I salute, these touch, these clasp and fold
      As though a hand were in my hand to hold,
Or through mine ears a mourning musical
      Of many mourners rolled.

I among these, I also, in such station
      As when the pyre was charred, and piled the sods,
      And offering to the dead made, and their gods,
The old mourners had, standing to make libation,
      I stand, and to the gods and to the dead
      Do reverence without prayer or praise, and shed
Offering to these unknown, the gods of gloom,
      And what of honey and spice my seedlands bear,
      And what I may of fruits in this chilled air,
And lay, Orestes-like, across the tomb
      A curl of severed hair.

But by no hand nor any treason stricken,
      Not like the low-lying head of Him, the King,
      The flame that made of Troy a ruinous thing,
Thou liest, and on this dust no tears could quicken
      There fall no tears like theirs that all men hear
      Fall tear by sweet imperishable tear
Down the opening leaves of holy poets' pages.
      Thee not Orestes, not Electra mourns;
      But bending us-ward with memorial urns
The most high Muses that fufil all ages
      Weep, and our God's heart yearns.

For, sparing of his sacred strength, not often
      Among us darkling here the lord of light
      Makes manifest his music and his might
In hearts that open and in lips that soften
      With the soft flame and heat of songs that shine.
      Thy lips indeed he touched with bitter wine,

And nourished them indeed with bitter bread;
        Yet surely from his hand thy soul's food came,
        The fire that scarred thy spirit at his flame
Was lighted, and thine hungering heart he fed
        Who feeds our hearts with fame.

Therefore he too now at thy soul's sunsetting,
        God of all suns and songs, he too bends down
        To mix his laurel with thy cypress crown,
And save thy dust from blame and from forgetting.
        Therefore he too, seeing all thou wert and art,
        Compassionate, with sad and sacred heart,
Mourns thee of many his children the last dead,
        And hallows with strange tears and alien sighs
        Thine unmelodious mouth and sunless eyes,
And over thine irrevocable head
        Sheds light from the under skies.

And one weeps with him in the ways Lethean,
        And stains with tears her changing bosom chill:
        That obscure Venus of the hollow hill,
That thing transformed which was the Cytherean,
        With lips that lost their Grecian laugh divine
        Long since, and face no more called Erycine;
A ghost, a bitter and luxurious god.
        Thee also with fair flesh and singing spell
        Did she, a sad and second prey, compel
Into the footless places once more trod,
        And shadows hot from hell.

And now no sacred staff shall break in blossom,
        No choral salutation lure to light
        A spirit sick with perfume and sweet night
And love's tired eyes and hands and barren bosom.
        There is no help for these things; none to mend
        And none to mar; not all our songs, O friend,
Will make death clear or make life durable.
        Howbeit with rose and ivy and wild vine
        And with wild notes about this dust of thine
At least I fill the place where white dreams dwell
        And wreathe an unseen shrine.

Sleep; and if life was bitter to thee, pardon,
    If sweet, give thanks; thou hast no more to live;
    And to give thanks is good, and to forgive.
Out of the mystic and the mournful garden
    Where all day through thine hands in barren braid
    Wove the sick flowers of secrecy and shade,
Green buds of sorrow and sin, and remnants grey,
    Sweet-smelling, pale with poison, sanguine-hearted,
    Passions that sprang from sleep and thoughts that
        started,
Shall death not bring us all as thee one day
    Among the days departed?

For thee, O now a silent soul, my brother,
    Take at my hands this garland, and farewell.
    Thin is the leaf, and chill the wintry smell,
And chill the solemn earth, a fatal mother,
    With sadder than the Niobean womb,
    And in the hollow of her breasts a tomb.
Content thee, howsoe'er, whose days are done;
    There lies not any troublous thing before,
    Nor sight nor sound to war against thee more,
For whom all winds are quiet as the sun,
    All waters as the shore.

Choruses from Atalanta in Calydon

1.

    When the hounds of spring are on winter's traces,
      The mother of months in meadow or plain
    Fills the shadows and windy places
      With lisp of leaves and ripple of rain;
    And the brown bright nightingale amorous
    Is half assuaged for Itylus,
    For the Thracian ships and the foreign faces,
      The tongueless vigil, and all the pain.

    Come with bows bent and with emptying of quivers,
      Maiden most perfect, lady of light,
    With a noise of winds and many rivers,
      With a clamour of waters, and with might;

Bind on thy sandals, O thou most fleet,
Over the splendour and speed of thy feet;
For the faint east quickens, the wan west shivers,
   Round the feet of the day and the feet of the night.

Where shall we find her, how shall we sing to her,
   Fold our hands round her knees, and cling?
O that man's heart were as fire and could spring to her,
   Fire, or the strength of the streams that spring!
For the stars and the winds are unto her
As raiment, as songs of the harp-player;
For the risen stars and the fallen cling to her,
   And the southwest-wind and the west-wind sing.

For winter's rains and ruins are over,
   And all the season of snows and sins;
The days dividing lover and lover,
   The light that loses, the night that wins;
And time remembered is grief forgotten,
And frosts are slain and flowers begotten,
And in green underwood and cover
   Blossom by blossom the spring begins.

The full streams feed on flowers of rushes,
   Ripe grasses trammel a travelling foot,
The faint fresh flame of the young year flushes
   From leaf to flower and flower to fruit;
And fruit and leaf are as gold and fire,
And the oat is heard above the lyre,
And the hooféd heel of a satyr crushes
   The chestnut-husk at the chestnut-root.

And Pan by noon and Bacchus by night,
   Fleeter of foot than the fleet-foot kid,
Follows with dancing and fills with delight
   The Maenad and the Bassarid;
And soft as lips that laugh and hide
The laughing leaves of the trees divide,
And screen from seeing and leave in sight
   The god pursuing, the maiden hid.

The ivy falls with the Bacchanal's hair
    Over her eyebrows hiding her eyes;
The wild vine slipping down leaves bare
    Her bright breast shortening into sighs,
The wild vine slips with the weight of its leaves,
But the berried ivy catches and cleaves
To the limbs that glitter, the feet that scare
    The wolf that follows, the fawn that flies.

2.

Before the beginning of years
    There came to the making of man
Time, with a gift of tears;
    Grief with a glass that ran;
Pleasure, with pain for leaven;
    Summer, with flowers that fell;
Remembrance fallen from heaven,
    And madness risen from hell;
Strength without hands to smite;
    Love that endures for a breath;
Night, the shadow of light,
    And life, the shadow of death.

And the high gods took in hand
    Fire, and the falling of tears,
And a measure of sliding sand
    From under the feet of the years;
And froth and drift of the sea;
    And dust of the labouring earth;
And bodies of things to be
    In the houses of death and of birth;
And wrought with weeping and laughter,
    And fashioned with loathing and love
With life before and after
    And death beneath and above,
For a day and a night and a morrow,
    That his strength might endure for a span
With travail and heavy sorrow,
    The holy spirit of man.

From the winds of the north and the south
   They gathered as unto strife;
They breathed upon his mouth,
   They filled his body with life;
Eyesight and speech they wrought
   For the veils of the soul therein,
A time for labour and thought,
   A time to serve and to sin;
They gave him light in his ways,
   And love, and a space for delight,
And beauty and length of days,
   And night, and sleep in the night.
His speech is a burning fire;
   With his lips he travaileth;
In his heart is a blind desire,
   In his eyes foreknowledge of death;
He weaves, and is clothed with derision;
   Sows, and he shall not reap;
His life is a watch or a vision
   Between a sleep and a sleep.

3.

Who hath given man speech? or who hath set therein
A thorn for peril and a snare for sin?
For in the word his life is and his breath,
   And in the word his death,
That madness and the infatuate heart may breed
   From the word's womb the deed
And life bring one thing forth ere all pass by,
Even one thing which is ours yet cannot die—
Death. Hast thou seen him ever anywhere,
Time's twin-born brother, imperishable as he
Is perishable and plaintive, clothed with care
   And mutable as sand,
But death is strong and full of blood and fair
And perdurable and like a lord of land?
Nay, time thou seest not, death thou wilt not see
Till life's right hand be loosened from thine hand
   And thy life-days from thee.

For the gods very subtly fashion
　　Madness with sadness upon earth:
Not knowing in any wise compassion,
　　Nor holding pity of any worth;
And many things they have given and taken,
　　And wrought and ruined many things;
The firm land they have loosed and shaken,
　　And sealed the sea with all her springs;
They have wearied time with heavy burdens
　　And vexed the lips of life with breath:
Set men to labour and given them guerdons,
　　Death, and great darkness after death:
Put moans into the bridal measure
　　And on the bridal wools a stain;
And circled pain about with pleasure,
　　And girdled pleasure about with pain;
And strewed one marriage-bed with tears and fire
For extreme loathing and supreme desire.

What shall be done with all these tears of ours?
　　Shall they make watersprings in the fair heaven
To bathe the brows of morning? or like flowers
Be shed and shine before the starriest hours,
　　Or made the raiment of the weeping Seven?
Or rather, O our masters, shall they be
Food for the famine of the grievous sea,
　　A great well-head of lamentation
Satiating the sad gods? or fall and flow
Among the years and seasons to and fro,
　　And wash their feet with tribulation
And fill them full with grieving ere they go?
　　Alas, our lords, and yet alas again,
Seeing all your iron heaven is gilt as gold
　　But all we smite thereat in vain;
Smite the gates barred with groanings manifold,
　　And all the floors are paven with our pain.
Yea, and with weariness of lips and eyes,
With breaking of the bosom, and with sighs,
　　We labour, and are clad and fed with grief
And filled with days we would not fain behold

And nights we would not hear of; we wax old,
  All we wax old and wither like a leaf.
We are outcast, strayed between bright sun and moon;
  Our light and darkness are as leaves of flowers,
Black flowers and white, that perish; and the noon
  As midnight, and the night as daylight hours.
  A little fruit a little while is ours,
    And the worm finds it soon.

But up in heaven the high gods one by one
  Lay hands upon the draught that quickeneth,
Fulfilled with all tears shed and all things done,
  And stir with soft imperishable breath
  The bubbling bitterness of life and death,
And hold it to our lips and laugh; but they
Preserve their lips from tasting night or day,
  Lest they too change and sleep, the fates that spun,
The lips that made us and the hands that slay;
  Lest all these change, and heaven bow down to none,
Change and be subject to the secular sway
  And terrene revolution of the sun.
Therefore they thrust it from them, putting time away.

I would the wine of time, made sharp and sweet
  With multitudinous days and nights and tears
  And many mixing savours of strange years,
Were no more trodden of them under feet,
  Cast out and spilt about their holy places:
That life were given them as a fruit to eat
And death to drink as water; that the light
Might ebb, drawn backward from their eyes, and night
  Hide for one hour the imperishable faces.
That they might rise up sad in heaven, and know
Sorrow and sleep, one paler than young snow,
  One cold as blight of dew and ruinous rain;
Rise up and rest and suffer a little, and be
Awhile as all things born with us and we,
  And grieve as men, and like slain men be slain.

For now we know not of them; but one saith
  The gods are gracious, praising God; and one,

When hast thou seen? or hast thou felt his breath
    Touch, nor consume thine eyelids as the sun,
Nor fill thee to the lips with fiery death?
    None hath beheld him, none
Seen above other gods and shapes of things,
Swift without feet and flying without wings,
Intolerable, not clad with death or life,
    Insatiable, not known of night or day,
The lord of love and loathing and of strife
    Who gives a star and takes a sun away;
Who shapes the soul, and makes her a barren wife
    To the earthly body and grievous growth of clay;
Who turns the large limbs to a little flame
    And binds the great sea with a little sand;
Who makes desire, and slays desire with shame;
    Who shakes the heaven as ashes in his hand;
Who, seeing the light and shadow for the same,
    Bids day waste night as fire devours a brand,
Smites without sword, and scourges without rod;
    The supreme evil, God.

Yea, with thine hate, O God, thou hast covered us,
    One saith, and hidden our eyes away from sight,
And made us transitory and hazardous,
    Light things and slight;
Yet have men praised thee, saying, He hath made man thus,
    And he doeth right.
Thou hast kissed us, and hast smitten; thou hast laid
Upon us with thy left hand life, and said,
Live: and again thou hast said, Yield up your breath,
And with thy right hand laid upon us death.
Thou hast sent us sleep, and stricken sleep with dreams,
Saying, Joy is not, but love of joy shall be;
Thou hast made sweet springs for all the pleasant streams,
In the end thou hast made them bitter with the sea.
Thou hast fed one rose with dust of many men;
    Thou hast marred one face with fire of many tears;
Thou hast taken love, and given us sorrow again;
    With pain thou hast filled us full to the eyes and ears.
Therefore because thou art strong, our father, and we
    Feeble; and thou art against us, and thine hand

Constrains us in the shallows of the sea
    And breaks us at the limits of the land;
Because thou hast bent thy lightnings as a bow,
    And loosed the hours like arrows; and let fall
Sins and wild words and many a wingéd woe
    And wars among us, and one end of all;
Because thou hast made the thunder, and thy feet
    Are as a rushing water when the skies
Break, but thy face as an exceeding heat
    And flames of fire the eyelids of thine eyes;
Because thou art over all who are over us;
    Because thy name is life and our name death;
Because thou art cruel and men are piteous,
    And our hands labour and thine hand scattereth;
Lo, with hearts rent and knees made tremulous,
    Lo, with ephemeral lips and casual breath,
        At least we witness of thee ere we die
That these things are not otherwise, but thus;
    That each man in his heart sigheth, and saith,
        That all men even as I,
All we are against thee, against thee, O God most high.

THOMAS HARDY

(1840–1928)

The Impercipient
(AT A CATHEDRAL SERVICE)

That with this bright believing band
    I have no claim to be,
That faiths by which my comrades stand
    Seem fantasies to me,
And mirage-mists their Shining Land,
    Is a strange destiny.

Why thus my soul should be consigned
    To infelicity,
Why always I must feel as blind
    To sights my brethren see,
Why joys they've found I cannot find,
    Abides a mystery.

Since heart of mine knows not that ease
    Which they know; since it be
That He who breathes All's Well to these
    Breathes no All's Well to me,
My lack might move their sympathies
    And Christian charity!

I am like a gazer who should mark
    An inland company
Standing upfingered, with, "Hark! hark!
    The glorious distant sea!"
And feel, "Alas, 'tis but yon dark
    And wind-swept pine to me!"

Yet I would bear my shortcomings
    With meet tranquillity,
But for the charge that blessed things
    I'd liefer not have be.
O, doth a bird deprived of wings
    Go earth-bound wilfully!

.   .   .

Enough. As yet disquiet clings
    About us. Rest shall we.

To an Unborn Pauper Child

Breathe not, hid Heart: cease silently,
And though thy birth-hour beckons thee,
        Sleep the long sleep:
        The Doomsters heap
Travails and teens around us here
And Time-wraiths turn our songsingings to fear.

Hark, how the people surge and sigh,
And laughters fail, and greetings die:
        Hopes dwindle; yea,
        Faiths waste away,
Affections and enthusiasms numb;
Thou canst not mend these things if thou dost come.

Had I the ear of wombéd souls
Ere their terrestrial chart unrolls,
  And thou wert free
  To cease, or be,
Then would I tell thee all I know,
And put it to thee: Wilt thou take Life so?

Vain vow! No hint of mine may hence
To theeward fly: to thy locked sense
  Explain none can
  Life's pending plan:
Thou wilt thy ignorant entry make
Though skies spout fire and blood and nations quake.

Fain would I, dear, find some shut plot
Of earth's wide wold for thee, where not
  One tear, one qualm,
  Should break the calm.
But I am weak as thou and bare;
No man can change the common lot to rare.

Must come and bide. And such are we—
Unreasoning, sanguine, visionary—
  That I can hope
  Health, love, friends, scope
In full for thee; can dream thou wilt find
Joys seldom yet attained by humankind!

Shut Out That Moon

Close up the casement, draw the blind,
  Shut out that stealing moon,
She wears too much the guise she wore
  Before our lutes were strewn
With years-deep dust, and names we read
  On a white stone were hewn.

Step not out on the dew-dashed lawn
  To view the Lady's Chair,
Immense Orion's glittering form,
  The Less and Greater Bear:
Stay in; to such sights we were drawn
  When faded ones were fair.

Brush not the bough for midnight scents
    That come forth lingeringly,
And wake the same sweet sentiments
    They breathed to you and me
When living seemed a laugh, and love
    All it was said to be.

Within the common lamp-lit room
    Prison my eyes and thought;
Let dingy details crudely loom,
    Mechanic speech be wrought:
Too fragrant was Life's early bloom,
    Too tart the fruit it brought!

The Conformers

Yes; we'll wed, my little fay,
    And you shall write you mine,
And in a villa chastely gray
    We'll house, and sleep, and dine.
    But those night-screened, divine,
    Stolen trysts of heretofore,
We of choice ecstasies and fine
            Shall know no more.

The formal faced cohue
    Will then no more upbraid
With smiting smiles and whisperings two
    Who have thrown less loves in shade.
    We shall no more evade
    The searching light of the sun,
Our game of passion will be played,
            Our dreaming done.

We shall not go in stealth
    To rendezvous unknown,
But friends will ask me of your health,
    And you about my own.

When we abide alone,
No leapings each to each,
But syllables in frigid tone
        Of household speech.

When down to dust we glide
Men will not say askance,
As now: "How all the country side
    Rings with their mad romance!"
But as they graveward glance
Remark: "In them we lose
A worthy pair, who helped advance
        Sound parish views."

Let Me Enjoy

Let me enjoy the earth no less
Because the all-enacting Might
That fashioned forth its loveliness
Had other aims than my delight.

About my path there flits a Fair,
Who throws me not a word or sign;
I'll charm me with her ignoring air,
And laud the lips not meant for mine.

From manuscripts of moving song
Inspired by scenes and souls unknown,
I'll pour out raptures that belong
To others, as they were my own.

And some day hence, toward Paradise
And all its blest—if such should be—
I will lift glad, afar-off eyes,
Though it contain no place for me.

Afterwards

When the Present has latched its postern behind my tremu-
        lous stay,
    And the May month flaps its glad green leaves like wings,
Delicate-filmed as a new-spun silk, will the neighbours say,
    "He was a man who used to notice such things?"

If it be in the dusk when, like an eyelid's soundless blink,
    The dewfall-hawk comes crossing the shades to alight
Upon the wind-warped upland thorn, a gazer may think,
    "To him this must have been a familiar sight."

If I pass during some nocturnal blackness, mothy and warm,
    When the hedgehog travels furtively over the lawn,
One may say, "He strove that such innocent creatures should
        come to no harm,
    But he could do little for them; and now he is gone."

If, when hearing that I have been stilled at last, they stand
        at the door,
    Watching the full-starred heavens that winter sees,
Will this thought rise on those who will meet my face no
        more,
    "He was one who had an eye for such mysteries?"

And will any say when my bell of quittance is heard in the
        gloom,
    And a crossing breeze cuts a pause in its outrollings,
Till they rise again, as they were a new bell's boom,
    "He hears it not now, but used to notice such things?"

HENRY AUSTIN DOBSON

(1840–1921)

On a Fan That Belonged
to the Marquise de Pompadour

Chicken-skin, delicate, white,
    Painted by Carlo Vanloo,
Loves in a riot of light,
    Roses and vaporous blue;
    Hark to the dainty *frou-frou!*

Picture above if you can,
   Eyes that would melt as the dew,—
This was the Pompadour's fan!

See how they rise at the sight,
   Thronging the *Œil de Bœuf* through,
Courtiers as butterflies bright,
   Beauties that Fragonard drew,
Talon-rouge, falbala, queue,
   Cardinal, Duke,—to a man,
   Eager to sigh or to sue,—
This was the Pompadour's fan!

Ah! but things more than polite
   Hung on this toy, *voyez-vous!*
Matters of state and of might,
   Things that great ministers do;
   Things that, maybe, overthrew
Those in whose brains they began;
   Here was the sign and the cue,—
This was the Pompadour's fan!

ENVOY

Where are the secrets it knew?
   Weavings of plot and of plan?
But where is the Pompadour, too?
   This was the Pompadour's *Fan!*

WILFRID SCAWEN BLUNT
(1840–1922)

FROM *Esther*

L

He who has once been happy is for aye
   Out of destruction's reach. His fortune then
Holds nothing secret, and Eternity,
   Which is a mystery to other men,
Has like a woman given him its joy.
   Time is his conquest. Life, if it should fret,
Has paid him tribute. He can bear to die.
   He who has once been happy! When I set

The world before me and survey its range,
 Its mean ambitions, its scant fantasies,
The shreds of pleasure which for lack of change
 Men wrap around them and call happiness,
The poor delights which are the tale and sum
Of the world's courage in its martyrdom;

LI

When I hear laughter from a tavern door,
 When I see crowds agape and in the rain
Watching on tiptoe and with stifled roar
 To see a rocket fired or a bull slain,
When misers handle gold, when orators
 Touch strong men's hearts with glory till they weep,
When cities deck their streets for barren wars
 Which have laid waste their youth, and when I keep
Calmly the count of my own life and see
 On what poor stuff my manhood's dreams were fed
Till I too learned what dole of vanity
 Will serve a human soul for daily bread,
—Then I remember that I once was young
And lived with Esther the world's gods among.

FROM *The Love Sonnets of Proteus*

AS TO HIS CHOICE OF HER

If I had chosen thee, thou shouldst have been
A virgin proud, untamed, immaculate,
Chaste as the morning star, a saint, a queen,
Scarred by no wars, no violence of hate.
Thou shouldst have been of soul commensurate
With thy fair body, brave and virtuous
And kind and just; and, if of poor estate,
At least an honest woman for my house.
I would have had thee come of honoured blood
And honourable nurture. Thou shouldst bear
Sons to my pride and daughters to my heart,
And men should hold thee happy, wise, and good.
Lo, thou art none of this, but only fair.
Yet must I love thee, dear, and as thou art.

HE HAS FALLEN FROM THE HEIGHT OF HIS LOVE

Love, how ignobly hast thou met thy doom!
Ill-seasoned scaffolding by which, full-fraught
With passionate youth and mighty hopes, we clomb
To our heart's heaven, fearing, doubting, naught!
Oh love, thou wert too frail for such mad sport,
Too rotten at thy core, designed too high:
And we who trusted thee our death have bought,
And bleeding on the ground must surely die.
—I will not see her. What she now may be
I care not. For the dream within my brain
Is fairer, nobler, and more kind than she;
And with that vision I can mock at pain.
God! Was there ever woman half so sweet,
Or death so bitter, or at such dear feet?

ON THE NATURE OF LOVE

You ask my love. What shall my love then be?
A hope, an aspiration, a desire?
The soul's eternal charter writ in fire
Upon the earth, the heavens, and the sea?
You ask my love. The carnal mystery
Of a soft hand, of finger-tips that press,
Of eyes that kindle and of lips that kiss,
Of sweet things known to thee and only thee?
You ask my love. What love can be more sweet
Than hope or pleasure? Yet we love in vain.
The soul is more than joy, the life than meat.
The sweetest love of all were love in pain,
And that I will not give. So let it be.
—Nay, give me any love, so it be love of thee.

IN ANSWER TO A QUESTION

Why should I hate you, love, or why despise
For that last proof of tenderness you gave?
The battle is not always to the brave,

Nor life's sublimest wisdom to the wise.
True courage often is in frightened eyes,
And reason in sweet lips that only rave.
There is a weakness stronger than the grave,
And blood poured out has overcome the skies.
—Nay, love, I honour you the more for this,
That you have rent the veil, and ushered in
A fellow soul to your soul's holy place.
And why should either blush that we have been
One day in Eden, in our nakedness?
—'Tis conscience makes us sinners, not our sin.

FAREWELL TO JULIET

Lame, impotent conclusion to youth's dreams
Vast as all heaven! See, what glory lies
Entangled here in these base stratagems,
What virtue done to death! O glorious sighs,
Sublime beseechings, high cajoleries,
Fond wraths, brave ruptures, all that sometime was
Our daily bread of gods beneath the skies,
How are ye ended, in what utter loss!
Time was, time is, and time is yet to come,
Till even time itself shall have its end.
These were eternal. And behold, a tomb!
Come, let us laugh and eat and drink. God send
What all the world must need one day as we,
Speedy oblivion, rest for memory.

ST. VALENTINE'S DAY

To-day, all day, I rode upon the Down,
With hounds and horsemen, a brave company.
On this side in its glory lay the sea,
On that the Sussex Weald, a sea of brown.
The wind was light, and brightly the sun shone,
And still we galloped on from gorse to gorse.
And once, when checked, a thrush sang, and my horse
Pricked his quick ears as to a sound unknown.

I knew the Spring was come. I knew it even
Better than all by this, that through my chase
In bush and stone and hill and sea and heaven
I seemed to see and follow still your face.
Your face my quarry was. For it I rode,
My horse a thing of wings, myself a god.

TO ONE ON HER WASTE OF TIME

Why practise, love, this small economy
Of your heart's favours? Can you keep a kiss
To be enjoyed in age? And would the free
Expense of pleasure leave you penniless?
Nay, nay. Be wise. Believe me, pleasure is
A gambler's token, only gold to-day.
The day of love is short, and every bliss
Untasted now is a bliss thrown away.
'Twere pitiful, in truth, such treasures should
Lie by like miser's crusts till mouldy grown.
Think you the hand of age will be less rude
In touching your sweet bosom than my own?
Alas, what matter, when our heads are grey,
Whether you loved or did not love to-day?

TO ONE WHO WOULD MAKE CONFESSION

Oh! leave the Past to bury its own dead.
The Past is naught to us, the Present all.
What need of last year's leaves to strew Love's bed?
What need of ghosts to grace a festival?
I would not, if I could, those days recall,
Those days not ours. For us the feast is spread,
The lamps are lit, and music plays withal.
Then let us love and leave the rest unsaid.
This island is our home. Around it roar
Great gulfs and oceans, channels, straits, and seas.
What matter in what wreck we reached the shore,
So we both reached it? We can mock at these
Oh! leave the Past, if Past indeed there be.
I would not know it. I would know but thee.

Song

Oh fly not, Pleasure, pleasant-hearted Pleasure,
 Fold me thy wings, I prithee, yet and stay.
For my heart no measure
Knows nor other treasure
 To buy a garland for my love to-day.

And thou too, Sorrow, tender-hearted Sorrow,
 Thou grey-eyed mourner, fly not yet away.
For I fain would borrow
Thy sad weeds to-morrow
 To make a mourning for love's yesterday.

The voice of Pity, Time's divine dear Pity,
 Moved me to tears. I dared not say them nay,
But went forth from the city
Making thus my ditty
 Of fair love lost for ever and a day.

FROM *The Wisdom of Merlyn*

What then is Merlyn's message, his word to thee weary of
 pain,
Man, on thy desolate march, thy search for an adequate
 cause, for a thread, for a guiding rein,
Still in the maze of thy doubts and fears, to bring thee thy joy
 again?

Thou hast tried to climb to the sky; thou hast called it a
 firmament;
Thou hast found it a thing infirm, a heaven which is no haven,
 a bladder punctured and rent,
A mansion frail as the rainbow mist, as thy own soul impotent.

Thou hast clung to a dream in thy tears; thou hast stayed thy
 rage with a hope;
Thou hast anchored thy wreck to a reed, a cobweb spread for
 thy sail, with sand for thy salvage rope;
Thou hast made thy course with a compass marred, a toy for
 thy telescope.

What hast thou done with thy days? Bethink thee, Man, that
    alone
Thou of all sentient things, hast learned to grieve in thy joy,
    hast earned thee the malison
Of going sad without cause of pain, a weeper and woe-begone.

Why? For the dream of a dream of another than this fair life
Joyous to all but thee, by every creature beloved in its spring-
    time of passion rife,
By every creature but only thee, sad husband with sadder
    wife,

Scared at thought of the end, at the simple logic of death,
Scared at the old Earth's arms outstretched to hold thee again,
    thou child of an hour, of a breath,
Seeking refuge with all but her, the mother that comforteth.

Merlyn's message is this: he would bid thee have done with
    pride.
What has it brought thee but grief, thy parentage with the
    Gods, thy kinship with beasts denied?
What thy lore of a life to come in a cloud-world deified?

O thou child which art Man, distraught with a shadow of ill!
O thou fool of thy dreams, thou gatherer rarely of flowers but
    of fungi of evil smell,
Poison growths of the autumn woods, rank mandrake and
    mort-morell!

Take thy joy with the rest, the bird, the beast of the field,
Each one wiser than thou, which frolic in no dismay, which
    seize what the seasons yield,
And lay thee down when thy day is done content with the
    unrevealed.

Take the thing which thou hast. Forget thy kingdom unseen.
Lean thy lips on the Earth; she shall bring new peace to thy
    eyes with her healing vesture green.
Drink once more at her fount of love, the one true hippocrene.

O thou child of thy fears! Nay, shame on thy childish part,
Weeping when called to thy bed. Take cheer. When the shad-
    ows come, when the crowd is leaving the mart,
Then shalt thou learn that thou needest sleep, Death's kindly
    arms for thy heart.

SIDNEY LANIER

(1842–1881)

FROM *The Symphony*

I speak for each no-tonguéd tree
That, spring by spring, doth nobler be,
And dumbly and most wistfully
His mighty prayerful arms outspreads
Above men's oft-unheeding heads,
And his big blessing downward sheds.
I speak for all-shaped blooms and leaves,
Lichens on stones and moss on eaves,
Grasses and grains in ranks and sheaves;
Broad-fronded ferns and keen-leafed canes,
And briery mazes bounding lanes,
And marsh-plants, thirsty-cupped for rains,
And milky stems and sugary veins;
For every long-armed woman-vine
That round a piteous tree doth twine;
For passionate odors, and divine
Pistils, and petals crystalline;
All purities of shady springs,
All shynesses of film-winged things
That fly from tree-trunks and bark-rings;
All modesties of mountain-fawns
That leap to covert from wild lawns,
And tremble if the day but dawns;
All sparklings of small beady eyes
Of birds, and sidelong glances wise
Wherewith the jay hints tragedies;
All piquancies of prickly burs,
And smoothnesses of downs and furs
Of eiders and of minivers;
All limpid honeys that do lie

At stamen-bases, nor deny
The humming-birds' fine roguery,
Bee-thighs, nor any butterfly;
All gracious curves of slender wings,
Bark-mottlings, fibre-spiralings,
Fern-wavings and leaf-flickerings;
Each dial-marked leaf and flower-bell
Wherewith in every lonesome dell
Time to himself his hours doth tell;
All tree-sounds, rustlings of pine-cones,
Wind-sighings, doves' melodious moans,
And night's unearthly under-tones;
All placid lakes and waveless deeps,
All cool reposing mountain-steeps,
Vale-calms and tranquil lotos-sleeps;—
Yea, all fair forms, and sounds, and lights,
And warmths, and mysteries, and mights,
Of Nature's utmost depths and heights,
—These doth my timid tongue present,
Their mouthpiece and leal instrument
And servant, all love-eloquent.

GERARD MANLEY HOPKINS

(1844–1889)

Heaven—Haven
(A NUN TAKES THE VEIL)

I have desired to go
    Where springs not fail,
To fields where flies no sharp and sided hail
    And a few lilies blow.

And I have asked to be
    Where no storms come,
Where the green swell is in the havens dumb,
    And out of the swing of the sea.

The Habit of Perfection

Elected Silence, sing to me
And beat upon my whorléd ear,
Pipe me to pastures still and be
The music that I care to hear.

Shape nothing, lips; be lovely-dumb:
It is the shut, the curfew sent
From there where all surrenders come
Which only makes you eloquent.

Be shelléd, eyes, with double dark
And find the uncreated light:
This ruck and reel which you remark
Coils, keeps, and teases simple sight.

Palate, the hutch of tasty lust,
Desire not to be rinsed with wine:
The can must be so sweet, the crust
So fresh that comes in fasts divine!

Nostrils, your careless breath that spend
Upon the stir and keep of pride,
What relish shall the censers send
Along the sanctuary side!

O feel-of-primrose hands, O feet
That want the yield of plushy sward,
But you shall walk the golden street
And you unhouse and house the Lord.

And, Poverty, be thou the bride
And now the marriage feast begun,
And lily-coloured clothes provide
Your spouse not laboured-at nor spun.

In the Valley of the Elwy

I remember a house where all were good
    To me, God knows, deserving no such thing:
    Comforting smell breathed at very entering,
Fetched fresh, as I suppose, off some sweet wood.
That cordial air made those kind people a hood
    All over, as a bevy of eggs the mothering wing
    Will, or mild nights the new morsels of spring:
Why, it seemed of course; seemed of right it should.

Lovely the woods, waters, meadows, combes, vales,
All the air things wear that build this world of Wales;
    Only the inmate does not correspond:
God, lover of souls, swaying considerate scales,
Complete thy creature dear O where it fails,
    Being mighty a master, being a father and fond.

The Starlight Night

Look at the stars! look, look up at the skies!
    O look at all the fire-folk sitting in the air!
    The bright boroughs, the circle-citadels there!
Down in dim woods the diamond delves! the elves'-eyes!
The grey lawns cold where gold, where quickgold lies!
    Wind-beat whitebeam! airy abeles set on a flare!
    Flake-doves sent floating forth at a farmyard scare!—
Ah well! it is all a purchase, all is a prize.

Buy then! bid then!—What?—Prayer, patience, alms, vows.
Look, look: a May-mess, like on orchard boughs!
    Look! March-bloom, like on mealed-with-yellow sallows!
These are indeed the barn; withindoors house
The shocks. This piece-bright paling shuts the spouse
    Christ home, Christ and his mother and all his hallows.

Pied Beauty

Glory be to God for dappled things—
   For skies of couple-colour as a brinded cow;
     For rose-moles all in stipple upon trout that swim;
Fresh-firecoal chestnut-falls; finches' wings;
    Landscape plotted and pieced—fold, fallow, and plough;
     And áll Trádes, their gear and tackle and trim.
All things counter, original, spare, strange;
   Whatever is fickle, freckled (who knows how?)
    With swift, slow; sweet, sour; adazzle, dim;
He fathers-forth whose beauty is past change:
         Praise him.

ANDREW LANG

(1844–1912)

The Odyssey

As one that for a weary space has lain
   Lulled by the song of Circe and her wine,
   In gardens near the pale of Proserpine,
Where that Aeaean isle forgets the main,
And only the low lutes of love complain,
   And only shadows of wan lovers pine;
   As such an one were glad to know the brine
Salt on his lips, and the large air again—

So gladly, from the songs of modern speech
   Men turn, and see the stars, and feel the free
   Shrill wind beyond the close of heavy flowers;
   And, through the music of the languid hours,
They hear like ocean on a western beach
   The surge and thunder of the Odyssey.

ARTHUR WILLIAM EDGAR O'SHAUGHNESSY
(1844–1881)

FROM *Ode*

We are the music-makers,
　　And we are the dreamers of dreams,
Wandering by lone sea-breakers,
　　And sitting by desolate streams;
World-losers and world-forsakers,
　　On whom the pale moon gleams:
Yet we are the movers and shakers
　　Of the world for ever, it seems.

With wonderful deathless ditties
We build up the world's great cities,
　　And out of a fabulous story
　　We fashion an empire's glory:
One man with a dream, at pleasure,
　　Shall go forth and conquer a crown;
And three with a new song's measure
　　Can trample an empire down.

We, in the ages lying
　　In the buried past of the earth,
Built Nineveh with our sighing,
　　And Babel itself with our mirth;
And o'erthrew them with prophesying
　　To the old of the new world's worth;
For each age is a dream that is dying,
　　Or one that is coming to birth.

ROBERT BRIDGES
(1844–1930)

Pater Filio

Sense with keenest edge unuséd,
　　Yet unsteel'd by scathing fire;
Lovely feet as yet unbruiséd
　　On the ways of dark desire;
Sweetest hope that lookest smiling
O'er the wilderness defiling!

Why such beauty, to be blighted
  By the swarm of foul destruction?
Why such innocence delighted,
  When sin stalks to thy seduction?
All the litanies e'er chaunted
Shall not keep thy faith undaunted.

I have pray'd the sainted Morning
  To unclasp her hands to hold thee;
From resignful Eve's adorning
  Stol'n a robe of peace to enfold thee;
With all charms of man's contriving
Arm'd thee for thy lonely striving.

Me too once unthinking Nature
  —Whence Love's timeless mockery took me,—
Fashion'd so divine a creature,
  Yea, and like a beast forsook me.
I forgave, but tell the measure
Of her crime in thee, my treasure.

To L.B.C.L.M.

I love all beauteous things,
  I seek and adore them;
God hath no better praise,
And man in his hasty days
  Is honoured for them.

I too will something make
  And joy in the making;
Altho' to-morrow it seem
Like the empty words of a dream
  Remembered on waking.

On a Dead Child

Perfect little body, without fault or stain on thee,
  With promise of strength and manhood full and fair!
    Though cold and stark and bare,
The bloom and the charm of life doth awhile remain on thee.

Thy mother's treasure wert thou;—alas! no longer
  To visit her heart with wondrous joy; to be
      Thy father's pride;—ah, he
Must gather his faith together, and his strength make stronger.

To me, as I move thee now in the last duty,
  Dost thou with a turn or gesture anon respond;
      Startling my fancy fond
With a chance attitude of the head, a freak of beauty.

Thy hand clasps, as 'twas wont, my finger, and holds it:
  But the grasp is the clasp of Death, heart-breaking and stiff;
      Yet feels to my hand as if
'Twas still thy will, thy pleasure and trust that enfolds it.

So I lay thee there, thy sunken eyelids closing,—
  Go lie thou there in thy coffin, thy last little bed!—
      Propping thy wise, sad head,
Thy firm pale hands across thy chest disposing.

So quiet! doth the change content thee?
  Death, whither hath he taken thee?
  To a world, do I think, that rights the disaster of this?
      The vision of which I miss,
Who weep for the body, and wish but to warm thee and
    awaken thee?

Ah! little at best can all our hopes avail us
  To lift this sorrow, or cheer us, when in the dark,
      Unwilling, alone we embark,
And the things we have seen and have known and have heard
    of, fail us.

ALICE MEYNELL

(1849–1922)

A Letter from a Girl to Her Own Old Age

    Listen, and when thy hand this paper presses,
    O time-worn woman, think of her who blesses
    What thy thin fingers touch, with her caresses.

O mother, for the weight of years that break thee!
O daughter, for slow time must yet awake thee,
And from the changes of my heart must make thee.

O fainting traveller, morn is grey in heaven.
Dost thou remember how the clouds were driven?
And are they calm about the fall of even?

Pause near the ending of thy long migration,
For this one sudden hour of desolation
Appeals to one hour of thy meditation.

Suffer, O silent one, that I remind thee
Of the great hills that stormed the sky behind thee,
Of the wild winds of power that have resigned thee.

Know that the mournful plain where thou must wander
Is but a grey and silent world, but ponder
The misty mountains of the morning yonder.

Listen:—the mountain winds with rain were fretting,
And sudden gleams the mountain-tops besetting.
I cannot let thee fade to death, forgetting.

What part of this wild heart of mine I know not
Will follow with thee where the great winds blow not,
And where young flowers of the mountain grow not.

      ✻   ✻   ✻   ✻

I have not writ this letter of divining
To make a glory of thy silent pining,
A triumph of thy mute and strange declining.

Only one youth, and the bright life was shrouded.
Only one morning, and the day was clouded.
And one old age with all regrets is crowded.

O hush, O hush! thy tears my words are steeping.
O hush, hush, hush! So full, the fount of weeping?
Poor eyes, so quickly moved, so near to sleeping?

Pardon the girl; such strange desires beset her.
Poor woman, lay aside the mournful letter
That breaks thy heart; the one who wrote, forget her.

The one who now thy faded features guesses,
With filial fingers thy grey hair caresses,
With mournful tears thy mournful twilight blesses.

Renouncement

I must not think of thee; and, tired yet strong,
　I shun the love that lurks in all delight—
　The love of thee—and in the blue heaven's height,
And in the dearest passage of a song.
Oh, just beyond the sweetest thoughts that throng
　This breast, the thought of thee waits hidden yet bright;
　But it must never, never come in sight;
I must stop short of thee the whole day long.
But when sleep comes to close each difficult day,
　When night gives pause to the long watch I keep,
And all my bonds I needs must loose apart,
Must doff my will as raiment laid away,—
　With the first dream that comes with the first sleep
I run, I run, I am gather'd to thy heart.

WILLIAM ERNEST HENLEY

(1849–1903)

I.M.
R. T. Hamilton Bruce

Out of the night that covers me,
　Black as the Pit from pole to pole,
I thank whatever gods may be
　For my unconquerable soul.

In the fell clutch of circumstance
　I have not winced nor cried aloud.
Under the bludgeonings of chance
　My head is bloody, but unbowed.

Beyond this place of wrath and tears
　Looms but the horror of the shade,
And yet the menace of the years
　Finds, and shall find, me unafraid.

It matters not how strait the gate,
    How charged with punishments the scroll,
I am the master of my fate:
    I am the captain of my soul.

"Fill a Glass with Golden Wine"

Fill a glass with golden wine,
    And the while your lips are wet
Set their perfume unto mine,
        And forget,
Every kiss we take and give
Leaves us less of life to live.

Yet again! your whim and mine
    In a happy while have met.
All your sweets to me resign,
        Nor regret
That we press with every breath,
Sighed or singing, nearer death.

To A.D.

The nightingale has a lyre of gold,
    The lark's is a clarion call,
And the blackbird plays but a boxwood flute,
    But I love him best of all.

For his song is all of the joy of life,
    And we in the mad, spring weather,
We two have listened till he sang
    Our hearts and lips together.

"On the Way to Kew"

On the way to Kew
By the river old and gray,
Where in the Long Ago
We laughed and loitered so,
I met a ghost to-day,

A ghost that told of you—
A ghost of low replies
And sweet, inscrutable eyes
Coming up from Richmond
As you used to do.

By the river old and gray,
The enchanted Long Ago
Murmured and smiled anew.
On the way to Kew,
March had the laugh of May,
The bare boughs looked aglow,
And old immortal words
Sang in my breast like birds,
Coming up from Richmond
As I used with you.

With the life of Long Ago
Lived my thoughts of you.
By the river old and gray
Flowing his appointed way
As I watched I knew
What is so good to know—
Not in vain, not in vain,
Shall I look for you again
Coming up from Richmond
On the way to Kew.

Epilogue to Rhymes and Rhythms

These, to you now, O, more than ever now—
Now that the Ancient Enemy
Has passed, and we, we two that are one, have seen
A piece of perfect Life
Turn to so ravishing a shape of Death
The Arch-Discomforter might well have smiled
In pity and pride,
Even as he bore his lovely and innocent spoil
From those home-kingdoms he left desolate.

Poor windlestraws
On the great, sullen, roaring pool of Time
And Chance and Change, I know!
But they are yours, as I am, till we attain
That end for which we make, we two that are one:
A little, exquisite Ghost
Between us, smiling with the serenest eyes
Seen in this world, and calling, calling still
In that clear voice whose infinite subtleties
Of sweetness, thrilling back across the grave,
Break the poor heart to hear:—
                    "Come, Dadsie, come!
Mama, how long—how long!"

ROBERT LOUIS STEVENSON

(1850–1894)

The Celestial Surgeon

If I have faltered more or less
In my great task of happiness;
If I have moved among my race
And shown no glorious morning face;
If beams from happy human eyes
Have moved me not; if morning skies,
Books, and my food, and summer rain
Knocked on my sullen heart in vain:—
Lord, thy most pointed pleasure take
And stab my spirit broad awake;
Or, Lord, if too obdurate I,
Choose thou, before that spirit die,
A piercing pain, a killing sin,
And to my dead heart run them in!

The Vagabond

Give to me the life I love,
    Let the lave go by me,
Give the jolly heaven above
    And the byway nigh me.

Bed in the bush with stars to see,
    Bread I dip in the river—
There's the life for a man like me,
    There's the life for ever.

Let the blow fall soon or late,
    Let what will be o'er me;
Give the face of earth around
    And the road before me.
Wealth I seek not, hope nor love,
    Nor a friend to know me;
All I seek the heaven above
    And the road below me.

Or let autumn fall on me
    Where afield I linger,
Silencing the bird on tree,
    Biting the blue finger:
White as meal the frosty field—
    Warm the fireside haven—
Not to autumn will I yield,
    Not to winter even!

Let the blow fall soon or late,
    Let what will be o'er me;
Give the face of earth around,
    And the road before me.
Wealth I ask not, hope nor love,
    Nor a friend to know me;
All I ask the heaven above,
    And the road below me.

Requiem

Under the wide and starry sky
Dig the grave and let me lie.
Glad did I live and gladly die,
    And I laid me down with a will.

This be the verse you grave for me:
Here he lies where he longed to be;
Home is the sailor, home from sea,
    And the hunter home from the hill.

OSCAR WILDE

(1856–1900)

FROM *The Ballad of Reading Gaol*

In Debtor's Yard the stones are hard,
    And the dripping wall is high,
So it was there he took the air
    Beneath the leaden sky,
And by each side a Warder walked,
    For fear the man might die.

Or else he sat with those who watched
    His anguish night and day;
Who watched him when he rose to weep,
    And when he crouched to pray;
Who watched him lest himself should rob
    Their scaffold of its prey.

The Governor was strong upon
    The Regulations Act:
The Doctor said that Death was but
    A scientific fact:
And twice a day the Chaplain called,
    And left a little tract.

And twice a day he smoked his pipe,
    And drank his quart of beer:
His soul was resolute, and held
    No hiding-place for fear;
He often said that he was glad
    The hangman's hands were near.

But why he said so strange a thing
    No Warder dared to ask:

For he to whom a watcher's doom
   Is given as his task,
Must set a lock upon his lips,
   And make his face a mask.

Or else he might be moved, and try
   To comfort or console:
And what should Human Pity do
   Pent up in Murderers' Hole?
What word of grace in such a place
   Could help a brother's soul?

With slouch and swing around the ring
   We trod the Fools' Parade!
We did not care: we knew we were
   The Devil's Own Brigade:
And shaven head and feet of lead
   Make a merry masquerade.

We tore the tarry rope to shreds
   With blunt and bleeding nails;
We rubbed the doors, and scrubbed the floors,
   And cleaned the shining rails:
And, rank by rank, we soaped the plank,
   And clattered with the pails.

We sewed the sacks, we broke the stones,
   We turned the dusty drill:
We banged the tins, and bawled the hymns,
   And sweated on the mill:
But in the heart of every man
   Terror was lying still.

So still it lay that every day
   Crawled like a weed-clogged wave:
And we forgot the bitter lot
   That waits for fool and knave,
Till once, as we tramped in from work,
   We passed an open grave.

With yawning mouth the yellow hole
    Gaped for a living thing;
The very mud cried out for blood
    To the thirsty asphalt ring:
And we knew that ere one dawn grew fair
    Some prisoner had to swing.

Right in we went, with soul intent
    On Death and Dread and Doom:
The hangman, with his little bag,
    Went shuffling through the gloom:
And each man trembled as he crept
    Into his numbered tomb.

That night the empty corridors
    Were full of forms of Fear,
And up and down the iron town
    Stole feet we could not hear,
And through the bars that hide the stars
    White faces seemed to peer.

He lay as one who lies and dreams
    In a pleasant meadow-land,
The watchers watched him as he slept,
    And could not understand
How one could sleep so sweet a sleep
    With a hangman close at hand.

But there is no sleep when men must weep
    Who never yet have wept:
So we—the fool, the fraud, the knave—
    That endless vigil kept,
And through each brain on hands of pain
    Another's terror crept.

Alas! it is a fearful thing
    To feel another's guilt!
For, right within, the sword of Sin
    Pierced to its poisoned hilt,
And as molten lead were the tears we shed
    For the blood we had not spilt.

The Warders with their shoes of felt
    Crept by each padlocked door,
And peeped and saw, with eyes of awe,
    Gray figures on the floor,
And wondered why men knelt to pray
    Who never prayed before.

All through the night we knelt and prayed,
    Mad mourners of a corse!
The troubled plumes of midnight were
    The plumes upon a hearse:
And bitter wine upon a sponge
    Was the savour of Remorse.

The grey cock crew, the red cock crew,
    But never came the day;
And crooked shapes of terror crouched
    In the corners where we lay:
And each evil sprite that walks by night
    Before us seemed to play.

    ❀   ❀   ❀   ❀   ❀

The morning wind began to moan,
    But still the night went on;
Through its giant loom the web of gloom
    Crept till each thread was spun:
And, as we prayed, we grew afraid
    Of the Justice of the Sun.

The moaning wind went wandering round
    The weeping prison-wall:
Till like a wheel of turning steel
    We felt the minutes crawl:
O moaning wind! what had we done
    To have such a seneschal?

At last I saw the shadowed bars,
    Like a lattice wrought in lead,
Move right across the whitewashed wall
    That faced my three-planked bed,
And I knew that somewhere in the world
    God's dreadful dawn was red.

At six o'clock we cleaned our cells,
  At seven all was still,
But the sough and swing of a mighty wing
  The prison seemed to fill,
For the Lord of Death, with icy breath,
  Had entered in to kill.

He did not pass in purple pomp,
  Nor ride a moon-white steed,
Three yards of cord and a sliding board
  Are all the gallows' need:
So with rope of shame the Herald came
  To do the secret deed.

We were as men who through a fen
  Of filthy darkness grope:
We did not dare to breathe a prayer,
  Or to give our anguish scope:
Something was dead in each of us,
  And what was dead was Hope.

For Man's grim Justice goes its way,
  And will not swerve aside:
It slays the weak, it slays the strong,
  It has a deadly stride:
With iron heel it slays the strong,
  The monstrous parricide!

We waited for the stroke of eight:
  Each tongue was thick with thirst:
For the stroke of eight is the stroke of Fate
  That makes a man accursed,
And Fate will use a running noose
  For the best man and the worst.

We had no other thing to do,
  Save to wait for the sign to come:
So, like things of stone in a valley lone,
  Quiet we sat and dumb:
But each man's heart beat thick and quick,
  Like a madman on a drum!

With sudden shock, the prison-clock
  Smote on the shivering air,
And from all the jail rose up a wail
  Of impotent despair,
Like the sound that frightened marshes hear
  From some leper in his lair.

And as one sees most dreadful things
  In the crystal of a dream,
We saw the greasy hempen rope
  Hooked to the blackened beam,
And heard the prayer the hangman's snare
  Strangled into a scream.

And all the woe that moved him so
  That he gave that bitter cry,
And the wild regrets, and the bloody sweats,
  None knew so well as I:
For he who lives more lives than one
  More deaths than one must die.

JOHN DAVIDSON

(1857–1909)

In Romney Marsh

As I went down to Dymchurch Wall,
  I heard the South sing o'er the land;
I saw the yellow sunlight fall
  On knolls where Norman churches stand.

And ringing shrilly, taut and lithe,
  Within the wind a core of sound,
The wire from Romney town to Hythe
  Alone its airy journey wound.

A veil of purple vapour flowed
  And trailed its fringe along the Straits;
The upper air like sapphire glowed;
  And roses filled Heaven's central gates.

Masts in the offing wagged their tops;
  The swinging waves pealed on the shore;
The saffron beach, all diamond drops
  And beads of surge, prolonged the roar.

As I came up from Dymchurch Wall,
  I saw above the Downs' low crest
The crimson brands of sunset fall,
  Flicker and fade from out the west.

Night sank: like flakes of silver fire
  The stars in one great shower came down;
Shrill blew the wind; and shrill the wire
  Rang out from Hythe to Romney town.

The darkly shining salt sea drops
  Streamed as the waves clashed on the shore;
The beach, with all its organ stops
  Pealing again, prolonged the roar.

Waiting

Within unfriendly walls
  We starve—or starve by stealth.
Oxen fatten in their stalls;
  You guard the harrier's health:
They never can be criminals,
  And can't compete for wealth.
    From the mansion and the palace
      Is there any help or hail
    For the tenants of the alleys,
      Of the workhouse and the jail?

Though lands await our toil,
  And earth half-empty rolls,
Cumberers of English soil,
  We cringe for orts and doles—
Prosperity's accustomed foil,
  Millions of useless souls.
    In the gutters and the ditches
      Human vermin festering lurk—
    We, the rust upon your riches;
      We, the flaw in all your work.

Come down from where you sit;
  We look to you for aid.
Take us from the miry pit,
  And lead us undismayed:
Say: "Even you, outcast, unfit,
  Forward with sword and spade!"
    And myriads of us idle
      Would thank you through our tears,
     Though you drove us with a bridle,
      And a whip about our ears.

From cloudy cape to cape
  The teeming waters seethe;
Golden grain and purple grape
  The regions overwreathe.
Will no one help us to escape?
  We scarce have room to breathe.
    You might try to understand us:
      We are waiting night and day
     For a captain to command us,
      And the word we must obey.

ALFRED EDWARD HOUSMAN

(1859–1936)

"Loveliest of Trees..."

Loveliest of trees, the cherry now
Is hung with bloom along the bough,
And stands about the woodland ride
Wearing white for Eastertide.

Now, of my threescore years and ten,
Twenty will not come again,
And take from seventy springs a score,
It only leaves me fifty more.

And since to look at things in bloom
Fifty springs are little room,
About the woodlands I will go
To see the cherry hung with snow.

"When I Was One-and-Twenty"

When I was one-and-twenty
    I heard a wise man say,
"Give crowns and pounds and guineas
    But not your heart away;
Give pearls away and rubies
    But keep your fancy free."
But I was one-and-twenty,
    No use to talk to me.

When I was one-and-twenty
    I heard him say again,
"The heart out of the bosom
    Was never given in vain;
'Tis paid with sighs a-plenty
    And sold for endless rue."
And I am two-and-twenty,
    And oh, 'tis true, 'tis true.

"Into My Heart an Air..."

Into my heart an air that kills
    From yon far country blows:
What are those blue remembered hills,
    What spires, what farms are those?

That is the land of lost content,
    I see it shining plain,
The happy highways where I went
    And cannot come again.

Epitaph on an Army of Mercenaries

These, in the day when heaven was falling,
    The hour when earth's foundations fled,
Followed their mercenary calling
    And took their wages and are dead.

Their shoulders held the sky suspended;
　　They stood, and earth's foundations stay;
What God abandoned, these defended,
　　And saved the sum of things for pay.

"I to My Perils"

I to my perils
　　Of cheat and charmer
　　Came clad in armour
　　　By stars benign;
Hope lies to mortals
　　And most believe her,
　　But man's deceiver
　　　Was never mine.

The thoughts of others
　　Were light and fleeting,
　　Of lovers' meeting
　　　Or luck or fame;
Mine were of trouble
　　And mine were steady,
　　So I was ready
　　　When trouble came.

For My Funeral

O thou that from thy mansion
　　Through time and place to roam,
Dost sent abroad thy children,
　　And then dost call them home,

That men and tribes and nations
　　And all thy hand hath made
May shelter them from sunshine
　　In thine eternal shade:

We now to peace and darkness
And earth and thee restore
Thy creature that thou madest
And wilt cast forth no more.

FRANCIS THOMPSON

(1859–1907)

The Hound of Heaven

I fled Him, down the nights and down the days;
  I fled Him, down the arches of the years;
I fled Him, down the labyrinthine ways
  Of my own mind; and in the midst of tears
I hid from Him, and under running laughter.
        Up vistaed hopes I sped;
        And shot, precipitated,
Adown Titanic glooms of chasméd fears,
  From those strong Feet that followed, followed after.
        But with unhurrying chase,
        And unperturbéd pace,
    Deliberate speed, majestic instancy,
        They beat—and a Voice beat
        More instant than the Feet—
    "All things betray thee, who betrayest Me."

        I pleaded, outlaw-wise,
By many a hearted casement, curtained red,
  Trellised with intertwining charities
(For, though I knew His love Who followéd,
        Yet was I sore adread
Lest, having Him, I must have naught beside);
But, if one little casement parted wide,
  The gust of His approach would clash it to.
Fear wist not to evade, as Love wist to pursue.
Across the margent of the world I fled,
  And troubled the gold gateways of the stars,
  Smiting for shelter on their clangéd bars;
        Fretted to dulcet jars
And silvern chatter the pale ports o' the moon.

I said to dawn, Be sudden; to eve, Be soon;
   With thy young skiey blossoms heap me over
      From this tremendous Lover!
Float thy vague veil about me, lest He see!
    I tempted all His servitors, but to find
My own betrayal in their constancy,
In faith to Him their fickleness to me,
   Their traitorous trueness, and their loyal deceit.
To all swift things for swiftness did I sue;
   Clung to the whistling mane of every wind,
      But whether they swept, smoothly fleet,
    The long savannahs of the blue;
     Or whether thunder-driven
    They clanged his chariot 'thwart a heaven
Plashy with flying lightnings round the spurn o' their feet:—
   Fear wist not to evade as Love wist to pursue.
     Still with unhurrying chase,
     And unperturbéd pace,
    Deliberate speed, majestic instancy,
     Came on the following Feet,
     And a Voice above their beat—
    "Naught shelters thee, who wilt not shelter Me."

I sought no more that after which I strayed
    In face of man or maid;
But still within the little children's eyes
    Seems something, something that replies;
They at least are for me, surely for me!
I turned me to them very wistfully;
But, just as their young eyes grew sudden fair
    With dawning answers there,
Their angel plucked them from me by the hair.
"Come then, ye other children, Nature's—share
With me" (said I) "your delicate fellowship;
    Let me greet you lip to lip,
    Let me twine with you caresses,
      Wantoning
    With our Lady-Mother's vagrant tresses,
      Banqueting
    With her in her wind-walled palace,
    Underneath her azured daïs,

Quaffing as your taintless way is,
    From a chalice
Lucent-weeping out of the dayspring.
        So it was done:
I in their delicate fellowship was one—
Drew the bolts of Nature's secrecies.
I knew all the swift importings
    On the wilful face of skies;
    I knew how the clouds arise
    Spuméd of the wild sea-snortings;
        All that's born or dies
    Rose and drooped with—made them shapers
Of mine own moods, or wailful or divine—
    With them joyed and was bereaven.
    I was heavy with the even,
    When she lit her glimmering tapers
    Round the day's dead sanctities.
    I laughed in the morning's eyes.
I triumphed and I saddened with all weather,
    Heaven and I wept together,
And its sweet tears were salt with mortal mine;
Against the red throb of its sunset-heart
        I laid my own to beat,
        And share commingling heat;
But not by that, by that, was eased my human smart.
In vain my tears were wet on Heaven's grey cheek.
For ah! we know not what each other says,
        These things and I; in sound *I* speak—
Their sound is but their stir, they speak by silences.
Nature, poor stepdame, cannot slake my drouth;
        Let her, if she would owe me,
Drop yon blue bosom-veil of sky, and show me
        The breasts o' her tenderness:
Never did any milk of hers once bless
        My thirsting mouth.
        Nigh and nigh draws the chase,
        With unperturbéd pace,
    Deliberate speed, majestic instancy;
        And past those noiséd Feet
        A voice comes yet more fleet—
"Lo! naught contents thee, who content'st not Me."

Naked I wait Thy love's uplifted stroke!
My harness piece by piece Thou hast hewn from me,
    And smitten me to my knee;
   I am defenceless utterly.
   I slept, methinks, and woke,
And, slowly gazing, find me stripped in sleep.
In the rash lustihead of my young powers,
   I shook the pillaring hours
And pulled my life upon me; grimed with smears,
I stand amid the dust o' the mounded years—
My mangled youth lies dead beneath the heap.
My days have crackled and gone up in smoke,
Have puffed and burst as sun-starts on a stream.
    Yea, faileth now even dream
The dreamer, and the lute the lutanist;
Even the linkéd fantasies, in whose blossomy twist
I swung the earth a trinket at my wrist,
Are yielding; cords of all too weak account
For earth with heavy griefs so overplussed.
    Ah! is Thy love indeed
A weed, albeit an amaranthine weed,
Suffering no flowers except its own to mount?
    Ah! must—
    Designer infinite!—
Ah! must Thou char the wood ere Thou canst limn with it?
My freshness spent its wavering shower i' the dust;
And now my heart is as a broken fount,
Wherein tear-droppings stagnate, spilt down ever
    From the dank thoughts that shiver
Upon the sighful branches of my mind.
    Such is; what is to be?
The pulp so bitter, how shall taste the rind?
I dimly guess what Time in mists confounds;
Yet ever and anon a trumpet sounds
From the hid battlements of Eternity;
Those shaken mists a space unsettle, then
Round the half-glimpséd turrets slowly wash again.
    But not ere him who summoneth
    I first have seen, enwound
With glooming robes purpureal, cypress-crowned;
His name I know, and what his trumpet saith.

Whether man's heart or life it be which yields
 Thee harvest, must Thy harvest fields
 Be dunged with rotten death?

  Now of that long pursuit
  Comes on at hand the bruit;
 That Voice is round me like a bursting sea:
  "And is thy earth so marred,
  Shattered in shard on shard?
 Lo, all things fly thee, for thou fliest Me!
 Strange, piteous, futile thing!
Wherefore should any set thee love apart?
Seeing none but I makes much of naught"
  (He said)
"And human love needs human meriting:
  How hast thou merited—
Of all man's clotted clay the dingiest clot?
  Alack, thou knowest not
How little worthy of any love thou art!
Whom wilt thou find to love ignoble thee
  Save Me, save only Me?
All which I took from thee I did but take,
  Not for thy harms,
But just that thou might'st seek it in My arms.
  All which thy child's mistake
Fancies as lost, I have stored for thee at home;
  Rise, clasp My hand, and come!"
  Halts by me that footfall:
  Is my gloom, after all,
 Shade of His hand, outstretched caressingly?
  "Ah, fondest, blindest, weakest,
  I am He whom thou seekest!
Thou dravest love from thee, who dravest Me."

VICTOR PLARR

(1863–1929)

Epitaphium Citharistriae

Stand not uttering sedately
 Trite oblivious praise above her!
Rather say you saw her lately
 Lightly kissing her last lover.

Whisper not "There is a reason
  Why we bring her no white blossom:"
Since the snowy bloom's in season,
  Strow it on her sleeping bosom:

Oh, for it would be a pity
  To o'erpraise her or to flout her:
She was wild, and sweet, and witty—
  Let's not say dull things about her.

GEORGE SANTAYANA

(1863–1952)

Ode

My heart rebels against my generation,
That talks of freedom and is slave to riches,
And, toiling 'neath each day's ignoble burden,
      Boasts of the morrow.

No space for noonday rest or midnight watches,
No purest joy of breathing under heaven!
Wretched themselves, they heap, to make them happy,
      Many possessions.

But thou, O silent Mother, wise, immortal,
To whom our toil is laughter,—take, divine one,
This vanity away, and to thy lover
      Give what is needful:—

A staunch heart, nobly calm, averse to evil,
The windy sky for breath, the sea, the mountain,
A well-born, gentle friend, his spirit's brother,
      Ever beside him.

What would you gain, ye seekers, with your striving,
Or what vast Babel raise you on your shoulders?
You multiply distresses, and your children
      Surely will curse you.

O leave them rather friendlier gods, and fairer
Orchards and temples, and a freer bosom!
What better comforter have we, or what other
      Profit in living,

Than to feed, sobered by the truth of Nature,
Awhile upon her bounty and her beauty,
And hand her torch of gladness to the ages
      Following after?

She hath not made us, like her other children,
Merely for peopling of her spacious kingdoms,
Beasts of the wild, or insects of the summer,
      Breeding and dying.

But also that we might, half knowing, worship
The deathless beauty of her guiding vision,
And learn to love, in all things mortal, only
      What is eternal.

On the Death of a Metaphysician

Unhappy dreamer, who outwinged in flight
The pleasant region of the things I love,
And soared beyond the sunshine, and above
The golden cornfields and the dear and bright
Warmth of the hearth,—blasphemer of delight,
Was your proud bosom not at peace with Jove,
That you sought, thankless for his guarded grove,
The empty horror of abysmal night?
Ah, the thin air is cold above the moon!
I stood and saw you fall, befooled in death,
As, in your numbéd spirit's fatal swoon,
You cried you were a god, or were to be;
I heard with feeble moan your boastful breath
Bubble from depths of the Icarian sea.

"We Needs Must Be Divided..."

We needs must be divided in the tomb,
For I would die among the hills of Spain,
And o'er the treeless melancholy plain
Await the coming of the final gloom.
But thou—O pitiful!—wilt find scant room
Among thy kindred by the northern main,
And fade into the drifting mist again,
The hemlocks' shadow, or the pines' perfume.
Let gallants lie beside their ladies' dust,
In one cold grave, with mortal love inurned;
Let the sea part our ashes, if it must.
The souls fled thence which love immortal burned,
For they were wedded without bond of lust,
And nothing of our heart to earth returned.

WILLIAM BUTLER YEATS

(1865–1939)

A Faery Song

(SUNG BY THE PEOPLE OF FAERY OVER DIARMUID AND
GRANIA, IN THEIR BRIDAL SLEEP UNDER A CROMLECH)

We who are old, old and gay,
O so old!
Thousands of years, thousands of years,
If all were told:

Give to these children, new from the world,
Silence and love;
And the long dew-dripping hours of the night,
And the stars above:

Give to these children, new from the world,
Rest far from men.
Is anything better, anything better?
Tell us it then:

Us who are old, old and gay,
O so old!
Thousands of years, thousands of years,
If all were told.

The Lover Tells of the Rose in His Heart

All things uncomely and broken, all things worn out and old,
The cry of a child by the roadway, the creak of a lumbering
    cart,
The heavy steps of the ploughman, splashing the wintry
    mould,
Are wronging your image that blossoms a rose in the deeps
    of my heart.

The wrong of unshapely things is a wrong too great to be told;
I hunger to build them anew and sit on a green knoll apart,
With the earth and the sky and the water, re-made, like a
    casket of gold
For my dreams of your image that blossoms a rose in the
    deeps of my heart.

FROM The Land of Heart's Desire

The wind blows out of the gates of the day,
The wind blows over the lonely of heart,
And the lonely of heart is withered away;
While the fairies dance in a place apart,
Shaking their milk-white feet in a ring,
Tossing their milk-white arms in the air;
For they hear the wind laugh and murmur and sing
Of a land where even the old are fair,
And even the wise are merry of tongue;
But I heard a reed of Coolaney say—
"When the wind has laughed and murmured and sung,
The lonely of heart is withered away."

FROM Deirdre

"Why is it," Queen Edain said,
    "If I do but climb the stair
To the tower overhead,
    When the winds are calling there,

Or the gannets calling out,
  In waste places of the sky,
There's so much to think about,
  That I cry, that I cry?"

But her goodman answered her:
  "Love would be a thing of nought
Had not all his limbs a stir
  Born out of immoderate thought;
Were he anything by half,
  Were his measure running dry,
Lovers, if they may not laugh,
  Have to cry, have to cry."

But is Edain worth a song?
  Now the hunt begins anew?
Praise the beautiful and strong;
  Praise the redness of the yew;
Praise the blossoming apple-stem.
  But our silence had been wise.
What is all our praise to them,
  That have one another's eyes?

When Helen Lived

We have cried in our despair
That men desert,
For some trivial affair
Or noisy, insolent sport,
Beauty that we have won
From bitterest hours;
Yet we, had we walked within
Those topless towers
Where Helen walked with her boy,
Had given but as the rest
Of the men and women of Troy,
A word and a jest.

FROM A Prayer for My Daughter

I have walked and prayed for this young child an hour
And heard the sea-wind scream upon the tower,
And under the arches of the bridge, and scream
In the elms above the flooded stream;
Imagining in excited reverie
That the future years had come,
Dancing to a frenzied drum
Out of the murderous innocence of the sea.

May she be granted beauty and yet not
Beauty to make a stranger's eye distraught,
Or hers before a looking-glass, for such,
Being made beautiful overmuch,
Consider beauty a sufficient end,
Lose natural kindness and maybe
The heart-revealing intimacy
That chooses right, and never find a friend.

In courtesy I'd have her chiefly learned;
Hearts are not had as a gift but hearts are earned
By those that are not entirely beautiful;
Yet many, that have played the fool
For beauty's very self, has charm made wise,
And many a poor man that has roved,
Loved and thought himself beloved,
From a glad kindness cannot take his eyes.

My mind, because the minds that I have loved,
The sort of beauty that I have approved,
Prosper but little, has dried up of late,
Yet knows that to be choked with hate
May well be of all evil chances chief.
If there's no hatred in a mind
Assault and battery of the wind
Can never tear the linnet from the leaf.

An Intellectual hatred is the worst,
So let her think opinions are accursed.
Have I not seen the loveliest woman born
Out of the mouth of Plenty's horn,
Because of her opinionated mind
Barter that horn and every good
By quiet natures understood
For an old bellows full of angry wind?

And may her bridegroom bring her to a house
Where all's accustomed, ceremonious;
For arrogance and hatred are the wares
Peddled in the thoroughfares.
How but in custom and in ceremony
Are innocence and beauty born?
Ceremony's a name for the rich horn,
And custom for the spreading laurel tree.

Sailing to Byzantium

That is no country for old men. The young
In one another's arms, birds in the trees,
—Those dying generations—at their song,
The salmon-falls, the mackerel-crowded seas,
Fish, flesh, or fowl, commend all summer long
Whatever is begotten, born and dies.
Caught in that sensual music all neglect
Monuments of unageing intellect.

An aged man is but a paltry thing,
A tattered coat upon a stick, unless
Soul clap its hands and sing, and louder sing
For every tatter in its mortal dress,
Nor is there singing school but studying
Monuments of its own magnificence;
And therefore I have sailed the seas and come
To the holy city of Byzantium.

O sages standing in God's holy fire
As in the gold mosaic of a wall,
Come from the holy fire, perne in a gyre,
And be the singing-masters of my soul.
Consume my heart away; sick with desire
And fastened to a dying animal
It knows not what it is; and gather me
Into the artifice of eternity.

Once out of nature I shall never take
My bodily form from any natural thing,
But such a form as Grecian goldsmiths make
Of hammered gold and gold enamelling
To keep a drowsy Emperor awake;
Or set upon a golden bough to sing
To lords and ladies of Byzantium
Of what is past, or passing, or to come.

ARTHUR SYMONS

(1865–1945)

Declaration

Child, I will give you rings to wear,
And, if you love them, dainty dresses,
Flowers for your bosom and your hair,
And, if you love them, fond caresses;

And I will give you of my days,
And I will leave, when you require it,
My dreams, my books, my wonted ways,
Content if only you desire it.

Take for your own my life, my heart,
And for your love's sake I forgive you;
I only ask you for your heart,
Because I have no heart to give you.

Wanderer's Song

I have had enough of women, and enough of love,
But the land waits, and the sea waits, and day and night is
    enough;
Give me a long white road, and grey wide path of the sea,
And the wind's will and the bird's will, and the heart-ache
    still in me.

Why should I seek out sorrow, and give gold for strife?
I have loved much and wept much, but tears and love are
    not life;
The grass calls to my heart, and the foam to my blood cries
    up,
And the sun shines and the road shines, and the wine's in the
    cup.

I have had enough of wisdom, and enough of mirth,
For the way's one and the end's one, and it's soon to the
    ends of the earth;
And it's then good-night and to bed, and if heels or heart ache,
Well, it's sound sleep and long sleep, and sleep too deep to
    wake.

RUDYARD KIPLING

(1865–1936)

The Long Trail

There's a whisper down the field where the year has shot her
    yield,
  And the ricks stand grey to the sun,
Singing: "Over then, come over, for the bee has quit the
    clover,
  And your English summer's done."

    You have heard the beat of the off-shore wind,
    And the thresh of the deep-sea rain;
    You have heard the song—how long? how long?
    Pull out on the trail again!

Ha' done with the tents of Shem, dear lass,
We've seen the seasons through,
And it's time to turn on the old trail, our own trail, the
    out trail,
Pull out, pull out, on the Long Trail—the trail that is al-
    ways new!

It's North you may run to the rime-ringed sun
    Or South to the blind Horn's hate;
Or East all the way into Mississippi Bay,
    Or West to the Golden Gate—
        Where the blindest bluffs hold good, dear lass,
        And the wildest tales are true,
        And the men bulk big on the old trail, our own trail, the
            out trail,
        And life runs large on the Long Trail—the trail that is
            always new.

The days are sick and cold, and the skies are grey and old,
    And the twice-breathed airs blow damp;
And I'd sell my tired soul for the bucking beam-sea roll
    Of a black Bilbao tramp,
        With her load-line over her hatch, dear lass,
        And a drunken Dago crew,
        And her nose held down on the old trail, our own trail,
            the out trail
        From Cadiz south on the Long Trail—the trail that is
            always new.

There be triple ways to take, of the eagle or the snake,
    Or the way of a man with a maid;
But the sweetest way to me is a ship's upon the sea
    In the heel of the North-East Trade.
        Can you hear the crash on her bows, dear lass,
        And the drum of the racing screw,
        As she ships it green on the old trail, our own trail, the
            out trail,
        As she lifts and 'scends on the Long Trail—the trail that
            is always new?

See the shaking funnels roar, with the Peter at the fore,
 And the fenders grind and heave,
And the derricks clack and grate, as the tackle hooks the
  crate,
 And the fall-rope whines through the sheave;
  It's "Gang-plank up and in," dear lass,
  It's "Hawsers warp her through!"
  And it's "All clear aft" on the old trail, our own trail, the
   out trail,
  We're backing down on the Long Trail—the trail that is
   always new.

O the mutter overside, when the port-fog holds us tied,
 And the sirens hoot their dread,
When foot by foot we creep o'er the hueless viewless deep
 To the sob of the questing lead!
  It's down by the Lower Hope, dear lass,
  With the Gunfleet Sands in view,
  Till the Mouse swings green on the old trail, our own
   trail, the out trail,
  And the Gull Light lifts on the Long Trail—the trail that
   is always new.

O the blazing tropic night, when the wake's a welt of light
 That holds the hot sky tame,
And the steady fore-foot snores through the planet-powdered
  floors
 Where the scared whale flukes in flame!
  Her plates are flaked by the sun, dear lass,
  And her ropes are taut with dew,
  For we're booming down on the old trail, our own trail,
   the out trail,
  We're sagging south on the Long Trail—the trail that
   is always new.

Then home, get her home, where the drunken rollers comb,
 And the shouting seas drive by,
And the engines stamp and ring, and wet bows reel and
  swing,
 And the Southern Cross rides high!
  Yes, the old lost stars wheel back, dear lass,

That blaze in the velvet blue.
They're all old friends on the old trail, our own trail, the
out trail,
They're God's own guides on the Long Trail—the trail
that is always new.

Fly forward, O my heart, from the Foreland to the Start—
We're steaming all too slow,
And its twenty thousand mile to our little lazy isle
Where the trumpet-orchids blow!
You have heard the call of the off-shore wind
And the voice of the deep-sea rain:
You have heard the song. How long—how long?
Pull out on the trail again!

The Lord knows what we may find, dear lass,
And the Deuce knows what we may do—
But we're back once more on the old trail, our own trail, the
out trail,
We're down, hull-down, on the Long Trail—the trail that is
always new!

Screw-Guns

Smokin' my pipe on the mountings, sniffin' the mornin' cool,
I walks in my old brown gaiters along o' my old brown mule,
With seventy gunners be'ind me, and never a beggar forgets
It's only the pick of the Army that handles the dear little pets
—'Tss! 'Tss!
For you all love the screw-guns—the screw-guns they all
love you!
So when we call round with a few guns, o' course you
will know what to do—hoo! hoo!
Jest send in your Chief and surrender—it's worse if you
fights or you runs:
You can go where you please, you can skid up the trees,
but you don't get away from the guns!

They sends us along where the roads are, but mostly we goes
where they ain't.

We'd climb up the side of a sign-board an' trust to the stick
 o' the paint:
We've chivvied the Naga an' Looshai; we've given the Afree-
 deeman fits;
For we fancies ourselves at two thousand, we guns that are
 built in two bits—'Tss! 'Tss!
  For you all love the screw-guns . . .

If a man doesn't work, why, we drills 'im an' teaches 'im 'ow
 to behave.
If a beggar can't march, why, we kills 'im an' rattles 'im into
 'is grave.
You've got to stand up to our business an' spring without
 snatchin' or fuss.
D'you say that you sweat with the field-guns? By God, you
 must lather with us—'Tss! 'Tss!
  For you all love the screw-guns . . .

The eagles is screamin' around us, the river's a-moanin' below,
We're clear o' the pine an' the oak-scrub, we're out on the
 rocks an' the snow,
An' the wind is as thin as a whip-lash what carries away to
 the plains
The rattle an' stamp o' the lead-mules—the jinglety-jink o'
 the chains—'Tss! 'Tss!
  For you all love the screw-guns . . .

There's a wheel on the Horns o' the Mornin', an' a wheel on
 the edge o' the Pit,
An' a drop into nothin' beneath you as straight as a beggar
 can spit:
With the sweat runnin' out o' your shirt-sleeves, an' the sun
 off the snow in your face,
An' 'arf o' the men on the drag-ropes to hold the old gun in
 'er place—'Tss! 'Tss!
  For you all love the screw-guns . . .

Smokin' my pipe on the mountings, sniffin' the mornin' cool,
I climbs in my old brown gaiters along o' my old brown mule.
The monkey can say what our road was—the wild-goat 'e
 knows where we passed.

Stand easy, you long-eared old darlin's! Out drag-ropes! With
    shrapnel! Hold fast—'Tss! 'Tss!
    For you all love the screw-guns—the screw-guns they all
        love you!
    So when we take tea with a few guns, o' course you will
        know what to do—hoo! hoo!
    Jest send in your Chief an' surrender—it's worse if you
        fights or you runs:
    You may hide in the caves, they'll be only your graves,
        but you can't get away from the guns!

Shillin' a Day

My name is O'Kelly, I've heard the Revelly
From Birr to Bareilly, from Leeds to Lahore,
Hong-Kong and Peshawur,
Lucknow and Etawah,
And fifty-five more all endin' in "pore."
Black Death and his quickness, the depth and the thickness
Of sorrow and sickness I've known on my way,
But I'm old and I'm nervis,
I'm cast from the Service,
And all I deserve is a shillin' a day.

   Chorus: Shillin' a day,
               Bloomin' good pay—
               Lucky to touch it, a shillin' a day!

Oh, it drives me half crazy to think of the days I
Went slap for the Ghazi, my sword at my side,
When we rode Hell-for-leather
Both squadrons together,
That didn't care whether we lived or we died.
But it's no use despairin', my wife must go charin'
An' me commissairin', the pay-bills to better,
So if me you be'old
In the wet and the cold,
By the Grand Metropold, won't you give me a letter?

Full Chorus: Give 'im a letter—
'Can't do no better,
Late Troop-Sergeant-Major an'—runs with a
    letter!
Think what 'e's been,
Think what 'e's seen,
Think of his pension an'—
GAWD SAVE THE QUEEN!

Recessional
(1897)

God of our fathers, known of old,
  Lord of our far-flung battle-line,
Beneath whose awful Hand we hold
  Dominion over palm and pine—
Lord God of Hosts, be with us yet,
Lest we forget—lest we forget!

The tumult and the shouting dies;
  The Captains and the Kings depart:
Still stands Thine ancient sacrifice,
  An humble and a contrite heart.
Lord God of Hosts, be with us yet,
Lest we forget—lest we forget!

Far-called, our navies melt away;
  On dune and headland sinks the fire:
Lo, all our pomp of yesterday
  Is one with Nineveh and Tyre!
Judge of the Nations, spare us yet,
Lest we forget—lest we forget!

If, drunk with sight of power, we loose
  Wild tongues that have not Thee in awe,
Such boastings as the Gentiles use,
  Or lesser breeds without the Law—
Lord God of Hosts, be with us yet,
Lest we forget—lest we forget!

For heathen heart that puts her trust
    In reeking tube and iron shard,
All valiant dust that builds on dust,
    And guarding, calls not Thee to guard,
For frantic boast and foolish word—
Thy mercy on Thy people, Lord!

ERNEST DOWSON

(1867–1900)

Vitae Summa Brevis Spem Nos Vetat Incohare Longam

They are not long, the weeping and the laughter,
    Love and desire and hate:
I think they have no portion in us after
        We pass the gate.

They are not long, the days of wine and roses:
    Out of a misty dream
Our path emerges for a while, then closes
        Within a dream.

Non Sum Qualis Eram Bonae sub Regno Cynarae

Last night, ah, yesternight, betwixt her lips and mine
There fell thy shadow, Cynara! thy breath was shed
Upon my soul between the kisses and the wine;
And I was desolate and sick of an old passion,
    Yea, I was desolate and bow'd my head:
I have been faithful to thee, Cynara! in my fashion.

All night upon mine heart I felt her warm heart beat,
Night-long within mine arms in love and sleep she lay;
Surely the kisses of her bought red mouth were sweet;
But I was desolate and sick of an old passion,
    When I awoke and found the dawn was gray:
I have been faithful to thee, Cynara! in my fashion.

I have forgot much, Cynara! gone with the wind,
Flung roses, roses, riotously with the throng,
Dancing, to put thy pale lost lilies out of mind;
But I was desolate and sick of an old passion,
    Yea, all the time, because the dance was long:
I have been faithful to thee, Cynara! in my fashion.

I cried for madder music and for stronger wine,
But when the feast is finish'd and the lamps expire,
Then falls thy shadow, Cynara! the night is thine;
And I am desolate and sick of an old passion,
    Yea, hungry for the lips of my desire:
I have been faithful to thee, Cynara! in my fashion.

A.E.—GEORGE WILLIAM RUSSELL

(1867–1935)

Chivalry

I dreamed I saw that ancient Irish queen,
Who from her dun, as dawn had opened wide,
Saw the tall foemen rise on every side,
And gazed with kindling eye upon the scene,
And in delight cried, "Noble is their mien."
"Most kingly are they," her own host replied,
Praising the beauty, bravery, and pride
As if the foe their very kin had been.
And then I heard the innumerable hiss
Of human adders, nation with poisonous breath
Spitting at nation, as if the dragon's rage
Would claw the spirit, and I woke at this,
Knowing the soul of man was sick to death
And I was weeping in the Iron Age.

LIONEL JOHNSON

(1867–1902)

The Precept of Silence

I know you: solitary griefs,
Desolate passions, aching hours!
I know you: tremulous beliefs,
Agonized hopes, and ashen flowers!

The winds are sometimes sad to me;
The starry spaces, full of fear:
Mine is the sorrow on the sea,
And mine the sigh of places drear.

Some players upon plaintive strings
Publish their wistfulness abroad:
I have not spoken of these things
Save to one man, and unto God.

EDGAR LEE MASTERS

(1869–1950)

The Hill

Where are Elmer, Herman, Bert, Tom and Charley,
The weak of will, the strong of arm, the clown, the boozer,
        the fighter?
All, all, are sleeping on the hill.

One passed in a fever,
One was burned in a mine,
One was killed in a brawl,
One died in a jail,
One fell from a bridge toiling for children and wife—
All, all are sleeping, sleeping, sleeping on the hill.

Where are Ella, Kate, Mag, Lizzie and Edith,
The tender heart, the simple soul, the loud, the proud, the
        happy one?—
All, all, are sleeping on the hill.

One died in shameful child-birth,
One of a thwarted love,
One at the hands of a brute in a brothel,
One of a broken pride, in the search for heart's desire,
One after life in far-away London and Paris
Was brought home to her little space by Ella and Kate and
        Mag—
All, all are sleeping, sleeping, sleeping on the hill.

Where are Uncle Isaac and Aunt Emily,
And old Towny Kincaid and Sevigne Houghton,
And Major Walker who had talked
With venerable men of the revolution?—
All, all, are sleeping on the hill.

They brought them dead sons from the war,
And daughters whom life had crushed,
And their children, fatherless, crying—
All, all are sleeping, sleeping, sleeping on the hill.

Where is old Fiddler Jones
Who played with life all his ninety years,
Braving the sleet with bared breast,
Drinking, rioting, thinking neither of wife nor kin,
Nor gold, nor love, nor heaven?
Lo! he babbles of the fish-frys of long ago,
Of the horse-races of long ago at Clary's Grove,
Of what Abe Lincoln said
One time at Springfield.

Howard Lamson

Ice cannot shiver in the cold,
Nor stones shrink from the lapping flame.
Eyes that are sealed no more have tears;
Ears that are stopped hear nothing ill;
Hearts turned to silt are strange to pain;
Tongues that are dumb report no loss;
Hands stiffened, well may idle be;
No sigh is from a breathless breast.
Beauty may fade, but closed eyes see not;
Sorrow may wail, but stopped ears hear not;
Nothing to say is for dumb tongues.
The rolling earth rolls on and on
With trees and stones and winding streams—
My dream is what the hillside dreams!

EDWIN ARLINGTON ROBINSON

(1869–1935)

For a Dead Lady

No more with overflowing light
Shall fill the eyes that now are faded,
Nor shall another's fringe with night
Their woman-hidden world as they did.
No more shall quiver down the days
The flowing wonder of her ways,
Whereof no language may requite
The shifting and the many-shaded.

The grace, divine, definitive,
Clings only as a faint forestalling;
The laugh that love could not forgive
Is hushed, and answers to no calling;
The forehead and the little ears
Have gone where Saturn keeps the years;
The breast where roses could not live
Has done with rising and with falling.

The beauty, shattered by the laws
That have creation in their keeping,
No longer trembles at applause,
Or over children that are sleeping;
And we who delve in beauty's lore
Know all that we have known before
Of what inexorable cause
Makes Time so vicious in his reaping.

Momus

"Where's the need of singing now?"—
Smooth your brow,
Momus, and be reconciled,
For King Kronos is a child—
Child and father,
Or god rather,
And all gods are wild.

"Who reads Byron any more?"
Shut the door,
Momus, for I feel a draught;
Shut it quick, for some one laughed.—
"What's become of
Browning? Some of
Wordsworth lumbers like a raft?

"What are poets to find here?"—
Have no fear:
When the stars are shining blue
There will yet be left a few
Themes availing—
And these failing,
Momus, there'll be you.

Mr. Flood's Party

Old Eben Flood, climbing alone one night
Over the hill between the town below
And the forsaken upland hermitage
That held as much as he should ever know
On earth again of home, paused warily.
The road was his with not a native near;
And Eben, having leisure, said aloud,
For no man else in Tilbury Town to hear:

"Well, Mr. Flood, we have the harvest moon
Again, and we may not have many more;
The bird is on the wing, the poet says,
And you and I have said it here before.
Drink to the bird." He raised up to the light
The jug that he had gone so far to fill,
And answered huskily: "Well, Mr. Flood,
Since you propose it, I believe I will."

Alone, as if enduring to the end
A valiant armor of scarred hopes outworn,
He stood there in the middle of the road
Like Roland's ghost winding a silent horn.

Below him, in the town among the trees,
Where friends of other days had honored him,
A phantom salutation of the dead
Rang thinly till old Eben's eyes were dim.

Then, as a mother lays her sleeping child
Down tenderly, fearing it may awake,
He set the jug down slowly at his feet
With trembling care, knowing that most things break;
And only when assured that on firm earth
It stood, as the uncertain lives of men
Assuredly did not, he paced away,
And with his hand extended paused again:

"Well, Mr. Flood, we have not met like this
In a long time; and many a change has come
To both of us, I fear, since last it was
We had a drop together. Welcome home!"
Convivially returning with himself,
Again he raised the jug up to the light;
And with an acquiescent quaver said:
"Well, Mr. Flood, if you insist, I might.

"Only a very little, Mr. Flood—
For auld lang syne. No more, sir; that will do."
So, for the time, apparently it did,
And Eben evidently thought so too;
For soon amid the silver loneliness
Of night he lifted up his voice and sang,
Secure, with only two moons listening,
Until the whole harmonious landscape rang—

"For auld lang syne." The weary throat gave out,
The last word wavered, and the song was done.
He raised again the jug regretfully
And shook his head, and was again alone.
There was not much that was ahead of him,
And there was nothing in the town below—
Where strangers would have shut the many doors
That many friends had opened long ago.

LAURENCE BINYON

(1869–1943)

FROM *For the Fallen*

They went with songs to the battle, they were young,
Straight of limb, true of eye, steady and aglow.
They were staunch to the end against odds uncounted,
They fell with their faces to the foe.

They shall not grow old, as we that are left grow old:
Age shall not weary them, nor the years condemn.
At the going down of the sun and in the morning
We will remember them.

WILLIAM HENRY DAVIES

(1870–1940)

The Sailor to His Parrot

Thou foul-mouthed wretch! Why dost thou choose
    To learn bad language, and no good;
Canst thou not say, "The Lord be praised"
    As easy as "Hell's fire and blood"?

Why didst thou call the gentle priest
    A thief and a damned rogue; and tell
The deacon's wife, who came to pray,
    To hold her jaw and go to hell?

Thou art a foe, no friend of mine,
    For all my thoughts thou givest away;
Whate'er I say in confidence,
    Thou dost in evil hours betray.

Thy mind's for ever set on bad;
    I cannot mutter one small curse,
But thou dost make it endless song,
    And shout it to a neighbour's house.

Aye, swear to thy delight and ours,
    When here I welcome shipmates home,
And thou canst see abundant grog—
    But hold thy tongue when landsmen come.

Be dumb when widow Johnson's near,
    Be dumb until our wedding day;
And after that—but not before—
    She will enjoy the worst you say.

There is a time to speak and not;
    When we're together, all is well;
But damn thy soul—What! you damn *mine!*
    And you tell *me* to go to hell!

HILAIRE BELLOC

(1870–1953)

Discovery

Life is a long discovery, isn't it?
You only get your wisdom bit by bit.
If you have luck you find in early youth
How dangerous it is to tell the Truth;
And next you learn how dignity and peace
Are the ripe fruits of patient avarice.
You find that middle life goes racing past.
You find despair: and, at the very last,
You find as you are giving up the ghost
That those who loved you best despised you most.

LORD ALFRED DOUGLAS

(1870–1945)

The Dead Poet

I dreamed of him last night, I saw his face
All radiant and unshadowed of distress,
And as of old, in music measureless,
I heard his golden voice and marked him trace

Under the common thing the hidden grace,
And conjure wonder out of emptiness,
Till mean things put on beauty like a dress
And all the world was an enchanted place.

And then methought outside a fast locked gate
I mourned the loss of unrecorded words,
Forgotten tales and mysteries half said,
Wonders that might have been articulate,
And voiceless thoughts like murdered singing birds.
And so I woke and knew that he was dead.

CHARLOTTE MEW

(1870–1928)

Sea Love

Tide be runnin' the great world over:
    'Twas only last June month I mind that we
Was thinkin' the toss and the call in the breast of the lover
    So everlastin' as the sea.

Heer's the same little fishes that sputter and swim,
    Wi' the moon's old glim on the grey, wet sand;
An' him no more to me nor me to him
    Than the wind goin' over my hand.

Moorland Night

My face is wet against the grass—the moorland grass is wet—
My eyes are shut against the grass, against my lips there are
        the little blades,
        Over my head the curlews call,
    And now there is the night wind in my hair;
My heart is against the grass and the sweet earth;—it has
        gone still, at last.
        It does not want to beat any more,
            And why should it beat?
        This is the end of the journey;
            The Thing is found.

This is the end of all the roads—
Over the grass there is the night-dew
And the wind that drives up from the sea along the moorland
road;
I hear a curlew start out from the heath
And fly off, calling through the dusk,
The wild, long, rippling call.
The Thing is found and I am quiet with the earth.
Perhaps the earth will hold it, or the wind, or that bird's cry,
But it is not for long in any life I know. This cannot stay,
Not now, not yet, not in a dying world, with me, for very
long.
I leave it here:
And one day the wet grass may give it back—
One day the quiet earth may give it back—
The calling birds may give it back as they go by—
To some one walking on the moor who starves for love and
will not know
Who gave it to all these to give away;
Or, if I come and ask for it again,
Oh! then, to me.

NORA HOPPER

(1871–1906)

The Fairy Fiddler

'Tis I go fiddling, fiddling,
By weedy ways forlorn:
I make the blackbird's music
Ere in his breast 'tis born:
The sleeping larks I waken
'Twixt the midnight and the morn.

No man alive has seen me,
But women hear me play
Sometimes at the door or window,
Fiddling the souls away,—
The child's soul and the colleen's
Out of the covering clay.

None of my fairy kinsmen
   Make music with me now;
Alone the raths I wander
   Or ride the whitethorn bough;
But the wild swans they know me,
   And the horse that draws the plough.

STEPHEN CRANE

(1871–1900)

War Is Kind

Do not weep, maiden, for war is kind.
Because your lover threw wild hands toward the sky
And the affrighted steed ran on alone,
Do not weep.
War is kind.

    Hoarse, booming drums of the regiment,
    Little souls who thirst for fight,
    These men were born to drill and die.
    The unexplained glory flies above them,
    Great is the battle-god, great, and his kingdom—
    A field where a thousand corpses lie.

Do not weep, babe, for war is kind.
Because your father tumbled in the yellow trenches,
Raged at his breast, gulped and died,
Do not weep.
War is kind.

    Swift blazing flag of the regiment,
    Eagle with crest of red and gold,
    These men were born to drill and die.
    Point for them the virtue of slaughter,
    Make plain to them the excellence of killing
    And a field where a thousand corpses lie.

Mother whose heart hung humble as a button
On the bright splendid shroud of your son,
Do not weep.
War is kind.

"A Newspaper Is..."

A newspaper is a collection of half-injustices
Which, bawled by boys from mile to mile,
Spreads its curious opinion
To a million merciful and sneering men,
While families cuddle the joys of the fireside
When spurred by tale of dire lone agony.
A newspaper is a court
Where every one is kindly and unfairly tried
By a squalor of honest men.
A newspaper is a market
Where wisdom sells its freedom
And melons are crowned by the crowd.
A newspaper is a game
Where his error scores the player victory
While another's skill wins death.
A newspaper is a symbol;
It is feckless life's chronicle,
A collection of loud tales,
Concentrating eternal stupidities,
That in remote ages lived unhaltered,
Roaming through a fenceless world.

RALPH HODGSON

(1871-   )

Time, You Old Gipsy Man

Time, you old gipsy man,
    Will you not stay,
Put up your caravan
    Just for one day?

All things I'll give you
Will you be my guest,
Bells for your jennet
Of silver the best,
Goldsmiths shall beat you
A great golden ring,

Peacocks shall bow to you,
Little boys sing.
Oh, and sweet girls will
Festoon you with may,
Time, you old gipsy,
Why hasten away?

Last week in Babylon,
Last night in Rome,
Morning, and in the crush
Under Paul's dome;
Under Paul's dial
You tighten your rein—
Only a moment, and off once again;
Off to some city
Now blind in the womb,
Off to another
Ere that's in the tomb.

Time, you old gipsy man,
   Will you not stay,
Put up your caravan
   Just for one day?

JOHN McCRAE

(1872–1918)

In Flanders Fields

In Flanders fields the poppies blow
Between the crosses, row on row,
   That mark our place; and in the sky
   The larks, still bravely singing, fly
Scarce heard amid the guns below.

We are the Dead. Short days ago
We lived, felt dawn, saw sunset glow,
   Loved and were loved, and now we lie
   In Flanders fields.

Take up our quarrel with the foe:
To you from failing hands we throw
    The torch; be yours to hold it high.
    If ye break faith with us who die
We shall not sleep, though poppies grow
    In Flanders fields.

FORD MADOX FORD

(1873–1939)

FROM On Heaven

. . . And my dear one sat in the shadows; very softly she
        wept:—
Such joy is in Heaven,
In the cool of the even,
After the burden and toil of the days,
After the heat and haze
In the vine-hills; or in the shady
Whispering groves in high passes up in the Alpilles
Guarding the castle of God.

And I went on talking towards her unseen face:
"So it is, so it goes, in this beloved place,
There shall be never a grief but passes; no, not any;
There shall be such bright light and no blindness;
There shall be so little awe and so much loving-kindness;
There shall be a little longing and enough care,
There shall be a little labour and enough of toil
To bring back the lost flavour of our human coil;
Not enough to taint it;
And all that we desire shall prove as fair as we can paint it."
For, though that may be the very hardest trick of all
God set Himself, who fashioned this goodly hall,
Thus He has made Heaven;
Even Heaven.

For God is a good man; God is a kind man;
In the darkness He came walking to our table beneath the
        planes,

And spoke
So kindly to my dear,
With a little joke,
Giving Himself some pains
To take away her fear
Of His Stature,
So as not to abash her,
In no way at all to dash her new pleasure beneath the planes,
In the cool of the even
In Heaven.

That, that is God's nature,
For God's a good brother, and God is no blind man,
And God's a good mother and loves sons who're rovers,
And God is our father and loves all good lovers,
He has a kindly smile for many a poor sinner;
He takes note to make it up to poor wayfarers on sodden
        roads;
Such as bear heavy loads
He takes note of, and of all that toil on bitter seas and frosty
        lands,
He takes care that they shall all have good at His hands;
Well He takes note of a poor old cook,
Cooking your dinner;
And much He loves sweet joys in such as ever took
Sweet joy on earth. He has a kindly smile for a kiss
Given in a shady nook.
And in the golden book
Where the accounts of His estate are kept,
All the round, golden sovereigns of bliss,
Known by poor lovers, married or never yet married,
Whilst the green world waked, or the black world quietly
        slept;
All joy, all sweetness, each sweet sigh that's sighed—
Their accounts are kept,
And carried
By the love of God to His own credit's side.
So that is why He came to our table to welcome my dear,
        dear bride,
In the cool of the even
In front of a café in Heaven.

A Solis Ortus Cardine...

Oh, quiet peoples sleeping bed by bed
Beneath grey roof-trees in the glimmering West,
We who can see the silver grey and red
Rise over No Man's Land—salute your rest.

Oh, quiet comrades, sleeping in the clay
Beneath a turmoil you need no more mark,
We who have lived through yet another day
Salute your graves at setting in of dark.

And rising from your beds or from the clay
You, dead, or far from lines of slain and slayers,
Thro' your eternal or your finite day
Give us your prayers!

WALTER DE LA MARE

(1873-1956)

An Epitaph

Here lies a most beautiful lady,
Light of step and heart was she;
I think she was the most beautiful lady
That ever was in the West Country.
But beauty vanishes; beauty passes;
However rare—rare it be;
And when I crumble, who will remember
This lady of the West Country?

The Listeners

"Is there anybody there?" said the Traveller,
      Knocking on the moonlit door;
And his horse in the silence champed the grasses
      Of the forest's ferny floor:
And a bird flew up out of the turret,
      Above the Traveller's head:

And he smote upon the door again a second time;
  "Is there anybody there?" he said.
But no one descended to the Traveller;
  No head from the leaf-fringed sill
Leaned over and looked into his grey eyes,
  Where he stood perplexed and still.
But only a host of phantom listeners
  That dwelt in the lone house then
Stood listening in the quiet of the moonlight
  To that voice from the world of men:
Stood thronging the faint moonbeams on the dark stair,
  That goes down to the empty hall,
Hearkening in an air stirred and shaken
  By the lonely Traveller's call.
And he felt in his heart their strangeness,
  Their stillness answering his cry,
While his horse moved, cropping the dark turf,
  'Neath the starred and leafy sky;
For he suddenly smote on the door, even
  Louder, and lifted his head:—
"Tell them I came, and no one answered,
  That I kept my word," he said.
Never the least stir made the listeners,
  Though every word he spake
Fell echoing through the shadowiness of the still house
  From the one man left awake:
Ay, they heard his foot upon the stirrup,
  And the sound of iron on stone,
And how the silence surged softly backward,
  When the plunging hoofs were gone.

All That's Past

Very old are the woods;
  And the buds that break
Out of the brier's boughs,
  When March winds wake.
So old with their beauty are—
  Oh, no man knows
Through what wild centuries
  Roves back the rose.

Very old are the brooks;
    And the rills that rise
Where snow sleeps cold beneath
    The azure skies
Sing such a history
    Of come and gone
Their every drop is as wise
    As Solomon.

Very old are we men;
    Our dreams are tales
Told in dim Eden
    By Eve's nightingales;
We wake and whisper awhile,
    But, the day gone by,
Silence and sleep like fields
    Of amaranth lie.

Clear Eyes

Clear eyes do dim at last,
    And cheeks outlive their rose.
Time, heedless of the past,
    No loving-kindness knows;
Chill unto mortal lip
    Still Lethe flows.

Griefs, too, but brief while stay,
    And sorrow, bring o'er,
Its salt tears shed away,
    Woundeth the heart no more.
Stealthily lave those waters
    That solemn shore.

Ah, then, sweet face burn on,
    While yet quick memory lives!
And Sorrow, ere thou art gone,
    Know that my heart forgives—
Ere yet, grown cold in peace,
    It loves not, nor grieves.

GILBERT KEITH CHESTERTON
(1874–1936)

Wine and Water

Old Noah he had an ostrich farm and fowls on the largest
scale,
He ate his egg with a ladle in an egg-cup big as a pail,
And the soup he took was Elephant Soup, and the fish he
took was Whale,
But they all were small to the cellar he took when he set out
to sail,
And Noah he often said to his wife when he sat down to dine,
"I don't care where the water goes if it doesn't get into the
wine."

The cataract of the cliff of heaven fell blinding off the brink
As if it would wash the stars away as suds go down a sink,
The seven heavens came roaring down for the throats of hell
to drink,
And Noah he cocked his eye and said, "It looks like rain, I
think,
The water has drowned the Matterhorn as deep as a Mendip
mine,
But I don't care where the water goes if it doesn't get into
the wine."

But Noah he sinned, and we have sinned; on tipsy feet we
trod,
Till a great big black teetotaller was sent to us for a rod,
And you can't get wine at a P. S. A., or chapel, or Eisteddfod,
For the Curse of Water has come again because of the wrath
of God,
And water is on the Bishop's board and the Higher Thinker's
shrine,
But I don't care where the water goes if it doesn't get into
the wine.

On a Prohibitionist Poem

Though Shakespeare's Mermaid, ocean's mightiest daughter,
With vintage could the seas incarnadine:
And Keats's name that was not writ in water
    Was often writ in wine;

Though wine that seeks the loftiest habitation
Went to the heads of Villon and Verlaine,
Yet Hiram Hopper needs no inspiration
    But water on the brain.

Elegy in a Country Churchyard

The men that worked for England
They have their graves at home:
And bees and birds of England
About the cross can roam.

But they that fought for England,
Following a falling star,
Alas, alas for England
They have their graves afar.

And they that rule in England,
In stately conclave met,
Alas, alas for England
They have no graves as yet.

ANONYMOUS

(19TH CENTURY)

"I Know Where I'm Going"

I know where I'm going,
I know who's going with me,
I know who I love,
But the dear knows who I'll marry.

I'll have stockings of silk,
Shoes of fine green leather,
Combs to buckle my hair
And a ring for every finger.

Feather beds are soft,
Painted rooms are bonny;
But I'd leave them all
To go with my love Johnny.

Some say he's dark,
I say he's bonny,
He's the flower of them all
My handsome, coaxing Johnny.

I know where I'm going,
I know who's going with me,
I know who I love,
But the dear knows who I'll marry.

TRUMBULL STICKNEY

(1874-1904)

Mnemosyne

It's autumn in the country I remember.

How warm a wind blew here about the ways!
And shadows on the hillside lay to slumber
During the long sun-sweetened summer-days.

It's cold abroad the country I remember.

The swallows veering skimmed the golden grain
At midday with a wing aslant and limber;
And yellow cattle browsed upon the plain.

It's empty down the country I remember.

I had a sister lovely in my sight:
Her hair was dark, her eyes were very sombre;
We sang together in the woods at night.

It's lonely in the country I remember.

The babble of our children fills my ears,
And on our hearth I stare the perished ember
To flames that show all starry thro' my tears.

It's dark about the country I remember.

There are the mountains where I lived. The path
Is slushed with cattle-tracks and fallen timber,
The stumps are twisted by the tempests' wrath.

But that I knew these places are my own,
I'd ask how came such wretchedness to cumber
The earth, and I to people it alone.

It rains across the country I remember.

AMY LOWELL

(1874–1925)

Little Ivory Figures Pulled with String

Is it the tinkling of mandolins which disturbs you?
Or the dropping of bitter-orange petals among the coffee-
cups?
Or the slow creeping of the moonlight between the olive-
trees?
*Drop! Drop! the rain
Upon the thin plates of my heart.*

String your blood to chord with this music,
Stir your heels upon the cobbles to the rhythm of a dance-
tune.
They have slim thighs and arms of silver;
The moon washes away their garments;
They make a pattern of fleeing feet in the branch shadows,

And the green grapes knotted about them
Burst as they press against one another.
  The rain knocks upon the plates of my heart,
  They are crumpled with its beating.

Would you drink only from your brains, Old Man?
See, the moonlight has reached your knees,
It falls upon your head in an accolade of silver.
Rise up on the music,
Fling against the moon-drifts in a whorl of young light
      bodies:
Leaping grape clusters,
Vine leaves tearing from a grey wall.
You shall run, laughing, in a braid of women,
And weave flowers with the frosty spines of thorns.
Why do you gaze into your glass,
And jar the spoons with your finger-tapping?
  The rain is rigid on the plates of my heart.
  The murmur of it is loud—loud.

ROBERT FROST

(1875-   )

The Pasture

I'm going out to clean the pasture spring;
I'll only stop to rake the leaves away
(And wait to watch the water clear, I may):
I shan't be gone long.—You come too.

I'm going out to fetch the little calf
That's standing by the mother. It's so young
It totters when she licks it with her tongue.
I shan't be gone long.—You come too.

My November Guest

My sorrow, when she's here with me,
    Thinks these dark days of autumn rain
Are beautiful as days can be;

She loves the bare, the withered tree;
　　She walks the sodden pasture lane.

Her pleasure will not let me stay.
　　She talks and I am fain to list:
She's glad the birds are gone away,
She's glad her simple worsted grey
　　Is silver now with clinging mist.

The desolate, deserted trees,
　　The faded earth, the heavy sky,
The beauties she so truly sees,
She thinks I have no eye for these,
　　And vexes me for reason why.

Not yesterday I learned to know
　　The love of bare November days
Before the coming of the snow;
But it were vain to tell her so,
　　And they are better for her praise.

After Apple-Picking

My long two-pointed ladder's sticking through a tree
Toward heaven still,
And there's a barrel that I didn't fill
Beside it, and there may be two or three
Apples I didn't pick upon some bough.
But I am done with apple-picking now.
Essence of winter sleep is on the night,
The scent of apples: I am drowsing off.
I cannot rub the strangeness from my sight
I got from looking through a pane of glass
I skimmed this morning from the drinking trough
And held against the world of hoary grass.
It melted, and I let it fall and break.
But I was well
Upon my way to sleep before it fell,
And I could tell
What form my dreaming was about to take.

Magnified apples appear and disappear.
Stem end and blossom end,
And every fleck of russet showing clear.
My instep arch not only keeps the ache,
It keeps the pressure of a ladder-round.
I feel the ladder sway as the boughs bend.
And I keep hearing from the cellar bin
The rumbling sound
Of load on load of apples coming in.
For I have had too much
Of apple-picking: I am overtired
Of the great harvest I myself desired.
There were ten thousand thousand fruit to touch,
Cherish in hand, lift down, and not let fall.
For all
That struck the earth,
No matter if not bruised or spiked with stubble,
Went surely to the cider-apple heap
As of no worth.
One can see what will trouble
This sleep of mine, whatever sleep it is.
Were he not gone,
The woodchuck could say whether it's like his
Long sleep, as I describe its coming on,
Or just some human sleep.

Storm Fear

When the wind works against us in the dark,
And pelts with snow
The lowly chamber window on the east,
And whispers with a sort of stifled bark,
The beast,
"Come out! Come out!"—
It costs no inward struggle not to go,
Ah, no!
I count our strength,
Two and a child,
Those of us not asleep subdued to mark
How the cold creeps as the fire dies at length,—

How drifts are piled
Dooryard and road ungraded,
Till even the comforting barn grows far away
And my heart owns a doubt
Whether 'tis in us to arise with day
And save ourselves unaided.

Mending Wall

Something there is that doesn't love a wall,
That sends the frozen-ground-swell under it,
And spills the upper boulders in the sun;
And makes gaps even two can pass abreast.
The work of hunters is another thing:
I have come after them and made repair
Where they have left not one stone on a stone,
But they would have the rabbit out of hiding,
To please the yelping dogs. The gaps I mean,
No one has seen them made or heard them made,
But at spring mending-time we find them there.
I let my neighbor know beyond the hill;
And on a day we meet to walk the line
And set the wall between us once again.
We keep the wall between us as we go.
To each the boulders that have fallen to each.
And some are loaves and some so nearly balls
We have to use a spell to make them balance:
"Stay where you are until our backs are turned!"
We wear our fingers rough with handling them.
Oh, just another kind of out-door game,
One on a side. It comes to little more:
There where it is we do not need the wall:
He is all pine and I am apple orchard.
My apple trees will never get across
And eat the cones under his pines, I tell him.
He only says, "Good fences make good neighbors."
Spring is the mischief in me, and I wonder
If I could put a notion in his head:
"Why do they make good neighbors? Isn't it
Where there are cows? But here there are no cows.

Before I built a wall I'd ask to know
What I was walling in or walling out,
And to whom I was like to give offence.
Something there is that doesn't love a wall,
That wants it down." I could say "Elves" to him,
But it's not elves exactly, and I'd rather
He said it for himself. I see him there
Bringing a stone grasped firmly by the top
In each hand, like an old-stone savage armed.
He moves in darkness as it seems to me,
Not of woods only and the shade of trees.
He will not go behind his father's saying.
And he likes having thought of it so well
He says again, "Good fences make good neighbors."

FROM *Two Witches*

THE WITCH OF COÖS

I stayed the night for shelter at a farm
Behind the mountain, with a mother and son,
Two old-believers. They did all the talking.

MOTHER. Folks think a witch who has familiar spirits
She could call up to pass a winter evening,
But won't, should be burned at the stake or something.
Summoning spirits isn't "Button, button,
Who's got the button," I would have them know.

SON. Mother can make a common table rear
And kick with two legs like an army mule.

MOTHER. And when I've done it, what good have I done?
Rather than tip a table for you, let me
Tell you what Ralle the Sioux Control once told me.
He said the dead had souls, but when I asked him
How could that be—I thought the dead were souls,
He broke my trance. Don't that make you suspicious
That there's something the dead are keeping back?
Yes, there's something the dead are keeping back.

SON. You wouldn't want to tell him what we have
Up attic, mother?

MOTHER. Bones—a skeleton.

SON. But the headboard of mother's bed is pushed
Against the attic door: the door is nailed.
It's harmless. Mother hears it in the night
Halting perplexed behind the barrier
Of door and headboard. Where it wants to get
Is back into the cellar where it came from.

MOTHER. We'll never let them, will we, son! We'll never!

SON. It left the cellar forty years ago
And carried itself like a pile of dishes
Up one flight from the cellar to the kitchen,
Another from the kitchen to the bedroom,
Another from the bedroom to the attic,
Right past both father and mother, and neither stopped it.
Father had gone upstairs; mother was downstairs.
I was a baby: I don't know where I was.

MOTHER. The only fault my husband found with me—
I went to sleep before I went to bed,
Especially in winter when the bed
Might just as well be ice and the clothes snow.
The night the bones came up the cellar-stairs
Toffile had gone to bed alone and left me,
But left an open door to cool the room off
So as to sort of turn me out of it.
I was just coming to myself enough
To wonder where the cold was coming from,
When I heard Toffile upstairs in the bedroom
And thought I heard him downstairs in the cellar.
The board we had laid down to walk dry-shod on
When there was water in the cellar in spring
Struck the hard cellar bottom. And then someone
Began the stairs, two footsteps for each step,
The way a man with one leg and a crutch,

Or a little child, comes up. It wasn't Toffile:
It wasn't anyone who could be there.
The bulkhead double-doors were double-locked
And swollen tight and buried under snow.
The cellar windows were banked up with sawdust
And swollen tight and buried under snow.
It was the bones. I knew them—and good reason.
My first impulse was to get to the knob
And hold the door. But the bones didn't try
The door; they halted helpless on the landing,
Waiting for things to happen in their favor.
The faintest restless rustling ran all through them.
I never could have done the thing I did
If the wish hadn't been too strong in me
To see how they were mounted for this walk.
I had a vision of them put together
Not like a man, but like a chandelier.
So suddenly I flung the door wide on him.
A moment he stood balancing with emotion,
And all but lost himself. (A tongue of fire
Flashed out and licked along his upper teeth.
Smoke rolled inside the sockets of his eyes.)
Then he came at me with one hand outstretched,
The way he did in life once; but this time
I struck the hand off brittle on the floor,
And fell back from him on the floor myself.
The finger-pieces slid in all directions.
(Where did I see one of those pieces lately?
Hand me my button-box—it must be there.)
I sat up on the floor and shouted, "Toffile,
It's coming up to you." It had its choice
Of the door to the cellar or the hall.
It took the hall door for the novelty,
And set off briskly for so slow a thing,
Still going every which way in the joints, though,
So that it looked like lightning or a scribble,
From the slap I had just now given its hand.
I listened till it almost climbed the stairs
From the hall to the only finished bedroom,
Before I got up to do anything;
Then ran and shouted, "Shut the bedroom door,

Toffile, for my sake!" "Company?" he said,
"Don't make me get up; I'm too warm in bed."
So lying forward weakly on the handrail
I pushed myself upstairs, and in the light
(The kitchen had been dark) I had to own
I could see nothing. "Toffile, I don't see it.
It's with us in the room though. It's the bones."
"What bones?" "The cellar bones—out of the grave."
That made him throw his bare legs out of bed
And sit up by me and take hold of me.
I wanted to put out the light and see
If I could see it, or else mow the room,
With our arms at the level of our knees,
And bring the chalk-pile down. "I'll tell you what—
It's looking for another door to try.
The uncommonly deep snow has made him think
Of his old song, *The Wild Colonial Boy,*
He always used to sing along the tote road.
He's after an open door to get outdoors.
Let's trap him with an open door up attic."
Toffile agreed to that, and sure enough,
Almost the moment he was given an opening,
The steps began to climb the attic stairs.
I heard them. Toffile didn't seem to hear them.
"Quick!" I slammed to the door and held the knob.
"Toffile, get nails." I made him nail the door shut
And push the headboard of the bed against it.
Then we asked was there anything
Up attic that we'd ever want again.
The attic was less to us than the cellar.
If the bones liked the attic, let them have it.
Let them stay in the attic. When they sometimes
Come down the stairs at night and stand perplexed
Behind the door and headboard of the bed,
Brushing their chalky skull with chalky fingers,
With sounds like the dry rattling of a shutter,
That's what I sit up in the dark to say—
To no one any more since Toffile died.
Let them stay in the attic since they went there.
I promised Toffile to be cruel to them
For helping them be cruel once to him.

SON. We think they had a grave down in the cellar.

MOTHER. We know they had a grave down in the cellar.

SON. We never could find out whose bones they were.

MOTHER. Yes, we could too, son. Tell the truth for once.
They were a man's his father killed for me.
I mean a man he killed instead of me.
The least I could do was to help dig their grave.
We were about it one night in the cellar.
Son knows the story: but 'twas not for him
To tell the truth, suppose the time had come.
Son looks surprised to see me end a lie
We'd kept all these years between ourselves
So as to have it ready for outsiders.
But tonight I don't care enough to lie—
I don't remember why I ever cared.
Toffile, if he were here, I don't believe
Could tell you why he ever cared himself. . . .

She hadn't found the finger-bone she wanted
Among the buttons poured out in her lap.
I verified the name next morning: Toffile.
The rural letter box said Toffile Lajway.

Fire and Ice

Some say the world will end in fire,
Some say in ice.
From what I've tasted of desire
I hold with those who favor fire.
But if it had to perish twice,
I think I know enough of hate
To say that for destruction ice
Is also great
And would suffice.

Stopping by Woods on a Snowy Evening

Whose woods these are I think I know.
His house is in the village though;
He will not see me stopping here
To watch his woods fill up with snow.

My little horse must think it queer
To stop without a farmhouse near
Between the woods and frozen lake
The darkest evening of the year.

He gives his harness bells a shake
To ask if there is some mistake.
The only other sound's the sweep
Of easy wind and downy flake.

The woods are lovely, dark and deep,
But I have promises to keep,
And miles to go before I sleep,
And miles to go before I sleep.

JOHN MASEFIELD

(1878–　　)

FROM *Reynard the Fox*

The cobbler bent at his wooden foot,
Beating sprigs in a broken boot;
He wore old glasses with thick horn rim,
He scowled at his work, for his sight was dim.
His face was dingy, his lips were grey,
From trimming sparrowbills day by day.
As he turned his boot he heard a noise
At his garden-end, and he thought, "It's boys."
Like a rocket shot to a ship ashore
The lean red bolt of his body tore,
Like a ripple of wind running swift on grass;
Like a shadow on wheat when a cloud blows past,
Like a turn at the buoy in a cutter sailing

When the bright green gleam lips white at the railing,
Like the April snake whipping back to sheath,
Like the gannets' hurtle on fish beneath,
Like a kestrel chasing, like a sickle reaping,
Like all things swooping, like all things sweeping,
Like a hound for stay, like a stag for swift,
With his shadow beside like spinning drift.

*   *   *   *   *

Past the gibbet-stock all stuck with nails,
Where they hanged in chains what had hung at jails,
Past Ashmundshowe where Ashmund sleeps,
And none but the tumbling peewit weeps,
Past Curlew Calling, the gaunt grey corner
Where the curlew comes as a summer mourner,
Past Blowbury Beacon, shaking his fleece,
Where all winds hurry and none brings peace;
Then down on the mile-long green decline,
Where the turf's like spring and the air's like wine
Where the sweeping spurs of the downland spill
Into Wan Brook Valley and Wan Dyke Hill.

*   *   *   *   *

On he went with a galloping rally
Past Maesbury Camp for Wan Brook Valley.
The blood in his veins went romping high,
"Get on, on, on, to the earth or die."
The air of the downs went purely past
Till he felt the glory of going fast,
Till the terror of death, though there indeed,
Was lulled for a while by his pride of speed.
He was romping away from the hounds and hunt,
He had Wan Dyke Hill and his earth in front,
In one mile more when his point was made
He would rest in safety from dog or spade;
Nose between paws he would hear the shout
Of the "Gone to earth!" to the hounds without,
The whine of the hounds, and their cat-feet gadding,
Scratching the earth, and their breath pad-padding;
He would hear the horn call hounds away,
And rest in peace till another day.

On Growing Old

Be with me, Beauty, for the fire is dying;
My dog and I are old, too old for roving.
Man, whose young passion sets the spindrift flying,
Is soon too lame to march, too cold for loving.
I take the book and gather to the fire,
Turning old yellow leaves; minute by minute
The clock ticks to my heart. A withered wire,
Moves a thin ghost of music in the spinet.
I cannot sail your seas, I cannot wander
Your cornland, nor your hill-land, nor your valleys
Ever again, nor share the battle yonder
Where the young knight the broken squadron rallies.
Only stay quiet while my mind remembers
The beauty of fire from the beauty of embers.

Beauty, have pity! for the strong have power,
The rich their wealth, the beautiful their grace,
Summer of man its sunlight and its flower,
Spring-time of man all April in a face.
Only, as in the jostling in the Strand,
Where the mob thrusts or loiters or is loud,
The beggar with the saucer in his hand
Asks only a penny from the passing crowd,
So, from this glittering world with all its fashion,
Its fire, and play of men, its stir, its march,
Let me have wisdom, Beauty, wisdom and passion,
Bread to the soul, rain when the summers parch.
Give me but these, and though the darkness close
Even the night will blossom as the rose.

EDWARD THOMAS

(1878–1917)

The Sign-Post

The dim sea glints chill. The white sun is shy,
And the skeleton weeds and the never-dry,
Rough, long grasses keep white with frost
At the hill-top by the finger-post;

The smoke of the traveller's-joy is puffed
Over hawthorn berry and hazel tuft.
I read the sign. Which way shall I go?
A voice says: You would not have doubted so
At twenty. Another voice gentle with scorn
Says: At twenty you wished you had never been born.
One hazel lost a leaf of gold
From a tuft at the tip, when the first voice told
The other he wished to know what 'twould be
To be sixty by this same post. "You shall see,"
He laughed—and I had to join his laughter—
"You shall see; but either before or after,
Whatever happens, it must befall.
A mouthful of earth to remedy all
Regrets and wishes shall be freely given;
And if there be a flaw in that heaven
'Twill be freedom to wish, and your wish may be
To be here or anywhere talking to me,
No matter what the weather, on earth,
At any age between death and birth,—
To see what day or night can be,
The sun and the frost, the land and the sea,
Summer, Autumn, Winter, Spring,—
With a poor man of any sort, down to a king,
Standing upright out in the air
Wondering where he shall journey, O where?"

CARL SANDBURG

(1878–   )

Chicago

Hog Butcher for the World,
Tool Maker, Stacker of Wheat,
Player with Railroads and the Nation's Freight Handler;
Stormy, husky, brawling,
City of the Big Shoulders:
They tell me you are wicked and I believe them, for I have
    seen your painted women under the gas lamps luring
    the farm boys.

And they tell me you are crooked and I answer: Yes, it is
    true I have seen the gunman kill and go free to kill
    again.
And they tell me you are brutal and my reply is: On the
    faces of women and children I have seen the marks
    of wanton hunger.
And having answered so I turn once more to those who
    sneer at this my city, and I give them back the sneer
    and say to them:
Come and show me another city with lifted head singing so
    proud to be alive and coarse and strong and cunning.
Flinging magnetic curses amid the toil of piling job on job,
    here is a tall bold slugger set vivid against the little
    soft cities;
Fierce as a dog with tongue lapping for action, cunning as a
    savage pitted against the wilderness,
    Bareheaded,
    Shoveling,
    Wrecking,
    Planning,
    Building, breaking, rebuilding.
Under the smoke, dust all over his mouth, laughing with
    white teeth,
Under the terrible burden of destiny laughing as a young
    man laughs,
Laughing even as an ignorant fighter laughs who has never
    lost a battle,
Bragging and laughing that under his wrist is the pulse, and
    under his ribs the heart of the people,
                Laughing!
Laughing the stormy, husky, brawling laughter of Youth,
    half-naked, sweating, proud to be Hog Butcher, Tool
    Maker, Stacker of Wheat, Player with Railroads and
    Freight Handler to the Nation.

Cool Tombs

    When Abraham Lincoln was shoveled into the tombs he
forgot the copperheads and the assassin . . . in the dust, in
the cool tombs.

And Ulysses Grant lost all thought of con men and Wall
Street, cash and collateral turned ashes . . . in the dust, in
the cool tombs.

Pocahontas' body, lovely as a poplar, sweet as a red haw
in November or a paw-paw in May, did she wonder, does
she remember? . . . in the dust, in the cool tombs?

Take any streetful of people buying clothes and groceries,
cheering a hero or throwing confetti and blowing tin horns
. . . tell me if the lovers are losers . . . tell me if any get
more than the lovers . . . in the dust . . . in the cool
tombs.

VACHEL LINDSAY
(1879–1931)

The Eagle That Is Forgotten

(JOHN P. ALTGELD. BORN DECEMBER 30, 1847;
DIED MARCH 12, 1902)

Sleep softly . . . eagle forgotten . . . under the stone.
Time has its way with you there, and the clay has its own.

"We have buried him now," thought your foes, and in secret
    rejoiced.
They made a brave show of their mourning, their hatred
    unvoiced,
They had snarled at you, barked at you, foamed at you, day
    after day,
Now you were ended. They praised you, . . . and laid you
    away.

The others that mourned you in silence and terror and truth,
The widow bereft of her crust, the boy without youth,
The mocked and the scorned and the wounded, the lame and
    the poor
That should have remembered forever, . . . remember no
    more.

Where are those lovers of yours, on what name do they call,
The lost, that in armies wept over your funeral pall?

They call on the names of a hundred high-valiant ones
A hundred white eagles have risen, the sons of your sons,
The zeal in their wings is a zeal that your dreaming began,
The valor that wore out your soul in the service of man.

Sleep softly, . . . eagle forgotten, . . . under the stone.
Time has its way with you there, and the clay has its own.
Sleep on, O brave-hearted, O wise man, that kindled the
　　flame—
To live in mankind is far more than to live in a name,
To live in mankind, far, far more . . . than to live in a
　　name.

HAROLD MONRO

(1879–1932)

Midnight Lamentation

When you and I go down
Breathless and cold,
Our faces both worn back
To earthly mould,
How lonely we shall be!
What shall we do,
You without me,
I without you?

I cannot bear the thought
You, first, may die,
Nor of how you will weep,
Should I.
We are too much alone;
What can we do
To make our bodies one:
You, me; I, you?

We are most nearly born
Of one same kind;
We have the same delight,
The same true mind.

Must we then part, we part;
Is there no way
To keep a beating heart
And light of day?

I could now rise and run
Through street on street
To where you are breathing—you,
That we might meet,
And that your living voice
Might sound above
Fear, and we two rejoice
Within our love.

How frail the body is,
And we are made
As only in decay
To lean and fade.
I think too much of death;
There is a gloom
When I can't hear your breath
Calm in some room.

O, but how suddenly
Either may droop;
Countenance be so white,
Body stoop.
Then there may be a place
Where fading flowers
Drop on a lifeless face
Through weeping hours.

Is then nothing safe?
Can we not find
Some everlasting life
In our one mind?
I feel it like disgrace
Only to understand
Your spirit through your word,
Or by your hand.

I cannot find a way
Through love and through;
I cannot reach beyond
Body, to you.
When you or I must go
Down evermore,
There'll be no more to say
—But a locked door.

WALLACE STEVENS

(1879–1955)

The Emperor of Ice-Cream

Call the roller of big cigars,
The muscular one, and bid him whip
In kitchen cups concupiscent curds.
Let the wenches dawdle in such dress
As they are used to wear, and let the boys
Bring flowers in last month's newspapers.
Let be be the finale of seem.
The only emperor is the emperor of ice-cream.

Take from the dresser of deal,
Lacking the three glass knobs, that sheet
On which she embroidered fantails once
And spread it so as to cover her face.
If her horny feet protrude, they come
To show how cold she is, and dumb.
Let the lamp affix its beam.
The only emperor is the emperor of ice-cream.

Peter Quince at the Clavier

I

Just as my fingers on these keys
Make music, so the self-same sounds
On my spirit make a music too.

Music is feeling then, not sound;
And thus it is that what I feel,
Here in this room, desiring you,
Thinking of your blue-shadowed silk,
Is music. It is like the strain
Waked in the elders by Susanna:

Of a green evening, clear and warm,
She bathed in her still garden, while
The red-eyed elders, watching, felt

The basses of their being throb
In witching chords, and their thin blood
Pulse pizzicati of Hosanna.

II

In the green evening, clear and warm,
Susanna lay.
She searched
The touch of springs,
And found
Concealed imaginings.
She sighed
For so much melody.

Upon the bank she stood
In the cool
Of spent emotions.
She felt, among the leaves,
The dew
Of old devotions.

She walked upon the grass,
Still quavering.
The winds were like her maids,
On timid feet,
Fetching her woven scarves,
Yet wavering.

A breath upon her hand
Muted the night.

She turned—
A cymbal clashed,
And roaring horns.

III

Soon, with a noise like tambourines,
Came her attendant Byzantines.

They wondered why Susanna cried
Against the elders by her side:

And as they whispered, the refrain
Was like a willow swept by rain.

Anon their lamps' uplifted flame
Revealed Susanna and her shame.

And then the simpering Byzantines
Fled, with a noise like tambourines.

IV

Beauty is momentary in the mind—
The fitful tracing of a portal;
But in the flesh it is immortal.

The body dies; the body's beauty lives.
So evenings die, in their green going,
A wave, interminably flowing.

So gardens die, their meek breath scenting
The cowl of Winter, done repenting.
So maidens die to the auroral
Celebration of a maiden's choral.

Susanna's music touched the bawdy strings
Of those white elders; but, escaping,
Left only Death's ironic scraping.
Now in its immortality, it plays
On the clear viol of her memory,
And makes a constant sacrament of praise.

Not Ideas about the Thing
but the Thing Itself

At the earliest ending of winter,
In March, a scrawny cry from outside
Seemed like a sound in his mind.

He knew that he heard it,
A bird's cry, at daylight or before,
In the early March wind.

The sun was rising at six,
No longer a battered panache above snow . . .
It would have been outside.

It was not from the vast ventriloquism
Of sleep's faded papier-mâché . . .
The sun was coming from outside.

That scrawny cry—it was
A chorister whose c preceded the choir.
It was part of the colossal sun,

Surrounded by its choral rings,
Still far away. It was like
A new knowledge of reality.

WILSON PUGSLEY MacDONALD

(1880–

Exit

Easily to the old
Opens the hard ground:
But when youth grows cold,
And red lips have no sound,
Bitterly does the earth
Open to receive
And bitterly do the grasses
In the churchyard grieve.

Cold clay knows how to hold
An agéd hand;
But how to comfort youth
It does not understand.
Even the gravel rasps
In a dumb way
When youth comes homing
Before its day.

Elizabeth's hair was made
To warm a man's breast,
And her lips called like roses
To be caressed;
But grim the Jester
Who gave her hair to lie
On the coldest lover
Under the cold sky.

But Elizabeth never knew
Nor will learn now,
How the long wrinkle comes
On the white brow;
Nor will she ever know,
In her robes of gloom,
How chill is a dead child
From a warm womb.

O clay, so tender
When a flower is born!
Press gently as she dreams
In her bed forlorn.
They who come early
Must weary of their rest—
Lie softly, then, as light
On her dear breast.

Unflowered is her floor,
Her roof is unstarred.
Is this then the ending—
Here, shuttered and barred?
Nay, not the ending;

She will awake
Or the heart of the earth
That enfolds her will break.

Easily to the old
Opens the hard ground:
But when youth grows cold,
And red lips have no sound,
Bitterly does the earth
Open to receive
And bitterly do the grasses
In the churchyard grieve.

RALPH CHAPLIN

(1880–   )

"Mourn Not the Dead . . ."

Mourn not the dead that in the cool earth lie—
Dust unto dust—
The calm sweet earth that mothers all who die
As all men must;

Mourn not your captured comrades who must dwell—
Too strong to strive—
Each in his steel-bound coffin of a cell, buried alive;

But rather mourn the apathetic throng—
The coward and the meek—
Who see the world's great anguish and its wrong
And dare not speak.

LASCELLES ABERCROMBIE

(1881–1938)

Epitaph

Sir, you shall notice me: I am the Man;
I am Good Fortune: I am satisfied.
All I desired, more than I could desire,
I have: everything has gone right with me.

Life was a hiding-place that played me false;
I croucht ashamed, and still was seen and scorned:
But now I am not seen. I was a fool,
And now I know what wisdom dare not know:
For I know Nothing. I was a slave, and now
I have ungoverned freedom and the wealth
That cannot be conceived: for I have Nothing.
I lookt for beauty and I longed for rest,
And now I have perfection: nay, I am
Perfection: I am nothing, I am dead.

JOSEPH CAMPBELL

(1881–   )

The Old Woman

As a white candle
In a holy place,
So is the beauty
Of an agéd face.

As the spent radiance
Of the winter sun,
So is a woman
With her travail done.

Her brood gone from her,
And her thoughts as still
As the waters
Under a ruined mill.

PADRAIC COLUM

(1881–   )

A Drover

To Meath of the pastures,
From wet hills by the sea,
Through Leitrim and Longford,
Go my cattle and me.

I hear in the darkness
Their slipping and breathing—
I name them the by-ways
They're to pass without heeding.

Then the wet, winding roads,
Brown bogs with black water,
And my thoughts on white ships
And the King o' Spain's daughter.

O farmer, strong farmer!
You can spend at the fair,
But your face you must turn
To your crops and your care;

And soldiers, red soldiers!
You've seen many lands,
But you walk two by two,
And by captain's commands!

O the smell of the beasts,
The wet wind in the morn,
And the proud and hard earth
Never broken for corn!

And the crowds at the fair,
The herds loosened and blind,
Loud words and dark faces,
And the wild blood behind!

(O strong men with your best
I would strive breast to breast,
I could quiet your herds
With my words, with my words!)

I will bring you, my kine,
Where there's grass to the knee,
But you'll think of scant croppings
Harsh with salt of the sea.

JAMES JOYCE

(1882–1941)

"I Hear an Army Charging . . ."

I hear an army charging upon the land,
   And the thunder of horses plunging, foam about their
     knees:
Arrogant, in black armour, behind them stand,
   Disdaining the reins, with fluttering whips, the charioteers.

They cry unto the night their battle-name:
   I moan in sleep when I hear afar their whirling laughter.
They cleave the gloom of dreams, a blinding flame,
   Clanging, clanging upon the heart as upon an anvil.

They come shaking in triumph their long, green hair:
   They come out of the sea and run shouting by the shore.
My heart, have you no wisdom thus to despair?
   My love, my love, my love, why have you left me alone?

She Weeps over Rahoon

Rain on Rahoon falls softly, softly falling,
Where my dark lover lies.
Sad is his voice that calls me, sadly calling,
At grey moonrise.

Love, hear thou
How soft, how sad his voice is ever calling.
Ever unanswered and the dark rain falling,
Then as now.

Dark too our hearts, O love, shall lie and cold
As his sad heart has lain
Under the moongrey nettles, the black mould
And muttering rain.

A Memory of the Players in a Mirror
at Midnight

They mouth love's language. Gnash
The thirteen teeth
Your lean jaws grin with. Lash
Your itch and quailing, nude greed of the flesh.
Love's breath in you is stale, worded or sung,
As sour as cat's breath,
Harsh of tongue.

This grey that stares
Lies not, stark skin and bone.
Leave greasy lips their kissing. None
Will choose her what you see to mouth upon.
Dire hunger holds his hour.
Pluck forth your heart, saltblood, a fruit of tears.
Pluck and devour!

JAMES STEPHENS
(1882–1950)

Deirdre

Do not let any woman read this verse!
It is for men, and after them their sons,
And their son's sons!

The time comes when our hearts sink utterly;
When we remember Deirdre, and her tale,
And that her lips are dust.

Once she did tread the earth: men took her hand;
They looked into her eyes and said their say,
And she replied to them.

More than two thousand years it is since she
Was beautiful: she trod the waving grass;
She saw the clouds.

Two thousand years! The grass is still the same;
The clouds as lovely as they were that time
When Deirdre was alive.

But there has been again no woman born
Who was so beautiful; not one so beautiful
Of all the women born.

Let all men go apart and mourn together!
No man can ever love her! Not a man
Can dream to be her lover!

No man can bend before her! No man say—
What could one say to her? There are no words
That one could say to her!

Now she is but a story that is told
Beside the fire! No man can ever be
The friend of that poor queen!

THOMAS ERNEST HULME

(1883–1917)

Autumn

A touch of cold in the Autumn night—
I walked abroad,
And saw the ruddy moon lean over a hedge
Like a red-faced farmer.
I did not stop to speak, but nodded,
And round about were the wistful stars
With white faces like town children.

Conversion

Light-hearted I walked into the valley wood
In the time of hyacinths,
Till beauty like a scented cloth

Cast over, stifled me. I was bound
Motionless and faint of breath
By loveliness that is her own eunuch.

Now pass I to the final river
Ignominiously, in a sack, without sound,
As any peeping Turk to the Bosphorus.

WILLIAM CARLOS WILLIAMS

(1883–   )

Peace on Earth

The Archer is wake!
The Swan is flying!
Gold against blue
An Arrow is lying.
There is hunting in heaven—
Sleep safe till tomorrow.

The Bears are abroad!
The Eagle is screaming!
Gold against blue
Their eyes are gleaming!
Sleep!
Sleep safe till tomorrow.

The Sisters lie
With their arms intertwining;
Gold against blue
Their hair is shining!
The Serpent writhes!
Orion is listening!
Gold against blue
His sword is glistening!
Sleep!
There is hunting in heaven—
Sleep safe till tomorrow.

The Yachts

contend in a sea which the land partly encloses
shielding them from the too heavy blows
of an ungoverned ocean which when it chooses

tortures the biggest hulls, the best man knows
to pit against its beating, and sinks them pitilessly.
Mothlike in mists, scintillant in the minute

brilliance of cloudless days, with broad bellying sails
they glide to the wind tossing green water
from their sharp prows while over them the crew crawls

ant like, solicitously grooming them, releasing,
making fast as they turn, lean far over and having
caught the wind again, side by side, head for the mark.

In a well guarded arena of open water surrounded by
lesser and greater craft which, sycophant, lumbering
and flittering follow them, they appear youthful, rare

as the light of a happy eye, live with the grace
of all that in the mind is feckless, free and
naturally to be desired. Now the sea which holds them

is moody, lapping their glossy sides, as if feeling
for some slightest flaw but fails completely.
Today no race. Then the wind comes again. The yachts

move, jockeying for a start, the signal is set and they
are off. Now the waves strike at them but they are too
well made, they slip through, though they take in canvas.

Arms with hands grasping seek to clutch at the prows.
Bodies thrown recklessly in the way are cut aside.
It is a sea of faces about them in agony, in despair

until the horror of the race dawns staggering the mind,
the whole sea become an entanglement of watery bodies
lost to the world bearing what they cannot hold. Broken,

beaten, desolate, reaching from the dead to be taken up
they cry out, failing, failing! their cries rising
in waves still as the skillful yachts pass over.

ANNA WICKHAM

(1884–   )

The Fresh Start

O give me back my rigorous English Sunday
And my well-ordered house, with stockings washed on Mon-
    day.
Let the House-Lord, that kindly decorous fellow,
Leave happy for his Law at ten, with a well-furled umbrella.
Let my young sons observe my strict house rules,
Imbibing Tory principles, at Tory schools.

Two years now I have sat beneath a curse
And in a fury poured out frenzied verse.
Such verse as held no beauty and no good
And was at best new curious vermin-food.

My dog is rabid, and my cat is lean,
And not a pot in all this place is clean.
The locks have fallen from my hingeless doors,
And holes are in my credit and my floors.

There is no solace for me, but in sooth
To have said baldly certain ugly truth.
Such scavenger's work was never yet a woman's,
My wardrobe's more a scarecrow's than a human's.

I'm off to the House-goddess for her gift.
"O give me Circumspection, Temperance, Thrift;
Take thou this lust of words, this fevered itching,
And give me faith in darning, joy of stitching!"

When this hot blood is cooled by kindly Time
Controlled and schooled, I'll come again to Rhyme.
Sure of my methods, morals and my gloves,
I'll write chaste sonnets of imagined Loves.

JAMES ELROY FLECKER

(1884–1915)

The Dying Patriot

Day breaks on England down the Kentish hills,
Singing in the silence of the meadow-footing rills,
Day of my dreams, O day!
  I saw them march from Dover, long ago,
  With a silver cross before them, singing low,
Monks of Rome from their home where the blue seas break
    in foam,
  Augustine with his feet of snow.

Noon strikes on England, noon on Oxford town,
  —Beauty she was statue cold—there's blood upon her
    gown:
Noon of my dreams, O noon!
  Proud and godly kings had built her, long ago,
  With her towers and tombs and statues all arow,
With her fair and floral air and the love that lingers there,
  And the streets where the great men go!

Evening on the olden, the golden sea of Wales,
When the first star shivers and the last wave pales:
O evening dreams!
  There's a house that Britons walked in, long ago,
  Where now the springs of ocean fall and flow,
And the dead robed in red and sea-lilies overhead
  Sway when the long winds blow.

Sleep not, my country: though night is here, afar
Your children of the morning are clamorous for war:
Fire in the night, O dreams!
  Though she send you as she sent you, long ago,
  South to desert, east to ocean, west to snow,
West of these out to seas colder than the Hebrides I must go
  Where the fleet of stars is anchored and the young Star-
    captains glow.

DAVID HERBERT LAWRENCE

(1885–1930)

FROM *The Virgin Mother*

I kiss you good-bye, my darling,
Our ways are different now;
You are a seed in the night-time,
I am a man, to plough
The difficult glebe of the future
For seed to endow.

I kiss you good-bye, my dearest,
It is finished between us here.
Oh, if I were calm as you are,
Sweet and still on your bier!
Oh God, if I had not to leave you
Alone, my dear.

Is the last word now uttered?
Is the farewell said?
Spare me the strength to leave you
Now you are dead.
I must go, but my soul lies helpless
Beside your bed.

River Roses

By the Isar, in the twilight
We were wandering and singing,
By the Isar, in the evening
We climbed the huntsman's ladder and sat swinging
In the fir-tree overlooking the marshes,
While river met with river, and the ringing
Of their pale-green glacier water filled the evening.

By the Isar, in the twilight
We found the dark wild roses
Hanging red at the river; and simmering
Frogs were singing, and over the river closes
Was savour of ice and roses; and glimmering

Fear was abroad. We whispered: "No one knows us.
Let it be as the snake disposes
Here in this simmering marsh."

Song of a Man Who Has Come Through

Not I, not I, but the wind that blows through me!
A fine wind is blowing the new direction of Time.
If only I let it bear me, carry me, if only it carry me!
If only I am sensitive, subtle, oh, delicate, a winged gift!
If only, most lovely of all, I yield myself and am borrowed
By the fine, fine wind that takes its course through the chaos
        of the world
Like a fine, an exquisite chisel, a wedge-blade inserted;
If only I am keen and hard like the sheer tip of a wedge
Driven by invisible blows,
The rock will split, we shall come at the wonder, we shall
        find the Hesperides.

> Oh, for the wonder that bubbles into my soul,
> I would be a good fountain, a good well-head,
> Would blur no whisper, spoil no expression.

> What is the knocking?
> What is the knocking at the door in the night?
> It is somebody wants to do us harm.

> No, no, it is the three strange angels.
> Admit them, admit them.

Sinners

> The big mountains sit still in the afternoon light,
>   Shadows in their lap;
> The bees roll round in the wild-thyme with delight.

> We sitting here among the cranberries
>   So still in the gap
> Of rock, distilling our memories,

Are sinners! Strange! The bee that blunders
     Against me goes off with a laugh.
A squirrel cocks his head on the fence, and wonders

What about sin?—For, it seems
     The mountains have
No shadow of us on their snowy forehead of dreams

As they ought to have. They rise above us
     Dreaming
For ever. One even might think that they love us.

Little red cranberries cheek to cheek,
Two great dragon-flies wrestling;
You, with your forehead nestling
Against me, and bright peak shining to peak—

There's a love-song for you!—Ah, if only
     There were no teeming
Swarms of mankind in the world, and we were less lonely!

Bavarian Gentians

Not every man has gentians in his house
in soft September, at slow, sad Michaelmas.

Bavarian gentians, big and dark, only dark
darkening the day-time torch-like with the smoking blueness
     of Pluto's gloom,
ribbed and torch-like, with their blaze of darkness spread
     blue
down flattening into points, flattened under the sweep of
     white day
torch-flower of the blue-smoking darkness, Pluto's dark-blue
     daze,
black lamps from the halls of Dis, burning dark blue,
giving off darkness, blue darkness, as Demeter's pale lamps
     give off light,
lead me then, lead me the way.

Reach me a gentian, give me a torch
let me guide myself with the blue, forked torch of this flower
down the darker and darker stairs, where blue is darkened
on blueness,
even where Persephone goes, just now, from the frosted
September
to the sightless realm where darkness is awake upon the dark
and Persephone herself is but a voice
or a darkness invisible enfolded in the deeper dark
of the arms Plutonic, and pierced with the passion of dense
gloom,
among the splendour of torches of darkness, shedding dark-
ness on the lost bride and her groom.

Ship of Death

I sing of autumn and the falling fruit
and the long journey towards oblivion.

The apples falling like great drops of dew
to bruise themselves an exit from themselves.

Have you built your ship of death, oh, have you?
Build then your ship of death, for you will need it!

Can man his own quietus make
with a bare bodkin?

With daggers, bodkins, bullets man can make
a bruise or break of exit for his life
but is that a quietus, oh tell me, is it quietus?

Quietus is the goal of the long journey,
the longest journey towards oblivion.

Slips out the soul, invisible one, wrapped still
in the white shirt of the mind's experiences
and folded in the dark-red, unseen
mantle of the body's still mortal memories.

Frightened and alone, the soul slips out of the house
or is pushed out
to find himself on the crowded, arid margins of existence.

Oh, it is not so easy, I tell you it is not so easy
to set softly forth on the longest journey, the longest journey.

It is easy to be pushed out of the silvery city of the body
through any breach in the wall,
thrust out on to the grey grey beaches of shadow,
the long marginal stretches of existence, crowded with lost
        souls
that intervene between our tower and the shaking sea of the
        beyond.

Oh build your ship of death, oh build it in time
and build it lovingly, and put it between the hands of your
        soul.

Once outside the gate of the walled silvery life of days,
once outside upon the grey marsh beaches, where lost souls
        moan
in millions, unable to depart,
having no boat to launch upon the shaken, soundless
deepest and longest of seas,
once outside the gate,
what will you do, if you have no ship of the soul?

Oh pity the dead that are dead but cannot take
the journey, still they moan and beat
against the silvery adamant walls of this our exclusive exist-
        ence.
They moan and beat, they gnash, they rage,
they fall upon the new outcoming souls with rage,
and they send arrows of anger, bullets and bombs of frustra-
        tion
over the adamant walls of this, our by-no-means impregnable
        existence.

Pity, oh pity the poor dead that are only ousted from life,
and crowd there on the grey mud beaches of the margins,

gaunt and horrible,
waiting, waiting till at last the ancient boatman with the
         common barge
shall take them abroad, towards the great goal of oblivion.

Pity the poor gaunt dead that cannot die
into the distance with receding oars,
but must roam like outcast dogs on the margins of life,
and think of them, and with the soul's deep sigh
waft nearer to them the bark of delivery.

But, for myself, but for my soul, dear soul,
let me build a little ship with oars and food
and little dishes, and all accoutrements
dainty and ready for the departing soul.
And put it between the hands of the trembling soul.

So that when the hour comes, and the last door closes behind
         him,
he shall slip down the shores invisible
between the half-visible hordes
to where the furthest and longest sea
touches the margins of our life's existence
with wincing unwilling waves.

And launching there his little ship,
wrapped in the dark-red mantle of the body's memories,
the little, slender soul sits swiftly down, and takes the oars,
and draws away, away, away towards the dark depths,
fathomless deep ahead, far, far from the grey shores
that fringe with shadow all this world's existence.

Over the sea, over the furthest sea
on the longest journey,
past the jutting rocks of shadow,
past the lurking octopus arms of agonised memory,
past the strange whirlpools of remembered greed,
through the dead weed of a life-time's falsity,
slow, slow, my soul in his little ship,
on the most soundless of all seas,
taking the longest journey.

Pulling the long oars of a life-time's courage,
drinking the confident water from the little jug,
and eating the brave bread of a wholesome knowledge,
row, little soul, row on,
on the longest journey, towards the greatest goal;

Neither straight nor crooked, neither here nor there,
but shadows folded on deeper shadows,
and deeper, to a core of sheer oblivion,
like the convolutions of shadow-shell,
or deeper, like the foldings and involvings of a womb.

Drift on, drift on, my soul, towards the most pure,
most dark oblivion.
And at the penultimate porches, the dark-red mantle
of the body's memories slips and is absorbed
into the shell-like, womb-like convoluted shadow.

And round the great final bend of unbroken dark,
the skirt of the spirit's experience has melted away,
the oars have gone from the boat, and the little dishes
gone, gone, and the boat dissolves like pearl,
as the soul at last slips perfect into the goal, the core
of sheer oblivion and of utter peace,
the womb of silence in the living night.

Ah peace, ah lovely peace, most lovely lapsing
of this my soul into the plasm of peace.

Oh lovely last, last lapse of death, into pure oblivion,
at the end of the longest journey
peace, complete peace!
But can it be that also it is procreation?

Oh build your ship of death,
oh build it!
Oh, nothing matters but the longest journey.

EZRA POUND

(1885–)

Δώρια

Be in me as the eternal moods
   of the bleak wind, and not
As transient things are—
   gaiety of flowers.
Have me in the strong loneliness
   of sunless cliffs
And of grey waters.
   Let the gods speak softly of us
In days hereafter,
   The shadowy flowers of Orcus
Remember thee.

The Return

See, they return; ah, see the tentative
Movements, and the slow feet,
The trouble in the pace and the uncertain
Wavering!

See, they return, one, and by one,
With fear, as half-awakened;
As if the snow should hesitate
And murmur in the wind,
   and half turn back;
These were the "Wing'd-with-Awe,"
  Inviolable.

Gods of the wingéd shoe!
With them the silver hounds
   sniffing the trace of air!

Haie! Haie!
     These were the swift to harry;
These the keen-scented;
These were the souls of blood.

Slow on the leash,
    pallid the leash-men!

FROM *Canto LXXXI*

What thou lovest well remains,
        the rest is dross
What thou lov'st well shall not be reft from thee
What thou lov'st well is thy true heritage
Whose world, or mine or theirs
        or is it of none?
First came the seen, then thus the palpable
    Elysium, though it were in the halls of hell,
What thou lovest well is thy true heritage

The ant's a centaur in his dragon world.
Pull down thy vanity, it is not man
Made courage, or made order, or made grace,
    Pull down thy vanity, I say pull down.
Learn of the green world what can be thy place
In scaled invention or true artistry,
Pull down thy vanity,
        Paquin pull down!
The green casque has outdone your elegance.

"Master thyself, then others shall thee beare"
    Pull down thy vanity
Thou art a beaten dog beneath the hail,
A swollen magpie in a fitful sun,
Half black half white
Nor knowst'ou wing from tail
Pull down thy vanity
        How mean thy hates
Fostered in falsity,
        Pull down thy vanity,
Rathe to destroy, niggard in charity,
Pull down thy vanity,
        I say pull down.

But to have done instead of not doing
        this is not vanity
To have, with decency, knocked
That a Blunt should open
        To have gathered from the air a live tradition

or from a fine old eye the unconquered flame
This is not vanity.
Here error is all in the not done,
all in the diffidence that faltered.

ELINOR WYLIE

(1885–1928)

The Eagle and the Mole

Avoid the reeking herd,
Shun the polluted flock,
Live like that stoic bird,
The eagle of the rock.

The huddled warmth of crowds
Begets and fosters hate;
He keeps, above the clouds,
His cliff inviolate.

When flocks are folded warm,
And herds to shelter run,
He sails above the storm,
He stares into the sun.

If in the eagle's track
Your sinews cannot leap,
Avoid the lathered pack,
Turn from the steaming sheep.

If you would keep your soul
From spotted sight or sound,
Live like the velvet mole;
Go burrow underground

And there hold intercourse
With roots of trees and stones,
With rivers at their source,
And disembodied bones.

SIEGFRIED SASSOON

(1886-   )

Aftermath

Have you forgotten yet? . . .
For the world's events have rumbled on since those gagged
     days,
Like traffic checked awhile at the crossing of city ways:
And the haunted gap in your mind has filled with thoughts
     that flow
Like clouds in the lit heaven of life; and you're a man re-
     prieved to go,
Taking your peaceful share of Time, with joy to spare.
But the past is just the same,—and War's a bloody game . . .
Have you forgotten yet? . . .
Look down, and swear by the slain of the War that you'll
     never forget?

Do you remember the dark months you held the sector at
     Mametz,—
The nights you watched and wired and dug and piled sand-
     bags on parapets?
Do you remember the rats; and the stench
Of corpses rotting in front of the front-line trench,—
And dawn coming, dirty-white, and chill with a hopeless
     rain?
Do you ever stop and ask, "Is it all going to happen again?"

Do you remember that hour of din before the attack,—
And the anger, the blind compassion that seized and shook
     you then
As you peered at the doomed and haggard faces of your
     men?
Do you remember the stretcher-cases lurching back
With dying eyes and lolling heads,—those ashen-grey
Masks of the lads who once were keen and kind and gay?

Have you forgotten yet? . . .
Look up, and swear by the green of the Spring that you'll
     never forget.

H.D.
(HILDA DOOLITTLE)

(1886–   )

Sitalkas

Thou art come at length
more beautiful
than any cool god
in a chamber under
Lycia's far coast,
than any high god
who touches us not
here in the seeded grass,
aye, than Argestes
scattering the broken leaves.

Lethe

Nor skin nor hide nor fleece
  Shall cover you,
Nor curtain of crimson nor fine
Shelter of cedar-wood be over you,
  Nor the fir-tree
  Nor the pine.

Nor sight of whin nor gorse
  Nor river-yew,
Nor fragrance of flowering bush,
Nor wailing of reed-bird to waken you,
  Nor of linnet,
  Nor of thrush.

Nor word nor touch nor sight
  Of lover, you
Shall long through the night but for this:
The roll of the full tide to cover you
  Without question,
  Without kiss.

FROM *Hymen*

Never more will the wind
Cherish you again,
Never more will the rain.

Never more
Shall we find you bright
In the snow and wind.

The snow is melted,
The snow is gone,
And you are flown:

Like a bird out of our hand,
Like a light out of our heart,
You are gone.

ROBINSON JEFFERS
(1887–   )

Signpost

Civilized, crying how to be human again: this will tell you
      how.
Turn outward, love things, not men, turn right away from
      humanity,
Let that doll lie. Consider if you like how the lilies grow,
Lean on the silent rock until you feel its divinity
Make your veins cold, look at the silent stars, let your eyes
Climb the great ladder out of the pit of yourself and man.
Things are so beautiful, your love will follow your eyes;
Things are the God, you will love God, and not in vain,
For what we love, we grow to it, we share its nature. At
      length
You will look back along the stars' rays and see that even
The poor doll humanity has a place under heaven.
Its qualities repair their mosaic around you, the chips of
      strength
And sickness; but now you are free, even to become human,
But born of the rock and the air, not of a woman.

Shine, Perishing Republic

While this America settles in the mould of its vulgarity, heav-
ily thickening to empire,
And protest, only a bubble in the molten mass, pops and
sighs out, and the mass hardens,

I sadly smiling remember that the flower fades to make fruit,
the fruit rots to make earth
Out of the mother; and through the spring exultances, ripe-
ness and decadence; and home to the mother.

You making haste haste on decay: not blameworthy; life is
good, be it stubbornly long or suddenly
A mortal splendor: meteors are not needed less than moun-
tains: shine, perishing republic.

But for my children, I would have them keep their distance
from the thickening center; corruption
Never has been compulsory, when the cities lie at the mon-
ster's feet there are left the mountains.

And boys, be in nothing so moderate as in love of man, a
clever servant, insufferable master.
There is the trap that catches noblest spirits, that caught—
they say—God, when he walked on earth.

EDITH SITWELL

(1887–   )

An Old Woman Laments in Spring-Time

I walk on grass as soft as wool,
Or fluff that our old fingers pull
From beaver or from miniver,—
Sweet-sounding as a dulcimer,—

A poor old woman creeping where
The young can never pry and stare.
I am so old, I should be gone,—
Too old to warm in the kind sun

My wrinkled face; my hat that flaps
Will hide it, and my cloak has laps
That trail upon the grass as I
Like some warm shade of spring creep by.

And all the laden fruit-boughs spread
Into a silver sound, but dead
Is the wild dew I used to know,
Nor will the morning music grow.

I sit beneath these coral boughs
Where the air's silver plumage grows
And flows like water with a sigh.
Fed with sweet milk of lilies, I

Still feel the dew like amber gums,
That from the richest spice-tree comes,
Drip down upon my turbanned head,
Trembling and ancient as the Dead,

Beneath these floating branches' shade.
Yet long ago, a lovely maid,
On grass, a fading silver tune
Played on an ancient dulcimer,
(And soft as wool of miniver)

I walked like a young antelope,
And Day was but an Ethiop,
Beside my fairness shining there—
Like black shade seemed the brightest air

When I was lovely as the snows,—
A fading starriness that flows . . .
Then, far-off Death seemed but the shade
That those heavenly branches made.

EDWIN MUIR

(1887–   )

The Road

There is a road that turning always
    Cuts off the country of Again.
Archers stand there on every side
    And as it runs time's deer is slain,
    And lies where it has lain.

The busy clock shows never an hour.
    All flies and all in flight must tarry.
The hunter shoots the empty air
    Far on before the quarry,
    Which falls though nothing's there to parry.

The lion couching in the centre
    With mountain head and sunset brow
Rolls down the everlasting slope
    Bones picked an age ago,
    And the bones rise up and go.

There the beginning finds the end
    Before beginning ever can be,
And the great runner never leaves
    The starting and the finishing tree,
    The budding and the fading tree.

There the ship sailing safe in harbour
    Long since in many a sea was drowned.
The treasure burning in her hold
    So near will never be found,
    Sunk past all sound.

There a man on a summer evening
    Reclines at ease upon his tomb
And is his mortal effigy.
    And there within the womb,
    The cell of doom,

The ancestral deed is thought and done,
        And in a million Edens fall
A million Adams drowned in darkness,
        For small is great and great is small,
        And a blind seed all.

LEONARD BACON

(1887–1954)

Chorus from a Tragedy

The world is no longer good.
Men's hearts no more are kind.
There is coldness in the mind,
Bitterness in the blood.
And I am not resigned.

When they talk of burning things
That touch me to the heart,
They trammel music and art,
They wither Ariel's wings
Or tear his pinions apart,

Anatomizing, digesting,
Drying the sap that ran
Once in the brain of man
Riotous and unresting,
Guiltless of plot or plan.

There is no pulse in the vein.
And the staunch muscle has slacked.
A blight has devoured the bract.
Color dies to a stain.
Wisdom dwindles to fact.

And I feel as dead as the asb
Of an unregarded fire.
The elements of desire,
Lovely and wild and rash,
Separate and retire.

We shall not have things as they were,
Not as they were before.
If I had the heart to restore,
Would the chestnut thicken its burr?
Would the olive leaf once more?

MARIANNE MOORE

(1887-   )

Silence

My father used to say,
"Superior people never make long visits,
have to be shown Longfellow's grave
or the glass flowers at Harvard.
Self-reliant like the cat—
that takes its prey to privacy,
the mouse's limp tail hanging like a shoelace from its mouth—
they sometimes enjoy solitude,
and can be robbed of speech
by speech which has delighted them.
The deepest feeling always shows itself in silence;
not in silence, but restraint."
Nor was he insincere in saying, "Make my house your inn."
Inns are not residences.

A Talisman

Under a splintered mast,
Torn from the ship and cast
    Near her hull,

A stumbling shepherd found
Embedded in the ground,
    A seagull

Of lapis lazuli,
A scarab of the sea,
    With wings spread—

Curling its coral feet,
Parting its beak to greet
Men long dead.

Poetry

I, too, dislike it: there are things that are important beyond
        all this fiddle.
    Reading it, however, with a perfect contempt for it, one
        discovers in
    it, after all, a place for the genuine.
        Hands that can grasp, eyes
        that can dilate, hair that can rise
            if it must, these things are important not because a

high-sounding interpretation can be put upon them but be-
        cause they are
    useful. When they become so derivative as to become un-
        intelligible
    the same thing may be said for all of us, that we
        do not admire what
        we cannot understand: the bat
            holding on upside down or in quest of something to

eat, elephants pushing, a wild horse taking a roll, a tireless
        wolf under
    a tree, the immovable critic twitching his skin like a horse
        that feels a flea, the base-
    ball fan, the statistician—
        nor is it valid
            to discriminate against "business documents and

school-books"; all these phenomena are important. One must
        make a distinction
    however: when dragged into prominence by half poets, the
        result is not poetry,
    nor till the poets among us can be
        "literalists of
        the imagination"—above
            insolence and triviality and can present

for inspection, "imaginary gardens with real toads in them,"
      shall we have
   it. In the meantime, if you demand on the one hand,
   the raw material of poetry in
      all its rawness and
      that which is on the other hand
         genuine, you are interested in poetry.

In Distrust of Merits

Strengthened to live, strengthened to die for
      medals and positioned victories?
They're fighting, fighting, fighting the blind
      man who thinks he sees,—
who cannot see that the enslaver is
enslaved; the hater, harmed. O shining O
            firm star, O tumultuous
                  ocean lashed till small things go
            as they will, the mountainous
                  wave makes us who look, know

depth. Lost at sea before they fought! O
      star of David, star of Bethlehem,
O black imperial lion
      of the Lord—emblem
of a risen world—be joined at last, be
joined. There is hate's crown beneath which all is
            death; there's love's without which none
                  is king; the blessed deeds bless
            the halo. As contagion
                  of sickness makes sickness,

contagion of trust can make trust. They're
      fighting in deserts and caves, one by
one, in battalions and squadrons;
      they're fighting that I
may yet recover from the disease, My
Self; some have it lightly; some will die. "Man

wolf to man?" And we devour
        ourselves. The enemy could not
have made a greater breach in our
        defenses. One pilot-

ing a blind man can escape him, but
        Job disheartened by false comfort knew
that nothing is so defeating
        as a blind man who
can see. O alive who are dead, who are
proud not to see, O small dust of the earth
        that walks so arrogantly,
                trust begets power and faith is
        an affectionate thing. We
                vow, we make this promise

to the fighting—it's a promise—"We'll
        never hate black, white, red, yellow, Jew,
Gentile, Untouchable." We are
        not competent to
make our vows. With set jaw they are fighting,
fighting, fighting,—some we love whom we know,
        some we love but know not—that
                hearts may feel and not be numb.
        It cures me; or am I what
                I can't believe in? Some

in snow, some on crags, some in quicksands,
        little by little, much by much, they
are fighting fighting fighting that where
        there was death there may
be life. "When a man is prey to anger,
he is moved by outside things; when he holds
        his ground in patience patience
                patience, that is action or
        beauty," the soldier's defense
                and hardest armor for

the fight. The world's an orphans' home. Shall
        we never have peace without sorrow?

without pleas of the dying for
      help that won't come? O
quiet form upon the dust, I cannot
look and yet I must. If these great patient
         dyings—all these agonies
            and woundbearings and bloodshed—
      can teach us how to live, these
         dyings were not wasted.

Hate-hardened heart, O heart of iron,
      iron is iron till it is rust.
There never was a war that was
      not inward; I must
fight till I have conquered in myself what
causes war, but I would not believe it.
         I inwardly did nothing.
            O Iscariotlike crime!
         Beauty is everlasting
           and dust is for a time.

RUPERT BROOKE

(1887–1915)

The Hill

Breathless, we flung us on the windy hill,
    Laughed in the sun, and kissed the lovely grass.
    You said, "Through glory and ecstasy we pass;
Wind, sun, and earth remain, the birds sing still,
When we are old, are old . . ." "And when we die
    All's over that is ours; and life burns on
Through other lovers, other lips," said I,
    "Heart of my heart, our heaven is now, is won!"

"We are earth's best, that learnt her lesson here.
    Life is our cry. We have kept the faith!" we said;
    "We shall go down with unreluctant tread
Rose-crowned into the darkness!" . . . Proud we were,
And laughed, that had such brave true things to say,
    —And then you suddenly cried, and turned away.

The Soldier

If I should die, think only this of me:
　That there's some corner of a foreign field
That is for ever England. There shall be
　In that rich earth a richer dust concealed;
A dust whom England bore, shaped, made aware;
　Gave, once, her flowers to love, her ways to roam,
A body of England's breathing English air,
　Washed by the rivers, blest by suns of home.

And think, this heart, all evil shed away,
　A pulse in the eternal mind, no less
　　Gives somewhere back the thoughts by England given;
Her sights and sounds; dreams happy as her day;
　And laughter, learnt of friends; and gentleness,
　　In hearts at peace, under an English heaven.

ALAN SEEGER

(1888–1916)

"I Have a Rendezvous with Death"

I have a rendezvous with Death
At some disputed barricade,
When Spring comes back with rustling shade
And apple-blossoms fill the air—
I have a rendezvous with Death
When Spring brings back blue days and fair.

It may be he shall take my hand
And lead me into his dark land
And close my eyes and quench my breath—
It may be I shall pass him still.
I have a rendezvous with Death
On some scarred slope of battered hill,
When Spring comes round again this year
And the first meadow-flowers appear.

God knows 'twere better to be deep
Pillowed in silk and scented down,

Where Love throbs out in blissful sleep,
Pulse nigh to pulse, and breath to breath,
Where hushed awakenings are dear . . .
But I've a rendezvous with Death
At midnight in some flaming town,
When Spring trips north again this year,
And I to my pledged word am true,
I shall not fail that rendezvous.

THOMAS STEARNS ELIOT
(1888–   )

The Love Song of J. Alfred Prufrock

*S'io credcssi che mia risposta fosse
A persona che mai tornasse al mondo,
Questa fiamma staria senza più scosse.
Ma perciocché giammai di questo fondo
Non tornò vivo alcun, s'i'odo il vero
Senza tema d'infamia ti rispondo.*

Let us go then, you and I,
When the evening is spread out against the sky
Like a patient etherised upon a table;
Let us go, through certain half-deserted streets,
The muttering retreats
Of restless nights in one-night cheap hotels
And sawdust restaurants with oyster-shells:
Streets that follow like a tedious argument
Of insidious intent
To lead you to an overwhelming question . . .
Oh, do not ask, "What is it?"
Let us go and make our visit.

In the room the women come and go
Talking of Michelangelo.

The yellow fog that rubs its back upon the window-panes,
The yellow smoke that rubs its muzzle on the window-panes
Licked its tongue into the corners of the evening,
Lingered upon the pools that stand in drains,
Let fall upon its back the soot that falls from chimneys,

Slipped by the terrace, made a sudden leap,
And seeing that it was a soft October night,
Curled once about the house, and fell asleep.

And indeed there will be time
For the yellow smoke that slides along the street,
Rubbing its back upon the window-panes;
There will be time, there will be time
To prepare a face to meet the faces that you meet;
There will be time to murder and create,
And time for all the works and days of hands
That lift and drop a question on your plate;
Time for you and time for me,
And time yet for a hundred indecisions,
And for a hundred visions and revisions,
Before the taking of a toast and tea.

In the room the women come and go
Talking of Michelangelo.

And indeed there will be time
To wonder, "Do I dare?" and, "Do I dare?"
Time to turn back and descend the stair,
With a bald spot in the middle of my hair—
(They will say: "How his hair is growing thin!")
My morning coat, my collar mounting firmly to the chin,
My necktie rich and modest, but asserted by a simple pin—
(They will say: "But how his arms and legs are thin!")
Do I dare
Disturb the universe?
In a minute there is time
For decisions and revisions which a minute will reverse.

For I have known them all already, known them all:—
Have known the evenings, mornings, afternoons,
I have measured out my life with coffee spoons;
I know the voices dying with a dying fall
Beneath the music from a farther room.
    So how should I presume?

And I have known the eyes already, known them all—
The eyes that fix you in a formulated phrase,
And when I am formulated, sprawling on a pin,
When I am pinned and wriggling on the wall,
Then how should I begin
To spit out all the butt-ends of my days and ways?
   And how should I presume?

And I have known the arms already, known them all—
Arms that are braceleted and white and bare
(But in the lamplight, downed with light brown hair!)
Is it perfume from a dress
That makes me so digress?
Arms that lie along a table, or wrap about a shawl.
   And should I then presume?
   And how should I begin?

.   .   .   .   .

Shall I say, I have gone at dusk through narrow streets
And watched the smoke that rises from the pipes
Of lonely men in shirt-sleeves, leaning out of windows? . . .

I should have been a pair of ragged claws
Scuttling across the floors of silent seas.

.   .   .   .   .

And the afternoon, the evening, sleeps so peacefully!
Smoothed by long fingers,
Asleep . . . tired . . . or it malingers,
Stretched on the floor, here beside you and me.
Should I, after tea and cakes and ices,
Have the strength to force the moment to its crisis?
But though I have wept and fasted, wept and prayed,
Though I have seen my head (grown slightly bald) brought
     in upon a platter,
I am no prophet—and here's no great matter;
I have seen the moment of my greatness flicker,
And I have seen the eternal Footman hold my coat, and
     snicker,
And in short, I was afraid.

And would it have been worth it, after all,
After the cups, the marmalade, the tea,
Among the porcelain, among some talk of you and me,
Would it have been worth while,
To have bitten off the matter with a smile,
To have squeezed the universe into a ball
To roll it toward some overwhelming question,
To say: "I am Lazarus, come from the dead,
Come back to tell you all, I shall tell you all"—
If one, settling a pillow by her head,
   Should say: "That is not what I meant at all.
   That is not it, at all."

And would it have been worth it, after all,
Would it have been worth while,
After the sunsets and the dooryards and the sprinkled streets,
After the novels, after the teacups, after the skirts that trail
      along the floor—
And this, and so much more?—
It is impossible to say just what I mean!
But as if a magic lantern threw the nerves in patterns on a
      screen:
Would it have been worth while
If one, settling a pillow or throwing off a shawl,
And turning toward the window, should say:
   "That is not it at all,
   That is not what I meant, at all."

    .   .   .   .   .

No! I am not Prince Hamlet, nor was meant to be;
Am an attendant lord, one that will do
To swell a progress, start a scene or two,
Advise the prince; no doubt, an easy tool,
Deferential, glad to be of use,
Politic, cautious, and meticulous;
Full of high sentence, but a bit obtuse;
At times, indeed, almost ridiculous—
Almost, at times, the Fool.

I grow old . . . I grow old . . .
I shall wear the bottoms of my trousers rolled.

Shall I part my hair behind? Do I dare to eat a peach?
I shall wear white flannel trousers, and walk upon the beach.
I have heard the mermaids singing, each to each.

I do not think that they will sing to me.

I have seen them riding seaward on the waves
Combing the white hair of the waves blown back
When the wind blows the water white and black.

We have lingered in the chambers of the sea
By sea-girls wreathed with seaweed red and brown
Till human voices wake us, and we drown.

La Figlia Che Piange

O quam te memorem virgo . . .

Stand on the highest pavement of the stair—
Lean on a garden urn—
Weave, weave the sunlight in your hair—
Clasp your flowers to you with a pained surprise—
Fling them to the ground and turn
With a fugitive resentment in your eyes:
But weave, weave the sunlight in your hair.

So I would have had him leave,
So I would have had her stand and grieve,
So he would have left
As the soul leaves the body torn and bruised,
As the mind deserts the body it has used.
I should find
Some way incomparably light and deft,
Some way we both should understand,
Simple and faithless as a smile and shake of the hand.

She turned away, but with the autumn weather
Compelled my imagination many days,
Many days and many hours:
Her hair over her arms and her arms full of flowers.

And I wonder how they should have been together!
I should have lost a gesture and a pose.
Sometimes these cogitations still amaze
The troubled midnight and the noon's repose.

"Eyes That Last I Saw in Tears"

Eyes that last I saw in tears
Through division
Here in death's dream kingdom
The golden vision reappears
I see the eyes but not the tears
This is my affliction

This is my affliction
Eyes I shall not see again
Eyes of decision
Eyes I shall not see unless
At the door of death's other kingdom
Where, as in this,
The eyes outlast a little while
A little while outlast the tears
And hold us in derision.

FROM *Four Quartets*

(FROM *Burnt Norton*)

V

Words move, music moves
Only in time; but that which is only living
Can only die. Words, after speech, reach
Into the silence. Only by the form, the pattern,
Can words or music reach
The stillness, as a Chinese jar still
Moves perpetually in its stillness.
Not the stillness of the violin, while the note lasts,
Not that only, but the co-existence,
Or say that the end precedes the beginning,

And the end and the beginning were always there
Before the beginning and after the end.
And all is always now. Words strain,
Crack and sometimes break, under the burden,
Under the tension, slip, slide, perish,
Decay with imprecision, will not stay in place,
Will not stay still. Shrieking voices
Scolding, mocking, or merely chattering,
Always assail them. The Word in the desert
Is most attacked by voices of temptation,
The crying shadow in the funeral dance,
The loud lament of the disconsolate chimera.

The detail of the pattern is movement,
As in the figure of the ten stairs.
Desire itself is movement
Not in itself desirable;
Love is itself unmoving,
Only the cause and end of movement,
Timeless, and undesiring
Except in the aspect of time
Caught in the form of limitation
Between un-being and being.
Sudden in a shaft of sunlight
Even while the dust moves
There rises the hidden laughter
Of children in the foliage
Quick now, here, now, always—
Ridiculous the waste sad time
Stretching before and after.

JOHN CROWE RANSOM

(1888–   )

Tom, Tom, the Piper's Son

Grim in my little black coat as the sleazy beetle,
And gone of hue,
Lonely, a man reputed for softening little,
Loving few—

Mournfully going where men assemble, unfriended, pushing
With laborious wares,
And glaring with little grey eyes at whom I am brushing,
Who would with theirs—

Full of my thoughts as I trudge here and trundle yonder,
Eyes on the ground,
Tricked by white birds or tall women into no wonder,
And no sound—

Yet privy to great dreams, and secret in vainglory,
And hot and proud,
And poor and bewildered, and longing to hear my own story
Rehearsed aloud—

How I have passed, involved in these chances and choices,
By certain trees
Whose tiny attent auricles receive the true voices
Of the wordless breeze—

And against me the councils of spirits were not then dark-
        ened
Who thereby house,
As I set my boots to the path beneath them, and hearkened
To the talking boughs—

How one said, "This ambulant worm, he is strangely other
Than they suppose"—
But one, "He was sired by his father and damned by his
        mother,
And acknowledges those"—

And then: "Nay, nay—this man is a changeling, and knows
        not—
This was a Prince
From a far great kingdom—and should return, but goes
        not—
Long years since"—

But like a King I was subject to a King's condition,
And I marched on,
Not testing at eavesdrop the glory of my suspicion,
And the talkers were gone—

And duly appeared I on the very clock-throb appointed
In the litten room,
Nor was hailed with that love that leaps to the Heir anointed:
"Hush, hush, he is come!"

CONRAD AIKEN

(1889-   )

FROM *Time in the Rock*

XX

And you who love, you who attach yourselves
to another mouth, who in the depth of night
speak without speech act without conscious action
in all that lamentable struggle to be another
to make that other yourself, to find that other,
to make two one

           who would be tree and earth
cloud and ocean, movement and stillness,
object and shadow

           what can we learn from you
pathetic ones, poor victims of the will,
wingless angels who beat with violent arms,
what can we learn from your tragic effort

is there a secret here, an unambiguous
message, a leaf blown from another star,
that thus all stand and watch you, thus all envy,
all emulate? must we be violent too?

O patience, let us be patient and discern
in this lost leaf all that can be discerned;
and let us learn, from this sad violence learn,
all that in midst of violence can be learned.

Blind Date

No more the swanboat on the artificial lake
its paddled path through neon lights shall take;
the stars are turned out on the immortal Ferris wheel,
dark and still are the cars of the Virginia Reel.
Baby, it is the last of all blind dates,
and this we keep with the keeper of the golden gates.

For the last time, my darling, the chute-the-chutes,
the Tunnel of Love, the cry "all men are brutes,"
the sweaty dance-hall with the juke-box playing,
pretzels and beer, and our young love a-Maying:
baby, it is the last of all blind dates,
and this we keep with the keeper of the golden gates.

The radios in a thousand taxis die;
at last man's music fades from the inhuman sky;
as, short or long, fades out the impermanent wave
to find in the ether or the earth its grave.
Baby, it is the last of all blind dates,
and this we keep with the keeper of the golden gates.

Hold hands and kiss, it will never come again,
look in your own eyes and remember the deep pain,
how hollow the world is, like a bubble burst,
yes, and all beauty by some wretchedness accursed!
Baby, it is the last of all blind dates,
and this we keep with the keeper of the golden gates.

Love now the footworn grass, the trampled flowers,
and the divided man of crowds, for he is ours—
love him, yes, love him now, this sundered being,
who most himself seeks when himself most fleeing—
baby, it is the last of all blind dates,
and this we keep with the keeper of the golden gates.

But look—the scenic railway is flashed from red to green—
and swiftly beneath our feet as this machine
our old star plunges down the precipitous sky,
down the hurrahs of space! So soon to die!—
But baby, it is the last of all blind dates;
and we shall keep it with the keeper of the golden gates.

ISAAC ROSENBERG

(1890–1918)

Break of Day in the Trenches

The darkness crumbles away—
It is the same old druid Time as ever.
Only a live thing leaps my hand—
A queer sardonic rat—
As I pull the parapet's poppy
To stick behind my ear.
Droll rat, they would shoot you if they knew
Your cosmopolitan sympathies
(And God knows what antipathies).
Now you have touched this English hand
You will do the same to a German—
Soon, no doubt, if it be your pleasure
To cross the sleeping green between.
It seems you inwardly grin as you pass
Strong eyes, fine limbs, haughty athletes
Less chanced than you for life,
Bonds to the whims of murder,
Sprawled in the bowels of the earth,
The torn fields of France.
What do you see in our eyes
As the shrieking iron and flame
Hurled through still heavens?
What quaver—what heart aghast?
Poppies whose roots are in man's veins
Drop, and are ever dropping;
But mine in my ear is safe,
Just a little white with the dust.

OSBERT SITWELL

(1892–   )

Mrs. Southern's Enemy

Even as the shadows of the statues lengthen,
While, when the glowing glass below is broken,
The plunging images are shaken,
For the young, blue-wingéd god is woken,

Sighs, stretches, shivers, till his muscles strengthen
So he can trample down the flowers, forsaken
By their droning, golden-liveried lovers, tumble
Among them till their red mouths tremble,
Already in the ancient house, whose shadow dies
With the slow opening of its hundred eyes,
Already, even then, Night the Black Panther
Is slinking, creeping down the corridors,
Lithe-swinging on her velvet paws,
Sharpening her treacherous claws
To frighten children.

And then it is
        I seem to see again
That grey typhoon we knew as Mrs. Southern,
Spinning along the darkened passages,
Watching things, tugging things,
Seeing to things,
        And putting things to rights.
Oh, would that the cruel daylight too,
Could give us back again
Dear Mrs. Southern,
Dear selfless, blue-lipped Mrs. Southern,
Cross, mumbling and transparent Mrs. Southern,
With her grey hair,
        Grey face,
          And thinly-bitter smile,
In wide blue skirt, white-spotted, and white apron;
On the very top of her head she carried a cap,
An emblem of respect and respectability, while
As though she were a Hindu charmer of snakes,
Her hair lay coiled and tame at the back of her head.
But her actual majesty was really the golden glory,
Through which she moved, a hurrying fly
Enshrined in rolling amber,
As she spun along in a twisting column of golden atoms,
A halo of gold motes above and about her,
A column of visible, virtuous activity.
Her life was a span of hopeless conflict,
For she battled against Time,
That never-vanquished and invisible foe.

She did not recognise her enemy,
She thought him Dust:
But what is Dust,
Save Time's most lethal weapon,
His faithful ally and our sneaking foe,
Through whom Time steals and covers all we know,
The very instrument through whom he overcame
Great Nineveh and Rome and Carthage,
Ophir and Trebizond and Ephesus,
Now deep, all deep, so deep in dust?
   Even the lean and arid archaeologist,
    Who bends above the stones, and peers and ponders,
    Will be his, too, one day.
Dust loads the dice,
Then challenges to play,
Each layer of dust upon a chair or table
A tablet to his future victory.
And Dust is cruel, no victory despising,
However slight,
And Dust is greedy, eats the very bones;
So that, in the end, still not content
With trophies such as Helen of Troy,
Or with the conquering golden flesh of Cleopatra
   (She, perhaps, understood the age-long battle,
    For did she not prefer to watch her pearl
    Dissolve in amber wine,
    Thus herself enjoying
    Its ultimate disintegration,
    Than let Dust conquer such a thing of beauty?
    Was not the asp, fruit-hidden,
    The symbol of such understanding?),
He needs must seize upon Mrs. Southern,
Poor mumbling, struggling, blue-lipped Mrs. Southern,
For Dust is insatiate and invincible.

FROM *England Reclaimed*

Sound out, proud trumpets,
   And you, bugles, blow
     Over the English Dead,

Not slain in battle, in no sense sublime,
These rustic figures caught at last by Time,
And yet their blood was warm and red
As any roses that in England grow
To these anonymous armies of the Dead.
        Blow, bugles, blow;
Sound out, proud trumpets, let your brazen thunder
    Wake them, to make them pass
    Before us under the wide sky.
    Thunder, drums and trumpets, thunder,
    Wake them, to rise from where they lie
Under,
        Under
                Under
                    The green grass
                Under the wide grey sky.

ARCHIBALD MacLEISH

(1892–   )

You, Andrew Marvel

And here face down beneath the sun
And here upon earth's noonward height
To feel the always coming on
The always rising of the night:

To feel creep up the curving east
The earthy chill of dusk and slow
Upon those under lands the vast
And ever climbing shadow grow

And strange at Ecbatan the trees
Take leaf by leaf the evening strange
The flooding dark about their knees
The mountains over Persia change

And now at Kermanshah the gate
Dark empty and the withered grass
And through the twilight now the late
Few travelers in the westward pass

And Baghdad darken and the bridge
Across the silent river gone
And through Arabia the edge
Of evening widen and steal on

And deepen on Palmyra's street
The wheel rut in the ruined stone
And Lebanon fade out and Crete
High through the clouds and overblown

And over Sicily the air
Still flashing with the landward gulls
And loom and slowly disappear
The sails above the shadowy hulls

And Spain go under and the shore
Of Africa the gilded sand
And evening vanish and no more
The low pale light across that land

Nor now the long light on the sea:

And here face downward in the sun
To feel how swift how secretly
The shadow of the night comes on . . .

"Not Marble nor the Gilded Monuments"

The praisers of women in their proud and beautiful poems,
Naming the grave mouth and the hair and the eyes,
Boasted those they loved should be forever remembered:
These were lies.

The words sound but the face in the Istrian sun is forgotten.
The poet speaks but to her dead ears no more.
The sleek throat is gone—and the breast that was troubled to
    listen:
Shadow from door.

Therefore I will not praise your knees nor your fine walking
Telling you men shall remember your name as long

As lips move or breath is spent or the iron of English
Rings from a tongue.

I shall say you were young and your arms straight, and your
    mouth scarlet:
I shall say you will die and none will remember you:
Your arms change, and none remember the swish of your
    garments,
Nor the click of your shoe.

Not with my hand's strength, not with difficult labor
Springing the obstinate words to the bones of your breast
And the stubborn line to your young stride and the breath to
    your breathing
And the beat to your haste
Shall I prevail on the hearts of unborn men to remember.

(What is a dead girl but a shadowy ghost
Or a dead man's voice but a distant and vain affirmation
Like dream words most)

Therefore I will not speak of the undying glory of women.
I will say you were young and straight and your skin fair
And you stood in the door and the sun was a shadow of
    leaves on your shoulders
And a leaf on your hair—

I will not speak of the famous beauty of dead women:
I will say the shape of a leaf lay once on your hair.
Till the world ends and the eyes are out and the mouths broken
Look! It is there!

EDNA ST. VINCENT MILLAY
(1892–1950)

"Oh, Sleep Forever in the Latmian Cave"

Oh, sleep forever in the Latmian cave,
Mortal Endymion, darling of the Moon!
Her silver garments by the senseless wave
Shouldered and dropped and on the shingle strewn,

Her fluttering hand against her forehead pressed,
Her scattered looks that trouble all the sky,
Her rapid footsteps running down the west—
Of all her altered state, oblivious lie!
Whom earthen you, by deathless lips adored,
Wild-eyed and stammering to the grasses thrust,
And deep into her crystal body poured
The hot and sorrowful sweetness of the dust:
Whereof she wanders mad, being all unfit
For mortal love, that might not die of it.

FROM *Sonnets*

XIX

What lips my lips have kissed, and where, and why,
I have forgotten, and what arms have lain
Under my head till morning; but the rain
Is full of ghosts to-night, that tap and sigh
Upon the glass and listen for reply,
And in my heart there stirs a quiet pain
For unremembered lads that not again
Will turn to me at midnight with a cry.
Thus in the winter stands the lonely tree,
Nor knows what birds have vanished one by one,
Yet knows its boughs more silent than before:
I cannot say what loves have come and gone,
I only know that summer sang in me
A little while, that in me sings no more.

WILFRED OWEN

(1893–1918)

Greater Love

Red lips are not so red
    As the stained stones kissed by the English dead.
Kindness of wooed and wooer
Seems shame to their love pure.
O Love, your eyes lose lure
    When I behold eyes blinded in my stead!

Your slender attitude
   Trembles not exquisite like limbs knife-skewed,
Rolling and rolling there
Where God seems not to care;
Till the fierce Love they bear
   Cramps them in death's extreme decrepitude.

Your voice sings not so soft,—
   Though even as wind murmuring through raftered loft,—
Your dear voice is not dear,
Gentle, and evening clear,
As theirs whom none now hear,
   Now earth has stopped the piteous mouths that coughed.

Heart, you were never hot,
   Nor large, nor full like hearts made great with shot;
And though your hand be pale,
Paler are all which trail
Your cross through flame and hail:
   Weep, you may weep, for you may touch them not.

The Show

My soul looked down from a vague height with Death,
As unremembering how I rose or why,
And saw a sad land, weak with sweats of dearth,
Gray, cratered like the moon with hollow woe,
And fitted with great pocks and scabs of plagues.

Across its beard, that horror of harsh wire,
There moved thin caterpillars, slowly uncoiled.
It seemed they pushed themselves to be as plugs
Of ditches, where they writhed and shrivelled, killed.

By them had slimy paths been trailed and scraped
Round myriad warts that might be little hills.

From gloom's last dregs these long-strung creatures crept
And vanished out of dawn down hidden holes.

(And smell came up from those foul openings
As out of mouths, or deep wounds deepening.)

On dithering feet upgathered, more and more,
Brown strings, towards strings of gray, with bristling spines,
All migrants from green fields, intent on mire.

Those that were gray, of more abundant spawns,
Ramped on the rest and ate them and were eaten.

I saw their bitten backs curve, loop, and straighten,
I watched those agonies curl, lift, and flatten.

Whereat, in terror what that sight might mean
I reeled and shivered earthward like a feather.

And Death fell with me, like a deepening moan.
And He, picking a manner of worm, which half had hid
Its bruises in the earth, but crawled no further,
Showed me its feet, the feet of many men,
And the fresh-severed head of it, my head.

Anthem for Doomed Youth

What passing-bells for these who die as cattle?
    Only the monstrous anger of the guns.
    Only the stuttering rifles' rapid rattle
Can patter out their hasty orisons.
No mockeries for them from prayers or bells,
    Nor any voice of mourning save the choirs,—
The shrill, demented choirs of wailing shells;
    And bugles calling for them from sad shires.

What candles may be held to speed them all?
    Not in the hands of boys, but in their eyes
Shall shine the holy glimmers of good-byes.
    The pallor of girls' brows shall be their pall;
Their flowers the tenderness of silent minds,
And each slow dusk a drawing-down of blinds.

ALDOUS HUXLEY

(1894–   )

Ninth Philosopher's Song

God's in His Heaven: He never issues
  (Wise man!) to visit this world of ours.
Unchecked the cancer gnaws our tissues,
  Stops to lick chops and then again devours.

Those find, who most delight to roam
  'Mid castles of remotest Spain,
That there's, thank Heaven, no place like home;
  So they set out upon their travels again.

Beauty for some provides escape,
  Who gains a happiness in eyeing
The gorgeous buttocks of the ape
  Or Autumn sunsets exquisitely dying.

And some to better worlds than this
  Mount up on wings as frail and misty
As passion's all-too-transient kiss
  (Though afterwards—oh, *omne animal triste!*)

But I, too rational by half
  To live but where I bodily am,
Can only do my best to laugh,
  Can only sip my misery dram by dram.

While happier mortals take to drink,
  A dolorous dipsomaniac,
Fuddled with grief I sit and think,
  Looking upon the bile when it is black.

Then brim the bowl with atrabilious liquor!
  We'll pledge our Empire vast across the flood:
For Blood, as all men know, than Water's thicker,
  But Water's wider, thank the Lord, than Blood.

Frascati's

Bubble-breasted swells the dome
Of this my spiritual home,
From whose nave the chandelier,
Schaffhausen frozen, tumbles sheer.
We in the round balcony sit,
Lean o'er and look into the pit
Where feed the human bears beneath,
Champing with their gilded teeth.
What negroid holiday makes free
With such priapic revelry?
What songs? What gongs? What nameless rites?
What gods like wooden stalagmites?
What steams of blood or kidney pie?
What blasts of Bantu melody?
Ragtime . . . But when the wearied Band
Swoons to a waltz, I take her hand,
And there we sit in blissful calm,
Quietly sweating palm to palm.

MARK VAN DOREN

(1894-   )

Epitaphs: For a Fickle Man

Two women had these words engraved:
The first and last of whom he tired.
One told the other, while they lived,
The thing between them he desired.
What now it is they do not know,
Or where he seeks it round the sun.
They only ask the wind to blow,
And that his will be ever done.

The End

I sing of ghosts and people under ground,
Or if they live, absented from green sound.
Not that I dote on death or being still;

But what men would is seldom what they will,
And there is farthest meaning in an end
Past the wild power of any word to mend.
The telltale stalk, and silence at the close,
Is most that may be read of man or rose.
Death is our outline, and a stillness seals
Even the living heart that loudest feels.
I am in love with joy, but find it wrapped
In a queer earth, at languages unapt;
With shadows sprinkled over, and no mind
To speak for them and prove they are designed.
I sing of men and shadows, and the light
That none the less shines under them by night.
Then lest I be dog enemy of day,
I add old women talking by the way;
And, not to grow insensible to noise,
Add gossip girls and western-throated boys.

EDWARD ESTLIN CUMMINGS

(1894–   )

Song

All in green went my love riding
on a great horse of gold
into the silver dawn.

four lean hounds crouched low and smiling
the merry deer ran before.

Fleeter be they than dappled dreams
the swift sweet deer
the red rare deer.

four red roebuck at a white water
the cruel bugle sang before.

Horn at hip went my love riding
riding the echo down
into the silver dawn.

four lean hounds crouched low and smiling
the level meadows ran before.

Softer be they than slippered sheep
the lean lithe deer
the fleet flown deer.

Four fleet does at a gold valley
the famished arrow sang before.

Bow at belt went my love riding
riding the mountain down
into the silver dawn.

four lean hounds crouched low and smiling
the sheer peaks ran before.

Paler be they than daunting death
the sleek slim deer
the tall tense deer.

Four tall stags at a green mountain
the lucky hunter sang before.

All in green went my love riding
on a great horse of gold
into the silver dawn.

four lean hounds crouched low and smiling
my heart fell dead before.

"the Cambridge ladies who live
in furnished souls"

the Cambridge ladies who live in furnished souls
are unbeautiful and have comfortable minds
(also, with the church's protestant blessings
daughters, unscented shapeless spirited)
they believe in Christ and Longfellow, both dead,

are invariably interested in so many things—
at the present writing one still finds
delighted fingers knitting for the is it Poles?
perhaps. While permanent faces coyly bandy
scandal of Mrs. N and Professor D
. . . the Cambridge ladies do not care, above
Cambridge if sometimes in its box of
sky lavender and cornerless, the
moon rattles like a fragment of angry candy

"what if a much of a which of a wind"

what if a much of a which of a wind
gives the truth to summer's lie;
bloodies with dizzying leaves the sun
and yanks immortal stars awry?
Blow king to beggar and queen to seem
(blow friend to fiend:blow space to time)
—when skies are hanged and oceans drowned,
the single secret will still be man

what if a keen of a lean wind flays
screaming hills with sleet and snow:
strangles valleys by ropes of thing
and stifles forests in white ago?
Blow hope to terror;blow seeing to blind
(blow pity to envy and soul to mind)
—whose hearts are mountains,roots are trees,
it's they shall cry hello to the spring

what if a dawn of a doom of a dream
bites this universe in two,
peels forever out of his grave
and sprinkles nowhere with me and you?
Blow soon to never and never to twice
(blow life to isn't:blow death to was)
—all nothing's only our hugest home;
the most who die,the more we live

HOWARD PHELPS PUTNAM

(1894–1948)

Hasbrouck and the Rose

Hasbrouck was there and so were Bill
And Smollet Smith the poet, and Ames was there.
After his thirteenth drink, the burning Smith,
Raising his fourteenth trembling in the air,
Said, "Drink with me, Bill, drink up to the Rose."
But Hasbrouck laughed like old men in a myth,
Inquiring, "Smollet, are you drunk? What rose?"
And Smollet said, "I drunk? It may be so;
Which comes from brooding on the flower, the flower
I mean toward which mad hour by hour
I travel brokenly; and I shall know,
With Hermes and the alchemists—but, hell,
What use is it talking that way to you?
Hard-boiled, unbroken egg, what can you care
For the enfolded passion of the Rose?"
Then Hasbrouck's voice rang like an icy bell:
"Arcane romantic flower, meaning what?
Do you know what it meant? Do I?
We do not know.
Unfolded pungent rose, the glowing bath
Of ecstasy and clear forgetfulness;
Closing and secret bud one might achieve
By long debauchery—
Except that I have eaten it, and so
There is no call for further lunacy.
In Springfield, Massachusetts, I devoured
The mystic, the improbable, the Rose.
For two nights and a day, rose and rosette,
And petal after petal and the heart,
I had my banquet by the beams
Of four electric stars which shone
Weakly into my room, for there,
Drowning their light and gleaming at my side,
Was the incarnate star
Whose body bore the stigma of the Rose.
And that is all I know about the flower;

I have eaten it—it has disappeared.
There is no Rose."

Young Smollet Smith let fall his glass; he said
"Oh Jesus, Hasbrouck, am I drunk or dead?"

ROBERT GRAVES

(1895–   )

The Bards

The bards falter in shame, their running verse
Stumbles, with marrow-bones the drunken diners
Pelt them for their delay.
It is a something fearful in the song
Plagues them—an unknown grief that like a churl
Goes common-place in cowskin
And bursts unheralded, crowing and coughing,
An unpilled holly-club twirled in his hand,
Into their many-shielded, samite-curtained,
Jewel-bright hall where twelve kings sit at chess
Over the white-bronze pieces and the gold;
And by a gross enchantment
Flails down the rafters and leads off the queens—
The wild-swan-breasted, the rose-ruddy-cheeked,
Raven-haired daughters of their admiration—
To stir his black pots and to bed on straw.

The Climate of Thought

The climate of thought has seldom been described.
It is no terror of Caucasian frost,
Nor yet that brooding Hindu heat
For which a loin-rag and a dish of rice
Suffice until the pestilent monsoon.
But, without winter, blood would run too thin;
Or, without summer, fires would burn too long.
In thought the seasons run concurrently.

Thought has a sea to gaze, not voyage on;
And hills, to rough the edge of the bland sky,
Not to be climbed in search of blander prospect;
Few birds, sufficient for such caterpillars
As are not fated to turn butterflies;
Few butterflies, sufficient for the flowers
That are the luxury of a full orchard;
Wind, sometimes, in the evening chimneys; rain
On the early morning roof, on sleepy sight;
Snow streaked upon the hilltop, feeding
The fond brook at the valley-head
That greens the valley and that parts the lips;
The sun, simple, like a country neighbour;
The moon, grand, not fanciful with clouds.

Counting the Beats

You, love, and I,
(He whispers) you and I,
And if no more than only you and I
What care you or I?

Counting the beats,
Counting the slow heart beats,
The bleeding to death of time in slow heart beats,
Wakeful they lie.

Cloudless day,
Night, and a cloudless day;
Yet the huge storm will burst upon their heads one day
From a bitter sky.

Where shall we be,
(She whispers) where shall we be,
When death strikes home, O where then shall we be
Who were you and I?

Not there but here,
(He whispers) only here,

As we are, here, together, now and here,
Always you and I.

Counting the beats,
Counting the slow heart beats,
The bleeding to death of time in slow heart beats,
Wakeful they lie.

EDMUND BLUNDEN
(1896–   )

Into the Salient

Sallows like heads in Polynesia,
With few and blood-stuck hairs,
Mud-layered cobble-stones,
Soldiers in smoky sheds, blackening uniforms and walls with
  their cookery;
Shell-holes in roofs, in roads,
Even in advertisements
Of bicycles and beer;
The Middle Ages gone to sleep, and woken up to this—
A salvo, four flat slamming explosions.
When you come out the wrong side of the ruin, you are
  facing Hill Sixty,
Hill Sixty is facing you.
You have been planted on the rim of a volcano,
Which will bring forth its fruit, at any second.
Better to be shielded from these facts;
There is a cellar, or was just now.
If the wreck isn't knocked in on us all,
We may emerge past the two Belgian policemen,
The owners' representatives,
Standing in their capes on the steps of the hollow estaminet
Open at all hours to all the winds
At the Poperinghe end of Ypres.
O if we do, if time will pass in time,
We will march
With rifles butt-upwards, in our teeth, any way you like,
Into seven days of country where you come out any door.

An Infantryman

Painfully writhed the few last weeds upon those houseless
uplands,
  Cleft pods had dropt their blackened seeds into the tram-
  pled clay,
Wind and rain were running loose, and icy flew the whiplash;
  Masked guns like autumn thunder drummed the outcast
  year away.

Hidden a hundred yards ahead with winter's blinding pas-
sion,
  The mule-track appeared half dead, even war's hot blood
  congealed;
The half-dug trenches brimmed like troughs, the camps lay
  slushed and empty,
  Unless those bitter whistlings proved Death's army in the
  field.

Over the captured ridge above the hurt battalion waited,
  And hardly had sense left to prove if ghost or living passed
From hole to hole with sunken eyes and slow ironic orders,
  While fiery fountains burst and clanged—and there your
  lot was cast.

Yet I saw your health and youth go brightening the vortex,
  The ghosts on guard, the storm uncouth were then no
  match for you;
You smiled, you sang, your courage rang, and to this day I
  hear it,
  Sunny as a May-day dance, along that spectral avenue.

STEPHEN VINCENT BENÉT

(1898–1943)

FROM *John Brown's Body*

This is the hidden place that hiders know.
This is where hiders go.
Step softly, the snow that falls here is different snow,

The rain has a different sting.
Step softly, step like a cloud, step softly as the least
Whisper of air against the beating wing,
And let your eyes be sealed
With two blue muscadines
Stolen from secret vines
Or you will never find, in the lost field,
The table spread, the signs of the hidden feast.

This is where hiders live.
This is the tentative
And outcast corner where hiders steal away
To bake their hedgehogs in a lump of clay,
To raise their crops and children wild and shy
And let the world go by
In accidental marches of armed wrath
That stumble blindly past the buried path.
Step softly, step like a whisper, but do not speak
Or you will never see
The furriness curled within the hollow tree,
The shadow-dance upon the wilderness creek.

This is the hiders' house.
This is the ark of pine-and-willow-boughs.
This is the quiet place.
You may call now, but let your call be sweet
As clover-honey strained through silver sieves
And delicate as the dust upon the moth
Or you will never find your fugitives.
Call once, and call again,
Then, if the lifted strain
Has the true color and substance of the wild,
You may perceive, if you have lucky eyes,
Something that ran away from being wise
And changed silk ribbons for a greener cloth,
Some budding-horned and deer-milk-suckled child,
Some lightness, moving toward you on light feet,
Some girl with indolent passion in her face.

HART CRANE

(1899–1932)

Voyages: II

—And yet this great wink of eternity,
Of rimless floods, unfettered leewardings,
Samite sheeted and processioned where
Her undinal vast belly moonward bends,
Laughing the wrapt inflections of our love;

Take this Sea, whose diapason knells
On scrolls of silver snowy sentences,
The sceptered terror of whose sessions rends
As her demeanors motion well or ill,
All but the pieties of lovers' hands.

And onward, as bells off San Salvador
Salute the crocus lusters of the stars,
In these poinsettia meadows of her tides,—
Adagios of islands, O my Prodigal,
Complete the dark confessions her veins spell.

Mark how her turning shoulders wind the hours,
And hasten while her penniless rich palms
Pass superscription of bent foam and wave,—
Hasten, while they are true,—sleep, death, desire,
Close round one instant in one floating flower.

Bind us in time, O seasons clear, and awe.
O minstrel galleons of Carib fire,
Bequeath us to no earthly shore until
Is answered in the vortex of our grave
The seal's wide spindrift gaze toward paradise.

FROM *The Bridge*

THE RIVER

Stick your patent name on a signboard
brother—all over—going west—young man
Tintex—Japalac—Certain-teed Overalls ads

and land sakes! under the new playbill ripped
in the guaranteed corner—see Bert Williams what?
Minstrels when you steal a chicken just
save me the wing for if it isn't
Erie it ain't for miles around a
Mazda—and the telegraphic night coming on Thomas
a Ediford—and whistling down the tracks
a headlight rushing with the sound—can you
imagine—while an EXPRESS makes time like
SCIENCE—COMMERCE and the HOLYGHOST
RADIO ROARS IN EVERY HOME WE HAVE THE NORTHPOLE
WALLSTREET AND VIRGINBIRTH WITHOUT STONES OR
WIRES OR EVEN RUNning brooks connecting ears
and no more sermons windows flashing roar
Breathtaking—as you like it . . . eh?

                              So the 20th Century—so
whizzed the Limited—roared by and left
three men, still hungry on the tracks, ploddingly
watching the tail lights wizen and converge, slip-
ping gimleted and neatly out of sight.

The last bear, shot drinking in the Dakotas,
Loped under wires that span the mountain stream.
Keen instruments, strung to a vast precision
Bind town to town and dream to ticking dream.
But some men take their liquor slow—and count
—Though they'll confess no rosary nor clue—
The river's minute by the far brook's year.
Under a world of whistles, wires and steam
Caboose-like they go ruminating through
Ohio, Indiana—blind baggage—
To Cheyenne tagging . . . Maybe Kalamazoo.

Time's renderings, time's blendings they construe
As final reckonings of fire and snow;
Strange bird-wit, like the elemental gist
Of unwalled winds they offer, singing low
My Old Kentucky Home and *Casey Jones,*
Some Sunny Day. I heard a road-gang chanting so.
And afterwards, who had a colt's eyes—one said,

"Jesus! O I remember watermelon days!" And sped
High in a cloud of merriment, recalled
"—And when my Aunt Sally Simpson smiled," he drawled—
"It was almost Louisiana, long ago."

"There's no place like Booneville though, Buddy,"
One said, excising a last burr from his vest,
"—For early trouting." Then peering in the can,
"—But I kept on the tracks." Possessed, resigned,
He trod the fire down pensively and grinned,
Spreading dry shingles of a beard. . . .

                                    Behind
My father's cannery works I used to see
Rail-squatters ranged in nomad raillery,
The ancient men—wifeless or runaway
Hobo-trekkers that forever search
An empire wilderness of freight and rails.
Each seemed a child, like me, on a loose perch,
Holding to childhood like some termless play.
John, Jake, or Charley, hopping the slow freight
—Memphis to Tallahassee—riding the rods,
Blind fists of nothing, humpty-dumpty clods.

Yet they touch something like a key perhaps.
From pole to pole across the hills, the states
—They know a body under the wide rain;
Youngsters with eyes like fjords, old reprobates
With racetrack jargon,—dotting immensity
They lurk across her, knowing her yonder breast
Snow-silvered, sumac-stained or smoky blue—
Is past the valley-sleepers, south or west.
—As I have trod the rumorous midnights, too,

And past the circuit of the lamp's thin flame
(O Nights that brought me to her body bare!)
Have dreamed beyond the print that bound her name.
Trains sounding the long blizzards out—I heard
Wail into distances I knew were hers.

Papooses crying on the wind's long mane
Screamed redskin dynasties that fled the brain,
—Dead echoes! But I knew her body there,
Time like a serpent down her shoulder, dark,
And space, an eaglet's wing, laid on her hair.

Under the Ozarks, domed by Iron Mountain,
The old gods of the rain lie wrapped in pools
Where eyeless fish curvet a sunken fountain
And re-descend with corn from querulous crows.
Such pilferings make up their timeless eatage,
Propitiate them for their timber torn
By iron, iron—always the iron dealt cleavage!
They doze now, below axe and powder horn.

And Pullman breakfasters glide glistening steel
From tunnel into field—iron strides the dew—
Straddles the hill, a dance of wheel on wheel.
You have a half-hour's wait at Siskiyou,
Or stay the night and take the next train through.
Southward, near Cairo passing, you can see
The Ohio merging,—borne down Tennessee;
And if it's summer and the sun's in dusk
Maybe the breeze will lift the River's musk
—As though the waters breathed that you might know
Memphis Johnny, Steamboat Bill, Missouri Joe.
Oh, lean from the window, if the train slows down,
As though you touched hands with some ancient clown,
—A little while gaze absently below
And hum *Deep River* with them while they go.

Yes, turn again and sniff once more—look see,
O Sheriff, Brakeman and Authority—
Hitch up your pants and crunch another quid,
For you, too, feed the River timelessly.
And few evade full measure of their fate;
Always they smile out eerily what they seem.
I could believe he joked at heaven's gate—
Dan Midland—jolted from the cold brake-beam.

Down, down—born pioneers in time's despite,
Grimed tributaries to an ancient flow—
They win no frontier by their wayward plight,
But drift in stillness, as from Jordan's brow.

You will not hear it as the sea; even stone
Is not more hushed by gravity . . . But slow,
As loth to take more tribute—sliding prone
Like one whose eyes were buried long ago

The River, spreading, flows—and spends your dream.
What are you, lost within this tideless spell?
You are your father's father, and the stream—
A liquid theme that floating niggers swell.

Damp tonnage and alluvial march of days—
Nights turbid, vascular with silted shale
And roots surrendered down of moraine clays:
The Mississippi drinks the farthest dale.

O quarrying passion, undertowed sunlight!
The basalt surface drags a jungle grace
Ocherous and lynx-barred in lengthening might;
Patience! and you shall reach the biding place!

Over De Soto's bones the freighted floors
Throb past the City storied of three thrones.
Down two more turns the Mississippi pours
(Anon tall ironsides up from salt lagoons)

And flows within itself, heaps itself free.
All fades but one thin skyline 'round . . . Ahead
No embrace opens but the stinging sea;
The River lifts itself from its long bed,

Poised wholly on its dream, a mustard glow
Tortured with history, its one will—flow!
—The passion spreads in wide tongues, choked and slow,
Meeting the Gulf, hosannas silently below.

ALLEN TATE

(1899-   )

Shadow and Shade

The shadow streamed into the wall—
The wall, break-shadow in the blast;
We lingered wordless while a tall
Shade enclouded the shadow's cast.

The torrent of the reaching shade
Broke shadow into all its parts,
What then had been of shadow made
Found exigence in fits and starts

Where nothing properly had name
Save that still element the air,
Burnt the sea of universal frame
In which impounded now we were:

I took her hand, I shut her eyes
And all her shadow clove with shade,
Shadow was crushed beyond disguise
But, being fear, was unafraid.

I asked fair shadow at my side:
What more shall fiery shade require?
We lay there in the immense tide
Of shade and shadowy desire

And saw the dusk assail the wall,
The black surge, mounting, crash the stone!
Companion of this lust, we fall,
I said, lest we should die alone.

Ode to the Confederate Dead

Row after row with strict impunity
The headstones yield their names to the element,
The wind whirrs without recollection;
In the riven troughs the splayed leaves

Pile up, of nature the casual sacrament
To the seasonal eternity of death,
Then driven by the fierce scrutiny
Of heaven to their business in the vast breath,
They sough the rumor of mortality.

Autumn is desolation in the plot
Of a thousand acres where these memories grow
From the inexhaustible bodies that are not
Dead, but feed the grass row after rich row.
Think of the autumns that have come and gone—
Ambitious November with the humors of the year,
With a particular zeal for every slab,
Staining the uncomfortable angels that rot
On the slabs, a wing chipped here, an arm there:
The brute curiosity of an angel's stare
Turns you, like them, to stone,
Transforms the heaving air,
Till plunged to a heavier world below
You shift your sea-space blindly
Heaving, turning like the blind crab.

> Dazed by the wind, only the wind
> The leaves flying, plunge

You know who have waited by the wall
The twilit certainty of an animal;
Those midnight restitutions of the blood
You know—the immitigable pines, the smoky frieze
Of the sky, the sudden call; you know the rage—
The cold pool left by the mounting flood—
The rage of Zeno and Parmenides.
You who have waited for the angry resolution
Of those desires that should be yours tomorrow,
You know the unimportant shrift of death
And praise the vision
And praise the arrogant circumstance
Of those who fall
Rank upon rank, hurried beyond decision—
Here by the sagging gate, stopped by the wall.

Seeing, seeing only the leaves
Flying, plunge and expire

Turn your eyes to the immoderate past
Turn to the inscrutable infantry rising
Demons out of the earth—they will not last.
Stonewall, Stonewall—and the sunken fields of hemp,
Shiloh, Antietam, Malvern Hill, Bull Run.
Lost in that orient of the thick and fast
You will curse the setting sun.

Cursing only the leaves crying
Like an old man in a storm

You hear the shout—the crazy hemlocks point
With troubled fingers to the silence which
Smothers you, a mummy, in time.
                                        The hound bitch
Toothless and dying, in a musty cellar
Hears the wind only.

                              Now that the salt of their blood
Stiffens the saltier oblivion of the sea,
Seals the malignant purity of the flood,
What shall we who count our days and bow
Our heads with a commercial woe
In the ribboned coats of grim felicity,
What shall we say of the bones, unclean,
Whose verdurous anonymity will grow?
The ragged arms, the ragged heads and eyes
Lost in these acres of the insane green?
The gray lean spiders come, they come and go;
In a tangle of willows without light
The singular screech-owl's bright
Invisible lyric seeds the mind
With the furious murmur of their chivalry.

We shall say only, the leaves
Flying, plunge and expire

We shall say only, the leaves whispering
In the improbable mist of nightfall
That flies on multiple wing:
Night is the beginning and the end
And in between the ends of distraction
Waits mute speculation, the patient curse
That stones the eyes, or like the jaguar leaps
For his own image in a jungle pool, his victim.

What shall we say who have knowledge
Carried to the heart? Shall we take the act
To the grave? Shall we, more hopeful, set up the grave
In the house? The ravenous grave?

                              Leave now
The shut gate and the decomposing wall:
The gentle serpent, green in the mulberry bush,
Riots with his tongue through the hush—
Sentinel of the grave who counts us all!

LÉONIE ADAMS

(1899-   )

Country Summer

Now the rich cherry, whose sleek wood,
And top with silver petals traced
Like a strict box its gems encased,
Has spilt from out that cunning lid,
All in an innocent green round,
Those melting rubies which it hid;
With moss ripe-strawberry-encrusted,
So birds get half, and minds lapse merry
To taste the deep-red lark's-bite berry,
And blackcap-bloom is yellow-dusted.

The wren that thieved it in the eaves
A trailer of the rose could catch
To her poor droopy sloven thatch,
And side by side with the wren's brood—
O lovely time of beggars' luck—

Opens the quaint and hairy bud;
And full and golden is the yield
Of cows that never have to house,
But all night nibble under boughs,
Or cool their sides in the moist field.

Into the rooms flow meadow airs,
The warm farm baking smell's blown round.
Inside and out, and sky and ground
Are much the same; the wishing star,
Hesperus, kind and early born,
Is risen only finger-far;
All stars stand close in summer air,
And tremble, and look mild as amber;
When wicks are lighted in the chamber,
They are like stars which settled there.

Now straightening from the flowery hay,
Down the still light the mowers look,
Or turn, because their dreaming shook,
And they waked half to other days,
When left alone in yellow stubble,
The rusty-coated mare would graze.
Yet thick the lazy dreams are born,
Another thought can come to mind,
But like the shivering of the wind,
Morning and evening in the corn.

SACHEVERELL SITWELL

(1900-   )

Variation on a Theme by John Lyly

What mournful metamorphosis
Changed my days: mocked time that flies:
My life, a beating clock that is,
Turning to endless song that dies:
So while I sigh here as a reed,
I, dying, live, that lived, indeed?

The hills' green tumbling fields I climbed
For hollow music from the shore,
That with the cooling wind's voice rhymed,
Both mingling through the wood's green core;
Till leaves and branches both do sing
With wind and water echoing.

One day I trod the river bank
And sang into the gentle wind,
The wood god tangled, wet and dank,
Leaped through the leaves and came behind;
He ran with goat's feet, chasing me,
Until I fell back wearily.

My heart, that beating clock, stopped dead,
And I was changed into a brake;
My limbs that cheated him, my head,
All turned to reed that wind can shake;
So do I mock time, blowing here;
One winter's sighs make not a year.

He comes and cuts himself a quill,
To make my image with his breath;
He tries at mine, his lips, to fill,
But music mocks him like my death;
No sooner a shrill note he blows,
Than it has fled, as water flows.

And so this ghost of me escapes,
It flies from him each time he plays;
And I shall never feel his rapes,
Till music in a reed pipe stays;
Till then, he'll find me still a reed,
Though sighing at his breath, indeed.

KENNETH SLESSOR

(1901–   )

Metempsychosis

Suddenly to become John Benbow, walking down William
    Street
With a tin trunk and a five-pound note, looking for a place
    to eat,
And a peajacket the colour of a shark's behind
That a Jew might buy in the morning . . .

To fry potatoes (God save us!) if you feel inclined,
Or to kiss the landlady's daughter, and no one mind,
In a peel-paper bedroom with a whistling jet
And a picture of the Holy Virgin . . .

Wake in a shaggy bale of blankets with a fished-up cigarette,
Picking over "Turfbird's Tattle" for a Sunday morning bet,
With a bottle in the wardrobe easy to reach
And a blast of onions from the landing . . .

Tattooed with foreign ladies' tokens, a heart and dagger
    each,
In places that make the delicate female inquirer screech,
And over a chest smoky with gunpowder-blue—
Behold!—a mermaid piping through a coach-horn!

Banjo-playing, firing off guns, and other momentous things
    to do,
Such as blowing through peashooters at hawkers to improve
    the view—

Suddenly paid-off and forgotten in Woolloomooloo . . .

Suddenly to become John Benbow. . . .

ROY CAMPBELL

(1902–1957)

The Zebras

From the dark woods that breathe of fallen showers,
Harnessed with level rays in golden reins,
The zebras draw the dawn across the plains
Wading knee-deep among the scarlet flowers.
The sunlight, zithering their flanks with fire,
Flashes between the shadows as they pass
Barred with electric tremors through the grass
Like wind along the gold strings of a lyre.
Into the flushed air snorting rosy plumes
That smoulder round their feet in drifting fumes,
With dove-like voices call the distant fillies,
While round the herds the stallion wheels his flight,
Engine of beauty volted with delight,
To roll his mare among the trampled lilies.

FROM *Talking Bronco*

THE VOLUNTEER'S REPLY TO THE POET
("WILL IT BE SO AGAIN?")

. . . So the soldier replied to the Poet,
Oh yes! it will all be the same,
But a bloody sight worse, and you know it
Since you have a hand in the game:
And you'll be the first in the racket
To sell us a similar dope,
Wrapped up in a rosier packet,
But noosed with as cunning a rope.
You coin us the catchwords and phrases
For which to be slaughtered; and then,
While thousands are blasted to blazes,
Sit picking your nose with your pen.
We know what you're bursting to tell us,
By heart. It is all very fine.
We must swallow the bait that you sell us
And pay for your Hook and your Line.
But his pride for a soldier suffices

Since someone must carry the can;
In war, or depression, or crisis,
It's what you expect of a man.
But when we have come to the Isthmus
That bridges the Slump to the War,
We shall contact a new Father Christmas
Like the one we contacted before,
Deploring the one he replaces
Like you do (it's part of the show!)
But with those same mincing grimaces
And that mealy old kisser we know!
And he'll patent a cheap cornucopia
For all that our purse can afford,
And rent us a flat in Utopia
With dreams for our lodging and board.
And we'll hand in our Ammo and Guns
As we handed them in once before,
And we'll lock them up safe; till our sons
Are conscripted for Freedom once more.
We can die for our faith by the million
And laugh at our bruises and scars,
But hush! for the Poet-Civilian
Is weeping, between the cigars.
Mellifluous, sweeter than Cadbury's,
The M.O.I. Nightingale (Hush!)
Is lining his pockets with Bradburies
So his feelings come out with a rush,
For our woes are the cash in his kitty
When his voice he so kindly devotes
In sentiment, pathos, and pity,
To bringing huge lumps to our throats
Of our widows, and sweethearts, and trollops,
Since it sells like hot cakes to the town
As he doles out the Goitre in dollops
And the public is gulping it down.
Oh well may he weep for the soldier,
Who weeps at a guinea a tear,
For although his invention gets mouldier,
It keeps him his job in the rear.
When my Mrs. the organ is wheeling
And my adenoids wheeze to the sky,

He will publish the hunger I'm feeling
And rake in his cheque with a sigh:
And when with a trayful of matches
And laces, you hawk in the street,
O comrades, in tatters and patches,
Rejoice! since we're in for a treat:
For when we have died in the gutter
To safeguard his income and state,
Be sure that the Poet will utter
Some beautiful thoughts on our Fate!

CECIL DAY LEWIS

(1904–   )

FROM *From Feathers to Iron*

XIV

Now the full-throated daffodils,
Our trumpeters in gold,
Call resurrection from the ground
And bid the year be bold.

To-day the almond tree turns pink,
The first flush of the spring;
Winds loll and gossip through the town
Her secret whispering.

Now too the bird must try his voice
Upon the morning air;
Down drowsy avenues he cries
A novel great affair.

He tells of royalty to be;
How with her train of rose
Summer to coronation comes
Through waving wild hedgerows.

To-day crowds quicken in a street,
The fish leaps in the flood:
Look there, gasometer rises,
And here bough swells to bud.

For our love's luck, our stowaway,
Stretches in his cabin;
Our youngster joy barely conceived
Shows up beneath the skin.

Our joy was but a gusty thing
Without sinew or wit,
An infant flyaway; but now
We make a man of it.

PHYLLIS McGINLEY

(1905–   )

Midcentury Love Letter

Stay near me. Speak my name. Oh, do not wander
By a thought's span, heart's impulse, from the light
We kindle here. You are my sole defender
(As I am yours) in this precipitous night,
Which over earth, till common landmarks alter,
Is falling, without stars, and bitter cold.
We two have but our burning selves for shelter.
Huddle against me. Give me your hand to hold.

So might two climbers lost in mountain weather
On a high slope and taken by the storm,
Desperate in the darkness, cling together
Under one cloak and breathe each other warm.
Stay near me. Spirit, perishable as bone,
In no such winter can survive alone.

WILLIAM EMPSON

(1906–   )

Missing Dates

Slowly the poison the whole blood stream fills.
It is not the effort nor the failure tires.
The waste remains, the waste remains and kills.

It is not your system or clear sight that mills
Down small to the consequence a life requires;
Slowly the poison the whole blood stream fills.

They bled an old dog dry yet the exchange rills
Of young dog blood gave but a month's desires;
The waste remains, the waste remains and kills.

It is the Chinese tombs and the slag hills
Usurp the soil, and not the soil retires.
Slowly the poison the whole blood stream fills.

Not to have fire is to be a skin that shrills.
The complete fire is death. From partial fires
The waste remains, the waste remains and kills.

It is the poems you have lost, the ills
From missing dates, at which the heart expires.
Slowly the poison the whole blood stream fills.
The waste remains, the waste remains and kills.

WYSTAN HUGH AUDEN

(1907-   )

"O for Doors to Be Open"

O for doors to be open and an invite with gilded edges
To dine with Lord Lobcock and Count Asthma on the plat-
    inum benches,
With the somersaults and fireworks, the roast and the smack-
    ing kisses—
        Cried the cripples to the silent statue,
        The six beggared cripples.

And Garbo's and Cleopatra's wits to go astraying,
In a feather ocean with me to go fishing and playing
Still jolly when the cock has burst himself with crowing—
        Cried the six cripples to the silent statue,
        The six beggared cripples.

And to stand on green turf among the craning yelling faces,
Dependent on the chestnut, the sable, the Arabian horses,
And me with a magic crystal to foresee their places—
　　　Cried the six cripples to the silent statue,
　　　The six beggared cripples.

And this square to be a deck, and these pigeons sails to rig
And to follow the delicious breeze like a tantony pig
To the shaded feverless islands where the melons are big—
　　　Cried the six cripples to the silent statue,
　　　The six beggared cripples.

And these shops to be turned to tulips in a garden bed,
And me with my stick to thrash each merchant dead
As he pokes from a flower his bald and wicked head—
　　　Cried the six cripples to the silent statue,
　　　The six beggared cripples.

And a hole in the bottom of heaven, and Peter and Paul
And each smug surprised saint like parachutes to fall,
And every one-legged beggar to have no legs at all—
　　　Cried the six cripples to the silent statue,
　　　The six beggared cripples.

Ballad: "O What Is That Sound . . ."

O what is that sound which so thrills the ear
　　Down in the valley drumming, drumming?
Only the scarlet soldiers, dear,
　　The soldiers coming.

O what is that light I see flashing so clear
　　Over the distance brightly, brightly?
Only the sun on their weapons, dear,
　　As they step lightly.

O what are they doing with all that gear;
　　What are they doing this morning, this morning?
Only the usual maneuvers, dear,
　　Or perhaps a warning.

O why have they left the road down there,
  Why are they suddenly wheeling, wheeling?
Perhaps a change in the orders, dear;
  Why are you kneeling?

O haven't they stopped for the doctor's care,
  Haven't they reined their horses, their horses?
Why, they are none of them wounded, dear,
  None of these forces.

O is it the parson they want, with white hair;
  Is it the parson, is it, is it?
No, they are passing his gateway, dear,
  Without a visit.

O it must be the farmer who lives so near,
  It must be the farmer, so cunning, so cunning?
They have passed the farm already, dear,
  And now they are running.

O where are you going? Stay with me here!
  Were the vows you swore me deceiving, deceiving?
No, I promised to love you, dear,
  But I must be leaving.

O it's broken the lock and splintered the door,
  O it's the gate where they're turning, turning;
Their feet are heavy on the floor
  And their eyes are burning.

In Memory of W. B. Yeats

I

He disappeared in the dead of winter:
The brooks were frozen, the airports almost deserted,
And snow disfigured the public statues;
The mercury sank in the mouth of the dying day.
O all the instruments agree
The day of his death was a dark cold day.

Far from his illness
The wolves ran on through the evergreen forests,
The peasant river was untempted by the fashionable quays;
By mourning tongues
The death of the poet was kept from his poems.

But for him it was his last afternoon as himself,
An afternoon of nurses and rumors;
The provinces of his body revolted,
The squares of his mind were empty,
Silence invaded the suburbs,
The current of his feeling failed: he became his admirers.

Now he is scattered among a hundred cities
And wholly given over to unfamiliar affections;
To find his happiness in another kind of wood
And be punished under a foreign code of conscience.
The words of a dead man
Are modified in the guts of the living.

But in the importance and noise of tomorrow
When the brokers are roaring like beasts on the floor of the
        Bourse,
And the poor have the sufferings to which they are fairly
        accustomed,
And each in the cell of himself is almost convinced of his
        freedom;
A few thousand will think of this day
As one thinks of a day when one did something slightly
        unusual.
O all the instruments agree
The day of his death was a dark cold day.

II

You were silly like us: your gift survived it all;
The parish of rich women, physical decay,
Yourself; mad Ireland hurt you into poetry.
Now Ireland has her madness and her weather still,
For poetry makes nothing happen: it survives
In the valley of its saying where executives
Would never want to tamper; it flows south

From ranches of isolation and the busy griefs,
Raw towns that we believe and die in; it survives,
A way of happening, a mouth.

III

Earth, receive an honored guest;
William Yeats is laid to rest:
Let the Irish vessel lie
Emptied of its poetry.

Time that is intolerant
Of the brave and innocent,
And indifferent in a week
To a beautiful physique,

Worships language and forgives
Everyone by whom it lives;
Pardons cowardice, conceit,
Lays its honours at their feet.

Time that with this strange excuse
Pardoned Kipling and his views,
And will pardon Paul Claudel,
Pardons him for writing well.

In the nightmare of the dark
All the dogs of Europe bark,
And the living nations wait,
Each sequestered in its hate;

Intellectual disgrace
Stares from every human face,
And the seas of pity lie
Locked and frozen in each eye.

Follow, poet, follow right
To the bottom of the night,
With your unconstraining voice
Still persuade us to rejoice;

With the farming of a verse
Make a vineyard of the curse,
Sing of human unsuccess
In a rapture of distress;

In the deserts of the heart
Let the healing fountain start,
In the prison of his days
Teach the free man how to praise.

LOUIS MacNEICE

(1907–   )

Aubade

Having bitten on life like a sharp apple
Or, playing it like a fish, been happy,

Having felt with fingers that the sky is blue,
What have we after that to look forward to?

Not the twilight of the gods but a precise dawn
Of sallow and grey bricks, and newsboys crying war.

Bagpipe Music

It's no go the merry-go-round, it's no go the rickshaw,
All we want is a limousine and a ticket for the peepshow.
Their knickers are made of crêpe-de-chine, their shoes are
          made of python,
Their halls are lined with tiger rugs and their walls with
          heads of bison.

John MacDonald found a corpse, put it under the sofa,
Waited till it came to life and hit it with a poker,
Sold its eyes for souvenirs, sold its blood for whiskey,
Kept its bones for dumb-bells to use when he was fifty.

It's no go the Yogi-Man, it's no go Blavatsky,
All we want is a bank balance and a bit of skirt in a taxi.

Annie MacDougall went to milk, caught her foot in the
    heather,
Woke to hear a dance record playing of Old Vienna.
It's no go your maidenheads, it's no go your culture,
All we want is a Dunlop tyre and the devil mend the punc-
    ture.

The Laird o'Phelps spent Hogmannay declaring he was
    sober;
Counted his feet to prove the fact and found he had one foot
    over.
Mrs. Carmichael had her fifth, looked at the job with re-
    pulsion,
Said to the midwife "Take it away; I'm through with over-
    production."

It's no go the gossip column, it's no go the Ceilidh,
All we want is a mother's help and a sugar-stick for the baby.

Willie Murray cut his thumb, couldn't count the damage,
Took the hide of an Ayrshire cow and used it for a bandage.
His brother caught three hundred cran when the seas were
    lavish,
Threw the bleeders back in the sea and went upon the
    parish.

It's no go the Herring Board, it's no go the Bible,
All we want is a packet of fags when our hands are idle.

It's no go the picture palace, it's no go the stadium,
It's no go the country cot with a pot of pink geraniums.
It's no go the Government grants, it's no go the elections,
Sit on your arse for fifty years and hang your hat on a
    pension.

It's no go my honey love, it's no go my poppet;
Work your hands from day to day, the winds will blow the
    profit.
The glass is falling hour by hour, the glass will fall for ever,
But if you break the bloody glass you won't hold up the
    weather.

KATHLEEN RAINE

(1908–   )

The Pythoness

I am that serpent-haunted cave
Whose navel breeds the fates of men.
All wisdom issues from a hole in the earth:
The gods form in my darkness, and dissolve again.

From my blind womb all kingdoms come,
And from my grave seven sleepers prophesy.
No babe unborn but wakens to my dream,
No lover but at last entombed in me shall lie.

I am that feared and longed-for burning place
Where man and phoenix are consumed away,
And from my low polluted bed arise
New sons, new suns, new skies.

THEODORE ROETHKE

(1908–   )

Big Wind

Where were the greenhouses going,
Lunging into the lashing
Wind driving water
So far down the river
All the faucets stopped?—
So we drained the manure-machine
For the steam plant,
Pumping the stale mixture
Into the rusty boilers,
Watching the pressure gauge
Waver over to red,
As the seams hissed
And the live steam
Drove to the far
End of the rose-house,
Where the worst wind was,
Creaking the cypress window-frames,

Cracking so much thin glass
We stayed all night,
Stuffing the holes with burlap;
But she rode it out,
That old rose-house,
She hove into the teeth of it,
The core and pith of that ugly storm,
Ploughing with her stiff prow,
Bucking into the wind-waves
That broke over the whole of her,
Flailing her sides with spray,
Flinging long strings of wet across the roof-top,
Finally veering, wearing themselves out, merely
Whistling thinly under the wind-vents;
She sailed into the calm morning,
Carrying her full cargo of roses.

STEPHEN SPENDER

(1909–   )

Thoughts during an Air Raid

Of course, the entire effort is to put myself
Outside the ordinary range
Of what are called statistics. A hundred are killed
In the outer suburbs. Well, well, I carry on.
So long as the great "I" is propped upon
This girdered bed which seems more like a hearse,
In the hotel bedroom with flowering wallpaper
Which rings in wreathes above, I can ignore
The pressure of those names under my fingers
Heavy and black as I rustle the paper,
The wireless wail in the lounge margin.
Yet supposing that a bomb should dive
Its nose right through this bed, with me upon it?
The thought is obscene. Still, there are many
To whom my death would be only a name,
One figure in a column. The essential is
That all the "I"s should remain separate
Propped up under flowers, and no one suffer
For his neighbour. Then horror is postponed

For everyone until it settles on him
And drags him to that incommunicable grief
Which is all mystery or nothing.

"I Think Continually of Those . . ."

I think continually of those who were truly great.
Who, from the womb, remembered the soul's history
Through corridors of light where the hours are suns,
Endless and singing. Whose lovely ambition
Was that their lips, still touched with fire,
Should tell of the Spirit, clothed from head to foot in song.
And who hoarded from the Spring branches
The desires falling across their bodies like blossoms.

What is precious is never to forget
The delight of the blood drawn from ageless springs
Breaking through rocks in worlds before our earth.
Never to deny its pleasure in the morning simple light
Nor its grave evening demand for love.
Never to allow gradually the traffic to smother
With noise and fog, the flowering of the Spirit.

Near the snow, near the sun, in the highest fields,
See how these names are fêted by the waving grass,
And by the streamers of white cloud
And whispers of wind in the listening sky.
The names of those who in their lives fought for life,
Who wore at their hearts the fire's centre.
Born of the sun, they travelled a short while toward the sun,
And left the vivid air signed with their honour.

FREDERIC PROKOSCH

(1909–   )

Eclogue

No one dies cleanly now,
All, all of us rot away:
No longer down the wood

Angelic shapes delight
The innocent and gay.
Poisonous things are spared,
The gifted are the sad
And solitude breeds hate.
Yellow is every bough,
No one dies cleanly now.

All, all of us rot away.
In broken barges drift
The warm and cinnamon-skinned
And in black Europe's wind
The ice-edged lanterns sway.
The carousels are silent,
The towns are torn by sea
And in their coiling streets
The dragon snares his prey
Till all of us rot away!

No longer down the wood
May the tall victor lead
The shy swan-breasted maid
Or generous pageants move.
The loved are sick of love,
Love is strangled with words:
Beauty sighs in her bed:
The faithful, calm and good
Follow the songs of birds
No longer down the wood.

Angelic shapes delight
Only the perpetual child.
The murderer plans his night
And the green hunter's horn
Drives the unwanted wild.
O mourn, willows, weep!
Till the clear spring return
And to the warming heart
The curious wonders creep;
A cry; a living sleep.

WILLIAM ROBERT RODGERS

(1909-   )

Neither Here nor There

In that land all is and nothing's ought;
No owners or notices, only birds;
No walls anywhere, only lean wire of words
Worming brokenly out from eaten thought;
No oats growing, only ankle-lace grass
Easing and not resenting the feet that pass;
No enormous beasts, only names of them;
No bones made, bans laid, or boons expected,
No contracts, entails, hereditaments,
Anything at all that might tie or hem.

In that land all's lackadaisical;
No lakes of coddled spawn, and no locked ponds
Of settled purpose, no netted fishes;
But only inkling streams and running fronds
Fritillaried with dreams, weedy with wishes;
No arrogant talk is heard, haggling phrase,
But undertones, and hesitance, and haze;
On clear days mountains of meaning are seen
Humped high on the horizon; no one goes
To con their meaning, no one cares or knows.

In that land all's flat, indifferent; there
Is neither springing house nor hanging tent,
No aims are entertained, and nothing is meant,
For there are no ends and no trends, no roads,
Only follow your nose to anywhere.
No one is born there, no one stays or dies,
For it is a timeless land, it lies
Between the act and the attrition, it
Marks off bound from rebound, make from break, tit
From tat, also today from tomorrow.
No Cause there comes to term, but each departs
Elsewhere to whelp its deeds, expel its darts;
There are no homecomings, of course, no good-byes
In that land, neither yearning nor scorning,
Though at night there is the smell of morning.

ELIZABETH BISHOP

(1911–   )

The Fish

I caught a tremendous fish
and held him beside the boat
half out of water, with my hook
fast in a corner of his mouth.
He didn't fight.
He hadn't fought at all.
He hung a grunting weight,
battered and venerable
and homely. Here and there
his brown skin hung in strips
like ancient wall-paper,
and its pattern of darker brown
was like wall-paper:
shapes like full-blown roses
stained and lost through age.
He was speckled with barnacles,
fine rosettes of lime,
and infested
with tiny white sea-lice,
and underneath two or three
rags of green weed hung down.
While his gills were breathing in
the terrible oxygen
—the frightening gills
fresh and crisp with blood,
that can cut so badly—
I thought of the coarse white flesh
packed in like feathers,
the big bones and the little bones,
the dramatic reds and blacks
of his shiny entrails,
and the pink swim-bladder
like a big peony.
I looked into his eyes
which were far larger than mine
but shallower, and yellowed,

the irises backed and packed
with tarnished tinfoil
seen through the lenses
of old scratched isinglass.
They shifted a little, but not
to return my stare.
—It was more like the tipping
of an object toward the light.
I admired his sullen face,
the mechanism of his jaw,
and then I saw
that from his lower lip
—if you could call it a lip—
grim, wet, and weapon-like,
hung five old pieces of fish-line,
or four and a wire leader
with the swivel still attached,
with all their five hooks
grown firmly in his mouth.
A green line, frayed at the end
where he broke it, two heavier lines,
and a fine black thread
still crimped from the strain and snap
when it broke and he got away.
Like medals with their ribbons
frayed and wavering,
a five-haired beard of wisdom
trailing from his aching jaw.
I stared and stared
and victory filled up
the little rented boat,
from the pool of bilge
where oil had spread a rainbow
around the rusted engine
to the bailer rusted orange,
the sun-cracked thwarts,
the oarlocks on their strings,
the gunnels—until everything
was rainbow, rainbow, rainbow!
And I let the fish go.

GEORGE BARKER

(1913-)

Sonnet to My Mother

Most near, most dear, most loved and most far,
Under the window where I often found her
Sitting as huge as Asia, seismic with laughter,
Gin and chicken helpless in her Irish hand,
Irresistible as Rabelais but most tender for
The lame dogs and hurt birds that surround her,—
She is a procession no one can follow after
But be like a little dog following a brass band.

She will not glance up at the bomber or condescend
To drop her gin and scuttle to a cellar,
But lean on the mahogany table like a mountain
Whom only faith can move, and so I send
O all my faith and all my love to tell her
That she will move from mourning into morning.

To Any Member of My Generation

What was it you remember?—the summer mornings
Down by the river at Richmond with a girl,
And as you kissed, clumsy in bathing costumes,
History guffawed in a rosebush. O what a warning—
If only we had known, if only we had known!
And when you looked in mirrors was this meaning
Plain as the pain in the centre of a pearl?
Horrible tomorrow in goddamning postures
Making absurd the past we cannot disown?

Whenever we kissed we cocked the future's rifles
And from our wildoat words, like dragons' teeth,
Death underfoot now arises. When we were gay
Dancing together in what we hoped was life,
Who was it in our arms but the whores of death
Whom we have found in our beds today, today?

DELMORE SCHWARTZ

(1913–   )

FROM *The Repetitive Heart*

III

All clowns are masked and all *personae*
Flow from choices; sad and gay, wise,
Moody and humorous are chosen faces,
And yet not so! For all are circumstances,
Given, like a tendency
To colds or like blond hair and wealth,
Or war and peace or gifts for mathematics,
Fall from the sky, rise from the ground, stick to us
In time, surround us: Socrates is mortal.

Gifts and choices! All men are masked,
And we are clowns who think to choose our faces
And we are taught in time of circumstances
And we have colds, blond hair and mathematics,
For we have gifts which interrupt our choices,
And all our choices grasp in Blind Man's Buff:
"My wife was very different, after marriage,"
"I practise law, but botany's my pleasure,"
Save postage stamps or photographs,
But save your soul! Only the past is immortal.

Decide to take a trip, read books of travel,
Go quickly! Even Socrates is mortal,
Mention the name of happiness: it is
Atlantis, Ultima Thule, or the limelight,
Cathay or Heaven. But go quickly
And remember: there are circumstances,
And he who chooses chooses what is given,
And he who chooses is ignorant of Choice,
—Choose love, for love is full of children,
Full of choices, children choosing
Botany, mathematics, law and love,
So full of choices! So full of children!
And the past is immortal, the future is inexhaustible!

KARL SHAPIRO

(1913–   )

Buick

As a sloop with a sweep of immaculate wing on her delicate
    spine
And a keel as steel as a root that holds in the sea as she
    leans,
Leaning and laughing, my warm-hearted beauty, you ride,
    you ride,
You tack on the curves with parabola speed and a kiss of
    good-bye,
Like a thoroughbred sloop, my new high-spirited spirit, my
    kiss.

As my foot suggests that you leap in the air with your hips
    of a girl,
My finger that praises your wheel and announces your voices
    of song,
Flouncing your skirts, you blueness of joy, you flirt of polite-
    ness,
You leap, you intelligence, essence of wheelness with silvery
    nose,
And your platinum clocks of excitement stir like the hairs of
    a fern.

But how alien you are from the booming belts of your birth
    and the smoke
Where you turned on the stinging lathes of Detroit and
    Lansing at night
And shrieked at the torch in your secret parts and the amo-
    rous tests,
But now with your eyes that enter the future of roads you
    forget;
You are all instinct with your phosphorous glow and your
    streaking hair.

And now when we stop it is not as the bird from the shell
    that I leave
Or the leathery pilot who steps from his bird with a sneer
    of delight,

And not as the ignorant beast do you squat and watch me
    depart,
But with exquisite breathing you smile, with satisfaction of
    love,
And I touch you again as you tick in the silence and settle
    in sleep.

HENRY REED

(1914–   )

Lessons of the War: Naming of Parts

Today we have naming of parts. Yesterday,
We had daily cleaning. And tomorrow morning,
We shall have what to do after firing. But today,
Today we have naming of parts. Japonica
Glistens like coral in all of the neighbouring gardens,
    And today we have naming of parts.

This is the lower sling swivel. And this
Is the upper sling swivel, whose use you will see,
When you are given your slings. And this is the piling swivel,
Which in your case you have not got. The branches
Hold in the gardens their silent, eloquent gestures,
    Which in our case we have not got.

This is the safety-catch, which is always released
With an easy flick of the thumb. And please do not let me
See anyone using his finger. You can do it quite easy
If you have any strength in your thumb. The blossoms
Are fragile and motionless, never letting anyone see
    Any of them using their finger.

And this you can see is the bolt. The purpose of this
Is to open the breech, as you see. We can slide it
Rapidly backwards and forwards: we call this
Easing the spring. And rapidly backwards and forwards
The early bees are assaulting and fumbling the flowers:
    They call it easing the Spring.

They call it easing the Spring: it is perfectly easy
If you have any strength in your thumb: like the bolt,
And the breech, and the cocking-piece, and the point of
      balance,
Which in our case we have not got; and the almond-blossom
Silent in all of the gardens and the bees going backwards
      and forwards,
    For today we have naming of parts.

DYLAN THOMAS

(1914–1953)

"The Force That through the Green Fuse . . ."

The force that through the green fuse drives the flower
Drives my green age; that blasts the roots of trees
Is my destroyer.
And I am dumb to tell the crooked rose
My youth is bent by the same wintry fever.

The force that drives the water through the rocks
Drives my red blood; that dries the mouthing streams
Turns mine to wax.
And I am dumb to mouth unto my veins
How at the mountain spring the same mouth sucks.

The hand that whirls the water in the pool
Stirs the quicksand; that ropes the blowing wind
Hauls my shroud sail.
And I am dumb to tell the hanging man
How of my clay is made the hangman's lime.

The lips of time leech to the fountain head;
Love drips and gathers, but the fallen blood
Shall calm her sores.
And I am dumb to tell a weather's wind
How time has ticked a heaven round the stars.

And I am dumb to tell the lover's tomb
How at my sheet goes the same crooked worm.

"Light Breaks Where No Sun Shines"

Light breaks where no sun shines;
Where no sea runs, the waters of the heart
Push in their tides;
And, broken ghosts with glowworms in their heads,
The things of light
File through the flesh where no flesh decks the bones.

A candle in the thighs
Warms youth and seed and burns the seeds of age;
Where no seed stirs,
The fruit of man unwrinkles in the stars,
Bright as a fig;
Where no wax is, the candle shows its hairs.

Dawn breaks behind the eyes;
From poles of skull and toe the windy blood
Slides like a sea;
Nor fenced, nor staked, the gushers of the sky
Spout to the rod
Divining in a smile the oil of tears.

Night in the sockets rounds,
Like some pitch moon, the limit of the globes;
Day lights the bone;
Where no cold is, the skinning gales unpin
The winter's robes;
The film of spring is hanging from the lids.

Light breaks on secret lots,
On tips of thought where thoughts smell in the rain;
When logics die,
The secret of the soil grows through the eye,
And blood jumps in the sun;
Above the waste allotments the dawn halts.

Fern Hill

Now as I was young and easy under the apple boughs
About the lilting house and happy as the grass was green,
  The night above the dingle starry,
   Time let me hail and climb
  Golden in the heydays of his eyes,
And honored among wagons I was prince of the apple towns
And once below a time I lordly had the trees and leaves
   Trail with daisies and barley
  Down the rivers of the windfall light.

And as I was green and carefree, famous among the barns
About the happy yard and singing as the farm was home,
  In the sun that is young once only,
   Time let me play and be
  Golden in the mercy of his means,
And green and golden I was huntsman and herdsman, the
    calves
Sang to my horn, the foxes on the hills barked clear and cold,
   And the sabbath rang slowly
  In the pebbles of the holy streams.

All the sun long it was running, it was lovely, the hay
Fields high as the house, the tunes from the chimneys, it was
    air
  And playing, lovely and watery
   And fire green as grass.
  And nightly under the simple stars
As I rode to sleep the owls were bearing the farm away,
All the moon long I heard, blessed among stables, the night-
    jars
  Flying with the ricks, and horses
   Flashing into the dark.

And then to awake, and the farm, like a wanderer white
With the dew, come back, the cock on his shoulder: it was
    all
  Shining, it was Adam and maiden,
   The sky gathered again
  And the sun grew round that very day.
So it must have been after the birth of the simple light

In the first, spinning place, the spellbound horses walking
    warm
      Out of the whinnying green stable
        On to the fields of praise.

And honored among foxes and pheasants by the gay house
Under the new made clouds and happy as the heart was long,
      In the sun born over and over,
        I ran my heedless ways,
      My wishes raced through the house high hay
And nothing I cared, at my sky blue trades, that time allows
In all his tuneful turning so few and such morning songs
      Before the children green and golden
        Follow him out of grace,

Nothing I cared, in the lamb white days, that time would
    take me
Up to the swallow thronged loft by the shadow of my hand,
      In the moon that is always rising,
        Nor that riding to sleep
      I should hear him fly with the high fields
And wake to the farm forever fled from the childless land.
Oh as I was young and easy in the mercy of his means,
      Time held me green and dying
      Though I sang in my chains like the sea.

Do Not Go Gentle into That Good Night

    Do not go gentle into that good night,
    Old age should burn and rave at close of day;
    Rage, rage against the dying of the light.

    Though wise men at their end know dark is right,
    Because their words had forked no lightning they
    Do not go gentle into that good night.

    Good men, the last wave by, crying how bright
    Their frail deeds might have danced in a green bay,
    Rage, rage against the dying of the light.

Wild men who caught and sang the sun in flight,
And learn, too late, they grieved it on its way,
Do not go gentle into that good night.

Grave men, near death, who see with blinding sight
Blind eyes could blaze like meteors and be gay,
Rage, rage against the dying of the light.

And you, my father, there on the sad height,
Curse, bless, me now with your fierce tears, I pray.
Do not go gentle into that good night.
Rage, rage against the dying of the light.

ROBERT LOWELL

(1917–   )

The Quaker Graveyard in Nantucket

(FOR WARREN WINSLOW, DEAD AT SEA)

*Let man have dominion over the fishes of the sea
and the fowls of the air and the beasts and the whole
earth, and every creeping creature that moveth upon
the earth.*

I

A brackish reach of shoal off Madaket,—
The sea was still breaking violently and night
Had steamed into our North Atlantic Fleet,
When the drowned sailor clutched the drag-net. Light
Flashed from his matted head and marble feet,
He grappled at the net
With the coiled, hurdling muscles of his thighs:
The corpse was bloodless, a botch of reds and whites,
Its open, staring eyes
Were lustreless dead-lights
Or cabin-windows on a stranded hulk
Heavy with sand. We weight the body, close
Its eyes and heave it seaward whence it came,
Where the heel-headed dogfish barks its nose
On Ahab's void and forehead; and the name
Is blocked in yellow chalk.

Sailors, who pitch this portent at the sea
Where dreadnoughts shall confess
Its hell-bent deity,
When you are powerless
To sand-bag this Atlantic bulwark, faced
By the earth-shaker, green, unwearied, chaste
In his steel scales: ask for no Orphean lute
To pluck life back. The guns of the steeled fleet
Recoil and then repeat
The hoarse salute.

II

Whenever winds are moving and their breath
Heaves at the roped-in bulwarks of this pier,
The terns and sea-gulls tremble at your death
In these home waters. Sailor, can you hear
The Pequod's sea wings, beating landward, fall
Headlong and break on our Atlantic wall
Off 'Sconset, where the yawing S-boats splash
The bellbuoy, with ballooning spinnakers,
As the entangled, screeching mainsheet clears
The blocks: off Madaket, where lubbers lash
The heavy surf and throw their long lead squids
For blue-fish? Sea-gulls blink their heavy lids
Seaward. The winds' wings beat upon the stones,
Cousin, and scream for you and the claws rush
At the sea's throat and wring it in the slush
Of this old Quaker graveyard where the bones
Cry out in the long night for the hurt beast
Bobbing by Ahab's whaleboats in the East.

III

All you recovered from Poseidon died
With you, my cousin, and the harrowed brine
Is fruitless on the blue beard of the god,
Stretching beyond us to the castles in Spain,
Nantucket's westward haven. To Cape Cod
Guns, cradled on the tide,
Blast the eelgrass about a waterclock

Of bilge and backwash, roil the salt and sand
Lashing earth's scaffold, rock
Our warships in the hand
Of the great God, where time's contrition blues
Whatever it was these Quaker sailors lost
In the mad scramble of their lives. They died
When time was open-eyed,
Wooden and childish; only bones abide
There, in the nowhere, where their boats were tossed
Sky-high, where mariners had fabled news
Of Is, the whited monster. What it cost
Them is their secret. In the sperm-whale's slick
I see the Quakers drown and hear their cry:
"If God himself had not been on our side,
If God himself had not been on our side,
When the Atlantic rose against us, why,
Then it had swallowed us up quick."

IV

This is the end of the whaleroad and the whale
Who spewed Nantucket bones on the thrashed swell
And stirred the troubled waters to whirlpools
To send the Pequod packing off to hell:
This is the end of them, three-quarters fools,
Snatching at straws to sail
Seaward and seaward on the turntail whale,
Spouting out blood and water as it rolls,
Sick as a dog to these Atlantic shoals:
Clamavimus, O depths. Let the sea-gulls wail

For water, for the deep where the high tide
Mutters to its hurt self, mutters and ebbs.
Waves wallow in their wash, go out and out,
Leave only the death-rattle of the crabs,
The beach increasing, its enormous snout
Sucking the ocean's side.
This is the end of running on the waves;
We are poured out like water. Who will dance
The mast-lashed master of Leviathans
Up from this field of Quakers in their unstoned graves?

V

When the whale's viscera go and the roll
Of its corruption overruns this world
Beyond tree-swept Nantucket and Wood's Hole
And Martha's Vineyard, Sailor, will your sword
Whistle and fall and sink into the fat?
In the great ash-pit of Jehoshaphat
The bones cry for the blood of the white whale,
The fat flukes arch and whack about its ears,
The death-lance churns into the sanctuary, tears
The gun-blue swingle, heaving like a flail,
And hacks the coiling life out: it works and drags
And rips the sperm-whale's midriff into rags,
Gobbets of blubber spill to wind and weather,
Sailor, and gulls go round the stoven timbers
Where the morning stars sing out together
And thunder shakes the white surf and dismembers
The red flag hammered in the mast-head. Hide
Our steel, Jonas Messias, in Thy side.

VI

OUR LADY OF WALSINGHAM

There once the penitents took off their shoes
And then walked barefoot the remaining mile;
And the small trees, a stream and hedgerows file
Slowly along the munching English lane,
Like cows at the old shrine, until you lose
Track of your dragging pain.
The stream flows down under the druid tree,
Shiloah's whirlpools gurgle and make glad
The castle of God. Sailor, you were glad
And whistled Sion by that stream. But see:

Our Lady, too small for her canopy,
Sits near the altar. There's no comeliness
At all or charm in that expressionless
Face with its heavy eyelids. As before,
This face, for centuries a memory,
Non est species, neque decor,

Expressionless, expresses God: it goes
Past castled Sion. She knows what God knows,
Not Calvary's Cross nor crib at Bethlehem
Now, and the world shall come to Walsingham.

VII

The empty winds are creaking and the oak
Splatters and splatters on the cenotaph,
The boughs are trembling and a gaff
Bobs on the untimely stroke
Of the greased wash exploding on a shoal-bell
In the old mouth of the Atlantic. It's well;
Atlantic, you are fouled with the blue sailors,
Sea-monsters, upward angel, downward fish:
Unmarried and corroding, spare of flesh,
Mart once of supercilious, wing'd clippers;
Atlantic, where your bell-trap guts its spoil
You could cut the brackish winds with a knife
Here in Nantucket, and cast up the time
When the Lord God formed man from the sea's slime
And breathed into his face the breath of life,
And blue-lung'd combers lumbered to the kill.
The Lord survives the rainbow of his will.

RICHARD WILBUR

(1921–   )

After the Last Bulletins

After the last bulletins the windows darken
And the whole city founders easily and deep,
Sliding on all its pillows
To the thronged Atlantis of personal sleep,

And the wind rises. The wind rises and bowls
The day's litter of news in the alleys. Trash
Tears itself on the railings,
Soars and falls with a soft crash,

Tumbles and soars again. Unruly flights
Scamper the park, and taking a statue for dead
Strike at positive eyes,
Batter and flap the stolid head

And scratch the noble name. In empty lots
Our journals spiral in a fierce noyade
Of all we thought to think,
Or caught in corners cramp and wad

And twist our words. And some from gutters flail
Their tatters at the tired patrolman's feet,
Like all that fisted snow
That cried beside his long retreat

Damn you! damn you! to the emperor's horse's heels.
Oh none too soon through the air white and dry
Will the clear announcer's voice
Beat like a dove, and you and I

From the heart's anarch and responsible town
Rise by the subway-mouth to life again,
Bearing the morning papers,
And cross the park where saintlike men,

White and absorbed, with stick and bag remove
The litter of the night, and footsteps rouse
With confident morning sound
The songbirds in the public boughs.

INDEX OF POETS

*(Pages 1–654 are in Volume One; pages 655–1253
in Volume Two.)*

INDEX OF FIRST LINES AND TITLES

(Pages 1–654 are in Volume One; pages 655–1253
in Volume Two.)

ACKNOWLEDGMENTS

The editor wishes to express his gratitude for permission to reprint selections from the works of those authors listed below. The listing shows the volume or volumes from which the selections from each poet's work were taken, and the individuals or firms from whom permission was obtained. When dates are given, they refer to United States copyright registration, not necessarily the dates of the volumes mentioned. Permissions for poems that have been added to the Revised, Mid-Century Edition are acknowledged on pages 1296–1297.

ORIGINAL EDITION

ABERCROMBIE, LASCELLES: Poems. Oxford University Press, Oxford.

A.E. (GEORGE WILLIAM RUSSELL): Collected Poems. 1926. The Macmillan Company, N.Y.

AIKEN, CONRAD: Time in the Rock. Copr. 1932, 1933, 1934, 1935, 1936 by Conrad Aiken. Charles Scribner's Sons, N.Y.

AUDEN, W. H.: "Look, Stranger!" from On This Island, 1937. Random House, Inc., N.Y. Also from Look, Stranger! Faber & Faber Ltd, London.

BACON, LEONARD: Bullinger Bound and Other Poems. Copr. 1938 by Leonard Bacon. Harper & Brothers, N.Y.

BELLOC, HILAIRE: Sonnets and Verse. Sheed & Ward, Inc., N.Y.

BENÉT, STEPHEN VINCENT: John Brown's Body. Copr. 1927, 1928 by Stephen Vincent Benét. Published by Farrar & Rinehart, N.Y.

BINYON, LAURENCE: Collected Poems. 1922. The Macmillan Company, N.Y.

BLUNDEN, EDMUND: Poems, 1914–1930. A. D. Peters, agent, London.

BRIDGES, ROBERT: Poems. Oxford University Press, Oxford.

BROOKE, RUPERT: The Collected Poems of Rupert Brooke. Copr. 1915 by Dodd, Mead & Company, Inc., N.Y. Complete Poems. McClelland & Stewart Ltd., Toronto. The author's representative and Sidgwick & Jackson Ltd., London.

CAMPBELL, ROY: Adamastor. Faber & Faber Ltd, London.

CHAPLIN, RALPH: Bars and Shadows. 1921. Nellie Seeds Nearing, Ridgewood, N.J., and the author.

CHESTERTON, G. K.: The Collected Poems of G. K. Chesterton. Copr. 1911, 1932 by Dodd, Mead & Company, Inc., N.Y. The executrix and Methuen & Co., Ltd., London.

CLOUGH, ARTHUR HUGH: Last four lines of "The Latest Decalogue" from Oxford Anthology of English Poetry. 1935. Oxford University Press, N.Y.

COLUM, PADRAIC: Wild Earth. 1916. The Macmillan Company, N.Y.

CUMMINGS, E. E.: Collected Poems. Copr. 1923, 1925, 1931, 1935, 1938 by E. E. Cummings. Published by Harcourt, Brace and Company, Inc., N.Y.

DAVIDSON, JOHN: "In Romney Marsh" from Ballads and Songs; "Waiting" from Fleet Street Eclogues. John Lane The Bodley Head Ltd, London. Both in Fleet Street and Other Poems. Modern Library, N.Y.

DAVIES, WILLIAM HENRY: The Poems of W. H. Davies. Oxford University Press, N.Y. Jonathan Cape Ltd, London.

DE LA MARE, WALTER: Collected Poems. 1941. Henry Holt and Company, N.Y. Faber & Faber Ltd, London.

DICKINSON, EMILY: The Poems of Emily Dickinson, edited by Martha Dickinson Bianchi and Alfred Leete Hampson. Reprinted

M

ACKNOWLEDGMENTS [1294]

by permission of Little, Brown & Company, Boston.

DOUGLAS, LORD ALFRED: *Sonnets and Lyrics.* The author.

ELIOT, T. S.: *Collected Poems of T. S. Eliot.* Copr. 1934, 1936 by Harcourt, Brace and Company, Inc., N.Y. Faber & Faber Ltd, London.

FORD, FORD MADOX: *Collected Poems of Ford Madox Ford.* 1936. Oxford University Press, N.Y.

FROST, ROBERT: *Collected Poems.* 1939, 1941. Henry Holt & Company, N.Y.

HARDY, THOMAS: *Collected Poems.* 1925. The Macmillan Company, N.Y.

H.D. (HILDA DOOLITTLE): *Collected Poems of H.D.* 1925. Liveright Publishing Corp., N.Y.

HODGSON, RALPH: *Poems.* 1917. The Macmillan Company, N.Y.

HOUSMAN, A. E.: "I to my perils" and "For my funeral" from *More Poems.* 1936. Leland Hayward, Inc., N.Y. "Epitaph on an Army of Mercenaries" from *Last Poems.* 1922. All others from *A Shropshire Lad,* Authorized Edition, 1924. Henry Holt and Company, N.Y.

HUXLEY, ALDOUS: *Leda.* Copr. 1929 by Aldous Huxley. Harper & Brothers, N.Y. The Macmillan Company Ltd., Toronto. The author and Chatto & Windus, London.

JEFFERS, ROBINSON: "Shine, Perishing Republic" from *Roan Stallion, Tamar.* 1925. "Signpost" from *Solstice and Other Poems.* 1935. Random House, Inc., N.Y.

JOYCE, JAMES: *Collected Poems.* 1918, 1927. The Viking Press, Inc., N.Y.

KIPLING, RUDYARD: All from *Rudyard Kipling's Verse, Inclusive Edition, 1885-1932.* Copr. 1891-1932. Reprinted by permission from Doubleday, Doran and Company, Inc., N.Y. "Recessional" from *The Five Nations;* all others from *Barrack Room*
Ballads. The Macmillan Company Ltd., London and Toronto.

LAWRENCE, D. H.: "The Ship of Death" and "Bavarian Gentians" from *Last Poems.* Copr. 1933 by Frieda Lawrence. All others from *Collected Poems.* 1929. The Viking Press, Inc., N.Y. Mrs. Frieda Lawrence and William Heinemann, Ltd., London.

LEWIS, C. DAY: *Collected Poems.* 1935. Random House, Inc., N.Y. From *Feathers to Iron.* Hogarth Press, London, and the author.

LOWELL, AMY: "Little Ivory Figures Pulled with String" from *Pictures of the Floating World.* 1919. Houghton Mifflin Company, Boston.

MACDONALD, WILSON: *Out of the Wilderness.* 1926. The author.

MACLEISH, ARCHIBALD: *Poems, 1924-1933.* 1925. Houghton Mifflin Company, Boston.

MACNEICE, LOUIS: *Poems.* 1937. Random House, Inc., N.Y. Faber & Faber Ltd, London.

MASEFIELD, JOHN: *Poems.* 1935. The Macmillan Company, N.Y.

MASTERS, EDGAR LEE: *Spoon River Anthology.* 1916. The author.

MCCRAE, JOHN: *In Flanders Fields and Other Poems.* 1919. G. P. Putnam's Sons, N.Y.

MEREDITH, GEORGE: *Poems.* Revised edition Copr. 1897, 1898 by George Meredith. Charles Scribner's Sons, N.Y. Constable & Co. Ltd., London.

MEW, CHARLOTTE: "Sea Love" from *The Farmer's Bride.* "Moorland Night" from *The Rambling Sailor.* The Poetry Bookshop, London.

MEYNELL, ALICE: *Poems.* Copr. 1923 by Wilfrid Meynell. Charles Scribner's Sons, N.Y.

MILLAY, EDNA ST. VINCENT: "Oh, Sleep Forever" from *Fatal Interview.* Copr. 1931 by Edna St. Vincent Millay. "What Lips My Lips" from *The Harp Weaver and Other Poems.* Copr. 1920, 1921, 1922, 1923 by Edna St. Vincent Millay. Published by Harper & Brothers, N.Y.

MITCHELL, SILAS WEIR: *Collected Poems.* 1914. The Pennsylvania Company, Philadelphia.

MONRO, HAROLD: *The Earth for Sale.* The Poetry Bookshop, London, and Mrs. Harold Monro.

MOORE, MARIANNE: "Silence" from *Selected Poems.* 1935. The Macmillan Company, N.Y. "A Talisman" from *Observations.* 1924. The author.

OWEN, WILFRED: *Poems.* Mrs. Owen and Chatto & Windus, London.

PLARR, VICTOR: *In the Dorian Mood.* John Lane The Bodley Head Ltd, London.

POUND, EZRA: *Personae: The Collected Poems of Ezra Pound.* 1926. Liveright Publishing Corp., N.Y., and Virginia Rice, agent.

PROKOSCH, FREDERIC: *Carnival.* Copr. 1938 by Harper & Brothers, N.Y. The author and Chatto & Windus, London.

PUTNAM, HOWARD PHELPS: *Five Seasons.* 1931. Charles Scribner's Sons, N.Y.

RANSOM, JOHN CROWE: *Chills and Fever.* 1924. Alfred A. Knopf, Inc., N.Y.

ROBINSON, EDWIN ARLINGTON: "Mr. Flood's Party" from *Collected Poems.* 1937. The Macmillan Company, N.Y. "For a Dead Lady" and "Momus" from *The Town down the River.* Copr. 1910 by Charles Scribner's Sons, N.Y.

ROSENBERG, ISAAC: *Poems.* William Heinemann, Ltd., London.

SANDBURG, CARL: *Cornhuskers,* 1918. Henry Holt and Company, N.Y.

SANTAYANA, GEORGE: *Poems.* Copr. 1901, 1923 by Charles Scribner's Sons, N.Y. Constable & Co. Ltd., London.

SASSOON, SIEGFRIED: *Picture Show.* Published by E. P. Dutton & Co., N.Y.

SCHWARTZ, DELMORE: *In Dreams Begin Responsibilities.* 1939. New Directions, Norfolk, Conn.

SEEGER, ALAN: *Poems.* 1916. Charles Scribner's Sons, N.Y.

SPENDER, STEPHEN: *The Still Centre.* Faber & Faber Ltd, London.

STEPHENS, JAMES: *Collected Poems.* 1926. The Macmillan Company, N.Y.

STEVENS, WALLACE: *Harmonium.* 1923. Alfred A. Knopf, Inc., N.Y.

SWINBURNE, ALGERNON CHARLES: *Collected Poetical Works.* Harper & Brothers, N.Y. *Complete Works.* William Heinemann, Ltd., London.

SYMONS, ARTHUR: *Poems.* Dodd, Mead & Company, Inc., N.Y. William Heinemann, Ltd., London.

TATE, ALLEN: *Selected Poems.* 1937. Charles Scribner's Sons, N.Y.

THOMAS, DYLAN: *The World I Breathe.* 1939. New Directions, Norfolk, Conn. *The Map of Love.* J. M. Dent & Sons, Ltd., London.

VAN DOREN, MARK: *The Collected Poems of Mark Van Doren.* 1939. Henry Holt and Company, N.Y., and the author.

WICKHAM, ANNA: *The Contemplative Quarry* and *The Man with a Hammer.* 1921. Harcourt, Brace and Company, Inc., N.Y.

WILLIAMS, WILLIAM CARLOS: *Complete Collected Poems of William Carlos Williams.* 1938. New Directions, Norfolk, Conn.

WYLIE, ELINOR: *Nets to Catch the Wind* in *Collected Poems of Elinor Wylie.* 1921. Alfred A. Knopf, Inc., N.Y.

YEATS, WILLIAM BUTLER: "The Land of Heart's Desire" and "Deirdre" from *Collected Plays.* 1934. All others from *Collected Poems.* 1933. The Macmillan Company, N.Y.

REVISED, MID-CENTURY EDITION

ADAMS, LÉONIE: *Poems: A Selection.* Copr. 1954 by Léonie Adams. Funk & Wagnalls Company, N.Y.

AIKEN, CONRAD: "Blind Date" from *Collected Poems.* Copr. 1953 by Conrad Aiken. Oxford University Press, Inc., N.Y.

AUDEN, W. H.: "Ballad," Copr. 1937 by Random House, Inc., and "In Memory of W. B. Yeats," Copr. 1940 by W. H. Auden, both from *The Collected Poetry of W. H. Auden.* By permission of Random House, Inc., N.Y.

BARKER, GEORGE: *Selected Poems.* Copr. 1941 by the Macmillan Company, N.Y. By permission of the author.

BISHOP, ELIZABETH: *Poems: North and South—A Cold Spring.* Copr. 1946 by Elizabeth Bishop. Houghton Mifflin Company, Boston.

CAMPBELL, ROY: "The Volunteer's Reply to the Poet" from *Talking Bronco.* Henry Regnery Company, Chicago.

CRANE, HART: *The Collected Poems of Hart Crane.* Copr. 1933 by Liveright, Inc. By permission of Liveright Publishing Corporation, N.Y.

CUMMINGS, E. E.: "the Cambridge ladies who live in furnished souls" and "what if a much of a which of a wind" from *Poems, 1923–1954.* Copr. © 1923, 1944, 1951 by E. E. Cummings. Harcourt, Brace and Company, Inc., N.Y. By permission of Brandt & Brandt, N.Y.

ELIOT, T. S.: Part V of "Burnt Norton" from *Four Quartets.* Copr. 1943 by T. S. Eliot. Harcourt, Brace and Company, Inc., N.Y.

EMPSON, WILLIAM: *Collected Poems of William Empson.* Copr. 1935, 1940, 1949 by William Empson. Harcourt, Brace and Company, Inc., N.Y.

FROST, ROBERT: "The Witch of Coös" from "Two Witches," "Fire and Ice," and "Stopping by Woods on a Snowy Evening" from *Complete Poems of Robert Frost.* Copr. 1930, 1949 by Henry Holt and Company, Inc., N.Y. By permission of the publisher.

GRAVES, ROBERT: *Collected Poems 1955.* Copr. 1955 by Robert Graves. Doubleday & Company, Inc., N.Y. By permission of the author.

LINDSAY, VACHEL: *Collected Poems.* Copr. 1913 by The Macmillan Company, N.Y. By permission of the publisher.

LOWELL, ROBERT: *Lord Weary's Castle.* Copr. 1944, 1946 by Robert Lowell. Harcourt, Brace and Company, Inc., N.Y.

MACNEICE, LOUIS: "Bagpipe Music" from *Poems, 1925–1940.* Copr. 1937, 1939 by Louis MacNeice. Random House, Inc., N.Y.

MCGINLEY, PHYLLIS: *The Love Letters of Phyllis McGinley.* Copr. 1953, 1954 by Phyllis McGinley. The Viking Press, Inc., N.Y. "Midcentury Love Letter" originally appeared in *The New Yorker.*

MOORE, MARIANNE: "Poetry" and "In Distrust of Merits" from *Collected Poems.* Copr. 1951 by Marianne Moore. The Macmillan Company, N.Y.

MUIR, EDWIN: *Collected Poems, 1921–1951.* Grove Press, Inc., N.Y.

OWEN, WILFRED: "The Show" from *Poems of Wilfred Owen.* All rights reserved. New Directions, publishers, Norfolk, Connecticut.

POUND, EZRA: "From 'Canto LXXXI'" from *The Cantos.* Copr. 1934, 1937, 1940, 1948 by Ezra Pound. New Directions, publishers, Norfolk, Connecticut.

RAINE, KATHLEEN: *The Pythoness and Other Poems.* Farrar, Straus and Cudahy, Inc., N.Y.

REED, HENRY: *A Map of Verona and Other Poems.* Copr. 1947 by Henry Reed. Harcourt, Brace and Company, Inc., N.Y.

RODGERS, W. R.: *Europa and the Bull.* Copr. 1952 by W. R. Rodgers. Farrar, Straus and Cudahy, Inc., N.Y.

ROETHKE, THEODORE: *The Lost Son and Other Poems.* Copr. © 1947 by the United Chapter of Phi Beta Kappa. Doubleday & Company, Inc., N.Y.

SANDBURG, CARL: "Chicago" from *Chicago Poems.* Copr. 1916 by Henry Holt and Company, Inc., N.Y.; Copr. 1944 by Carl Sandburg. By permission of the publisher.

SHAPIRO, KARL: *Poems, 1940–1953.* Copr. 1942 by Karl Jay Shapiro. Random House, Inc., N.Y.

SLESSOR, KENNETH: *Poems.* 1957. Angus and Robertson, Sydney.

SPENDER, STEPHEN: "I Think Continually of Those . . ." from *Collected Poems, 1928–1953.* Copr. 1934 by The Modern Library, Inc. By permission of Random House, Inc., N.Y.

STEVENS, WALLACE: "The Emperor of Ice Cream" and "Not Ideas about the Thing but the Thing Itself" from *The Collected Poems of Wallace Stevens.* Copr. 1931, 1954 by Wallace Stevens. Alfred A. Knopf, Inc., N.Y.

STICKNEY, TRUMBULL: *The Poems of Trumbull Stickney.* Copr. 1905 by L. M. Stickney. Houghton Mifflin Company, Boston. By permission of the author's brother, Henry A. Stickney.

TATE, ALLEN: "Ode to the Confederate Dead" from *Poems, 1922–1947.* Copr. 1932 by Charles Scribner's Sons. By permission of the publisher.

THOMAS, DYLAN. "Fern Hill" and "Do Not Go Gentle into That Good Night" from *Collected Poems of Dylan Thomas.* Copr. 1952, 1953 by Dylan Thomas. New Directions, publishers, Norfolk, Connecticut.

WILBUR, RICHARD: *Things of This World.* Copr. © 1956 by Richard Wilbur. Harcourt, Brace and Company, Inc., N.Y.

WILLIAMS, WILLIAM CARLOS: "The Yachts" from *The Collected Earlier Poems of William Carlos Williams.* Copr. 1938, 1951 by William Carlos Williams. New Directions, publishers, Norfolk, Connecticut.